THE SHAPE OF SPIRITUALITY

THE SHAPE OF SPIRITUALITY

THE PUBLIC SIGNIFICANCE OF A NEW RELIGIOUS FORMATION

EDITED BY DICK HOUTMAN AND GALEN WATTS

Columbia University Press *New York*

Columbia University Press
Publishers Since 1893
New York   Chichester, West Sussex

Copyright © 2024 Columbia University Press
All rights reserved

Library of Congress Cataloging-in-Publication Data
Names: Houtman, Dick, editor. | Watts, Galen, editor.
Title: The shape of spirituality : the public significance of a new religious formation / edited by Dick Houtman and Galen Watts. Description: New York : Columbia University Press, [2024] |
Includes bibliographical references.
Identifiers: LCCN 2024010782 (print) | LCCN 2024010783 (ebook) |
ISBN 9780231216845 (hardback) | ISBN 9780231216852 (trade paperback) |
ISBN 9780231561372 (ebook)
Subjects: LCSH: Spirituality—United States—History—21st century. | UnitedStates— Religion—21st century.|Non- church- affiliated people—United States.
Classification: LCC BL624 .S479 2024 (print) | LCC BL624 (ebook) |
DDC 204.0973—dc23/eng/20240402

Cover design: Milenda Nan Ok Lee
Cover photo: Vorachit Cherdpradith / Shutterstock

CONTENTS

Acknowledgments vii

Introduction: Spirituality—Privatized
Pseudo-Religion? 1
GALEN WATTS AND DICK HOUTMAN

1 How Spirituality Grew up and out of Christianity 39
LINDA WOODHEAD

2 The Cultic Milieu and the Spiritual Turn:
The Need for Theoretical Revision 59
COLIN CAMPBELL

3 Holistic Healing and the Reestablishment of
Religion in the United States 87
CANDY GUNTHER BROWN

4 Spiritualizing Therapy: How Psychologists Use
Spirituality to Counter the Hyperindividualistic
Spirit of Therapy 125
MICHAL PAGIS AND ORLY TAL

5 The Spiritual Impulse in Silicon Valley: A Content and
   Discourse Analysis of *Wired* Magazine, 2001–2020   151
   PAUL K. McCLURE AND CHRISTOPHER M. PIEPER

6 Lagged Identities and the Underestimated
   Civic Significance of Spirituality   177
   EVAN STEWART, TIM DACEY, AND JAIME KUCINSKAS

7 When the Spiritual Is Political: Self-Realization
   and the Quest for Social Justice   209
   GALEN WATTS

8 A Startling Alliance? Spirituality, Populism,
   and Antivaccination Protest   241
   DICK HOUTMAN AND STEF AUPERS

9 Conspirituality: An (Un)happy Marriage of
   Conspiracy Theories and Spirituality?   267
   JARON HARAMBAM

Bibliography   299
Contributors   337
Index   341

ACKNOWLEDGMENTS

Over the last two decades the scholarship on spirituality has grown exponentially. Given the prevalence of "spiritual" discourse and practice in late modern societies, even vehement critics have had to reckon with its presence, if only to downplay or dismiss it. At the same time, the staggering growth of scholarship and commentary on spirituality has not brought with it a similar growth in understanding. On the contrary: the sociology of spirituality remains rife with both confusion and controversy. While most agree that a "spiritual turn" has taken place, precisely what this entails or means is a matter of frenzied academic and moral debate. What is more, the closest thing to a consensus in the field is informed, regrettably, by secularization theory—that long-standing if beleaguered paradigm in the sociology of religion, which subsumes all religious change under a metanarrative of decline. As a result, the sociology of spirituality has for too long been characterized by a bizarre mix of analytic puzzlement, moral disapproval, and dogmatic certainty—which is to say, a lot of heat and little light.

It is a central task of this volume to change this. While the project was officially conceived in 2020 (a "pandemic baby," as they say), its origins lie much further back. Dick began studying spirituality back in the early 2000s, when few sociologists paid the topic any mind. Inspired by the first wave of scholarship on "New Age" spirituality (particularly the work of Wouter Hanegraaff in the Netherlands and Paul Heelas in Britain), he and a number of close collaborators sought to flesh out the cultural logic undergirding the spiritual turn, and with it the changing religious landscape of late modernity. Over the past two decades, he has consistently made the case in articles and books that despite the undeniable decline of traditional Christianity in Western modernity, the shift from "religion" to "spirituality" signals religious transformation of an epochal kind that holds far-reaching social and political implications. It remains a source of enduring frustration for us both that neither sociologists of religion nor sociologists more generally have yet to take this message seriously.

While we had the idea for an edited volume on the sociology of spirituality upon meeting at the 2019 meeting of the Society for the Scientific Study of Religion, at the time Dick was based in Belgium while Galen was completing his doctorate in Canada, and thus little action was taken until in 2020 Galen became a Banting Postdoctoral Fellow working with Dick at KU Leuven's Center for Sociological Research (CeSO). This provided us the freedom and institutional resources to brainstorm the kind of volume we wanted to produce. In conceptualizing the project, we decided that we wanted to bring together leading scholars of spirituality whose work on the topic resonated with our own cultural sociological approach in order to accomplish two things: first, to provide a theoretically sound, analytically clear, and practicable account of spirituality that could inform empirical research, and second, to make vivid through a series of case studies covering distinct institutional spheres the prevalence, persistence, and power of spirituality in twenty-first century societies. Put another way: we wanted to produce a book that would make clear to sociologists of all stripes *what spirituality is* and *why it matters.*

We began by making a list of the contributors we hoped to recruit. Thankfully, nearly everyone we approached agreed to participate. Owing to the pandemic, our plans to meet in person were repeatedly delayed, but in the spring of 2022 we finally had the great fortune of convening a group of scholars in Leuven's historic and picturesque Groot Begijnhof for a two-day book workshop. This gathering was intimate, collegial, and extremely productive. For many participants it embodied the best of academic life—spirited conversation in an environment of intellectual charity, curiosity, and humility. And this experience was made all the more gratifying in light of the previous years of social distancing and isolation. Over the course of the workshop, two key takeaways crystallized which would come to form the backbone of the book. First, the dominance of secularization theory in the sociology of religion has undermined sociologists' ability to recognize and appreciate the public significance of spirituality (not to mention the pivotal role it has played in marginalizing the sociology of religion within the discipline). Second, a cultural sociological approach to spirituality in fact helps us to understand many of the central cultural conflicts raging today. Thus, we remain convinced that the book has as much of importance to say to sociologists in general as it does to those interested only in religion.

For their avid participation in the workshop, we would like to thank Stef Aupers, Candy Gunther Brown, Colin Campbell, Mar Griera, Franz Höllinger, Jaron Harambam, Linda Woodhead, and Nurit Zaidman. While they did not attend the workshop, we would also like to extend a thank you to Timothy Dacey, Jaime Kucinskas, Paul McClure, Michal Pagis,

Christopher Pieper, Evan Stewart, and Orly Tal for agreeing to take part in the book project. It has been a great honor to converse and work with such brilliant scholars. Without a doubt, one of the greatest privileges of academic life is having the opportunity to learn from learned folk like these. We remain tremendously grateful to all who intrepidly contributed a chapter and whose willingness to take editorial directions and meet deadlines made our lives as editors much easier than they otherwise would have been.

We would like to thank the two anonymous readers for their comments on an earlier version of the manuscript, which undoubtedly helped us to hone our arguments. We would also like to thank the entire team at Columbia University Press for shepherding us through the publication process. Last, we wish to extend a heartful thank you to CUP's Wendy Lochner for believing in the project.

This book would not have been possible were it not for the support of various organizations and people. We would first like to thank the Center for Sociological Research at KU Leuven for serving as an extraordinary site of collegiality, social support, and rigorous social scientific research. We particularly wish to single out its Cultural Sociology Reading Group, which has institutionalized an ethos of intellectual camaraderie and done much to spread the word about the virtues of cultural sociology. Dick would particularly like to thank his intellectual buddy Stef Aupers, in close collaboration with whom he first embarked on the sociological study of spirituality and religious change almost a quarter of a century ago. He is also grateful for the fortunate decision by the Social Sciences and Humanities Research Council of Canada (SSHRC) to grant Galen a Banting Postdoctoral Fellowship (2020–2022), without which our immensely stimulating, pleasurable, and productive collaboration in Leuven would probably not have materialized. Galen, for his part, would like to thank SSHRC for the autonomy, flexibility, and financial support attached to that fellowship. He would also like to thank the Flanders Research Foundation (FWO) for providing him with a Junior Postdoctoral Fellowship (2022–2023), which was equally critical for ensuring that the necessary time and energy could be devoted to moving this project from mere idea to material reality. He would also like to extend thanks to his colleagues and friends at KU Leuven, whose company and companionship made his stay in Belgium sincerely wonderful. Furthermore, he would like to thank the Sociology and Legal Studies Department at the University of Waterloo for making his dreams come true—that is, allowing him to be a full-time academic back in his native Canada. Closer to home, he would like to thank his parents for their unconditional support and his sister, Kelsey, for her invaluable friendship. And last, but not least, he wishes to thank his lovely wife, Chantel, for everything she is and everything she does, and his beautiful children, Audrey and Emerson, for reminding him, each and every day, what truly matters.

Dick Houtman, Leuven
Galen Watts, Waterloo

THE SHAPE OF SPIRITUALITY

INTRODUCTION

Spirituality—Privatized Pseudo-Religion?

GALEN WATTS AND DICK HOUTMAN

The religious tide is turning in the West. Once the bastion of Christendom, it has become increasingly fitting to speak of a "post-Christian" civilization. The trends that began roundabout the 1960s have continued unabated, leaving many religious leaders in a state of perennial frustration and angst. They have looked on with uncomprehending horror as their membership numbers have dwindled, their moral authority has been neutered, and their congregants have increasingly become what in earlier centuries would have been deemed heretical but in the twenty-first century has become a humdrum norm. Though some forms of Christianity have managed to muster an admirable defense against this mass exodus away from the churches owing to the contemporary appeal of charismatic evangelicalism (itself a unique species of religiosity), and with immigration offering something like a last line of defense, these exceptions prove the rule. Indeed, the fastest growing religion in the West, so we are told, is "nonreligion," with Europe leading the way and America hot on its heels.[1] It is no doubt for this reason that esteemed philosopher and religious observer Charles Taylor has felt it right and proper to declare ours a "secular age."[2]

But are we as secular as we suppose? It depends on what we mean by this not uncontroversial or uncontested term. For while it remains undeniably true that today's cultural inertia seems to bode poorly for the established churches, we are simultaneously presented with trends that complicate any one-dimensional story of religious decline. We are speaking of the now commonplace semantic shift from "religion" to "spirituality"—what scholars call the "spiritual turn"—which has spread like wildfire across the West, stoking the curiosity and ire of popular and academic commentators alike.

A recent survey conducted by the Pew Research Center reports that about one in five Americans identifies as "spiritual but not religious" (or, as has become the fashion in academic circles, SBNR).[3] The number of SBNRs in Western Europe is also substantial.[4] What is more, judging by the Ngram Viewer on Google books, it seems that the popularity of "spirituality" is at an all-time-high.[5] This semantic shift is all the more surprising in light of the fact that, historically, "spirituality" and "religion" have been largely tethered conceptually. As Boaz Huss notes, the "spiritual" was once juxtaposed to the corporeal and the material, whereas today, these concepts are closely aligned, with the "spiritual" increasingly considered antithetical to the "religious," a development that would have stunned our medieval forebears.[6]

Acknowledging the semantic shift from "religion" to "spirituality," scholars have noted that the two terms are used in varying ways across social contexts and combined at different rates. For instance, Nancy Ammerman observes that in America most scholars continue to see these terms as overlapping rather than polar opposites, while Joantine Berghuijs, Jos Pieper, and Cok Bakker point out that in Europe the hardline distinction is far more common.⁷ These findings raise questions about whether or not the shift from "religion" to "spirituality" is indicative of a more fundamental process of substantive religious transformation.⁸

The hypothesis that all that has changed is the labels people use, and nothing more, would perhaps be plausible if the semantic shift were not synchronous with a slew of unprecedented developments in the West. Yoga, once the exclusive remit of Hindu sages, has become a national pastime for middle-class Westerners.⁹ Mindfulness, the ancient Buddhist practice, has been incorporated into secondary school curriculums and sports training programs. (In 2009, Americans are reported to have spent $4.2 billion on mindfulness-related practices and products.)¹⁰ Complementary and Alternative Medicine (CAM)—not so long ago the trifling site of what were widely considered quacks—increasingly informs mainstream health care.¹¹ Not surprisingly, corporations have jumped onto the bandwagon, too, giving life to the "workplace spirituality movement" and countless personal development seminars in the name of increased worker productivity and shareholder profits.¹² Meanwhile, the size of the "mind, body, spirit" section in the local bookstore seems to double with each passing year. Celebrities like British comedian and media personality Russell Brand, actress Gwyneth Paltrow, and two-time Democratic presidential candidate Marianne Williamson famously advocate the benefits of a "spiritual" life. And we have seen a marked interest in practices once associated with "New Age"—astrology, crystals, reiki, and more—leading media pundits to proclaim we are living in "The Age of Aquarius, All Over Again!"¹³ All in all, then, when it comes to the religious landscape of the West, there are serious and significant developments afoot.

Of course, we are far from the first to point this out. For decades sociologists have been aware of these changes. Yet we must confess: the discipline as a whole has done a poor job making sense of them. Why? One reason, we believe, derives from a lack of sensitivity to religion within mainstream sociology; whether they will admit it or not, most sociologists seem to think of religion as either "old news" or a foreign import, relevant to historians and those who study non-Western societies, perhaps, but not to those of us who study twenty-first-century liberal democracies.[14] However, as we see it this is only half an explanation. The other reason stems from deeply entrenched assumptions within the sociology of religion. These are first that spirituality is not "real" religion and second that although it may be widespread, spirituality lacks cultural coherence and thus public significance.

Consider the following examples from prominent sociologists of religion: the late Bryan Wilson characterized spirituality as representing " 'the religion of your choice,' the highly privatized preference that reduces religion to the significance of pushpin, poetry, or popcorns."[15] David Voas and Alasdair Crockett have maintained that what goes by "spirituality" has "little personal, let alone social, significance."[16] Bryan Turner has similarly written, "it is not self-evident that spirituality, which is by definition a somewhat private practice, will have any long-term significant consequences."[17] Finally, in his uniquely colorful fashion, Steve Bruce has argued that "spirituality" amounts to "a damp squib," lacks significance beyond the domestic realm, and cannot sustain a distinctive way of life.[18]

Each of these claims follow from the logic of secularization theory, which theorizes "spirituality" as "privatized." However, this notion of "privatization" is in fact quite ambiguous, because it entails no less than three distinct meanings, all invoked in the above claims about spirituality: (1) "privatized" as entailing religion that is merely a matter of consumer preference, free of cultural imperatives; (2) "privatized" as playing no role in public institutional spheres; and (3) "privatized" as domesticated and psychologized, and thus without political significance.[19] This volume argues that none of these characterizations of "privatized" actually fits contemporary spirituality. To substantiate this claim, in this introduction we critically interrogate the burgeoning, yet fragmented and dispersed, specialized scholarship on spirituality that has emerged over the last two decades.[20] In the process, we lay the groundwork for a cultural sociological approach to the study of spirituality that makes clear (1) that spirituality is underwritten by a unifying cultural logic, (2) that it has increasingly found its way into public institutions, and (3) that it is far from politically insignificant.

Animating this volume, then, is the conviction that assessments of the public significance of spirituality significantly depend upon the theoretical frameworks we use to study it, for we can only see what our tools allow us to; and, moreover, that the dominance of secularization theory has obscured the myriad ways that spirituality increasingly seeps into, suffuses, and restructures the public sphere in Western liberal democracies. In sum, the central contributions of this volume are twofold: first, to advance an empirically grounded cultural sociological framework with which to make sense of the shift from "religion" to "spirituality," and second, to make the case that sociologists who wish to understand the cultural changes and conflicts taking place in the West (and beyond) must take the spiritual turn seriously.

"SPIRITUALITY" AS "LESS-THAN-REAL" RELIGION?

A Submerged Christian Norm of "Real" Religion

In the sociology of religion, and in academic literature on spirituality generally, it has become something of a truism that "spirituality" sans "religion" is a mere "residual religiosity" or "alternative spirituality,"[21] which lacks the institutional structures, ideological coherence, and committed membership that traditional Christian religion entails. Interestingly, this is the dominant view not only among those who see the spiritual turn as a mere manifestation of secularization,[22] but also among those on the ground who favor "spirituality" and self-identify as "spiritual but not religious" (SBNR). Thus, among both sociologists of religion and those who identify as SBNR, "spirituality" is generally construed as radically different from, and even incompatible with, "religion."

But do these tendencies to emphasize the differences between "religion" and "spirituality" justify the view that the latter is not "real religion?" According to the logic of secularization theory, they do. Being a catch-all term for a multitude of social processes,[23] secularization theory basically highlights three social processes with allegedly profound consequences for religion and its public significance: institutional differentiation, pluralization, and privatization. *Institutional differentiation* captures the process whereby the religious sphere becomes only one subsystem among many, no longer functioning as a shared "sacred canopy" for society as a whole.[24] Resultantly, modern societies are characterized by the proliferation of independent life worlds and social spheres (e.g., politics, the economy, religion, etc.), or, in other words, by *pluralization*—a social process, so the story goes, that undermines the "taken-for-grantedness" of religion. This supposedly leads to the *privatization* of religion: banned from the public realm, it becomes a private issue. While this notion of privatization is not unambiguous, as we noted earlier, secularization theorists agree that in all three relevant respects modernity transforms religion into a mere simulacrum of what it once was.[25]

In truth, it is difficult to deny that Christianity is not faring well in the West. The hypothesis that more and more westerners are becoming less and less religious has been strongly supported by empirical research.[26] This applies even to the United States, a country regularly invoked by sociologists of religion as a counterexample.[27] Except for a few pockets of vibrancy, the overarching trend is decidedly toward decline of the types of religion that flourished in the nineteenth century.[28] Yet it seems premature to pronounce the death knell of religion in the West.

For one, the survey metrics invoked normalize traditional Christian religion. From the types of questions asked to the very wording of questions, the World Values Survey, the European Social Survey, the European Values Study, and other similar international survey programs are largely informed by an overly narrow and Christocentric conception of religion, which focuses on church attendance and all sorts of typically Christian beliefs (in God, heaven, hell, etc.). The resulting metrics are, in effect, tracking the kind of religiosity that once enveloped the West but that, as Linda Woodhead persuasively argues in this volume, is increasingly on the defense.[29]

For another, secularization theory's incessant representation—either explicitly or implicitly—of traditional Christian religion as "the real thing" raises the question of whether the theory should be thought of as a neutral scientific hypothesis at all. As we see it, it is at least as much a folk theory that naturalizes

Christian religion and as such reflects the interests of the established Christian churches (even while it delivers them endlessly bad news).[30] Inclusive and encompassing as its notion of "religion" may sound, secularization theory is not a theory about what modernity does to religion per se, but rather about what it does to Christian religion as the West has known it for centuries. That is, the theory privileges religious decline over religious change and defines religious diversity away. Further, it forces the latter onto its Procrustean bed of "religion" versus "nonreligion," identifying Christian religion as "real" and all other varieties of religion as "less-than-real." Secularization theory, in a word, fails to acknowledge religious difference: all that matters is the degree to which non-Christian religion is *less* religious than Christian religion rather than how it is *differently* religious. Anyone vaguely familiar with sociological work on "spirituality" knows the outcome: incessant portrayals of spirituality as lacking good-old Christianity's ideological coherence and public significance. As Linda Woodhead has observed, the enduring presence of a submerged norm of "real religion" has led sociologists of religion to perceive spirituality as "less-than-real" religion.[31] Because it does not fit the traditional Christian model, it is often disregarded or theorized out of sight.[32]

While the days when religious authority encompassed the entire social fabric have surely passed,[33] the pivotal theoretical question is whether institutional differentiation heralds a decline of religion tout court, irrespective of the *type of religion* in question. The alternative hypothesis is clear enough: that traditional Christian religion is more vulnerable to differentiation than spirituality. Indeed, analyses of survey data for the Netherlands, for instance, have demonstrated that the decline of traditional Christian religion in the postwar period has coincided with a proliferation of spirituality.[34] Now, we do not deny the merits of secularization theory for explaining the decline of traditional Christianity. By no means. Yet we do contend that to adequately track and come to grips with what today thrives as "spirituality" in the West, secularization theory's restrictive and parochial notion of religion needs to be abandoned. Furthermore, this can easily be done without engaging in futile debates about what religion "really" or "essentially" is. It suffices to pragmatically point out that even a superficial glance at the work of the early twentieth-century pioneers of the sociological study of religion makes it abundantly clear that none of them equated religion with traditional Christian religion.

Spirituality as Mystical Religion

Max Weber understood religion (albeit without defining it explicitly) in terms of its promise of salvation from suffering, by telling its adherents how to relate to a supernatural realm—that is, what to do and what to abstain from.[35] More specifically, Weber distinguished four ideal types of theodicy: religion may be either *ascetic* or *mystical* (requiring that believers think of themselves, respectively, as either "tools" or "vessels" of the divine), and it may be either *inner-worldly* or *other-worldly* (oriented toward and enmeshed in the mundane world of business and politics, or concerned, in monastic or hermitic fashion, with a strictly defined religious realm). The four ideal types that result from the combination of these two analytical distinctions inform Weber's comparative analysis of the world religions, the original goal of which was to explain why Protestantism's innerworldly asceticism contributed to a breakthrough of rationalized modernity in the West, while Buddhism, Hinduism, and Confucianism did not.[36] It follows that Weber's notion of religion is not restricted to traditional Christianity, but rather accounts for much more than Western-style monotheism.

The same applies for Emile Durkheim's conception of religion, which doesn't even refer to a supernatural realm—that is, to gods or spirits. Rather, Durkheim defines religion by the way communities imagine and coconstitute the distinction between the "sacred" and the "profane," along with how they engage in ritual practices aimed at protecting the former from pollution by the latter. Specifically, in Durkheim's hands religion refers to "a unified system of beliefs and practices relative to sacred things, that is to say, things set apart and forbidden—beliefs and practices which unite into one single community called a Church, all those who adhere to them."[37] Religion, then, is a collective or social phenomenon—there are no religions of one—which includes both ritual practices and collective representations. Needless to say, unlike Weber, Durkheim does not limit his conception to the "real" world religions. In fact, from a Durkheimian perspective, one could even think of science as a modern religious form, which sacralizes the scientific method and expertise while profaning or polluting traditional religion.[38]

The Weberian and Durkheimian notions of religion are obviously far from identical and in certain respects incompatible, but our only aim here is to convince the reader that it is misconceived to define "real" religion in the overly narrow Christian sense naturalized by secularization theory. In fact, such a parochial understanding of religion only emerged when after the classical period of Weber and Durkheim, the Christian churches transformed sociology of religion into a specialized sociology to serve their own needs, in effect cutting it off from general sociology.[39] Thomas Luckmann has trenchantly critiqued the resulting tendency among sociologists of religion of accepting "the self-interpretations—and the ideology—of religious institutions as valid definitions of the range of their subject matter."

For this tendency, Luckmann warned, caused secularization theorists to overlook or dismiss important religious changes occurring right before their eyes: "What are usually taken as symptoms of the decline of traditional Christianity may be symptoms of a more revolutionary change: the replacement of the institutional specialization of religion by a new social form of religion." In breaking from the herd mentality that he felt reigned in the sociology of religion of his day, Luckmann proposed that with differentiation, pluralization, and privatization comes not just decline but also the emergence of a "market of 'ultimate' significance" in which religious consumers shop for strictly personal packages of meaning, based on their individual biographies.[40] What he pointed out back in the 1960s was basically a massive proliferation of mystical religion as already identified in the beginning of the twentieth century by Ernst Troeltsch,[41] a sociologically inclined Protestant theologian and intellectual sparring partner of Max Weber. Given sociology of religion's tendency to reproduce the self-understandings of the Christian churches, it should come as no surprise that mystical religion was marginalized in the reception of Troeltsch's work, while those that were more compatible with traditional Christian religion became fetishized.[42] The latter are that of *church religion* (whose exemplar is the Catholic Church) and *sect religion* (whose exemplar is puritan Protestantism). *Mystical religion* differs profoundly from each of these: it lacks both church religion's hierarchical leadership and organizational structure and sect religion's explicit creed. Instead, it breathes a marked egalitarian ethos and relativizes boundaries between insiders and outsiders.[43]

Carefully distinguishing between mystical religion as the exclusive remit of religious virtuosos and a more general mysticism, Troeltsch observes that the latter "sees itself as the real universal heart of all religion, of which the various myth-forms are merely outer garment." What is more, he contends that from within such "spiritual religion," "all that is ecclesiastical, historic, dogmatic, objective, and authoritative is changed into a mere means of stimulation, into that which arouses that personal experience which alone is valuable, and on which alone the hope of salvation is founded. This is a theology of the subjective consciousness of salvation, and no longer one which confines itself to the objective facts of redemption."[44] This mystical religion, which despises submission to religion's "outer forms," has since the 1960s become increasingly widespread in the West.[45] Indeed, its characteristic suspicion of "all that is ecclesiastical, historic, dogmatic, objective, and authoritative" informs its typical fluidity and fleetingness. Individual groups and associations come and go, giving the impression of high turnover rates, weak ties and connections, superficial adherence, social instability, and a lack of cultural or ideological coherence, but all this is not true of the wider milieu to which the various spiritual "cults" belong. This is why back in the 1970s Colin Campbell presciently warned sociologists that the study of individual spiritual groups or associations was best replaced by a focus on the wider "cultic milieu"—an array of networks, groups, activities, and services, which collectively comprise the institutional heartland of deviant belief-systems in modern society.[46] Doing otherwise, he argues, would risk missing the forest for the trees.[47] Heeding this line of thought, Paul Heelas and Linda Woodhead have argued that the religiosity informing what nowadays goes by "spirituality" finds its institutional home in what they call the *holistic milieu*.[48]

Historical scholarship on the complex genealogical origins of spirituality has pointed out that despite its seeming affinities with ancient Eastern and Indigenous traditions such as Buddhism, Taoism, and Hinduism, its roots lie chiefly in the eighteenth and nineteenth centuries. Specifically, it bears the imprints of movements as diverse as English and German Romanticism, early Methodism, liberal Protestantism (especially Quakerism, Unitarianism, and Universalism), New England transcendentalism, Swedenborgism, Helena Blavatsky's Theosophy, American New Thought, spiritualism, and mesmerism, among others.[49] Much like Troeltsch's account of mystical religion these movements have typically been ignored, or downplayed, in the official religious histories of the West, basically because their presence has considerably troubled twentieth-century religious elites. Nonetheless, far from living on the cultural fringes, these movements and the religious tradition they embody are in fact "located at the heart of Western modernity," while at the same time having transcended and troubled the lines which ostensibly distinguish West from East.[50] Indeed, as Linda Woodhead makes clear in her chapter in this volume, the tradition of spirituality has had a long, entangled, and embattled relationship with traditional Christianity, which, in recent years, has seen spirituality shift from a position of cultural marginality to one of dominance. A similar argument, also in this volume, is made by Colin Campbell who now argues that it no longer makes sense to speak of spirituality as belonging to the "cultic milieu," since it increasingly saturates society's cultural mainstream.

IS SPIRITUALITY AS CULTURALLY INCOHERENT AS THEY SAY IT IS?

The Cultural Logic of Spirituality

While Luckmann's early critique of the parochial concerns that underlie secularization theory was surely well taken, it has also stimulated an intellectually pernicious underestimation of the cultural coherence of spirituality that pesters empirical research up to the present day. For while many of those who have followed in Luckmann's footsteps have stressed, contra secularization theory, that the shift from "religion" to "spirituality" is evidence of religious transformation, they have simultaneously, in line with secularization theory, characterized spirituality as a form of pseudo- or vicarious religion, which lacks cultural coherence and ideological consistency.[51] For instance, in his treatises on spirituality in American life at the end of the twentieth century, American sociologist Robert Wuthnow speaks of a "shift from dwelling to seeking," with individuals engaging in "spiritual tinkering" oriented by their idiosyncratic preferences.[52] Similarly, Wade Clark Roof describes the religious landscape of the United States as a "spiritual supermarket" where a "reflexive spirituality" reigns.[53] A number of other scholars have claimed to see in spirituality all the hallmarks of "postmodernity,"[54] with its incessant bricolage, syncretism, and alleged rejection of metanarratives. In all these depictions Luckmann's image of the individual consumer, picking and choosing freely, unencumbered by institutions or cultural imperatives, shines through. Yet the conviction that massively variegated spiritual practices on the ground prove the cultural incoherence of spirituality is fundamentally flawed, and it remains a principal source of misunderstanding.[55] For, on the contrary, most talk of "spirituality" is best conceived as signaling a coherent mystical religious tradition, one that has longstanding roots in the West but that takes varying discursive forms in different periods.[56]

What are the central cultural capstones of this tradition? While it is to some extent arbitrary to distinguish what is *central* from what is merely *peripheral*, we propose three principal precepts that set spirituality apart from traditional Christian religion—precepts that are logically interrelated and largely uncontested among experts on the issue. They revolve around

(1) *religious ontology* (what the divine "is"); (2) *religious epistemology* (how knowledge of spiritual truth can be attained); and (3) *religious soteriology* (how one can be saved and redeemed from suffering). The divine is here conceived as an omnipresent immanent spirit or life force rather than a transcendent or otherworldly God (*ontology*); religious truth is seen as attainable through personal experience rather than through sacred texts (*epistemology*); and salvation from suffering is seen as demanding a pursuit of authentic selfhood rather than conformity to externally imposed demands (*soteriology*).

RELIGIOUS ONTOLOGY: AN IMMANENT CONCEPTION OF THE DIVINE

Spirituality boasts a notion of the divine as an omnipresent and immanent spirit, energy or life force that permeates all of the world and the universe. This resonates loudly and clearly in the utterance heard so often nowadays among the "spiritual but not religious": "I don't believe in a personal God, but I do believe that there is something." This construal of the divine as an omnipresent and constantly present "energy," "power," or "life force" differs profoundly from traditional Christianity. For the latter to a greater or lesser extent entails a transcendent and otherworldly personal God, who has created the world and the universe, who has revealed religious truth, who makes ethical demands on his followers to engage in a pious religious life, and who has the capacity to interfere in human and earthly matters. "Monistic" or "holistic" spirituality thus differs from Christian dualism that conceives of God as inhabiting a world of His own and that as such sets the divine apart from the world.

Such religious dualism is exemplified by the puritan Protestantism that Weber singled out in *The Protestant Ethic and the Spirit of Capitalism*.[57] Far more than other strains of Christian religion, it construes the divine as an omnipotent God, who is radically divorced from the world He created and who is immune to magical manipulation. This antimagical posture is enshrined in Calvin's doctrine of predestination, according to which there is nothing that believers can do to secure salvation, because it is God who sovereignly decides this. This sharp dualism sets Calvinism apart from not only Eastern religions like Hinduism and Buddhism but also other strains of Christianity. For instance, Catholicism permits much more leeway for the presence of the divine in the world, best exemplified by its least dualistic, mystical renditions (e.g., Hildegard of Bingen, Meister Eckhart, Francis of Assisi). What is more, charismatic Christianity and Pentecostalism patently reject puritan dualism, adopting instead a more monistic conception of the divine, which places "primary emphasis upon the individual's immediate experience of the Spirit of God."[58] For charismatics, then, God is both immanent and transcendent, accessible through experience, while also otherworldly, thereby making charismatic Christianity and Pentecostalism Christianized versions of spirituality.[59] In a somewhat similar fashion, while most of those who identify as "spiritual" deny the existence of supernatural beings, this is not always and necessarily the case. Especially contemporary forms of occultism and esotericism, although monistic, posit the existence of personal spirits, angels, and demons that can be summoned or exorcized by magical means. Spirituality's religious ontology thus affords diverse theological interpretations.

RELIGIOUS EPISTEMOLOGY: PERSONAL EXPERIENCE

The traditional Christian conception of the divine as a transcendent otherworldly God is logically associated with a doctrinal epistemology, where truth is believed to be contained in a sacred text, originating in God's revelation. Spirituality's approach to religious truth, on the other hand, discourages such an epistemology in favor of personal experience. This follows logically from spirituality's immanent conception of the divine: because matter and spirit are considered interconnected, human beings are understood as, in effect, knots in a field of spiritual energy that connects them to "everything." As Paul Heelas observes, it follows that "the person is, in essence, spiritual." This self-ethic informs a conception of feelings, intuitions and emotions as emanations of "the God within": "The inner realm, and the inner realm alone, is held to serve as the source of authentic vitality, creativity, love, tranquility, wisdom, power, authority and all those other qualities which are held to comprise the perfect life."[60] In contrast to traditional Christian religion, then, the divine is not situated "out there" to be believed in and obeyed, but rather "in here" to be experienced. Feelings, intuitions, and emotions thus entail the spiritual counterpart of God-revealed truth and God-ordained ethical demands. As a spiritual mechanism of "inner" knowing they inform the adherent of what is true and what is not, what they must do and what they must abstain from. This "experiential" route to truth, known as "gnosis" in the more specialized literature, entails a rejection of the two epistemologies that have since the Enlightenment struggled for cultural dominance in the West—"reason" as embodied by science, and "faith" as central to doctrinal religion.[61] Indeed, it is owing to its experiential epistemology that spirituality intentionally excises religion's "outer myth-forms," as Troeltsch called them, defining them as unnecessary to authentic religious life.

RELIGIOUS SOTERIOLOGY: SALVATION THROUGH SELF-REALIZATION

Taking seriously the messages of the divine within—conceived as one's "true," "spiritual" or "natural" self—is considered the path to redemption. For the cause of suffering, on this view, is letting the outer world overburden and colonize "who one 'really' is," that is, the spiritual source within. A staple of spirituality is therefore that moral guidance follows from attuning oneself to "the voice within," or "listening to one's heart." Authority—both epistemic and moral—is seen as lying *within* rather than *without*, with the aim of connecting to one's "true self," understood as a divine source of ethical inspiration that guides the way to a free and authentic life. Indeed, spirituality holds that the ultimate purpose of life is to realize one's "true self" by overcoming and transcending society—its institutions, norms, and conventions—viewed as a source of corruption, ignorance, and evil. Spirituality thus entails a form of cultural criticism: leading a "spiritual" life requires overcoming the alienation caused by externally imposed standards. Shedding these culturally conditioned layers enables one to become "whole" by realizing the full potential of the pure and pristine "true self" within. This is the spiritual rendition of salvation from suffering: leading a fully authentic life that expresses who one truly is and that entails an escape from society's alienating cultural and institutional routines.

Spirituality in the New Age and Human Potential Movements

It was not until the 1960s that spirituality became a phenomenon to reckon with. Its key carrier movements during this period were the New Age movement, the Human Potential movement, and the charismatic evangelical movement. Though few scholars have given it much notice, these seemingly disparate movements were uncannily similar, sharing a commitment to the three precepts we outlined earlier. In other words, they reflect distinct iterations of spirituality.[62]

Of course, they also differed in important respects, which serves to illuminate the internal diversity of the spiritual turn. For instance, it was New Agers who popularized talk of "spirituality" without "religion." Indeed, many SBNRs today, while they may not care to admit it, carry forward the legacies of the New Age.[63] The Human Potential movement, by contrast, was an ostensibly secular, primarily academic movement pioneered by maverick psychologists who rejected the cultural pessimism of Freud.[64] That said, the line demarcating the New Age from the Human Potential movement is basically impossible to draw.[65] The two overlapped considerably, with New Agers enthusiastically borrowing from the ideas of humanistic psychologists such as Abraham Maslow and Carl Rogers, while the latter regularly invoked the language of "spirituality."

Charismatic Christians, conversely, generally do not reject the term "religion" but instead tend to self-identify as "religious and spiritual."[66] Yet this semantic divergence belies the underlying cultural similarities. Many contemporary Charismatics embrace ideas that have their origins in the Human Potential movement, and while many would vehemently deny it, as Campbell points out, charismatic Christianity "bears considerable resemblance to the New Age movement."[67] However, one crucial dividing line revolves around political ideology. Members of both the New Age and Human Potential movements tended to embrace the processes of liberalization the 1960s set in motion. Indeed, this explains why those who today self-identify as SBNR—in large measure descendants of these two movements—tend to be socially progressive, embracing postmaterialist and "green" values.[68] By contrast, charismatic evangelicals tend to be more socially conservative and in turn are far more comfortable with the language of theism.[69]

We highlight the shared affinities between these types of spirituality because few sociologists have paid them much mind, but also because it usefully highlights the Christocentric bias of much sociology of religion. For it should come as no surprise that there exists an abundance of sociological scholarship devoted to the study of charismatic Christianity,[70] while the study of spirituality in its New Age and Human Potential forms has largely languished. Here again, an implicit norm of "real" religion informed by traditional Christianity has functioned to privilege those forms of religiosity which embrace the language and labels of Christian theism over those which do not. It is indeed curious that while sociologists of religion have seen no problem with charging SBNR spirituality with cultural incoherence and public insignificance, few have made these claims about charismatic Christian "spirituality." In light of this academic asymmetry, we focus in this volume on spirituality in its New Age and Human Potential forms, for it is this type of spirituality that is the least studied and most misunderstood aspect of the spiritual turn.[71]

Mistaking Heterogeneous Spiritual Practices for Cultural Incoherence

Even though charismatic evangelicalism shares the three aforementioned precepts that make for spirituality's cultural coherence, it nevertheless differs markedly from New Age and Human Potential spiritualities. This is because while the latter embrace *religious universalism*, *bricolage*, and *seekership*, all these are absent in charismatic Christianity.

The dismissive stance vis-à-vis institutional authority normalized by New Age and Human Potential spiritualities discourages strong identifications with dogmas and institutions, because taking the routines, doctrines, and rituals of just one of these seriously at the cost of others entails precisely the type of conformity to external authority that is seen as the main source of suffering, alienation and unfreedom. This does not mean, however, that SBNRs reject religious traditions tout court. They rather hold that the latter's idiosyncrasies and particularisms need to be sidestepped, while what they have in common needs to be foregrounded. This is the doctrine of religious universalism, also known as "perennialism," which teaches that there are no religious traditions that are superior to others—that is, all world religions are equally valid. This is because they ultimately all worship the same divine life force that cannot be captured in human-made institutions and cannot be reduced to particular doctrines either. In fact, attempting to do either of these amounts to creating trivial, human-made differences between religious traditions.

Religious universalism entails an openness to religious diversity and an encouragement to incorporate and adopt ideas and techniques from the existing range of religious and psychospiritual traditions. The resulting practices of "bricolage" (or "syncretism") are as such informed by whatever "feels good," understood as emanations of the "spiritual voice from within," and give rise to a holistic milieu that boasts astonishing diversity and fragmentation. The spiritual "seekership" this entails differs profoundly from its Christian counterpart, because unlike the latter it is not informed by the hope or ambition of ultimately finding "the real thing" after careful consideration of everything on offer. It rather appreciates that the variegated offerings ultimately all refer to the same divine source and therefore aims to prevent "getting stuck" with just one of these in the mistaken belief that it is superior to others. Rather than aimed at finding "the truth" in a particularistic tradition, then, spiritual seekership breathes contempt for those docile and narrow-minded enough to believe that they alone are in possession of the truth. Given that life is a quest for wholeness and self-attainment, one must keep moving.

Sociology of religion's principal misunderstanding of spirituality is that it has almost consistently conceived of perennialism, bricolage, and seekership as its most important features. This has led sociologists of religion to mistake the massively heterogeneous and fleeting spiritual practices on the ground for an absence of shared cultural precepts. It is precisely the interlocking ontological, epistemological, and soteriological precepts, however, that not only provide spirituality with cultural coherence but also lead SBNRs to embrace religious universalism, indulge in practices of bricolage and syncretism, and engage in seekership. Sociologists' misplaced focus on their diverse and disparate spiritual activities, while neglecting the underlying cultural logic that structures their choices, has led to a misconstrual of the former as "proving" a lack of cultural coherence. It is in fact precisely the other way around: spirituality's typically neglected cultural coherence gives rise to massively variegated spiritual practices on the ground.[72]

Given spirituality's distrust of religious dogmas and institutions and its encouragement to "follow one's personal spiritual path" by taking one's experiences, feelings, and intuitions seriously, it simply cannot exist otherwise than as a "spiritual supermarket" with the individual spiritual seeker/consumer ruling sovereign. Yet religious bricolage, syncretism, and seekership are not evidence of a postmodern skepticism toward metanarratives, but solid proof of a new religious metanarrative that has increasingly risen to prominence in the West—a metanarrative that paradoxically blinds its critics and adherents alike to its cultural coherence.

IS SPIRITUALITY AS PUBLICLY INSIGNIFICANT AS THEY SAY IT IS?

Spirituality in Public Institutions

Overlooking the religious metanarrative that underlies the staggering diversity of spiritual practices on the ground, we agree with Véronique Altglas that sociologists of religion need to be critiqued for their tendency to "overestimate personal subjectivity, 'choice,' and 'freedom,'" ignoring the nature and availability of the cultural resources mobilized, and more importantly, the degree to which subjectivities are *themselves* socially constituted.[73] Stef Aupers and Dick Houtman have similarly critiqued the scholarship on spirituality from a cultural sociological point of view, observing that it is actually *un*sociological, because it neglects, or even explicitly denies, the cultural shaping of spiritual practices and identities.[74] What to the untrained eye might appear a mere chaotic spiritual supermarket with individual consumers freely picking and choosing whatever their idiosyncratic tastes and preferences lead them to fancy is, in fact, underwritten by a stable and coherent cultural logic.

This logic not only accounts for the diversity on the ground but also makes public institutions amenable to spirituality. For instance, what once went by Complementary and Alternative Medicine (CAM), but which now goes by Complementary and Integrative Health,[75] has since the 1960s made major inroads into Western health care. Informed by the notion of a spirit that connects "everything," and hence mind and body, it dismisses modern biomedicine's mind-body dualism to pose a drastically different model of health, disease, and healing.[76] While CAM has obviously not overhauled biomedicine, it increasingly competes with this paradigm in defining matters of health and disease. Drawing on decades of research, Candy Gunther Brown boldly argues herein that discourses of holistic healing have been institutionalized within mainstream medicine to such an extent that spirituality represents the new "religious establishment." Meanwhile, Michal Pagis and Orly Tal take a different perspective on spirituality's incorporation into health care—specifically, psychotherapeutic practice. Based on fieldwork with therapists in Israel, they document how these healthcare professionals draw upon spirituality to challenge the individualistic and amoral assumptions so often naturalized in secular psychotherapy. Pagis and Tal thereby challenge the widespread view that spirituality is itself a source of rugged individualism and moral degradation.

Spirituality has also made major inroads into the world of work.[77] In the wake of the "expressive revolution" of the 1960s, we have seen a marked shift away from stifling rationalized, hierarchical, and bureaucratic organizations to much flatter ones, with self-steering, flexible, and proactive employees held up as the new norm.[78] Self-help books catering to new entrants into the labor market boast precisely such a shift; earlier advice to conform to the roles and rules predetermined by one's work organization has increasingly given way to the common sense that work should be the medium through which one pursues one's passions and achieves personal growth.[79] Whereas this new ideal of self-steering, flexible, and proactive employees comes strikingly close to spiritual ideals of personal authenticity, individual freedom, and self-development, sociologists of religion have unsurprisingly paid minimal attention to the "business spirituality" this dynamic has given rise to. Yet religious studies scholars and critical management theorists leave no doubt whatever about the pervasive role of spirituality in the modern workplace.[80] In their view the rise of workplace spirituality is best interpreted as resulting from, and responding to, the needs of late-modern neoliberal capitalism, be it by supplying "ideological justification for the capitalist exploitation of labour," "support[ing] the ideology of capitalism," or "participat[ing] in much broader cultural processes that uphold neoliberal capitalism."[81] Cultural studies scholars similarly understand spirituality as part and parcel of a neoliberal *episteme*, which disciplines its willing adherents to become "neoliberal subjects," that is, "flexible" and "proactive" employees adapted to the neoliberal order.[82] Often taking their cues from Michel Foucault, these scholars portray spirituality as a "technology of the self" that produces psychologized subjects who voluntarily regulate themselves in ways "consonant with contemporary political principles, moral ideals, and constitutional exigencies."[83]

This critical scholarship is as empirically important as it theoretically debatable. It is empirically important because it demonstrates convincingly that sociology of religion's virtual consensus regarding spirituality's cultural incoherence and public insignificance has been built on quicksand. For what these studies convincingly show is that spirituality comes replete with its own moral imperatives and cultural scripts, which discursively produce a specific kind of subject that meets the needs of contemporary work organizations. Yet these studies are debatable on theoretical grounds owing to their dogmatic assertion that it is the ruling powers and interests of late-modern neoliberal capitalism that account for the circulation of spirituality, in effect treating spirituality as little more than a capitalist ideology outfitted for the twenty-first century.[84] This strikes us as overly simplistic and just as likely to impede progress in the sociological study of spirituality as sociology of religion's submerged traditional Christian norm of "real" religion. As we see it, the process more plausibly entails a latter-day version of the dynamics discussed in *The Protestant Ethic and the Spirit of Capitalism*: not so much an instance of an economic transformation giving rise to religious change, but rather an unintended consequence of religious change due to its "elective affinity" (*Wahlverwandtschaft*) with a process of economic transformation.

Spirituality's Wider Public Significance

The claim that the dissemination of spirituality, not least in the world of work, has occurred "in order to support the ideology of capitalism" is a textbook example of what Jeffrey Alexander and Philip Smith call a "weak" program in the sociology of culture—which they define by a tendency to reduce culture to an allegedly "more fundamental" material realm.[85] This is precisely what scholars in religious studies, critical management studies, and cultural studies do when they define spirituality as neoliberal ideology, be it as a superstructure to a capitalist base or as an instrument of discursive power. Another problem with such theoretical reductionism is that it rules out by mere definitional fiat any view of spirituality's public significance which is not the legitimation or sustenance of neoliberal capitalism. Thus, the chapters in this volume depart from this reductionist approach and instead analyze the more general public significance of spirituality by taking seriously its cultural logics.

In their chapter, Paul McClure and Christopher Pieper investigate the discursive particularities of spirituality in Silicon

Valley. Upon conducting a discourse analysis of *Wired* magazine, they found that spirituality is often championed in the tech sector as a means to achieve religious salvation through technological innovation. Furthermore, they contend that for better or worse, given the outsized influence of Silicon Valley in shaping contemporary cultural trends, this form of spirituality is likely to grow in prevalence. Evan Stewart, Tim Dacey, and Jaime Kucinskas analyze new survey data that demonstrate that spiritual practices are no less associated with civic engagement than more traditional religious ones. And they argue that the myth of "selfish spirituality" persists because of long-standing historical and cultural assumptions about the role of religion in civic life in the United States, which leads scholars and laypeople alike to assume that religious practices are more prosocial than spiritual ones. In line with these findings, Galen Watts shows how since the 1960s spirituality increasingly features in the progressive political imaginary—something secularization theorists and critical scholars alike have either denied or misconstrued. Acknowledging spirituality's unabashed methodological individualism, he demonstrates how it nonetheless plays out in tandem with leftist, structuralist political critiques of institutional racism and sexism. In this way, spiritual ideals of self-realization and personal transformation increasingly go hand in hand with institutional transformation, making for a far more radical political agenda than most realize.

Dick Houtman and Stef Aupers then discuss spiritual seekers' vaccine hesitancy, which gave rise to a startling alliance with the populist right during the COVID-19 pandemic. Yet, spiritual seekers engaged in such antivaccination protests despite markedly progressive political values that were in their case overridden by distinctly spiritual understandings of the sacred. The overcoming of their axiomatic spiritual inwardness and political quietism during the COVID-19 crisis had as such nothing to do with their political values. It stemmed from a spiritual understanding of vaccinations as desecrating and defiling nature's self-healing powers. Finally, Jaron Harambam investigates the relationship between spiritual seekers and the populist right in more empirical detail, focusing on their shared susceptibility to conspiracy theories. He highlights not only the remarkable convergence of their cultural logics but also the marked tensions and incompatibilities that exist between them. In doing so, Harambam not only deepens insight into the phenomenon of "conspirituality" but also challenges understandings of contemporary conspiracy culture as a unitary, homogeneous, and conflict-free phenomenon.[86]

What the West is witnessing today is not simply a process of secularization but also a societal-scale shift away from the traditional Christian models of religion that secularization theorists are obsessed with toward a strikingly different religious form. To be clear, we recognize that secularization and the spiritual turn are two distinct developments that are co-occuring.[87] Thus, in our view, secularization theory is less wrong than uninteresting—or at least incapable of properly tracking and illuminating the spiritual turn and its wider societal implications. Accordingly, we argue that the way forward entails discarding Luckmann's influential yet intellectually flawed account of privatized religion while at the same time heeding his call to reconnect the sociology of religion with general sociology. For the spiritual turn has major implications for any number of substantively specialized sociologies, ranging from organizational sociology and the sociology of work to political or environmental sociology, social policy, the sociology of science and medicine, and the sociology of culture. In a word, it is high time to demonstrate to a wider sociological audience spirituality's cultural logic and public significance in a range of ostensibly nonprivate and nonreligious realms. That is the aim of this volume.

NOTES

1. Lois Lee, *Recognizing the Non-religious: Reimagining the Secular* (Oxford: Oxford University Press, 2015); Elizabeth Drescher, *Choosing Our Religion: The Spiritual Lives of America's Nones* (Oxford: Oxford University Press, 2016); Joel Thiessen and Sarah Wilkins-Laflamme, *None of the Above: Nonreligious Identity in the US and Canada* (New York: New York University Press, 2020); Linda Woodhead, "The Rise of 'No Religion': Towards an Explanation," *Sociology of Religion: A Quarterly Review* 78, no. 3 (2016): 247–62.
2. Charles Taylor, *A Secular Age* (Cambridge, MA: Belknap Press of Harvard University Press, 2007).
3. Michael Lipka and Claire Gecewicz, "More Americans Now Say They're Spiritual but Not Religious," *Pew Research Center*, September 6, 2017, https://www.pewresearch.org/fact-tank/2017/09/06/more-americans-now-say-theyre-spiritual-but-not-religious/. The findings of this survey were reported on in a wide array of public media outlets, including *Vox* and *The Atlantic*.
4. Pew Research Center, "Being Christian in Western Europe," May 29, 2018, https://www.pewforum.org/2018/05/29/being-christian-in-western-europe/.
5. Adam Possamai, "Popular and Lived Religions," *Current Sociology* 63, no. 6 (2015): 792.
6. Boaz Huss, "Spirituality: The Emergence of a New Cultural Category and Its Challenge to the Religious and the Secular," *Journal of Contemporary Religion* 29, no. 1 (2014): 47–60; Philip Sheldrake, *Spirituality: A Brief History* (Chichester, UK: Wiley-Blackwell, 2013).
7. Nancy T. Ammerman, *Sacred Stories, Spiritual Tribes: Finding Religion in Everyday Life* (Oxford: Oxford University Press, 2014); see also Penny Long Marler and C. Kirk Hadaway, "'Being Religious' or 'Being Spiritual' in America: A Zero-Sum Proposition?," *Journal for the Scientific Study of Religion* 41, no. 1 (2002): 289–300; Brian Steensland, Lauren Chism Schmidt, and Xiaoyun Wang, "Spirituality: What Does It Mean and to Whom?," *Journal for the Scientific Study of Religion* 57, no. 3 (2018): 450–72.

8. Joantine Berghuijs, Jos Pieper, and Cok Bakker, "Being 'Spiritual' and Being 'Religious' in Europe: Diverging Life Orientations," *Journal of Contemporary Religion* 28, no. 1 (2013): 27.
9. Andrea Jain, *Selling Yoga: From Counterculture to Pop Culture* (Oxford: Oxford University Press, 2014).
10. Liza Cortois, Stef Aupers, and Dick Houtman, "The Naked Truth: Mindfulness and the Purification of Religion," *Journal of Contemporary Religion* 33, no. 2 (2018): 303–17; see also Michal Pagis, *Inward: Vipassana Meditation and the Embodiment of the Self* (Chicago: University of Chicago Press, 2019).
11. Candy Gunther Brown, *The Healing Gods: Complementary and Alternative Medicine in Christian America* (Oxford: Oxford University Press, 2013).
12. James Dennis LoRusso, *Spirituality, Corporate Culture, and American Business: The Neoliberal Ethic and the Spirit of Global Capital* (New York: Bloomsbury, 2017); Galen Watts and Dick Houtman, "Purification or Pollution? The Debate Over 'Workplace Spirituality,'" *Cultural Sociology* 17, no. 4 (2022): 439–56; Carolyn Chen, *Work Pray Code: When Work Becomes Religion in Silicon Valley* (Princeton, NJ: Princeton University Press, 2022).
13. David Brooks, "The Age of Aquarius, All Over Again!," *New York Times*, June 10, 2019.
14. Samuel L. Perry, "(Why) Is the Sociology of Religion Marginalized? Results from a Survey Experiment," *American Sociologist* 54, no. 3 (2023): 1–27.
15. Bryan Wilson, *Contemporary Transformations of Religion* (Oxford: Oxford University Press, 1976), 96.
16. David Voas and Alasdair Crockett, "Religion in Britain: Neither Believing nor Belonging," *Sociology* 39, no. 1 (2005): 14.
17. Bryan S. Turner, "Religion and Contemporary Sociological Theories," *Current Sociology* 62, no. 6 (2014): 782.
18. Steve Bruce, *Secular Beats Spiritual: The Westernization of the Easternization of the West* (Oxford: Oxford University Press, 2017), 179.
19. José Casanova, *Public Religions in the Modern World* (Chicago: University of Chicago Press, 1994).
20. This specialized literature has been largely ignored by sociology of religion, let alone sociology more generally, which has left it with next to no impact on either the sociological understanding of spirituality or the latter's integration into the core of sociology of religion. See Sharday Mosurinjohn and Galen Watts, "Religious Studies and the Spiritual Turn," *Method & Theory in the Study of Religion* 33, no. 5 (2021): 482–504. Indeed, few sociologists are even aware that such a literature exists, never mind what it's all about. In fact, this scholarship on

spirituality has rather had the opposite effect of turning the sociological study of spirituality into a narrowly specialized field in and of itself.
21. Voas and Crockett, "Religion in Britain," 14, 25.
22. Steve Bruce, *God Is Dead* (Malden, MA: Blackwell, 2002); Steve Bruce, *Secularization: In Defence of an Unfashionable Theory* (Oxford: Oxford University Press, 2011); Alasdair Crockett and David Voas, "Generations of Decline: Religious Change in 20th-Century Britain," *Journal for the Scientific Study of Religion* 45, no. 4 (2006): 567–84; David Voas, "The Rise and Fall of Fuzzy Fidelity in Europe," *European Sociological Review* 25, no. 2 (2009): 155–68; Tony Glendinning and Steve Bruce, "New Ways of Believing or Belonging: Is Religion Giving Way to Spirituality?," *British Journal of Sociology* 57, no. 3 (2006): 399–414; Detlef Pollack and Gert Pickel, "Religious Individualization or Secularization? Testing Hypotheses of Religious Change—The Case of Eastern and Western Germany," *British Journal of Sociology* 58, no. 4 (2007): 603–32; Joel Thiessen, *The Meaning of Sunday: The Practice of Belief in a Secular Age* (London: McGill-Queen's University Press, 2015); David Voas and Mark Chaves, "Is the United States a Counterexample to the Secularization Thesis?," *American Journal of Sociology* 121, no. 5 (2016): 1517–56.
23. Oliver Tschannen, "The Secularization Paradigm: A Systematization," *Journal for the Scientific Study of Religion* 30, no. 4 (1991): 396–415; Isabella Kasselstrand, Phil Zuckerman, and Ryan T. Cragun, *Beyond Doubt: The Secularization of Society* (New York: New York University Press, 2023).
24. Peter L. Berger, *The Sacred Canopy: Elements of A Sociological Theory of Religion* (New York: Anchor Books, 1967).
25. Bruce, *Secular Beats Spiritual*, 6.
26. Jörg Stolz, "Secularization Theories in the Twenty-First Century: Ideas, Evidence, and Problems (Presidential Address)," *Social Compass* 67, no. 2 (2020): 282–308.
27. Voas and Chaves, "Counterexample."
28. Callum G. Brown, *The Death of Christian Britain: Understanding Secularisation 1800–2000*, 2nd ed. (London: Routledge, 2009).
29. Dick Houtman, Paul Heelas, and Peter Achterberg, "Counting Spirituality? Survey Methodology After the Spiritual Turn," *Annual Review of the Sociology of Religion: New Methods in the Sociology of Religion* (2012): 25–44.
30. Courtney Bender et al., "Introduction: Religion on the Edge: De-centering and Re-centering," in *Religion on the Edge: De-centering and Re-centering the Sociology of Religion*, ed. Courtney Bender et al. (Oxford: Oxford University Press, 2013), 1–20.

31. Linda Woodhead, "Real Religion and Fuzzy Spirituality? Taking Sides in the Sociology of Religion," in *Religions of Modernity: Relocating the Sacred to the Self and the Digital*, ed. Stef Aupers and Dick Houtman (Leiden: Brill, 2010), 31–48.
32. Steven J. Sutcliffe, "New Age, World Religions and Elementary Forms," in *New Age Spirituality: Rethinking Religion*, ed. Steven J. Sutcliffe and Ingvild Saelid Gilhus (London: Routledge, 2014), 17–34.
33. Mark Chaves, "Secularization as Declining Religious Authority," *Social Forces* 72, no. 3 (1994): 749–74.
34. Dick Houtman and Peter Mascini, "Why Do Churches Become Empty, While New Age Grows? Secularization and Religious Change in the Netherlands," *Journal for the Scientific Study of Religion* 41, no. 3 (2002): 455–73; Dick Houtman and Stef Aupers, "The Spiritual Turn and the Decline of Tradition: The Spread of Post-Christian Spirituality in 14 Western Countries, 1981–2000," *Journal for the Scientific Study of Religion* 46, no. 3 (2007): 305–20; Dick Houtman and Stef Aupers. "Religions of Modernity: Relocating the Sacred to the Self and the Digital," in *Religions of Modernity: Relocating the Sacred to the Self and the Digital*, ed. Stef Aupers and Dick Houtman (Leiden: Brill, 2010), 1–30.
35. Max Weber, *The Sociology of Religion* (Boston: Beacon Press, 1963 [1922]).
36. For a concise summary see Randall Collins, "The Classical Tradition in Sociology of Religion," in *The SAGE Handbook of the Sociology of Religion*, ed. James A. Beckford and N. J. Demerath III (Los Angeles: Sage, 2007), 19–38.
37. Emile Durkheim, *The Elementary Forms of Religious Life*, ed. Karen E. Fields (New York: Free Press, 1995 [1912]), 44.
38. David Bloor, *Science and Social Imagery* (Chicago: University of Chicago Press, 1976); Dick Houtman, Stef Aupers, and Rudi Laermans, "Introduction: A Cultural Sociology of the Authority of Science," in *Science Under Siege: Contesting the Secular Religion of Scientism*, ed. Dick Houtman, Stef Aupers, and Rudi Laermans (New York: Palgrave Macmillan, 2021), 1–34.
39. Bryan Wilson, *Religion in Sociological Perspective* (Oxford: Oxford University Press, 1982).
40. Thomas Luckmann, *The Invisible Religion: The Problem of Religion in Modern Society* (New York: Macmillan, 1967), 26, 90–91, 104.
41. Ernst Troeltsch, *The Social Teachings of the Christian Churches (Two Volumes)* (Louisville, KY: Westminster/John Knox Press, 1992 [1912]).
42. Colin Campbell, "The Secret Religion of the Educated Classes," *Sociological Analysis* 39, no. 2 (1978): 146–56; William R. Garrett. "Maligned

Mysticism: The Maledicted Career of Troeltsch's Third Type," *Sociological Analysis* 36, no. 3 (1975): 205–23.
43. Troeltsch, *The Social Teachings of the Christian Churches*, 729.
44. Troeltsch, *The Social Teachings of the Christian Churches*, 734, 739.
45. Galen Watts, *The Spiritual Turn: The Religion of the Heart and the Making of Romantic Liberal Modernity* (Oxford: Oxford University Press, 2022); Galen Watts and Dick Houtman, "The Spiritual Turn and the Disenchantment of the World: Max Weber, Peter Berger and the Religion–Science Conflict," *Sociological Review* 71, no. 1 (2023): 261–79.
46. Colin Campbell, "The Cult, the Cultic Milieu and Secularisation," *A Sociological Yearbook of Religion in Britain* 5 (1972): 119–36.
47. Galen Watts, "Missing the Forest for the Trees: 'Spiritual' Religion in a Secular Age," *Toronto Journal of Theology* 34, no. 2 (2018): 243–56.
48. Paul Heelas and Linda Woodhead, *The Spiritual Revolution: Why Religion Is Giving Way to Spirituality* (Malden, MA: Blackwell, 2005).
49. Amanda Porterfield, *The Transformation of American Religion: The Story of a Late-Twentieth-Century Awakening* (Oxford: Oxford University Press, 2001); Robert C. Fuller, *Spiritual but not Religious: Understanding Unchurched America* (Oxford: Oxford University Press, 2001); Catherine Tumber, *American Feminism and the Birth of New Age Spirituality: Searching for the Higher Self, 1875–1915* (Lanham, MD: Rowman & Littlefield, 2002); Jeremy Carrette and Richard King, *Selling Spirituality: The Silent Takeover of Religion* (London: Routledge, 2005); Catherine L. Albanese, *A Republic of Mind and Spirit: A Cultural History of American Metaphysical Religion* (New Haven, CT: Yale University Press, 2007); Peter Van der Veer, "Spirituality in Modern Society," *Social Research* 76, no. 4 (2009): 1097–1120; Courtney Bender, *The New Metaphysicals: Spirituality and the American Religious Imagination* (Chicago: University of Chicago Press, 2010); Leigh Eric Schmidt, *Restless Souls: The Making of American Spirituality* (Berkeley: University of California Press, 2012); Arthur Versluis, *American Gurus: From Transcendentalism to New Age Religion* (Oxford: Oxford University Press, 2014); William B. Parsons and Robert C. Fuller, "Spiritual but Not Religious: A Brief Introduction," in *Being Spiritual but Not Religious: Past, Present, Future(s)*, ed. William B. Parsons (New York: Routledge, 2018), 15–29.
50. Van der Veer, "Spirituality in Modern Society," 1103; Colin Campbell, *The Easternization of the West: A Thematic Account of Cultural Change in the Modern Era* (Boulder, CO: Paradigm Publishers, 2007).
51. Wade Clark Roof, *A Generation of Seekers: The Spiritual Journeys of the Baby Boom Generation* (San Francisco: Harper, 1993); Danièle Hervieu-Léger, "Religion and Modernity in the French Context: For a New Approach to Secularization," *Sociological Analysis* 51, Special

Presidential Issue (1990): S15–S25; David Lyon, *Jesus in Disneyland: Religion in Postmodern Times* (Malden, MA: Polity Press, 2000).

52. Robert Wuthnow, *After Heaven: Spirituality in America since the 1950s* (Berkeley: University of California Press, 1998); Robert Wuthnow, *After the Baby Boomers: How Twenty- and Thirty-Somethings Are Shaping the Future of American Religion* (Princeton, NJ: Princeton University Press, 2007), 135.
53. Wade Clark Roof, *Spiritual Marketplace: Baby Boomers and the Remaking of American Religion* (Princeton, NJ: Princeton University Press, 1999).
54. Lyon, *Jesus in Disneyland*; Adam Possamai, "Alternative Spiritualities and the Cultural Logic of Late Capitalism," *Culture and Religion* 4, no. 1 (2003): 31–45.
55. This point is echoed by Brian Steensland, Jaime Kucinskas, and Anna Sun, eds., *Situating Spirituality: Context, Practice, and Power* (Oxford: Oxford University Press, 2022). While we view this collection as holding close affinities to our own, we also believe its theoretical pluralism inadvertently reinforces the impression that spirituality lacks cultural coherence.
56. Galen Watts has called this tradition "the religion of the heart." See *The Spiritual Turn*.
57. Max Weber, *The Protestant Ethic and the Spirit of Capitalism* (London: Routledge, 2005 [1904–5]).
58. Campbell, *The Easternization of the West*, 345.
59. Galen Watts, "The Religion of the Heart: 'Spirituality' in Late Modernity," *American Journal of Cultural Sociology* 10, no. 1 (2022): 1–33.
60. Paul Heelas, *The New Age Movement: The Celebration of the Self and the Sacralization of Modernity* (Oxford: Blackwell, 1996), 19.
61. Wouter J. Hanegraaff, *New Age Religion and Western Culture: Esotericism in the Mirror of Secular Thought* (Leiden: Brill, 1996), 519.
62. See Watts, *The Spiritual Turn*.
63. Paul Tromp, Anna Pless, and Dick Houtman, "Do 'Spiritual' Self-Identifications Signify Affinity with New Age Religion? Survey Evidence from the Netherlands," *Journal of Contemporary Religion*, February 28, 2024, https://www.tandfonline.com/doi/full/10.1080/13537903.2024.2315809. We recognize that "New Age" has become a deeply polluted term, which is why we use it only to delimit a particular historical movement, and not to speak of those who identify as "spiritual" today.
64. Jessica Grogan, *Encountering America: Humanistic Psychology, Sixties Culture & the Shaping of the Modern Self* (New York: HarperCollins, 2013).
65. Paul Heelas, "The Sacralization of the Self and New Age Capitalism," in *Social Change in Contemporary Britain*, ed. Nicholas Abercrombie and Alan Warde (Cambridge: Polity Press, 1992), 139–66.

66. This is not always the case; in some instances, charismatic Christians reject the term "religion" and instead speak of "faith." See Watts, "The Religion of the Heart."
67. Campbell, *The Easternization of the West*, 345
68. Gordon Lynch, *The New Spirituality: An Introduction to Progressive Belief in the Twenty-first Century* (London: I. B. Tauris, 2007); Franz Höllinger, "Does the Counter-Cultural Character of New Age Persist? Investigating Social and Political Attitudes of New Age Followers," *Journal of Contemporary Religion* 19, no. 3 (2004): 289–309; Franz Höllinger, "Value Orientations and Social Attitudes in the Holistic Milieu," *British Journal of Sociology* 68, no. 2 (2017): 293–313.
69. Ammerman, *Sacred Stories, Spiritual Tribes*, 41.
70. See, for instance, Harvey Cox, *Fire From Heaven: The Rise of Pentecostal Spirituality and the Reshaping of Religion in the Twenty-first Century* (New York: Addison-Wesley, 1995); David Martin, *Pentecostalism: The World Their Parish* (Oxford: Blackwell, 2002); Simon Coleman, *The Globalisation of Charismatic Christianity: Spreading the Gospel of Prosperity* (Cambridge: Cambridge University Press, 2000); Kate Bowler, *Blessed: A History of the American Prosperity Gospel* (Oxford: Oxford University Press, 2013).
71. Admittedly, scholars who study spirituality of this variety are in part responsible for this. One of the key impediments to progress within the sociology of spirituality has been the proliferation of analytic terms used to describe this particular religious form; the academic literature is littered with neologisms that serve only to exacerbate the misconception that spirituality is culturally incoherent and publicly insignificant. These include but are not limited to "self-spirituality," "self-religion," "subjective-life spirituality," "mind-body-spirit spirituality," "alternative spirituality," "New Age spirituality," "contemporary spirituality," "liberal gnosticism," 'spiritualities of life,' and "new spirituality."
72. Stef Aupers and Dick Houtman, "Beyond the Spiritual Supermarket: The Social and Public Significance of New Age Spirituality," *Journal of Contemporary Religion* 21, no. 2 (2006): 201–22.
73. Véronique Altglas, *From Yoga to Kabbalah: Religious Exoticism and the Logics of Bricolage* (Oxford: Oxford University Press, 2014), 8.
74. Aupers and Houtman, "Beyond the Spiritual Supermarket."
75. See Candy Gunther Brown's chapter in this volume.
76. Nadine Raaphorst and Dick Houtman, "A Necessary Evil that Does Not 'Really' Cure Disease: The Domestication of Biomedicine by Dutch Holistic General Practitioners," *Health: An Interdisciplinary Journal for the Social Study of Health, Illness and Medicine* 20, no. 3 (2016): 242–57.

77. Jaime Kucinskas, *The Mindful Elite: Mobilizing from the Inside Out* (New York: Oxford University Press, 2018); Chen, *Work Pray Code*.
78. Talcott Parsons and Gerald M. Platt, *The American University* (Cambridge, MA: Harvard University Press, 1973); Bernice Martin, *A Sociology of Contemporary Cultural Change* (Oxford: Blackwell, 1981); Luc Boltanski and Eve Chiapello, *The New Spirit of Capitalism* (London: Verso, 2005).
79. Kobe De Keere, "From a Self-Made to an Already-Made Man: A Historical Content Analysis of Professional Advice Literature," *Acta Sociologica* 57, no. 4 (2014): 311–24.
80. Kimberley J. Lau, *New Age Capitalism: Making Money East of Eden* (Philadelphia: University of Pennsylvania Press, 2000); Michael York, "New Age Commodification and Appropriation of Spirituality," *Journal of Contemporary Religion* 16, no. 3 (2001): 361–72; Emma Bell and Scott Taylor, "The Elevation of Work: Pastoral Power and the New Age Work Ethic," *Organization* 10, no. 2 (2003): 329–49; Carrette and King, *Selling Spirituality*; Matthew Wood, *Possession, Power and the New Age: Ambiguities of Authority in Neoliberal Societies* (Burlington, VT: Ashgate, 2007); Jean Comaroff, "The Politics of Conviction: Faith on the Neo-liberal Frontier," *Social Analysis* 53, no. 1 (2009): 17–38; Craig Martin, *Capitalizing Religion: Ideology and the Opiate of the Bourgeoisie* (London: Bloomsbury, 2014); James Dennis LoRusso, "Towards Radical Subjects: Workplace Spirituality as Neoliberal Governance in American Business," in *Spirituality, Organization and Neoliberalism: Understanding Lived Experiences*, ed. Emma Bell, Sorin Gog, Anca Simionca, and Scott Taylor (Cheltenham, UK: Edward Elgar, 2020), 1–26.
81. Emma Bell and Scott Taylor, "The Elevation of Work: Pastoral Power and the New Age Work Ethic," *Organization* 10, no. 2 (2003): 338; Carrette and King, *Selling Spirituality*, 17; James Dennis LoRusso, "Towards Radical Subjects," 3.
82. Majia Holmer Nadesan, "The Discourses of Corporate Spiritualism and Evangelical Capitalism," *Management Communication Quarterly* 13, no. 1 (1999): 3–42; Heidi Marie Rimke, "Governing Citizens Through Self-Help Literature," *Cultural Studies* 14, no. 1 (2000): 61–78; Sam Binkley, "Psychological Life as Enterprise: Social Practice and the Government of Neo-Liberal Interiority," *History of the Human Sciences* 24, no. 3 (2011): 83–102; Karmen Erjavec and Zala Volčič, "Management Through Spiritual Self-help Discourse in Post-socialist Slovenia," *Discourse and Communication* 3, no. 2 (2009): 123–43; Guy Redden, "Religion, Cultural Studies and New Age Sacralization of Everyday Life," *European Journal of Cultural Studies* 14, no. 6 (2011): 649–63; James Reveley, "Neoliberal Meditations: How Mindfulness

Training Medicalizes Education and Responsibilizes Young People," *Policy Futures in Education* 14, no. 4 (2016): 497–511; Ruth Williams, "Eat, Pray, Love: Producing the Female Neoliberal Spiritual Subject," *The Journal of Popular Culture* 47, no. 3 (2014): 613–33; Andrada Tobias, "Steps on Life Change and Spiritual Transformation: The Project of the Self," *Studia UBB Sociologia* 61, no. 2 (2016): 125–44; Farah Godrej, "The Neoliberal Yogi and the Politics of Yoga," *Political Theory* 45, no. 6 (2017): 772–800; Véronique Altglas, "Spirituality and Discipline: Not a Contradiction in Terms," in *Bringing Back the Social Into the Sociology of Religion: Critical Approaches*, ed. Véronique Altglas and Matthew Wood (Boston: Brill, 2018), 79–107; Ronald E. Pursuer, "Critical Perspectives on Corporate Mindfulness," *Journal of Management, Spirituality & Religion* 15, no. 2 (2018): 105–8; Andrea R. Jain, *Peace Love Yoga: The Politics of Global Spirituality* (Oxford: Oxford University Press, 2020).
83. Nikolas S. Rose, *Governing the Soul: The Shaping of the Private Self* (New York: Free Association Books, 1989), 261.
84. A closely related cliché within critical scholarship is the equally debatable and overly sweeping notion of the "neoliberal subject." This concept meanwhile appears to apply to virtually any subject, from social democrats to the most radical libertarians no matter their marked differences, as equally dominated by an imperial "neoliberalism" that moreover remains typically vague and poorly defined. See Galen Watts, "Are You a Neoliberal Subject? On the Uses and Abuses of a Concept," *European Journal of Social Theory* 25, no. 3 (2022): 458–76.
85. Carrette and King, *Selling Spirituality*, 17; Jeffrey C. Alexander and Philip Smith, "The Strong Program: Origins, Achievements, and Prospects," in *Handbook of Cultural Sociology*, ed. John R. Hall, Laura Grindstaff and Ming-Cheng Lo (London: Routledge, 2010), 13–24; Jeffrey C. Alexander, *The Meanings of Social Life: A Cultural Sociology* (Oxford: Oxford University Press, 2003).
86. Charlotte Ward and David Voas, "The Emergence of Conspirituality," *Journal of Contemporary Religion* 26, no. 1 (2011): 103–21.
87. Houtman and Mascini, "Why Do Churches Become Empty, While New Age Grows?"; Sarah Wilkins-Laflamme, "A Tale of Decline or Change? Working Toward a Complementary Understanding of Secular Transition and Individual Spiritualization Theories," *Journal for the Scientific Study of Religion* 60, no. 3 (2021): 516–39.

1

HOW SPIRITUALITY GREW UP AND OUT OF CHRISTIANITY

LINDA WOODHEAD

Spirituality and Christianity are often thought of as opposed traditions with distinct trajectories of development. In thinking about the rise of spirituality in the West, more attention is often given to the influence of Hindu, Buddhist, Indigenous, and other non-Christian influences. This is in accord with how spirituality generally wishes to present itself, in distinction from "traditional," "Western" religion. Here I suggest that spirituality can be fully understood only in terms of a close and constitutive relation with Christianity—a relationship that extends from its emergence in the late nineteenth century through to the present day but that weakens significantly from the late twentieth century on. I identify a number of phases in this tangled relationship of Christianity and spirituality, showing how and why spirituality moved from being a marginal alternative to Christianity in the Anglo-American Christian-heritage societies that are my focus to becoming part of the cultural mainstream. I chart a gradual cultural reversal whereby the once marginal in religious terms has changed places with the once mainstream.

LIBERAL CHRISTIANITY, COLONIALISM, AND THE EMERGENCE OF MODERN SPIRITUALITY

When "spirituality" first emerged as a significant and self-conscious cultural force in Britain and North America in the mid-nineteenth century, it did so chiefly on a stage that was offered by liberal varieties of Christianity like the World's Parliament of Religions, and as part of radical Christian and post-Christian reform movements.[1] Many of its pioneers and patrons were individuals who had abandoned efforts to reform their own churches and denominations and dedicated their efforts to creating new, post-Christian forms of spirituality. Typically, they abandoned a Trinitarian understanding of God for a more radically unitarian conception—the divine as the One, the All—as well as rejecting doctrines of hell, damnation, and original sin. They favored more open forms of organization that gave scope for leadership by educated and charismatic women as well as men, and they embraced a progressive ethos.

Colonialism was an important part of the context. Spirituality emerges when colonialism is at its height, with Western powers actively engaged in reshaping the geopolitical landscape to bring more territories, peoples, and cultures under their control. The British Empire plays the largest role in the early history of spirituality. One of its effects, from the eighteenth century onward, had been to bring into existence an educated, Westernized, bilingual, "native" cultural elite, particularly in India. A related effect was to introduce "modernizing" ideas whose impetus extended to religion. Encounter with Christian missionaries, with their critiques and denunciations of the backward and benighted "idolatrous" religions they encountered, acted as a stimulus for indigenous elites to defend and reform existing religious cultures.

Thus empire helped to shape the impetus, means, and leaders who would drive indigenous religious change and reform.[2] This led to both conservative, proto-fundamentalist movements on the one hand and reforming, modernizing currents on the other. With regard to the former in South Asia, Islamic, Buddhist, and Hindu reformers revisited their own traditions to excise "idolatrous" aspects and leave a purer, more ethical, and more monotheistic or monomystical core. This dynamic saw the creation of organizations like the Arya Samaj of Dayananda Saraswati in 1875. Even before that, a reforming-liberalizing trend saw the creation of organizations like the Brahmo Samaj of Rammohun Roy and Dwarkanath Tagore in 1830 with a universalist rather than exclusivist outlook.[3] It is in relation to this liberalizing reformation that we can understand the rise of modern spirituality.

By the late nineteenth century, the early rationalist phase of modernizing reform was supplemented by a romantic and philosophically idealist one. This was bound up with a revival of interest in the Advaitic (nondualist) tradition within Hinduism itself. The result was a turn toward a unitary monistic commitment: belief not in one God but in a single, ineffable divine "Unity" identified as the essence of all true religion. This "One" was said to lie beyond name and form, word and symbol, and differences and distinctions of race and religion. As such, it could serve as the perfect unifying point of all the world's religions—a perennial tradition that promised a new era of religious harmony for the whole world.

When such spirituality was presented by a succession of holy men and swamis to the West as "wisdom from the East" it won an enthusiastic following, not least among educated women. The period between 1890 and 1914 was one of intense activity. The World's Parliament of Religions held in Chicago in 1893 as part of the World's Columbian Exposition proved to be one of its most important events.[4] The Parliament's liberal Christian organizers brought religious liberals together from around the world, hoping to demonstrate that all had in common belief in one Father God and the brotherhood of man.

In practice, however, it was the more radical speakers at the World's Parliament of Religions, like Swami Vivekananda from India (influenced by the Brahmo Samaj but going beyond it), the Buddhist monk Dharmapala, and representatives of the new Theosophical movement like Annie Besant, who gained the most lasting celebrity. Vivekananda's speech presented key themes of the emerging spirituality.[5] At its heart is a vision of the divine who is "everywhere the pure and formless one."[6] Rather than being mediated by priests, scriptures, rituals, or organizations, this "God" is said to be accessible to all men and women (the latter being explicitly addressed by Vivekananda). All religions point to the one divine essence, he proclaimed, but "the East" has the special task of re-presenting the message to a West that is sunk in scientific materialism on the one hand and Christian dogmatism on the other. "Every other religion lays down a certain amount of fixed dogma, and tries to force the whole society through it," said Vivekananda, but "to the Hindu, the whole world of religion is only a travelling, a coming up, of different men and women, though various conditions and circumstances, to the same goal. Every religion is only an evolving of a god out of the material man; and the same god is the inspiration of them all. . . . It is the same light coming through different colours." Vivekananda went on to criticize Christianity for calling men and women sinners: "Sinners? It is a sin to call man so; it is a standing libel on human nature."⁷ The radical political implication was clear: the rule of white races and those who claim to be arbiters of eternal truth must end. The time is ripe for colonized peoples to save those who come to conquer them.

Christian reaction to this message was wary if not hostile. Only some followers of radical forms of Protestantism were receptive. Mainstream Christian liberals, including many of the organizers of the World's Parliament themselves, were critical. However adept speakers like Vivekananda were at insisting on how much they shared with their liberal Christian brethren, the differences were becoming clearer. Some more conservative Christians, both Protestant and Catholic, went on the offensive. One of the most outspoken was the popular writer and theologian of the time, the English lay Catholic G. K. Chesterton, who chose Annie Besant as the target of his most forceful critique. Her brand of Theosophical spirituality was for him the mirror image of orthodoxy. As he puts it in *Orthodoxy*: "By insisting especially on the immanence of God we get introspection, self-isolation, quietism, social indifference—Tibet. By insisting on the transcendence of God we get wonder, curiosity, moral and political adventure, righteous indignation—Christendom. Insisting that God is inside man, man is always inside himself. By insisting that God transcends man, man has transcended himself."⁸

Despite such attacks, the formless mysticism that had been developed in a colonial context grew in influence in the first part of the twentieth century and had some impact on Christian thinking. There was a revival of interest in mysticism in Christian circles, both Catholic and Anglican, as in Dean Inge's *Christian Mysticism* of 1899 and Evelyn Underhill's *Mysticism* of 1911.⁹ Such rapprochement would not presage a more substantial alignment of Christianity and spirituality, however, in the later twentieth century.[10]

ESOTERICISM AND CHRISTIANITY

The emergence of spirituality out of a mix of liberal Christian, romantic, and Asian influences is only one part of the origin story, and here too the Christian influence is apparent. Another important influence was "esotericism": the literate "occult" traditions that date from the Renaissance and earlier. Although Western esotericism has links to ancient sources, including Egyptian, Greco-Roman, and Kabbalistic ones, esoteric practices were revived and reinterpreted in the Renaissance by cultural elites including Freemasons and classical scholars. Many were practicing Christians belonging to more highly ritualized forms of Eastern Orthodox, Catholicism, and Anglicanism. Few repudiated Christianity altogether.

Despite the fact that esotericism is not really a tradition but a collection of fragments with varied historical and contextual origins, in the nineteenth century they were reassembled into new packages and organizational forms.[11] Some leading figures, like Madame Helena Blavatsky, the founder of Theosophy, distanced themselves from Christianity and appealed to a timeless wisdom communicated directly by mysterious adepts dwelling on remote Himalayan mountaintops. Others, like Anna Kingsford and some of the Masonic founders of the Hermetic Order of the Golden Dawn, the most influential of the nineteenth-century occult societies, remained committed to Christianity while seeking to recover its mystical and magical dimensions.[12]

Just like the formless mysticism of the early mystical, progressive spirituality discussed above, these esoteric forms proved attractive to educated people dissatisfied with contemporary Christianity and scientific materialism alike. They offered both women and men the opportunity to pursue intellectually rigorous and spiritually exciting paths in which they were active explorers, participants, and teachers. Although modern esotericism was typically tightly organized, highly ritualized, and hierarchical, both women and men could rise to high levels by ascending through stages of ritual initiation and spiritual prowess. They were rewarded with powerful and direct "occult" experience, intense fellowship, authority, and mystique.[13]

Even the occultists and mystics who eschewed Christianity operated in its shadow. Aleister Crowley's dark arts and diabolical, sexualized ritual magic are an inversion of a puritanical Christianity and what it most feared and forbade. At the other end of the spectrum, Evelyn Underhill, the author of *Mysticism*, was a member of the Hermetic Order of the Golden Dawn as well as a devout Christian.[14]

EARLY WICCA

Wicca, which arose in England in the 1940s, was neither straightforwardly esoteric nor Christian. Developed by a former Anglican priest, Gerald Gardner, it drew on a mix of sources, including the folklorist Margaret Murray's work on witches and some of Crowley's rituals. Its early advocates presented Wicca as an ancient pre-Christian religion, persecuted by the churches but kept alive in secret by small groups of women, organized into covens, across Europe and America. Its twin deities were male and female: the horned god and the goddess. It embraced elements of popular as well as high magic, including spells. Gardner writes with one sardonic eye on Christian practice and assumptions and claims that his intention is to keep the ancient tradition of witchcraft alive—but in "recording" its rituals, practices, and forms he is really creating a new, feminized, form of spirituality for the late modern world.[15]

With its female as well as male deities, its reverence for nature, embrace of magic, and sense of persecution at Christian hands, Wicca is easily interpreted as a form of modern spirituality that, unlike those reviewed before, truly owes little or nothing to Christianity. Historians have demonstrated otherwise. They have exploded the myth of a secret, underground tradition hidden from the churches and untouched by their teaching and practices, and shown that insofar as elements of pagan and pre-Christian practice were preserved, it was within Christianity in its many forms that this happened.[16]

Pearson reminds us that not only Gardner but several others attracted to early Wicca were ordained Christian clergy.[17] She positions Wicca within a nativist Christian strand that can be traced back to the Renaissance and finds expression in experiments in creating indigenous ethnic-national churches shorn of the "foreign" influences of both Catholic and Protestant versions of Christianity. The work was led by *episcopi vagantes* (wandering bishops) who championed churches that purportedly upheld ancient traditions polluted or abandoned by later Christianity (interest in "Celtic Christianity" is a recent manifestation of this tendency). Early Wicca is in direct continuity with this tradition, since it carries forward the idea of an ancient, indigenous religion native to the "green and pleasant land" of England that the Christian mystic and artist William Blake had celebrated. In its embrace of magic, the body, women, and sexuality it is also, like Crowley, pushed by rebellion against contemporary church teaching, and pulled by a romantic yearning to return to a pre-industrial era.

THE EXPERIENTIAL TURN IN RELIGION

Even those varieties of early spirituality that rebelled most fiercely against Christianity tended to create alternatives in its image. Christianity provided the template of a religion, with an educated clerisy with knowledge of ancient cultures and languages, sermons and theological tomes, and hierarchical forms of organization focused on collective ritual. It was "high" in at least two senses: tied into elite, educated culture and society and bound up with an idealist or Neoplatonic framework in which the body and the material must be transcended to rise to the spiritual realm.

Alongside such "high" forms of religion, however, there have always been more popular, pragmatic, and practice-based forms of religion and magic.[18] Their aim is not so much to interpret the world as to change it, or just cope with it. Regularly dismissed as "magic" and "superstition," such religiosity offers consolation, entertainment, healing, miracles, and divination. The growth of mass media gave it new scope. By the later nineteenth century, intriguing and entertaining spiritual and "paranormal" phenomena and practices were being widely publicized. Mysterious phenomena like faith-healing, mesmerism, psychic awareness, and vivid ways of communicating with the spirit world gained new audiences and celebrity practitioners.[19] Some of these, like spiritualism, took the form of churches and denominations that persist to this day; others remained local, sporadic, and much more loosely organized.

By the 1970s the authority of older forms of religion was being seriously challenged by developments with a more practical and experiential emphasis. Within Christianity this is clearest in the charismatic revival of the 1970s, which has had such a powerful influence on subsequent Protestant and to a lesser extent

Catholic Christianity around the world. The charismatic turn directly challenged more formal manifestations of Christianity and the clerical elites who guarded them. It offered individuals direct experience of the Spirit in ways that improved their lives in the here and now. Life-transforming experiences and worldly benefits—miracles, healing, prosperity—were exalted over theological learning, participation in "empty" rituals, and immersion in tradition.

A similar turn occurred in spirituality in the rise of what came to be called the New Age movement. It was fed by earlier streams of formless mysticism and esotericism, but also by psychotherapy, the human potential movement, countercultural music, mind-altering drugs, feminism, ecological concerns, and utopian hopes.[20] As with charismatic Christianity, what matters most in the New Age is "what works" and what is directly experienced in personal life. Both offer the promise of discovering and enhancing one's unique purpose and identity. Thus Rick Warren, a best-selling American Christian author, tells readers how to discover God's plan for them and live "a purpose-driven life," while a plethora of New Age groups and practices offer techniques to get in touch with one's true self and the "god within."[21] Both the New Age and charismatic Christianity bring people into closer contact with spiritual powers that are energizing, healing, and transforming. Such power can be accessed by individuals for themselves. No priests, rituals, or mediation are needed: what is on offer are tools, training, and support. They share a heady cosmic optimism: "God has a plan for the universe" (evangelical language) or "the universe is moving toward a new age of universal enlightenment" (New Age language)—in other words, all will be well.

Despite these similarities, New Age and Charismatic Christianity have typically regarded one another with suspicion and mistrust.[22] Some of this can be explained by very different ethics and aesthetics, some by identity politics and the historical oppositions traced above. Charismatic churches have tight moral and behavioral codes that emphasize the importance of the nuclear family, heterosexual gender roles, male headship, and restrictive codes of sexual conduct, dress, and self-presentation.[23] By contrast, the New Age is associated with sexual libertarianism, antiestablishment attitudes, and countercultural behavior. The differences are apparent in different styles of dress, deportment, and domestic decoration, as well as differing emotional programs and regimes.[24]

THE HOLISTIC TURN

In the "holistic" or "mind-body-spirit" variety of spirituality that overtook New Age in the 1990s and early 2000s, the practical and experiential turn took a more embodied form, with a stronger emphasis on health and well-being. Practices like yoga, reiki, and meditation grew in popularity and spread into healthcare, workplaces, and schools, while words like "chi," "chakras," and "karma" entered the popular vocabulary. This is the point at which spirituality goes mainstream and starts to pose a serious challenge to Christianity in Anglo-American countries.

Women were prominent in this development. When colleagues and I undertook a study of spirituality in 2000–2002 in Kendal, England, we found that 80 percent of those involved both as practitioners and clients were women.[25] The vast majority had been raised Christian but had turned from the churches. Many expressed a traditionally feminine concern with the care of others but wished to give this expression not through church-based and charitable activities but by setting up shop as holistic practitioners.[26] They offered practical techniques for managing relationships, emotions, and health. In contrast to idealist tendencies of earlier kinds of mysticism and Christianity, the aim is to enter more deeply into embodied and relational experience. The body ceases to be a burden or source of temptation and becomes the gateway to the spirit.[27]

While the barriers to entering churches have remained high—knowledge of the Bible, theology, and liturgy, acceptable deportment and self-presentation, and a self-denying sexual ethic—spirituality was easily aligned with a more liberal ethic and was adaptable to the capitalist marketplace of health, beauty, and well-being provision.[28] In Kendal we found that most of the practitioners of holistic well-being were exiles from either the churches or the National Health Service—or both. This was traditional women's work of care, and by failing to value it, or them, the churches lost perhaps their most important asset.[29]

At first some more liberal churches hosted things like yoga classes, but as the latter became more successful they became autonomous. A few churches have borrowed elements like meditation and mindfulness, but more have responded by repudiating it. In 2000, the Roman Catholic Church published *Jesus Christ the Bearer of the Water of Life: A Christian Reflection on the New Age*. The report acknowledges that spirituality is proving attractive to many and suggests that it should prompt the Church to recover aspects of its own spiritual provision. But the ideas of spirituality are criticized as defective both theologically and morally. It is repudiated as self-centered, antinomian, and socially corrupting. Evidently, even the world's largest church was now obliged to take spirituality seriously and to assess its own offerings in the light of its rival. By contrast, spirituality was increasingly relaxed about the relationship as it became part of the religious and cultural mainstream rather than something "alternative" to the dominant religion.

THE PARTING OF THE WAYS

In the line of development I have traced so far, spirituality grows from being a marginal "alternative" to Christianity taking root in its shadow to becoming so influential that even the Roman Catholic Church has to react. Opportunities for rapprochement and merger between Christianity and spirituality have opened up at various points but have largely been passed over. Despite small pockets of convergence, the bigger picture since the 1980s has been of a growing gulf between the churches and spirituality—with Christianity, under the growing influence of fundamentalism, becoming more conservative relative to wider social attitudes and spirituality moving in the opposite direction, in step with liberal opinion.

As spirituality has come out of the shadow of Christianity it has diversified. It now exhibits as much metaphysical, organizational, and political breadth as Christianity once did. In the twenty-first century one tendency, best exemplified by "mindfulness," has been to secularize selectively and align with science, thereby claiming the legitimacy to operate in public arenas like schools and workplaces.[30] A very different development sees spirituality eschewing the mainstream and aligning with conspiracy theories, something that accelerated under the COVID-19 pandemic.[31] Wellness "conspirituality" now takes many forms, from macho antivaxx influencers to back-to-nature, "bone-broth-making" feminine manifestations.[32] They share certain characteristics including an apocalyptic sense of living in the end times and representing a hidden, repressed and dangerous knowledge suppressed by the powers that be. (See Jaron Harambam's chapter in this volume.)

Diversification is now a feature not only of modern spirituality as a whole but also of the various strands within it. Paganism is the best example. In her "Pagan Census" of 2009–10, Helen Berger discovered twenty-two separate major pagan paths or identities. The three most popular are "Wiccan" or "Witch" (combined); then "Eclectic" and "Goddess Worshipper," followed by "Magic Worker," "Spiritual no labels," "Shaman," "Druid," and "Heathen."[33] Kathryn Rountree notes rival tendencies, including the prevalence of solitary practice on the one hand and the rise of tightly bounded and hierarchically organized heathen/reconstructionist groups on the other.[34] Heathenism, which looks back to the pre-Christian Scandinavian and Germanic gods, is now split between a "folkish" far right with racist and anti-Semitic tendencies and liberal, environmentally oriented elements fighting for the soul of the religion.[35]

Behind the diversity, paganism represents a break with Christianity much more profound than in earlier kinds of spirituality. In ethics, ontology, and "theology" (understanding of the divine) it is not in some kind of continuity with liberal, progressive versions of Christianity, as many earlier kinds of spirituality, including the holistic, have been, but has adopted a different template. It is nature-based and planetary rather than anthropocentric, as is evident in its ritual year, shaped as it is around planetary cycles rather than the life of Christ and the saints. It eschews an ethic of self-sacrifice and service in favor of one that is about realizing one's unique potential and helping close others do the same. And it relates to a plethora of gods, spirits, and supernatural beings, not an Almighty God.

FROM MARGIN TO MAINSTREAM

In the late nineteenth century, where this chapter begins, calling yourself a Christian of whatever denomination was the default position in Europe and America. This was the religious norm. It signaled majority belonging, national loyalty, and common decency. There were dissenting movements, of course, but they were largely Christian, particularly in the United States.[36] By the 2020s, where the chapter ends, this is no longer the case, even in America. In these increasingly plural societies it is no longer countercultural to describe oneself as "spiritual but not religious." Now it is "religion" that has more negative associations among many young people, being widely viewed as something intolerant and even abusive.[37] As the relationship between spirituality and Christianity has shifted, the former has gone from margin to mainstream. It has grown up and out of Christianity, and it has both walked out and been thrown out.

The century and a half considered here is marked by continuous change and adjustment, whereby spirituality becomes increasingly accepted. Many of its practices, concepts, and ideas have entered the language and popular culture and are popularized in the mass media, in film and fiction, and now by innumerable influencers through the internet and social media.

In the story I have told, spirituality starts out as a reforming movement within Christian and colonial contexts, defines itself over and against religion, and attains a clear profile and identity. Into the twentieth century, Christianity and spirituality develop in parallel, still with significant similarities including an idealist or Neoplatonic worldview, hierarchical forms of organization, and an eschatological horizon. The development of New Age and then holistic spirituality after the 1980s with their more therapeutic and this-worldly emphasis marks a turning point. There is a shift to the embodied and practical, to less hierarchical organization, and to female dominance. Spirituality inserts itself into social institutions from schools to hospitals. It goes mainstream, showing itself to be adaptable to a religious pluralism undergirded by law. By now it is Christianity that is reacting against spirituality rather than the other way round.

Today we see a more diversified landscape of spirituality. The growth of various kinds of paganism, both right-wing and left-wing, both tightly organized and solitary, alongside holistic spirituality, mindfulness, and conspirituality speaks of spirituality come of age. If anything, it exhibits even greater internal diversity and contention than Christianity did at the start of this story.

Like the word "Christianity," "spirituality" names a set of symbols, practices, and institutional resources that can be creatively reinterpreted and combined with new elements at different times and for different purposes. Spirituality has shown itself to be more flexible than Christianity, however, not because it has no authorities or sacred symbols but because its lack of centralized structures allows for an inflow of new entrants in every generation, taking power and offering fresh interpretations and manifestations, aided now by the internet.

None of this implies that spirituality has overtaken Christianity numerically, nor that it now has the same social and cultural influence that the churches once enjoyed.[38] The argument is rather about relative cultural influence and social acceptability. Insofar as a "reenchantment" can be discerned in Western societies today, it is spirituality rather than Christianity that is responsible.[39]

NOTES

1. Linda Woodhead, "The New Spirituality and the World's Parliament of Religions," in *Reinventing Christianity: Nineteenth Century Contexts*, ed. Linda Woodhead (Aldershot: Ashgate, 2001), 81–96; Leigh Eric Schmidt, *Restless Souls: The Making of American Spirituality* (New York: Harper San Francisco, 2005).
2. This task was additionally strengthened by the work of Western "Orientalist" scholars (in the language of the day) who came on the coattails of Empire but were active in recovering and celebrating the ancient texts and "Ur" cultures of the ancient "East." See David Kopf, *British Orientalism and the Bengal Renaissance: The Dynamics of Indian Modernization, 1773–1835* (Berkeley: University of California Press, 1969). The influence of other, sometimes countercultural, Westerners who showed an interest in the defense of ancient cultures also played a part. See, for example, Mary Lago, *Imperfect Encounter: The Letters of William Rothenstein and Rabindranath Tagore* (Cambridge, MA: Harvard University Press, 1972).
3. David Kopf, *The Brahmo Samaj and the Shaping of the Modern Indian Mind* (Princeton, NJ: Princeton University Press, 1979).
4. Richard Hughes Seager, *The Dawn of Religious Pluralism: Voices from the World's Parliament of Religions* (La Salle, IL: Open Court, 1993).
5. Ruth Harris, *Guru to the World: The Life and Legacy of Vivekananda* (Cambridge, MA: Belknap Press, 2022).
6. Vivekananda, "Hinduism," in *The World's Parliament of Religions*, ed. Henry Barrows (Chicago: Parliament Publishing Company, 1893), 2:972.
7. Vivekananda, "Hinduism," 976–77, 971.
8. G. K. Chesterton, *Orthodoxy* (London: Fontana, 1961 [1908]), 133.
9. Jane Shaw, *Pioneers of Modern Spirituality: The Neglected Anglican Innovators of a "Spiritual but Not Religious" Age* (London: Darton, Longman and Todd, 2017).
10. Later in the twentieth century liberal theologians like Rudolph Bultmann in Germany and John Robinson in Britain would offer accounts of God as "ultimate concern" and "depth of our being." These approaches had more in common with formless mysticism than Trinitarian orthodoxy. Heavily criticized by other Christian thinkers, they were eclipsed after the 1970s by more conservative and "neo-orthodox" views. Instead of being absorbed into mainstream Christianity and the churches, spirituality was forced outside them.
11. Wouter J. Hanegraaff, *New Age Religion and Western Culture: Esotericism in the Mirror of Secular Thought* (Albany: State University of New York Press, 1998).

12. Alex Owen, *The Place of Enchantment: British Occultism and the Culture of the Modern* (Chicago: University of Chicago Press, 2004).
13. Alex Owen, *The Darkened Room: Women, Power and Spiritualism in Late Victorian England* (London: Virago Press, 1989).
14. Shaw, *Pioneers of Modern Spirituality*.
15. Margot Adler, *Drawing Down the Moon: Witches, Druids, Goddess-Worshippers and Other Pagans in America Today*, rev. ed. (London: Penguin, 1986).
16. Ronald Hutton, *The Triumph of the Moon: A History of Modern Pagan Witchcraft* (Oxford: Oxford Paperbacks, 1995); Owen Davies and Willem de Blécourt, "Introduction: Beyond the Witch Trials," in *Beyond the Witch Trials: Witchcraft and Magic in Enlightenment Europe*, ed. Owen Davies and Willem de Blécourt (Manchester: Manchester University Press, 2004), 1–8.
17. Joanne Pearson, *Wicca and the Christian Heritage: Ritual, Sex and Magic* (New York: Routledge, 2007).
18. Owen Davies, *Cunning-Folk: Popular Magic in English History* (London: Bloomsbury, 2003).
19. Owen, *The Darkened Room*.
20. Some interpretations see New Age as growing out of esoteric spirituality (e.g., Hanegraaff, *New Age*), others out of formless mysticism: Paul Heelas, *The New Age Movement: The Celebration of the Self and the Sacralization of Modernity* (Oxford: Blackwell, 1996). My suggestion is that both are influential resources on which New Age and its many variants draw. See also Steven J. Sutcliffe, *Children of the New Age: A History of Spiritual Practices* (London: Routledge, 2003).
21. Rick Warren, *The Purpose Driven Life: What on Earth Am I Here For?* (Grand Rapids, MI: Zondervan, 2002); Heelas, *The New Age Movement*. Cultural commentators have tended to see these traits much more clearly in New Age and alternative spirituality—for example in the famous denunciation of the "expressive individualism" of "Sheila" in Robert Bellah et al., *Habits of the Heart: Individualism and Commitment in American Life* (Berkeley: University of California Press, 1985). It is interesting to note that Bellah in more recent essays acknowledges his mistake in not seeing that evangelical Christianity would be an equally if not more important social carrier of individualism in late-modern America. See Robert Bellah, "Flaws in the Protestant Code: Theological Roots of American Individualism," in *The Robert Bellah Reader*, ed. Robert Bellah and Steven M. Tipton (Durham, NC: Duke University Press, 2006), 225–45.
22. In research in Kendal in 2000–2002, I found that of all Christian groups, it was charismatic-evangelicals who were *least* likely to have any contact with New Age spirituality and vice versa. Even participating

in activities like yoga for purely physical reasons was regarded with suspicion by many evangelicals. In the most charismatic of the churches a full 60 percent of respondents agreed with the most negative statement offered in a survey of attitudes to spirituality: that "alternative or complementary non-church forms of spirituality are unacceptable for Christians." Data available at http://www.lancs.ac.uk/fss/projects/ieppp/kendal/.

23. Katie Gaddini, *The Struggle to Stay: Why Single Evangelical Women Are Leaving the Church* (New York: Columbia University Press, 2022).

24. Ole Riis and Linda Woodhead, *A Sociology of Religious Emotion* (Oxford: Oxford University Press, 2010).

25. Paul Heelas and Linda Woodhead, *The Spiritual Revolution: Why Religion Is Giving Way to Spirituality* (Malden, MA: Blackwell, 2005). Although middle- and lower-middle-class women played a central role in the success of holistic spirituality, it extends into the working class. During research in 2006 with Helen Berger in Asheville, North Carolina, for example, we visited a double-wide in a trailer park in an extremely poor area that both sold material paraphernalia associated with holistic spirituality (charms, crystals, tarot cards and so on) and had on hand a number of practitioners who were dealing with everyday issues including serious illness, depression, and even a sick pet. In the northwest of England, Janet Eccles's doctoral research has also discovered holistic practitioners whose homes serve as a regular port of call for those in the local area from all classes who need help, advice, and support with everyday problems—sometimes free of charge.

26. Eeva Sointu, *In Search of Wellbeing: Reflecting on the Use of Alternative and Complementary Medicines* (Lancaster, UK: Department of Sociology, Lancaster University, 2005).

27. Eeva Sointu and Linda Woodhead, "Holistic Spirituality, Gender, and Expressive Selfhood," *Journal for the Scientific Study of Religion* 47, no. 2 (2008): 259–76. Two hardly "bookish" books by American women bookend this holistic turn: Starhawk, *The Spiral Dance: A Rebirth of the Ancient Religion of the Great Goddess* (San Francisco: Harper, 1999) and Clarissa Pinkola Estés's *Women Who Run with the Wolves: Myths and Stories of the Wild Woman Archetype* (New York: Ballantine, 1992).

28. Galen Watts, *The Spiritual Turn: The Religion of the Heart and the Making of Romantic Liberal Modernity* (Oxford: Oxford University Press, 2022).

29. Frank Prochaska, *Christianity and Social Service in Modern Britain* (New York: Oxford University Press, 2006); Abby Day, *The Religious Lives of Older Laywomen: The Last Active Anglican Generation* (Oxford: Oxford University Press, 2017).

30. Alp Arat, " 'What It Means to Be Truly Human': The Postsecular Hack of Mindfulness," *Social Compass* 64, no. 2 (2017): 167–79.
31. David Robertson, *UFOs, Conspiracy Theories and the New Age: Millennial Conspiracism* (London: Bloomsbury, 2016); Anna Halafoff et al., "Selling (Con)spirituality and COVID-19 in Australia: Convictions, Complexity and Countering Dis/misinformation." *Journal for the Academic Study of Religion* 35, no. 2 (2022): 166–88.
32. See, for example, Derek Beres, Matthew Remski, and Julian Walker, "Russell Brand's Man Stans," *Conspirituality Podcast Series*, October 19, 2023, https://podcasts.apple.com/gb/podcast/176-russell-brands-man-stans/id1515827446?i=1000631850119; Sarah Wilson, "The Wellness Realm Has Fallen into Conspiritualism—I Have a Sense Why," *Guardian*, September 14, 2020.
33. Helen Berger, *Solitary Pagans: Contemporary Witches, Wiccans, and Others Who Practice Alone* (Columbia: University of South Carolina Press, 2019), 35. See also Helen A. Berger, Evan A. Leach, and Leigh S. Shaffer, *Voices from the Pagan Census: A National Survey of Witches and Neo-Pagans in the United States* (Columbia: University of South Carolina Press, 2003).
34. Kathryn Rountree, *Embracing the Witch and the Goddess: Feminist Ritual-Makers in New Zealand* (New York: Taylor and Francis, 2004).
35. Helen A. Berger, "The 'Sonnenrad' Used in Shooters' Manifestos: A Spiritual Symbol of Hate," *The Conversation*, May 27, 2022, https://theconversation.com/the-sonnenrad-used-in-shooters-manifestos-a-spiritual-symbol-of-hate-183319.
36. Stephen Bullivant, *Nonverts: The Making of Ex-Christian America* (New York: Oxford University Press, 2022).
37. Roberta Katz et al., *Gen Z, Explained: The Art of Living in a Digital Age* (Chicago: University of Chicago Press, 2021).
38. Paul Tromp, Anna Pless, and Dick Houtman, "A Smaller Pie with a Different Taste: The Evolution of the Western-European Religious Landscape," *Review of Religious Research* 64, no. 1 (2022) no. 1 (2022): 127–44.
39. Morris Berman, *The Re-enchantment of the World* (Ithaca, NY: Cornell University Press, 1981); Christopher Partridge, *The Re-enchantment of the West*, 2 vols. (New York: T&T Clark, 2005–6); Watts, *The Spiritual Turn*.

2

THE CULTIC MILIEU AND THE SPIRITUAL TURN

The Need for Theoretical Revision

COLIN CAMPBELL

In 1972 I introduced the notion of the "cultic milieu" in an attempt to direct the attention of sociologists of religion away from the essentially ephemeral phenomenon of cults to the more general and essentially cultural phenomenon of the milieu from which such organizations emerged (and back into which they usually quite quickly dissolved). This milieu I described as containing a range of esoteric, deviant, and unorthodox beliefs among which mystical and spiritual beliefs were commonplace. The article itself proved something of a slow burner, and it was quite a while before it received much notice. However, its current impact is far from negligible. Its citation count has increased from a mere 2 or 3 annually until as late as the early 1990s to an annual average of more than 40 in the last five years. What is more, even scholars beyond sociology and the study of religion have meanwhile come to embrace its argument as "prescient," "powerful," and "very useful."[1]

Yet, half a century later, the argument advanced in that article is in need of some theoretical revision. This is necessary because conceiving of spirituality as part and parcel of the cultic milieu has become less plausible due to its absorption into the cultural mainstream of the West.[2] This "spiritual turn" has prompted me not only to revise my understanding of the content of the milieu but also, more critically, to address the more serious problem of its conceptualization. Central to this problem is the question of whether the milieu needs to be defined *substantively* or *relationally*, and if indeed the latter approach is to be preferred, how best to conceptualize this dominant cultural realm and its relationship to the cultic milieu.

What this chapter offers, therefore, is a revision of my original argument about the cultic milieu. Empirically this is necessary because spirituality has become part of the Western cultural mainstream to such an extent that it can no longer be meaningfully considered part of the cultic milieu. This does not in itself necessarily make the concept of the cultic milieu redundant or obsolete. But it does direct attention to the unresolved problem of how precisely the milieu should be conceived, and in particular how it is related to the larger cultural system. What I suggest is that this system is best thought of as consisting of a trichotomy composed of a *cultural orthodoxy*, a *cultural mainstream*, and a *cultic milieu*.

THE FATE OF A CONCEPT

According to Jesper Aagaard Petersen, "A recurrent issue in the 40-year history of the concept of the cultic milieu is the pressing question: WHERE IS THE DAMN THING?"[3] His obvious frustration, arising as it clearly does from the difficulty of pinning down the empirical referent for the term, is shared by others. Hence Christopher Partridge, in his plea for its replacement by the term "occulture," suggests that its usage has been "stretched too far," having been used to encompass too broad a range of "ideologies and spiritualities." Partridge thus concludes, "The cultic milieu theory is currently not fit for purpose."[4]

And so, while the term may be widely used, this does not mean that there is also general agreement about its empirical referent, or even, it would appear, its usefulness. How is it that we can have such contrasting judgments? How is it that on the one hand the concept is judged to be powerful and useful, while on the other it is deemed impossible to locate and even no longer fit for purpose? I shall try to show that, paradoxically, both positions are fundamentally correct. In part this is because there are really two difficulties with the concept of the cultic milieu, and these are "What is it?" and "Where is it?" An answer to the first of these is relatively easy to give: it is usually conceived as a mélange of heterodox and esoteric beliefs, ideas, and associated movements ("diverse ideologies and spiritualities" in Partridge's words). However, the second question—Where is it to be found? or, more correctly, Where are its borders?—is much more difficult to answer.

It is in relation to the first question that various commentators have attested to its usefulness as a heuristic device, a means of focusing attention on a phenomenon that otherwise might have gone unnoticed. Thus, Jochen Scherer emphasizes that "the strength of the concept . . . lies in the fact that it draws attention to a continual dynamic process that is at the heart of the phenomenon under study," while Stephen Davies notes that what makes the concept "both powerful and very useful in understanding many contemporary phenomena" is that the various "fringe beliefs" found in the milieu "did not exist in isolation from each other . . . but mingled in a social space in which accepted and dominant ways of thinking about the world were rejected."[5] It is this view of the milieu as a kind of cultural cauldron or mixing pot that would appear to account for its appeal to commentators and researchers—an arena in which there is an active churning froth of ideas and beliefs, continually throwing up new cultural combinations that are then temporarily taken up by new associations or organizational forms, only to be radically changed or replaced by others.

At the same time there is considerable confusion and uncertainty about the milieu's parameters and hence how precisely it should be defined. In particular, it is unclear whether the cultic milieu should be defined in terms of its distinctive content, or its relationship with the larger societal cultural system, and if the latter, what form this relationship takes. This is the problem I hope to explore, and to help me do so I shall focus on two very different books, both of which make use of the concept of the cultic milieu. These are Wouter J. Hanegraaff's *New Age Religion and Western Culture: Esotericism in the Mirror of Secular Thought*, which was published in 1996, and Jeffrey Kaplan and Heléne Lööw's edited volume *The Cultic Milieu: Oppositional Subcultures in an Age of Globalization*, which was published in 2002.[6]

THE NEW AGE AND THE CULTIC MILIEU

I shall start with Hanegraaff's book. The important point to note in relation to the argument advanced in this volume is the question of timing. As Susan Joy Rennison observes, I proposed the concept of the cultic milieu, "before the emergence of 'New Age' as an analytical concept and so [I] make no reference to the New Age movement."[7] This is very true, although given the relevant dates, that omission is perhaps excusable. What is less excusable is that I failed to see the connection between the cultic milieu, as I outlined it in 1972, and the counterculture or "underground" of the 1960s, as the overlap was too obvious to be ignored, given the common interest in such subjects as astrology, Eastern religion, UFOs, vegetarianism, environmentalism, and the occult. Indeed, as many have noted, the 1960s counterculture very quickly morphed into the New Age movement, such that the term "New Age" has been widely employed to cover both the 1960s counterculture and the complete alternative movement that succeeded it—a point noted in *New Age Religion and Western Culture*. Then, critically, Hanegraaff goes on to observe that "with all the available evidence pointing in the same direction, it is natural to conclude that the New Age is either synonymous with the cultic milieu or that it represents a specific historical stage in the development of it." He continues by asserting that the New Age movement can be thought of as "the cultic milieu *having become conscious of itself* as constituting a more or less unified 'movement.'"[8]

If we accept Hanegraaff's claim that the New Age movement is indeed essentially identical with the cultic milieu, then we must also accept that the beliefs and practices that I identified as characteristic of the milieu in the 1970s have since become part of the cultural mainstream—or, at least, of *a* cultural mainstream.[9] This conclusion is inescapable because scholars who have studied the New Age movement all agree that it is not a phenomenon confined to the margins of contemporary society.[10] Thus, Paul Heelas says that it would be a mistake to assume that the New Age is only "a fringe curiosity." Rather, his conclusion is that it is "firmly entrenched as a cultural and practical resource" in contemporary society.[11] James R. Lewis, for his part, expresses the opinion that the New Age "is merely the most visible part of a more significant cultural shift," adding, "we are no longer talking about a marginal phenomenon. Rather we appear to be witnessing the birth of a new, truly pluralistic, Mainstream."[12] Finally, we have Philip Seddon —who as a Christian critic of the movement has little incentive to exaggerate its importance— writing, "the New Age is a spiritual movement of powerful proportions, analogous to the Renaissance or the Enlightenment."[13]

It follows that if we accept Hanegraaff's claim that "the New Age is synonymous with the cultic milieu," and Lewis's that the New Age movement is part of a "new, truly pluralistic mainstream" then we can no longer think of the cultic milieu as the realm of the deviant or unorthodox—at least not as long as this phenomenon is defined in terms of the substantive content I outlined in the 1970s. For it is indeed the case that many of the beliefs and practices that I identified in 1972 as hallmarks of cultic religious groups are today generally regarded as part of a pluralistic mainstream culture (at least in the Western world).[14] This is also true of the major Eastern world religions of Hinduism and Buddhism, as well as, relatedly, belief in reincarnation. But then it also tends to be the case with astrology, magic and witchcraft, meditation, and mediumship, together with what is known as alternative and complementary forms of medicine— all topics mentioned in the original article as typical features of the cultic milieu. It would seem therefore that if the terms "cultic milieu" and "New Age" refer to the same phenomenon then the former has outlived its usefulness.

But then, on reflection, it seems obvious that the ideas and beliefs that constitute orthodox accredited knowledge in a society will necessarily vary over time, as well as from one society to another. Consequently, it follows that the cultic milieu cannot be defined in terms of its substantive content. For to do so is necessarily to find oneself caught out by the ongoing processes of cultural change that characterize any society—as indeed I have been. Which therefore only leaves the possibility of defining the term by its relationship to the larger cultural system. And this is where the other book I mentioned comes in, Jeffrey Kaplan and Heléne Lööw's *The Cultic Milieu*.

THE CULTIC MILIEU RELATIONALLY CONCEIVED

Just a glance at the contents of this volume will immediately make clear that, in sharp contrast to the Hanegraaff book, we have lost touch with the cultic milieu as I outlined it in 1972—and hence any connection with Troeltsch's spiritual and mystic religion.[15] For here the concern is with what are referred to as "oppositional subcultures" (see the book's subtitle),[16] while examples included in the collection are the Branch Davidians, the Animal Liberation Front, the Church of Satan, the Black Panthers, Goths, neo-Nazis, and the Earth First! environmental movement. Now you may be wondering, as I did, quite what this diverse range of organizations and social movements might have in common that warrants them being identified as constituent ingredients of the cultic milieu. Strangely, Kaplan and Lööw do not give a straight answer to this question, being content to employ the single word "oppositional," as if that was all that needed to be said on the subject. In fact, they state, quite categorically, that "the cultic milieu is oppositional by nature."[17]

The problem with this of course is that describing the contents of the cultic milieu as "oppositional" still leaves two crucial questions unanswered. To what is it opposed? And what precisely is the nature of this opposition? (The answer to this second question rather presupposes that we know the answer to the first). Rather bizarrely, Kaplan and Lööw omit to say what the contents of the cultic milieu are supposedly opposed to, although they do make a passing reference to something they call "the dominant culture," presumably on the assumption that the reader will take for granted that this is what the milieu is "opposed to."[18] Even then the nature of this "opposition" remains obscure; it could be the unorthodox as opposed to the orthodox, the deviant as opposed to the normal, the accepted as opposed to the rejected, or that which is openly available as opposed to that which is suppressed. In the absence of any detailed discussion of what the cultic milieu is opposed to, such matters are left hanging in the air.

As you can see, the key feature of this attempt by Kaplan and Lööw to define the cultic milieu is that it is relational, that is, their conceiving of the milieu in terms of its distinctive relationship with the larger cultural system. What is more, this relationship is clearly conceived as dichotomous, there being just two items. Now, Kaplan and Lööw are not alone in defining the cultic milieu in this way, as most commentators also tend to contrast the cultic milieu with the larger societal culture (although not all use the word "oppositional"). The problem is that there is little standardization of terminology regarding "the other," against which the milieu is contrasted. So, while Kaplan and Lööw regard the milieu as opposed to "the dominant culture," others contrast it with "conventional beliefs and knowledge," or "ideas [found in] mainstream society."[19] Still others use the phrase "the dominant orthodoxy" or, more directly echoing Kaplan and Lööw, "the dominant societal culture."[20] Remarkable, in my view, is the lack of any attempt to clarify quite what we mean by these terms, let alone provide examples that would help the reader to grasp their meaning. What precisely is meant by "the dominant culture" or "the dominant orthodoxy" is left to one's imagination, as too is "the mainstream" or "ideas found in mainstream society." And yet, if we can't say with any certainty what cultural items are *not* to be found in the cultic milieu, how then can we be sure that we know what *is* to be found there?

Could it be that it is this failure to specify what the milieu is *not* that explains why, in Petersen's words, the cultic milieu has proved so difficult "to pin down?" Clearly what is needed to remedy this lack of definitional clarity is a specification of what is meant by the preceding terms. Given that I was responsible for launching the somewhat ambiguous term "cultic milieu" into academic discourse in the first place, I shall now endeavor to pin it down by specifying what might be a reasonable interpretation of phrases such as "the dominant culture," "the mainstream," "conventional beliefs and knowledge" or "the dominant orthodoxy."

The word "orthodox" is generally taken to mean, "established," "sound or correct in opinion or doctrine" or even "traditional," words that I take to imply that the belief or beliefs in question have been accredited by some officially recognized body. In this context the recognition may refer simply to the organization or institution and/or to the doctrine or dogma that it upholds. Thus, the Church of England, for example, could be said to be an officially recognized institution, given that it is a state church with representation in Parliament but also that it has official doctrines, for example in the form of the three creeds: the Nicene creed, Athanasius's creed, and the Apostles' creed. The other churches and religions represented in the United Kingdom could also be said to be part of "orthodoxy" in so far as they are also formally recognized as religious organizations with agreed statements of faith. In the secular sphere, what constitutes formal recognition is more difficult to pin down, but one would assume it would include knowledge that has been certified by the government for inclusion in school and college curricula, which is to say the national curriculum. If, however, one assumes that "orthodoxy" in this context means "generally accepted by experts in their field" and accepts the critical role played by professional and scientific organizations, then this would presumably mean that one would include such items as the theory of relativity, together with the standard theory or standard model in particle physics, as well as the theory of evolution in biology. In other words, if we are talking about orthodox knowledge, ideas, and beliefs, then we must be referring to material that has gone through some formal process of accreditation by an established, or officially approved, institution.

In addition to the idea of an orthodox culture (whether regarded as "dominant" or not) included in the phrases I have just listed are those that appear to refer to a different phenomenon, something called "the mainstream," "conventional beliefs and knowledge," "mainstream ideas and practices," or "mainstream accepted beliefs," terms that suggest to me something other than the orthodox.[21] For, as I understand it, the conventional refers to the ordinary, normal or expected, while mainstream ideas and beliefs would presumably refer to those accepted by most people. At first glance this sounds appropriate when attempting to identify the cultic milieu, and one can see why some people might assume that this corresponds to that which is orthodox. But the reality is that what most people believe differs significantly from orthodox knowledge as I have just outlined it. So we are faced with an interesting question. Is the cultic milieu opposed to orthodoxy or to the ideas found in the mainstream, given that they are not the same?

THE DEATH OF A DICHOTOMY

It is at this point that we become aware of the problem caused by using a simple dichotomous model of the cultural scene of modern industrial societies. For not everything that is outside of the established or formally approved cultural system is cultic. This becomes obvious once one realizes that what is identified as officially orthodox in contemporary British culture is adhered to only by a minority. To take one example, the beliefs embodied in the Anglican creeds mentioned earlier, although regularly chanted by those who attend church, would appear not to correspond to the actual beliefs of the UK population. For instance, a 2013 YouGov survey found that just 27 percent of the population believes that Jesus Christ was the son of God, while just 26 percent believes in the biblical account of the crucifixion.[22] In that sense, those who believe that Christ was born of a virgin and died and was resurrected hold to statistically deviant, if not actually unusual, beliefs. It is not quite the same when we turn to consider what might be considered scientific orthodoxy, since here the picture is more mixed. So, while a majority of the UK population believe in human-caused climate change, only about half believe in evolution.[23] There is, however, considerable support for conspiracy theories, such as the claim that the moon landings were staged.[24]

It is important to note, however, that mainstream or popular belief is not simply a matter of questioning or rejecting that which is orthodox. For the mainstream also consists of beliefs that are rejected by the spokespersons of orthodoxy. Consequently, in addition to rejecting some of the central tenets of the Christian faith, a sizeable minority of adults in the United Kingdom believe in reincarnation.[25] There is also a high level of belief in ghosts, fate, and superstitions such as crossing fingers for luck, taking care not to walk under ladders, or avoiding the number 13 in order to ward off bad luck—beliefs that are rejected by both religious and secular orthodoxy.[26] It follows from this that while it seems reasonable to define the cultic milieu as replete with beliefs and practices that are opposed to what is officially orthodox, it is wrong to claim that these same beliefs and practices are also opposed to the cultural mainstream, if by the latter term we mean what most people claim to believe. For what most people believe is anything but orthodox. On the other hand, it would clearly be absurd to suggest that the cultic milieu and the popular mainstream were one and the same. Consequently, we need to replace the prevailing dichotomous model with a *trichotomy*, one consisting of orthodoxy, the cultural mainstream, and the cultic milieu, so that the societal cultural system features a fissure between cultural orthodoxy and mainstream belief next to one between mainstream belief and the cultic.

Recognition that the cultural system of modern industrial society might be more usefully conceived of as a trichotomy than a dichotomy has a significant implication for the long-standing debate over whether late modernity is more aptly characterized as "secular," "religious," or—more commonly—"spiritual." All too often the tendency has been to dismiss "spirituality" on the grounds that it is a privatized, domesticated, and psychologized phenomenon of little social or public significance.[27] But recognizing that there is a significant cultural "mainstream" in contemporary Western societies, which differs markedly from orthodoxy without however embracing either secularity or being so outré or exotic as to be part of the cultic milieu, helps to frame this phenomenon in a new light. For it helps to direct attention to the fact that unorthodox beliefs can be both widespread and a significant influence on behavior, even if they do not necessarily give rise to formal institutions. Indeed, such beliefs occupy a crucial demotic "cultural space," defined as much by what is rejected as by that which is endorsed.

Still, replacing a dichotomy with a trichotomy necessarily raises an interesting question: What exactly constitutes the boundary between the mainstream and the cultic milieu? If the mainstream is separated from orthodoxy because it consists of beliefs that, although predominantly unorthodox, are widespread in society, how is this mainstream then separated from the cultic milieu? To answer this question I need to embark on a short semantic excursion concerning the word, "cult" (and hence, by definition, "cultic").

Apart from the well-known difficulties encountered in the sociology of religion in putting a clear and unambiguous meaning to this term it is also the case that, in ordinary usage, it is a pejorative. The term *cult* often has derogatory shades of meaning attached to it. Indeed, when used by a layperson, the term is basically "shorthand for 'a religion I don't like.'" And when applied to a group, the suggestion is that its teachings are extremist, false, or at least odd. Now, I imagine that in our capacity as scholars most of us would be only too quick to disassociate ourselves from such usage. After all, our task is the analysis and understanding of social phenomena, and to do that it is important that we should strive to remain as objective as possible. Which is all very understandable. However, in our anxiety to avoid being judgmental we may be making the mistake of overlooking a crucial aspect of reality. For the stigmatized character of the word "cult" is a social fact (or perhaps we should say a cultural fact), and these facts have consequences.

If, for example, sufficient people in a society consider a particular religious, quasi-religious, or secular organization to be "a cult," then the likelihood is that they will not only eschew any contact with it but also that they will also hold a strong negative attitude toward its members. It is very likely, for example, that they will regard belief in this "cult" as eccentric if not bizarre, and those who subscribe to it as weird. While dismissing the suggestion that the cultic milieu attracts people who are mentally unstable, Stephen Davies notes that a crucial feature of cultic beliefs is that most ordinary people consider those involved to be "simply nuts," and that "in every society there are a number of people who are predisposed to believe and accept things that the majority regard as bizarre or even insane."[28] The crucial part of this quote is that last phrase, "the majority regard as bizarre or even insane," because it is this that gives us the clue we need to identify the boundary between the mainstream and the cultic milieu. Seen in this light, cultic ideas, beliefs, and practices are not really distinguished by any intrinsic features. What distinguishes them is the fact that most people regard them as crazy.

After all, it cannot really be the case that most ordinary people reject cultic claims because they are at odds with establishment thinking, as they generally hold to beliefs that are unorthodox themselves. No, they reject cultic beliefs because they breach their sense of what is credible. Cultic claims are generally seen as contrary to what is deemed commonsensical and hence are viewed as outlandish or far-fetched, eccentric, even just plain silly, and consequently open to ridicule. Looked at in this way one could say that most cultic beliefs are rejected because ordinary people do not want to be thought of as weirdos.[29] At the same time, other cultic claims may be dismissed because they are seen as objectionable, offending against common decency, and hence regarded with distaste or disapproval. So while belief in evil and demonic possession is not uncommon, the cultic suggestion that it is acceptable to indulge in black magic or to worship Satan is likely to be dismissed as distasteful, if not repugnant.[30]

What I am pointing to is the existence of a cultural border or boundary that separates the officially unorthodox beliefs widely encountered among the general population and those characteristic of cultic groups—a loose and not very well-defined boundary, to be sure, and one that is porous enough for considerable movement back and forth. However, the border is real and is generally marked by a degree of skepticism, suspicion, ridicule, and even in some instances abhorrence and disgust on the part of the general populace.[31] One could say that, in general, most people have no trouble holding beliefs that are at odds with those endorsed by the guardians of cultural orthodoxy, whether it is belief in aliens, ghosts, fate, or astrology. But these beliefs are generally held lightly. In this way they are more like "half-beliefs."[32] At the same time, the fact that such officially erroneous beliefs are so widespread in society is helped in large measure by the extent to which magical and occult themes are routinely embedded in popular culture, even if such beliefs are also held in check to some degree, routinely divorced from any serious commitment, due to a residual, if begrudging, respect for authorized knowledge, whether scientific or religious in character. The dividing line between the mainstream and the cultic milieu can therefore be summarized as the difference between half-belief, in the sense that "there might be something in it," and a fully committed belief, in the sense that "there is an awful lot in it."

It follows from this that there are two crucial differences between popular unorthodox beliefs and genuinely cultic beliefs. The first is that what is held only lightly by the general population and generally has little impact on their behavior is the subject of a genuine commitment on the part of members of cultic organizations (belief versus half-belief). The second is that what for the public is merely a half-belief is for the cultist a stepping-stone on the path to a larger system of meaning, which impacts behavior. In this respect the cultic can be seen as an extended or developed form of popular belief, stretched to the extent of constituting a system of interlocking claims and assertions. An example will serve to illustrate the difference. In the

United Kingdom there is widespread popular belief not just in UFOs but also in the existence of aliens, even though this has been rejected time and again by both government and the scientific and astronomical communities.[33] However, while belief in aliens is common, believing that aliens are in effect "Cosmic Masters"—individuals with special psychic powers who have been controlling human destiny for thousands of years—is not only uncommon but would probably be regarded by most people as absurd, largely limited to members of the Aetherius Society.

Recognizing that there is this boundary between the cultic and the everyday makes it possible to see that not all cultic groups can be correctly described as adhering to unorthodox beliefs or practices. To take an example from the Kaplan and Lööw book, the Goth subculture principally comprises music and dress and is thus simply unconventional, intended to shock adults and express teenagers' independence, rather than oppose Judeo-Christian or scientific orthodoxy. It is also unclear whether it is accurate to describe unusual religious groups, such as the Druids, the Wiccans, or even the Church of Satan, as adhering to unorthodox beliefs. After all, it is not clear that these religious groups are any more opposed to the Judeo-Christian mainstream than is Islam or Buddhism. But then, crucially, most of these are formally recognized in law as accredited religious groups in their own right and hence effectively constitute part of "orthodox culture." So it might be more accurate to suggest that if indeed they warrant inclusion in the cultic milieu, it would be because they are at odds with mainstream public opinion, which is to say they constitute organizations that are seen as eccentric rather than unorthodox or oppositional.[34]

Of course, the reverse situation may also apply. Consider situations where beliefs that are generally considered quite acceptable by the public are nonetheless fundamentally opposed to those endorsed by the guardians of societal orthodoxy—for example, with astrology (and, as already noted, most superstitious belief and practice). The conclusion to be drawn is that not only is it the case that not everything that is unorthodox is cultic but also that not everything that is orthodox is necessarily noncultic. Essentially, a popular negative attitude is more significant than a lack of orthodoxy in determining what is cultic. Thus, although the cultic milieu has two boundaries, one with orthodox knowledge, understood as that which is accredited by official institutional bodies, and a second in the form of that which most people consider credible or acceptable at any one time, it is the latter that is the more significant. Consequently, the cultic milieu can be defined as an arena in which commonly considered eccentric ideas, beliefs, and practices are to be found. This is only a provisional definition because the norms involved relate to moral standards as well as matters of truth, and hence one needs to add that the cultic is also an arena in which one can find ideas, beliefs, or practices that are commonly regarded as objectionable.[35]

What this way of defining the cultic milieu strongly suggests is that this phenomenon works as a form of cultural control: a mechanism that sets limits to the degree of acceptable variation in a society's system of ideas and beliefs. For holding onto, or more properly publicly expressing, cultic beliefs is to be subject to social sanctions, with individuals forced to pay a price (in the form of mockery and ridicule) for doing so. Such sanctions are clearly meant to act as a deterrent, a means of restraining people from committing themselves to "crazy" beliefs.

What is interesting in this respect is the fact that throughout history there have been powerful forces at work aimed at setting firm limits to the beliefs that individuals were permitted to endorse. One can see this in the way that religious organizations promoted orthodoxy while employing all the sanctions at their disposal to stamp out heresy, both through efforts to restrict the ideas and beliefs that individuals could encounter,[36] and by subjecting heretics and apostates to excommunication, imprisonment, torture, or death. Not that such efforts ceased with the decline of the power and influence of established religion. For even today, in totalitarian societies round the globe, those who don't toe the ideological line are likely to be subject to fines, imprisonment, or "reeducation" or forced to recant.

Today, in Western liberal democracies, state power is no longer used in this way to force citizens to accept one set of beliefs, whether religious or secular in form. Some beliefs may well be prioritized, and as a consequence the organizations that promote them are granted special privileges (as is the case with the Church of England in the United Kingdom), but not only does dissent go unpunished, the right to freedom of religion or belief is generally upheld. The result, naturally enough, is that such societies tend to be not simply multicultural but also marked by a wide variety of forms of belief (and indeed nonbelief). Despite this, it seems highly unlikely that, even in societies as culturally diverse as these, absolutely any kind of belief will find acceptance. Indeed, there are good sociological reasons for believing that some limit on what people believe will still be necessary. That is, just as there are necessarily limits on the forms of overt behavior that people may display, so too will there be limits of some kind on the beliefs they can express. For some level of agreement on what is true is as necessary for the smooth running of society as an agreement on which forms of behavior are acceptable. However, given the abandonment of state-authorized controls, these limits are necessarily set through the operation of informal sanctions—such as ridicule and mockery, as mentioned before—enacted by ordinary people. In other words, these limits are set by popular opinion.[37] It is worth pondering at this point why people would bother to ridicule those who, in their opinion, hold "mad beliefs." No doubt there is some satisfaction to be had in poking fun at people unlike oneself, but it is also very possible that the need to mock those who espouse "crazy" beliefs stems from an underlying need to defend taken-for-granted truths or the verities upon which our view of reality is based.

To provide an example: in June 2020 there was a headline in the British popular newspaper *The Sun* reporting on how flat-earthers were being ridiculed on social media following the successful launch of the NASA and SPACEX falcon rocket into space.[38] What was happening was that people were pointing to the footage captured by cameras on the spacecraft showing a very definite curvature of the earth to poke fun at those who believed that the earth was flat. As reported in the article, "no sooner had the spacecraft taken off than the hashtag 'Flat Earth' was being thrown about online, and not by flat-earthers, but by those mocking the idea."[39] Significantly, these were not astronomers or even scientists, but ordinary people—people who were taking this opportunity to mock and ridicule those who expressed a belief they considered "nuts."

RESEARCHING THE CULTIC MILIEU

Until now the concept of a cultic milieu has largely been employed as a kind of catch-all category, one used to group together a range of bizarre or esoteric organizations and cultural movements under a common label. The principal advantage of this approach has been that it reveals how these diverse groups do not exist in isolation from each other but are on the contrary characterized by overlapping and interconnected ideas and beliefs, which collectively produce a range of cultural pathways that those of an inquiring mind can pursue. As Davies puts it, "People who dipped into the cultic milieu through following one idea would then find themselves exposed to and becoming interested in other heterodox notions."[40] However, recognizing that the milieu has this crucial boundary with the cultural mainstream makes it possible to expand the program of research beyond this focus on contents and make the milieu itself the object of study. Not only does this make it possible to study the flow of cultural material across this boundary, but it also opens the possibility of examining whether the milieu has expanded or contracted over time.

We have already encountered an example of cultural material that has in effect crossed the boundary, traveling from the milieu to the cultural mainstream. This of course is the New Age phenomenon so aptly described by Hanegraaff, a transition that occurred sometime between the 1960s and 1990s. As far as an example of cultural material and associated practices crossing in the opposite direction is concerned, a good example might be eugenics. Belief in the value and utility of eugenics was widespread through Western societies in the 1920s and 1930s, only to be discredited and consequently relegated to the cultic milieu in the late 1940s and early 1950s, following the shock discovery of the Holocaust and Nazi experiments aimed at promoting racial purity. As far as studying the size of the cultic milieu is concerned—and hence its relative significance in relation to the mainstream—the most obvious hypothesis that suggests itself is the suspicion that recent decades have seen an expansion of the cultic milieu at the expense of the cultural mainstream, and thus, to some degree also, of orthodoxy.

The suggestion that we are entering a new cultic age is the claim made by Ilya Somin, who asserts that, "Right now the size and influence of the CM [cultic milieu] is growing. Ever more people subscribe to fringe beliefs and the availability of the kinds of ideas that circulate in the cultic counterculture has increased dramatically."[41] Nor is he alone in thinking this. For instance, László Kürti goes so far as to proclaim, "this is the cultic age."[42] Why might this have happened? One reason might well be the move, noted earlier, of an essentially New Age philosophy from the cultic milieu into the cultural mainstream. Given that this movement endorses epistemological individualism and the polymorphous nature of truth, it is hardly surprising if the consequence is a turning away from orthodox doctrines.[43] But then the tendency to dismiss expert opinion is also strengthened by a libertarian political ideology that has championed the market and consumer choice against professional expertise. In that respect the authority of the "inner voice" is strengthened by the belief that the consumer—and indeed the citizen as voter—has the right to their own truth. On top of this has been the influence of the internet and social media, both of which have greatly favored fringe ideas, together with conspiracy theories of all kinds. In part this is because such ideas are so much easier to come across than was the case when they were confined to obscure pamphlets and magazines. Today bizarre ideas and extreme beliefs are literally only a few mouse clicks away. At the same time, those who hold cultic beliefs can now live out their existence in echo chambers or epistemic bubbles, knowing they will encounter only people who share their opinions.[44] People also favor social media as a source of news because they believe that the mainstream media is biased.

This is relevant to the erosion of the border between the mainstream and cultic beliefs, since it means that it is all too easy for those who hold cultic beliefs to evade the skepticism and ridicule of nonbelievers. Last, we need to note that all this has been happening against a background of a decline in the influence of the established churches, in which context we might recall Daniel Bell's assertion that when religions fail cults thrive.[45] The scientific worldview meanwhile, with its complex and increasingly impenetrable content, remains largely unavailable to most citizens.

THE NEED FOR THEORETICAL REVISION

In revisiting the cultic milieu nearly half a century after I first introduced the concept, I have focused my attention on the apparent paradox whereby it has become widely employed by scholars from a variety of disciplines, with commentators declaring the concept to be both "powerful" and "useful," while others have been highly critical of the idea, declaring that it has been "stretch[ed] too far" and is "impossible to pin down." I have suggested that this paradox arises from the fact that while the concept has directed attention to an intriguing and unique cultural phenomenon, it has proved difficult to define its parameters and hence to successfully outline its identity. Simply expressed, one can say that it is generally known what the milieu is, but not where it can be found. The two books I considered represent the two contrasting approaches to the resolution of this problem: to focus either on the content of the milieu or on its relationship to the larger cultural system. Unfortunately, it is logically impossible to define the milieu in terms of its content, since this will naturally change over time. Indeed, the emphasis placed in my 1972 article on esoteric forms of mysticism and spirituality as defining features of the milieu has proved misplaced, given that—following the spiritual turn—these phenomena have become very much part of the mainstream. But then successfully defining the milieu in terms of its relationship to the larger system has also proved elusive. The principal reason for this is the employment of a narrow dichotomous model by which a society's cultural system is simply split between the orthodox and the cultic. Recognizing that there is in fact a third party involved, something that we can call "the cultural mainstream," makes it somewhat easier to identify the milieu, since it shows that the cultic is not simply the unorthodox, the deviant, or the esoteric but also that its principal characteristic is that it consists of beliefs which most ordinary, sensible, or sane persons would consider eccentric, if not absurd. In other words, I am suggesting that the milieu is not best described as the home of the unorthodox, but rather the home of the eccentric.

I am conscious of the fact that in outlining the cultic milieu in the way that I have, especially in divorcing the definition of the concept from any specific content (such as Troeltsch's spiritual and mystic religion), I have rather left the sociology of religion behind. It remains the case of course that the milieu is replete with bizarre religious beliefs and associated groups, but the crucial feature of the milieu is that these are mixed in with—or overlap and interlink with—beliefs that that are more sociopolitical or pseudo-scientific in character. Indeed, it is this very mélange of beliefs and ideas (and associated practices) that characterizes the milieu. Consequently, while there is plenty of subject matter here for the sociologist of religion who has an interest in the weird or esoteric, the cultic milieu itself is unlikely to become an object of study, although it could be a useful introduction into the various ways in which religious and secular ideas and beliefs can become entangled.

The fact that focusing on the cultic milieu necessarily involves stepping outside of the sociology of religion was a point made in the original article where I noted that "some of the most interesting questions one can ask about this milieu concern not its internal anatomy but its relationship with the containing society and its orthodox culture." In addition, I said that any study of the cultic milieu necessarily had to be accompanied by "an examination of the total cultural system of which the milieu is a part."[46] This is a position that I have become more committed to in the intervening years. For, as should be apparent, I strongly believe that there cannot be any real understanding of any one part of the cultural system of a modern industrial society, whether it be a "subculture," a "counterculture," religion, or spirituality, unless there is a thorough understanding of the larger cultural system of which these are merely parts.

NOTES

1. Stephen Davies, "The Cultic Milieu and the Rise of the Violent Fringe," American Institute for Economic Research (AIER), August 7, 2019, https://www.aier.org/article/the-cultic-milieu-and-the-rise-of-violent-fringe/.
2. Wouter J. Hanegraaff, *New Age Religion and Western Culture: Esotericism in the Mirror of Secular Thought* (Leiden: Brill, 1996); Paul Heelas, *The New Age Movement: The Celebration of the Self and the Sacralization of Modernity* (Oxford: Blackwell, 2008); Galen Watts, *The Spiritual Turn: The Religion of the Heart and the Making of Romantic Liberal Modernity* (Oxford: Oxford University Press, 2022).
3. Jesper Aagaard Petersen, "The Black Helicopter: A Lecture in Hyperreality, Or Why Academese Matters," May 19, 2010, https://jespaa.wordpress.com/2010/05/19/a-lecture-in-hyperreality-or-why-academese-matters/.
4. Christopher Partridge, *The Re-Enchantment of the West*, vol. 1, *Alternative Spiritualities, Sacralization, Popular Culture and Occulture* (London: T&T Clark International, 2005), 34.
5. Jochen Scherer, " 'Truth Is What's True for Me?' Reassessing the Knowledge Claims of New Age Spirituality," PhD thesis, Bangor University, 2011; Davies, "The Cultic Milieu and the Rise of the Violent Fringe," 14.

6. Hanegraaff, *New Age Religion and Western Culture*; Jeffrey Kaplan and Heléne Lööw, ed., *The Cultic Milieu: Oppositional Subcultures in an Age of Globalization* (Walnut Creek, CA: Rowman & Littlefield, 2002).
7. Susan Joy Rennison, "Spiritual Evolution in the Cultic Milieu," April 2013, https://susanrennison.co.uk/Spiritual_Evolution_Cultic _Milieu_v2013.pdf.
8. Hanegraaff, *New Age Religion and Western Culture*, 16, 17 (emphasis in original).
9. Intriguingly, I had realized that Troeltsch's spiritual and mystical religion had become mainstream. Ernst Troeltsch, *The Social Teachings of the Christian Churches* (Louisville, KY: Westminster/John Knox Press, 1992 [1931]). Indeed, I discuss this in "The Secret Religion of the Educated Classes," *Sociological Analysis* 39, no. 2 (1978): 146–56. However, I completely failed to see the implication of this for the concept of the cultic milieu.
10. I will claim that I did predict the possibility that the cultic milieu might become mainstream. In the original article I do say that secularization, "may create circumstances favourable to the growth of the milieu and the further expansion of cultic beliefs throughout society," going on to suggest that progressive secularization could lead to the emergence, not of a secular scientific society but of one "centred on a blend of mysticism, magic and pseudo-science." Colin Campbell, "The Cult, the Cultic Milieu and Secularization," *A Sociological Yearbook of Religion in Britain* 5 (1972): 12.
11. Heelas, *The New Age Movement*, 105.
12. James R. Lewis and J. Gordon Melton, ed., *Perspectives on the New Age* (Albany: State University of New York Press, 1992), 2.
13. Philip Seddon, *The New Age: An Assessment* (Bramcote, UK: Grove Books, 1990), 3.
14. See Galen Watts, *The Spiritual Turn: The Religion of the Heart and the Making of Romantic Liberal Modernity* (Oxford: Oxford University Press, 2022).
15. I was obviously pleased when I first heard about this volume, using as it does the concept of the cultic milieu as its central theme. However, I should mention that I played no part in its initiation or planning. Indeed, it was not until the book was about to go into production that I first heard about it.
16. I would have thought that logic demanded that "oppositional subcultures" would be more aptly described as "countercultures."
17. Kaplan and Lööw, *The Cultic Milieu*, 4.
18. Kaplan and Lööw, *The Cultic Milieu*, 3, 4.
19. Davies, "The Cultic Milieu and the Rise of the Violent Fringe," 12; Paul Jackson, "Cultic Milieus and the Extreme Right," *Open Democracy*,

May 9, 2019, https://www.opendemocracy.net/en/cultic-milieus-and-extreme-right/.
20. Kitty Shropshire, "The Radical Right in the Cultic Milieu," *Center for the Analysis of the Radical Right*, August 21, 2020, https://www.radicalrightanalysis.com/2020/08/21/the-radical-right-in-the-cultic-milieu/; Stronged, "Campbell, Colin. The Cult, The Cultic Milieu and Secularization. A Sociological Yearbook of Religion in Britain, SCM Press London, 1972," *Honoured*, March 11, 2013, https://honoured.wordpress.com/2013/03/11/campbell-colin-the-cult-the-cultic-milieu-and-secularization-a-sociological-yearbook-of-religion-in-britain-scm-press-london-1972/.
21. Kaplan and Lööw, *The Cultic Milieu*, 4; Davies, "The Cultic Milieu and the Rise of the Violent Fringe," 1; Jackson, "Cultic Milieus and the Extreme Right," 1; Rennison, "Spiritual Evolution in the Cultic Milieu," 6. It follows that, as I see it, a term like "orthodox mainstream" is a contradiction. Ilya Somin, "The Growth of the Cultic Milieu and the Spread of Harmful Ideas," *Reason*, July 8, 2019, https://reason.com/volokh/2019/08/07/the-growth-of-the-cultic-milieu-and-the-spread-of-harmful-ideas/.
22. Humanists U.K., "Religion and Belief: Some Surveys and Statistics," n.d., https://humanists.uk/campaigns/religion-and-belief-some-surveys-and-statistics/.
23. Riazat Butt, "Half of Britons Do Not Believe in Evolution, Survey Finds," *Guardian*, February 1, 2009.
24. Victoria Waldersee, "Which Science-Based Conspiracy Theories Do Britons Believe?," 2019, https://yougov.co.uk/politics/articles/22839-which-science-based-conspiracy-theories-do-britons.
25. Faith Survey, UK Religion Survey 2017, https://faithsurvey.co.uk/uk-religion-survey.html.
26. Richard Wiseman, *UK Superstition Survey*, 2003, http://www.richardwiseman.com/resources/superstition_report.pdf.
27. See the introduction to this volume.
28. Davies, "The Cultic Milieu and the Rise of the Violent Fringe," 3.
29. See, as an illustration of this point, Jeffrey Kaplan's report that Aquino observed how what he calls "Hollywood Nazis" were regarded by most Americans as "refugees from the loony bin." Kaplan and Lööw, *The Cultic Milieu*, 236.
30. William Jordan, "8% of Britons Believe Horoscopes Can Predict the Future," July 3, 2015, https://yougov.co.uk/politics/articles/12731-8-of-Britons-believe-horoscopes-predict-the-future. What is judged eccentric obviously depends on what is familiar and unfamiliar. It is therefore necessarily a shifting boundary.

31. One can find clear echoes of this sense of the cultic as "unconventional" or "extremist," rather than oppositional, in language itself.
32. See Peter McKellar, *A Textbook of Human Psychology* (London: Cohen & West, 1952); Colin Campbell, "Half-Belief and the Paradox of Ritual Instrumental Activism: A Theory of Modern Superstition," *British Journal of Sociology* 47, no. 1 (1996): 151–65. The concept of "half-belief" was introduced by Peter McKellar in 1952. Originally used to refer to a contradiction between a statement of belief (or disbelief) and conduct, it was subsequently used by Kenneth Garwood to refer to a phenomenon that possessed "some of the qualities of belief and some of the qualities of disbelief." It may however be used to imply a stage in the transition from belief to disbelief or vice versa. See H. H. Price, *Belief: The Gifford Lectures* (London: Allen & Unwin, 1969), 302–14.
33. E&T Editorial Staff, "UFOS Hovering in the Mind of the British Public, Survey Reveals," Engineering and Technology, March 22, 2021, https://eandt.theiet.org/content/articles/2021/03/ufos-hovering-in-the-minds-of-the-british-public-according-to-survey/.
34. An interesting feature of the judgment of eccentricity is that the question of truth or falsity is largely sidestepped. The implication is certainly along the lines of "you wouldn't catch me believing something as mad as that," but this is as much because one would not want to be seen as the kind of person who believes that sort of thing as because it is obviously false. The preservation of image is paramount.
35. The fact that a belief or practice is at odds with orthodox opinion may be a crucial factor in persuading people of its eccentricity (e.g., the belief that the world is flat). However, being unorthodox may not be sufficient in itself to cause a belief to be regarded as eccentric, while some orthodox beliefs may themselves be seen as doubtful if not fully eccentric by many people (e.g., widespread doubts about the truth of the theory of evolution).
36. The Roman Catholic Church's index of banned books was such an attempt to limit access to knowledge and lasted until 1966.
37. It is important to stress that people are not sanctioned for simply having a different opinion or holding to different beliefs. Such differences are part and parcel of life in a multicultural, pluralistic society. What I am describing is different from disagreement because the rejected belief is considered so preposterous as not to warrant intellectual engagement. It is simply dismissed out of hand on the grounds that one does not argue with those who are seen, in effect, as "mad."
38. Charlotte Edwards, "Flat-Earthers Ridiculed on Social Media after Space-X Launch Footage Captures Curvature of Our Planet," *Sun*, June 1, 2020.

39. Edwards, "Flat-Earthers Ridiculed."
40. Davies, "The Cultic Milieu and the Rise of the Violent Fringe," 2.
41. Somin, "The Growth of the Cultic Milieu," 2.
42. László Kürti, "Neo-Shamanism, Psychic Phenomena and Media Trickery," in Kaplan and Lööw, *The Cultic Milieu*, 113.
43. See Scherer, "Truth Is What's True for Me?," cited by Rennison, "Spiritual Evolution in the Cultic Milieu," 5. There is also the fact that "spirituality" and notions of "wellness" can share affinities with right-wing views and conspiracy theories such as QAnon. See Jaron Harambam's "Conspirituality" in this volume.
44. University of Cambridge, Research, "Elvis Is Alive and the Moon Landings Were Faked: The (Conspiracy) Theory of Everything," October 25, 2016, https://www.cam.ac.uk/research/features/elvis-is-alive-and-the-moon-landings-were-faked-the-conspiracy-theory-of-everything; see also Esther Addley, "Study Shows that 60% of Britons Believe in Conspiracy Theories," *Guardian*, November 23, 2018.
45. Daniel Bell, "The Return of the Sacred: The Argument About the Future of Religion," *Zygon* 13, no. 3 (1978): 187–208. The full quotation reads, "When religions fail, cults appear. When the institutional framework of religions begins to break up, the search for direct experience which people can feel to be 'religious' facilitates the rise of cults" (202).
46. Campbell, "The Cult, the Cultic Milieu and Secularization," 129, 130.

3

HOLISTIC HEALING AND THE REESTABLISHMENT OF RELIGION IN THE UNITED STATES

CANDY GUNTHER BROWN

Holistic healing moved from the margins to the mainstream of U.S. culture during the second half of the twentieth century.[1] Observers tend to assume that secularization provides an explanation. This is not the case. Rather than disappearing, the religious foundations of holistic healing became less visible even as "mind-body-spirit" practices—such as yoga, meditation, chiropractic, reiki, and acupuncture—entered public institutions.[2] Religious invisibility enhanced the social, political, and legal influences of holistic healing to such an extent that we might describe the current state of affairs as a reestablishment of religion.[3] People who would reject healing practices premised on religion, especially if that religion is not Christian, accept practices advertised as better than modern medicine because both "scientifically validated" and "spiritual, but not religious." Through participation in embodied practices like yoga and mindfulness, people tend to embrace associated assumptions and worldviews, resulting in religious transformations.[4] This development did not result from chance, but from tactical marketing by holistic health promoters who presented their practices as nonreligious therapies.[5] Ironically, Christian consumers contributed to the decentering of Christianity in U.S. culture as their Word-centered theological lenses created a blind spot for the reciprocal interactions of mind, body, and spirit in embodied religions other than Christianity.[6] The result is anything but religious privatization.[7] Holistic healing has become embedded in public institutions, constraining consumer choice and legally reauthorizing public religion. This chapter first documents the institutionalization of holistic healing, then explains the vitalistic ontology, experiential epistemology, and social networks that give it cultural coherence, next theorizes supply-side and demand-side mechanisms of its mainstreaming, and finally considers its social, political, and legal significance.

THE INSTITUTIONALIZATION OF HOLISTIC HEALING

The term "holistic" healing, from Greek *holos* or whole, first circulated in the 1920s and gained traction in the 1970s, but "mind-body-spirit" medicine has a much longer, global history.[8] In the United States, holistic and biomedical healing have coexisted all along, but their relationship has changed over time. This occurred through three stages: consolidation of a medical mainstream, differentiation of holistic healing from mainstream medicine, and reintegration. European colonists brought with them to the Americas a mix of empirical medical knowledge and metaphysical folk wisdom, which they combined with Native American and African traditions.[9] A Supreme Court ruling, *Dent v. West Virginia* (1889), upheld the authority of a state medical examining board to prohibit irregularly trained physicians from practicing medicine.[10] Holistic healing did not disappear—a quarter of

American healers were "irregulars" in the 1930s. But the American Medical Association (AMA), formed in 1847, consolidated power during the first half of the twentieth century. In 1963, the AMA established a Committee on Quackery to eliminate "unscientific" practices such as chiropractic. However, the tides turned as the AMA lost a landmark federal appellate case, *Wilk v. American Medical Association* (1990); the ruling forbade the AMA from discriminating against chiropractors by disallowing medical referrals.[11]

By the 1990s, government support for holistic healing arose from the legislative as well as the judicial branch. In 1991 Congress budgeted $2 million to establish, within the National Institutes of Health, an Office of Alternative Medicine. Congress upgraded this office to the National Center for Complementary and Alternative Medicine in 1998, renaming it in 2014 as the National Center for Complementary and Integrative Health; in 2023, this center's annual budget approached $160 million.[12] Name changes mark the rising status of holistic healing from quackery to alternative to complementary to integrative, and now part of the medical mainstream.

Although still controversial, holistic healing has gained acceptance—and sometimes enthusiastic support—from conventionally trained medical doctors and hospitals. Symbolically, in 1998 the *Journal of the American Medical Association* devoted a special issue to clinical trials of seven unconventional therapies, four of which (chiropractic, acupuncture, yoga, and herbs) reported positive effects.[13] The American Hospital Association reports that 42 percent of U.S. hospitals offer integrative care, tripling between 2000 and 2010.[14] The Academic Consortium for Integrative Medicine & Health touts seventy-seven university health center members in 2023, sixty-eight of them in the United States, up from eight members in 1999.[15] Major medical research centers providing integrative care include the Cleveland Clinic, Duke, Georgetown, Johns Hopkins, Mass General/Brigham and Women's, Mayo Clinic, MD Anderson, UCLA, University of California San Francisco, and Yale University.[16] Typical offerings include homeopathy, hypnotherapy, meditation, yoga, aromatherapy, acupuncture, biofeedback, reiki, and guided imagery. There are critics, such as Steven Novella, a physician and professor of neurology at the Yale School of Medicine, who laments that his colleagues have "become witch doctors" and that patients are "being snookered."[17] Novella, however, belongs to a shrinking minority. Most U.S. medical providers will at least tolerate the integration of holistic modalities into conventional treatment plans—if for no other reason than that an "integrative" model sends a message to patients that holistic care is not a mutually exclusive "alternative" and that doctors should be informed about holistic treatments.[18]

Most U.S. healthcare consumers combine biomedical and holistic approaches. Fewer than 5 percent of Americans use only unconventional remedies. The most common conditions treated holistically are back problems (36 percent), anxiety (28 percent), headaches (27 percent), chronic pain (26 percent), and cancer (24 percent).[19] The National Health Interview Surveys for 2002, 2007, and 2012 reveal a trend of increased holistic usage.[20] A third (34 percent) of American adults acknowledged using at least one such approach in 2012; the most popular are dietary supplements, deep breathing, yoga, chiropractic, and meditation. There were also significant increases in use of homeopathy, acupuncture, and naturopathy. Even relatively less popular practices such as reiki attracted 1.1 million users, 0.5 percent of the U.S. population, in 2012.

The steadily growing popularity of yoga and meditation are particularly notable. Yoga practice among U.S. adults increased from 3 percent in 1976 to 5.1 percent in 2002 to 6.1 percent in 2007 to 9.5 percent in 2012 to 15 percent (36.7 million adults) in 2016.[21] Among children, yoga practice grew from 2.3 to 3.1 percent between 2007 and 2012.[22] Practices of mantra, mindfulness, or spiritual meditation increased from 7.6 percent in 2002 to 9.4 percent in 2007, with a modest rollback to 8.0 percent in 2012; from 2007 to 2012, the percentage of children who meditated rose from 1.3 to 1.6 percent.[23] The heyday of Transcendental Meditation (TM) was the late 1970s, when an estimated six million Americans recited TM mantras.[24] By 2023, the TM-based Maharishi International University had garnered $26 million in grants from the National Institutes of Health, as well as $4 million from the U.S. Department of Defense, for TM research.[25] However, in 2022 the Department of Veterans Affairs, responding to a complaint from a veteran disturbed by TM's religious foundations, discontinued an $8 million study of PTSD self-funded by TM supporters.[26] Since the 1970s, mindfulness meditation has surpassed TM in popularity. Between 1979 and 2023, the Center for Mindfulness at UMass Memorial Health taught Mindfulness-Based Stress Reduction (MBSR) to 25,000 individuals—and provided a model for thousands of MBSR programs in medical centers, schools, and other institutions worldwide.[27]

Public schools have played a major role in popularizing yoga and meditation among children. A 2015 survey of U.S. school-based yoga programs identified thirty-six organizations that had trained 5,400 instructors and offered yoga in 940 schools.[28] Between 2011 and 2016, one such organization, the K. P. Jois (a.k.a. Sonima/Pure Edge) Foundation, funded yoga and mindfulness programs for forty thousand students in 114 schools across the United States and in Kenya.[29] By 2023 Yoga Ed. was practiced by seventeen million children in twenty thousand schools.[30] Also by 2023, Mindful Schools had trained more than three million students and seventy thousand educators, while MindUP had introduced mindfulness to seven million children in fourteen countries.[31]

The integration of holistic health practices into mainstream U.S. medical and educational institutions is remarkable for at least two reasons—the absence of compelling scientific evidence and the presence of metaphysical underpinnings. Most studies of holistic healing that report efficacy are of such low quality that the results are inconclusive. Fewer than half of yoga studies published between 1967 and 2013 were randomized controlled trials (RCTs), and most had a sample size too small to determine a "clinically relevant difference."[32] Some studies of yoga in schools found "counterintuitive *increases* in negative mood state and perceived stress with the yoga."[33] Yoga results in more injuries than other forms of exercise, with 61 percent of practitioners reporting negative physical, emotional, or mental outcomes.[34] Out of nearly nineteen thousand meditation studies reviewed in 2014, only forty-seven were RCTs with active controls; the review found "no evidence that meditation programs were better than any active treatment," such as exercise or behavioral therapies.[35] Despite popular claims that "meditation changes your brain," the most rigorous studies have failed to find evidence of meditation-induced neuroplastic changes.[36] Although meditators self-report stress reduction to researchers, biological markers reveal *increased* stress after mindfulness practice by both adults and children.[37] Meditation-related difficulties reported include increased anxiety, anger, depressive affect, despair, acute psychotic episodes, and suicide attempts.[38] Despite an abundance of studies on acupuncture, systematic reviews "most often report that trials of acupuncture efficacy are equivocal or contradictory."[39] Blinded studies of Therapeutic Touch and reiki have found that healers cannot detect the "human energy fields" that they claim to manipulate.[40] Study results are similarly lackluster for other holistic therapies.

Even as U.S. hospitals might be expected to restrict their armamentarium to scientifically validated therapies, public institutions presumably avoid endorsing, let alone requiring, religious practices. The U.S. Constitution, as amended in 1791, prohibits the "establishment of religion" and protects its "free exercise." Since the 1960s the Supreme Court has intervened in public schools to prohibit religious practices such as prayer and devotional Bible reading, even when such practices are voluntary, since there is a risk of "indirect coercive pressure."[41] In 1979 a federal court prohibited teaching TM in public schools, even as an elective, on the grounds that religiously premised practices do "not shed that religiosity merely because they are presented as philosophy or science."[42] Nevertheless, the David Lynch Foundation for Consciousness-Based Education and World Peace, founded in 2005, continues to donate millions of dollars to public schools in exchange for teaching TM, rebranded as "Quiet Time"; parents are suing Chicago public schools for teaching TM-based Quiet Time.[43] School yoga programs also continue to proliferate, but have not reached federal courts; state court rulings have been mixed—with a California appellate court allowing school yoga despite a judge's determination that "yoga is religious," whereas a Pennsylvania Board of Education tribunal disallowed a yoga-based charter school because of its religious foundations.[44] Legal challenges have, however, done little to slow the proliferation of school meditation and yoga programs.

The U.S. government's religious regulations extend to public and private businesses. The U.S. Equal Employment Opportunity Commission (EEOC) protects employees against direct and "reverse" religious discrimination—the imposition of religious beliefs or practices by employers. The EEOC interprets Title VII of the Civil Rights Act of 1964 to safeguard "all aspects of religious observance and practice as well as belief."[45] In 2008, the EEOC singled out yoga, meditation, and biofeedback as "New Age" practices that employers must not require of objecting employees; in 2016, a federal court upheld an EEOC reverse discrimination claim.[46]

Even so, the institutional mainstreaming of holistic healing continues to accelerate. The significance of this development can be better understood by more closely examining the vitalistic ontology, experiential epistemology, and social networks that give holistic healing cultural coherence.

HOLISTIC HEALING'S CULTURAL COHERENCE

Vitalistic Ontology

The vitalistic ontology underpinning holistic healing encompasses notions of an impersonal energy field and personal spirits that must be harmonized or engaged to maintain health. Holistic healing presupposes that all reality is essentially one (monism), that this reality is more than physical (metaphysical), and that matter and energy, physical and nonphysical entities, exist in a continuum and constantly affect each other.[47]

The central, unifying premise is the existence, and possibility of manipulating, "vital" energy. This "energy" is variously termed qi, ki, prana, animal magnetism, vital breath, vital force, life force, biofields, or Innate Intelligence, concepts popularized as "the Force" by "Buddhist Methodist" George Lucas's 1977 blockbuster *Star Wars*.[48] Although the term "energy" can refer to measurable wavelengths and frequencies of electricity, light, sound, and magnetism, "vital" energy is by contrast "subtle"—undetectable by conventional scientific instruments.[49] Vital energy is more than a physical force. It is alive and life-giving, intelligent, and goal-directed, beneficently promoting homeostasis or balance.

Blockages or imbalances in the flow of vital energy from the universe through the human body presumably cause disease, often written as "dis-ease," or lack of ease. Holistic healing involves opening blockages or redirecting energy flows through the body's energy channels (nadis or meridians, joined at chakras), rebalancing opposing energy principles (yin and yang), or restoring harmonious equilibrium between human bodies and a divine principle that indwells the cosmos and flows through all things. Techniques include physical touch of the body or redirection of energy fields (auras) beyond the body using one's hands or instruments such as needles, or ingestion or external application of substances intended to restore energy balance.[50]

Vitalistic assumptions permeate healing methods that gained popular followings in Europe and North America between the nineteenth and twentieth centuries; significantly, vitalistic premises did not disappear as holistic healing entered the cultural mainstream. Take chiropractic as an example. Daniel David Palmer (1845–1913) reputedly "discovered" chiropractic in 1895 after experimenting with mesmerism and spiritualism; much like "cheiromancers," or palm readers, chiropractors "read" human destiny in the spine.[51] Palmer built what he called the "religion of chiropractic" on the "religious plank" of "Innate Intelligence"—a "segment of that Intelligence which fills the universe," synonymous with "the Greek's Theos, the Christian's God, the Hebrew Helohim, the Mahometan's Allah, Hahneman's [sic] Vital Force, New Thot's [Thought's] Divine Spark, the Indian's Great Spirit, Hudson's Subconscious Mind, the Christian Scientist's All

Goodness, the Allopath's Vis Medicatrix Nature." Chiropractors "adjusted" spines to remove blockages, or "subluxations," in the flow of Innate.[52]

Although certain modern chiropractors seeking medical legitimacy downplayed Palmer's influence—and replaced the terms "Innate" and "vitalism" with "homeostasis" and "holism" in outward-facing publications—vitalistic ideas continued to pervade publications written by chiropractors for one another.[53] Most modern chiropractors still identify Innate as the Universal Intelligence that must flow freely to maintain health. Only a few hundred out of more than sixty thousand chiropractors have renounced Palmer's hypothesis that subluxations cause disease.[54] A profession-wide survey conducted in 2003 found that 90 percent of chiropractors envision adjustments in expansive terms consistent with Palmer's overarching goal of restoring harmony with a universal life force; supermajorities agree that chiropractic scope of practice includes other vitalistic therapies, such as homeopathy and acupuncture.[55] Homeopathy, for instance, "potentize[s]" the "spiritlike medicinal power" latent in material substances so that it is "excited and enabled to act spiritually upon the vital forces"; understanding homeopathy's foundational premise calls into sharp relief the oddity that certain hospital online stores sell products such as homeopathic bee venom.[56] Similar to chiropractic and homeopathy, the goal of acupuncture—according to MGH physician Jian Kong—is "de qi," or to "obtain" the "vital energy."[57] Even in medical settings, vitalism persists.

Since the 1960s, Western and Eastern vitalistic traditions have increasingly intermingled, even in conventional medical settings. Therapeutic Touch founder and nursing professor Dolores Krieger (1921–2019) based her concept of energy on "Hindu" notions of prana, which she understands as essentially the same thing as "Chinese qi" and "Egyptian ka": it is "the life energy that is vital," which flows through "nonphysical channels called nadis" and operates through the "chakra system;" the "healing act" consists of a "human energy transfer."[58] The International Association of Reiki Professionals, many of whom are employed by hospitals as massage therapists, explains reiki as "spiritually guided life force energy," comparable to "the Chinese ling qi; the Indian maha para shakti; and the Western divine light."[59] The reiki healer places her hands several inches above the skin, in the "aura," to "cover the main chakra centers and the main meridian channels that the life force flows through."[60] Reiki healers may also "ask Guides or helping Deva [Nature Spirits]," as well as "angels, ascended masters, guides" and "other Light Be-ings to help with the healing."[61] Molecular biologist Jon Kabat-Zinn, a pioneer in introducing "Mindfulness-based Stress Reduction" (MBSR) into medical settings, encourages meditators to place their hands into *mudras* associated with "subtle or not-so-subtle energies," turning the palms up in receptivity to the "energy of the heavens."[62] Although holistic healers may disagree over how best to potentize vital energy, a core ontological premise is that this energy, whatever it is called and wherever it is practiced, provides a key to health and wholeness.

Experiential Epistemology

Practitioners of holistic healing claim to know that vital energy exists because of their personal experiences. Holistic healing's experiential epistemology can be distinguished from "'reason' as embodied by science and 'faith' as central to religion,"[63] in that individuals must personally engage with posited vital energy rather than learning about it from generalized principles or simply believing in its existence without sensory evidence. Nevertheless, holistic epistemology does still depend on both reason and faith in ascribing spiritual meanings to physical sensations. This can be seen, for example, in appeals to quantum physics or neuroscience and insistence of compatibility with orthodox Christian doctrines.[64] Discourses of holistic healing that privilege physical sensations and personal experiences—especially when framed with scientific or Christian language—can lead to a misconception that practices have been secularized when, instead, the physical is experienced as a conduit to the spiritual.

Every type of perception, including perceptions of spirit, emerge through an interplay of embodied sensations and mental hypotheses.[65] Spiritual energy fields and beings are by definition nonmaterial. Their existence cannot be perceived directly or detected with technological instruments but must be experienced. People claim to know that the spiritual realm is real through sensory evidence of apparent effects, interpreted through the lens of intuitive perception. Sensations described as heat, cold, tension, congestion, thickness, heaviness, pressure, emptiness, leadenness, static, tingling, pins and needles, or electricity, are commonly interpreted as evidence of energy blockage or imbalance, healing power, or the presence of either the Holy Spirit or evil spirits.[66] For instance, reiki master Pamela Miles understands "vibrations, pulsations, or oscillations—whatever you want to call them—a[s] the subtle form through which we experience Reiki. They are the spirit in spirituality."[67]

Coded as spiritual encounters, physical sensations accompanying holistic practice can be framed as direct experiences of the divine or transcendent. Ashtanga yoga developer Pattabhi Jois (1915–2009) adamantly denied that yoga postures are merely physical. This is because the human body is a "temple" and "inside that temple is atman, and that is God."[68] Performing yoga postures leads "very gradually to the realization of the non-difference between the jivatma, or indwelling Self of the individual, and the paramatma, or Universal Self." Jois explained his experiential epistemology: "You can lecture, you can talk about God, but when you practice correctly, you come to experience God inside." Jois is not unique. According to 81 percent of yoga practitioners surveyed, postural yoga helps them to "feel more connected to nature/universe/god/a higher power."[69] By similar logic, recitation of Transcendental Meditation mantras brings the meditator into direct contact with "transcendental reality," the "almighty creative intelligence," which in turn brings about the revelation that "you are God."[70] Buddhist meditation is likewise, in the words of former Jesuit priest and Zen teacher Ruben Habito, "an invitation to a direct experience."[71] Although perceptions arise within individual human bodies, interpretations are socially constructed.

Social Networks

Holistic healing is practiced in the context of social networks conducive to the circulation of shared beliefs and values. Yoga offers a revealing example. Of Americans who practice yoga, 48 percent do so in a gym, 45 percent in a yoga studio, 21 percent in a community center, 9 percent at a retreat center, and 9 percent in a school. New practitioners come to yoga through friends (33 percent), free classes (24 percent), relatives (15 percent), healthcare providers (11 percent), and work colleagues (7 percent). Quality of "social interaction" influences class selection for 14 percent of practitioners, and 66 percent seek out teachers who are "warm and friendly." Notably, practitioners report developing their understanding of yoga through social interactions with their yoga class (48 percent), friends (40 percent), and by reading internet articles (36 percent) and yoga magazines (17 percent).[72] Even inward-directed practices such as meditation are often practiced in group settings, such as classes and retreat centers.[73] Practice centers are sites for sharing information through fliers and testimonials about other practices premised on common assumptions.

Although individual consumers may choose from among many healing modalities, they encounter similar ontological and epistemological assumptions across the range of options offered through holistic social networks. Holistic therapists know one another, attend the same seminars, shop in the same health-food stores and bookstores, and refer clients to one another.[74] Naturopathic doctors counsel avoidance of "toxic" drugs, vaccination, radiation, and surgery while recommending a variety of holistic practices such as homeopathy, acupuncture, massage, and aromatherapy.[75]

Participation in multiple holistic healing practices increases opportunities for individuals to absorb ideas from holistic networks. For example, 69 percent of teenagers who practice karate also practice yoga.[76] One-third (36 percent) of yoga practitioners and two-thirds (69 percent) of yoga instructors report meditating, compared with 9 percent of nonpractitioners.[77] Consumers who have positive experiences with one practice labeled as "holistic," "mind-body-spirit," or "integrative" are more likely to try other products or services that share similar labels, a phenomenon that scholars describe as a "halo effect."[78] Practitioners report being led from one holistic modality to another. For instance, Catholic Margaret Lee Lyles notes that "Reiki leads us to other things that are an essential part in our healing process, such as Tai Chi or Qi Gong, yoga exercises, acupuncture, and different forms of meditation."[79] The more such therapies one explores through holistic social networks, the greater the reinforcement of ontological and epistemological assumptions undergirding a holistic or spiritual worldview.

Understanding the pervasiveness of vitalistic ontological and epistemological assumptions in holistic social networks calls attention to just how extraordinary it is that holistic healing has been integrated into public institutions. It is thus important to explore the supply-side and demand-side mechanisms by which this mainstreaming has occurred.

THE MAINSTREAMING OF HOLISTIC HEALING: HOW DID IT HAPPEN?

Secular Linguistic Tactics

The institutional mainstreaming of holistic healing did not occur by chance but required tactical marketing through linguistic and economic measures. Until recently promoters of holistic healing lacked institutional power necessary for strategic marketing campaigns and so relied on covert "tactics."[80] The primary linguistic tactic has been described variously by scholars as "camouflage," "code-switching," and "frontstage/backstage" behavior; it consists of "concealing and gradual exposure" of metaphysical foundations or moving between scientific and spiritual vocabularies depending on audience and purpose.[81] Holistic practitioners have themselves described their tactics as learning to "censor myself," employ "skillful means," "disguise," write "scripts," bring in a "Trojan horse," and as engaging in "Stealth Buddhism" or winning a "Vedic Victory."[82]

Often the same individuals describe the same practices differently depending on context. For example, the Yoga Alliance described yoga as "spiritual rather than fitness" when lobbying for a sales-tax exemption in 2014, but just three months later insisted that yoga is purely "secular," "physical fitness" when defending public-school yoga from litigation.[83] Yoga Ed. developer Tara Guber explained to *Hinduism Today* that she overcame objections from "fundamentalist Baptists" on an Aspen, Colorado, school board by relabeling "samadhi" as "oneness," "meditation" as "time in," and "pranayama" as "bunny breathing"; despite superficial linguistic repackaging, Guber expressed confidence that yoga practice would itself "go within, shift consciousness and alter beliefs."[84] MBSR-developer Jon Kabat-Zinn likewise assured readers of *Contemporary Buddhism* that MBSR communicates the "essence of the Buddha's teachings," even though he had for years "bent over backward" to conceal its Buddhist foundations when promoting it in medical settings. Once scientific studies made health professionals more accepting of mindfulness, Kabat-Zinn began to "articulate its origins and its essence" to healthcare providers—yet "not so much to the patients," whom he intentionally left uninformed about the "dharma that underlies the curriculum."[85] Similarly, in a password-protected section of the Center for Reiki Research *Including* Reiki in Hospitals website, reiki masters Ava Wolf and Janet Wing explain to other reiki healers "How We Got Reiki Into the Hospital." Although continuing to "trust the energy" when working with patients, they developed new "vocabulary so we could express our healing concepts in medical terminology." In addressing hospital administrators and patients, they defined reiki as "energy nutrition," an "effective touch therapy," and a "technique for stress reduction." They found that "the concept of Mind/Body/Spirit connection was acceptable," but "avoided references to channeling, auras, energy fields, guides, and spirituality."[86] Such linguistic flexibility has proved effective in bringing holistic healing into mainstream educational and medical institutions without jettisoning metaphysical foundations.

Many Christians have played a role in holistic mainstreaming through their efforts to "secularize" or "Christianize" practices by subtracting non-Christian language and adding prayers or Bible verses. Christianity—and its Protestant even more than its Catholic variants—privileges orthodox beliefs and verbal proclamation of those beliefs above orthopraxis. A Christian is one who will "declare with your mouth" and "believe in your heart" the risen Lord Jesus.[87] Practices like eating bread and wine or immersion in water are only religiously significant if labeled as communion or baptism. Christians may attend traditional yoga classes and relabel sun salutations as *Son* salutations or pranayama as breathing in the Holy Spirit. Others select "Christian" yoga alternatives such as Christoga or Yahweh Yoga, which relabel poses and add Bible verses. Christians uncomfortable with the term "yoga," because it connotes yoking with the Divine, choose programs at a further linguistic remove, such as WholyFit, Outstretched in Worship, or PraiseMoves.[88] Wheaton College yoga is "redeemed" because classes subtract "ancient (and sometimes religious) words" and add Christian prayers or Scripture.[89]

The principal litmus test employed by evangelicals evaluates "roots" and "fruits." Jesus said "I am the vine; you are the branches. If you remain in me and I in you, you will bear much fruit" and "every good tree bears good fruit, but a bad tree bears bad fruit.... Thus, by their fruit you will recognize them."[90] If historical origins of a practice, like reiki or yoga, seem suspect, then it is necessary to offer a Christianized version, set apart by linguistic modifications. Christians sometime speak of substituting ingredients in a recipe or refilling neutral containers with preferred contents.[91] The presumption is that intentions and words determine whether practices are religious or what kind of religion they express. If a practice works to improve health, or if it leads to Christ, then the fruits may be evaluated as good.

Christians come to holistic healing looking for good fruits—which they experience as lacking in their own traditions. Evangelical Protestants in particular have been described as the "backbone" of metaphysical religion in America; in point of fact, many evangelicals have had their backbones adjusted by chiropractors and other holistic healers.[92] Therapeutic Touch healer Judy Chuster, a Christian nurse, explains that "feeling the energy fields gives me something tangible."[93] One "devoted Southern Baptist church member" explains, "I get much more out of yoga and meditation than I ever get out of a sermon in church."[94] Certain evangelicals affirm that the Holy Spirit inspired the Bible and empowered Jesus's miracles, but envision the modern world in functionally naturalistic terms. By contrast, Pentecostal and charismatic Christians expect ongoing interventions by the Holy Spirit. Although Pentecostals insist that the Holy Spirit is a divine being, the third person of the Trinity, practices such as "laying on of hands," "anointing with oil," mailing of "prayer cloths," and "slaying in the spirit" readily bleed into notions that the Holy Spirit is a force that can be transferred.[95] Pentecostals sometimes seem to be persuaded by phenomenological similarities between charismatic and holistic healing—such as physical sensations of heat and tingling—that holistic healers achieve good fruits by tapping into the Holy Spirit, whether or not they realize that this is the source of their power.[96] Such Christians who are mollified by secular or Christian linguistic reframing of phenomenologically pleasant practices constitute a ready market for holistic goods and services.

Commodification

The second major marketing tactic is commodification of holistic healing. In part because of the historic dominance of Christianity in U.S. culture, Americans tend to associate "religion" with free goods and services. Jesus admonished his followers: "freely you have received; freely give."[97] Closer to home, many Americans criticize profit-seeking religious leaders—for instance "prosperity" preachers who promise financial blessings in exchange for donations—and also express suspicion that free gifts may be recruitment gimmicks.[98] By contrast, Americans are accustomed to paying for medical treatments and fitness services. Charging a fee implies that a product or service is therapeutic, rather than religious. Integrative medicine has become a $37 billion annual industry, and those most actively engaged in commercial exchanges often do so at the expense of less powerful cultural producers.[99] The first American certified as a reiki master, Hawayo Takata, was also the first person to charge for reiki, beginning in 1936. Sensing that Americans tend to associate higher fees with more valuable products, Takata certified three levels of reiki practitioners, collecting $10,000 from Level III reiki masters.[100] As certification options proliferated, reiki fees became more modest; all three degrees can now be obtained for as little as $500, making reiki training accessible to more people while still communicating commercial value.[101] In 2020 the average cost for a reiki treatment ranged from $60 to $80.[102] Exhibiting more of a hybrid marketing model, free introductory TM courses conclude with an invitation to enroll in fee-based courses. In the 1970s TM courses ran $125 for adults, $45 for students; as of 2023, a sliding-fee scale ranges from $420 to $980.[103] Somewhat different still, marketing MBSR as a medical program involved creating a hospital-based center that "bills like a clinic."[104] As of 2023, the Center for Mindfulness at UMass Memorial Medical Center charges $650 for an eight-week MBSR class, with discounts for hospital employees.[105] Discounts communicate special concern for groups such as students, hospital employees, and those who "need" services but cannot pay full price.

High fees denote high value, which feeds demand, but fees also erect financial access barriers. Philanthropic foundations meet and further stimulate demand by funding services.[106] For instance, the Urban Zen Foundation, created by "fashion icon" Donna Karan, brings reiki, meditation, yoga, and essential oils into U.S healthcare and educational institutions; Urban Zen offers institutional grants and individual scholarships for nurses and teachers to participate in training programs.[107] Between 2011 and 2016 the K. P. Jois USA Foundation (a.k.a. Sonima/Pure Edge), founded by hedge-fund billionaire Paul Tudor Jones and his wife Sonia, awarded more than $4 million in grants to introduce Ashtanga yoga and mindfulness meditation to K–6 students in the Encinitas Union School District in San Diego, California, and to develop curricula for use in other school districts.[108] Paul Tudor Jones also donated $12 million to his alma mater, the public University of Virginia, to endow a Contemplative Sciences Center that teaches "Buddhist Meditation for Free."[109] As a result of such philanthropic giving, the power to influence institutions like hospitals and schools shifts from experts in medicine or education, or even religious professionals, to those with money to fund—and/or internet savvy and social connections to market—the types of services and attendant belief systems that the philanthropists favor.[110] Institutions accepting grants invest resources of time and space on the premise that investments will increase health, productivity, and moral character needed to generate new capital amid globalization and neoliberal capitalism.[111] This in turn creates additional demand.

Consumer Demand

Demand for holistic healing cannot, however, be reduced to perception of commercial value. There are additional demand-side factors that vary by population. Hospitals administrators find themselves in the position of competing for patients. Of hospitals offering integrative medicine, 85 percent cite patient demand as a primary rationale.[112] Former CEO of Boston's Beth Israel Hospital Matt Fink explains that "if hospitals don't get involved in these kinds of programs they will lose patients because patients will go elsewhere."[113] Although patients pay $30 billion out-of-pocket annually for holistic services, insurance companies are increasingly willing to reimburse cost-effective, albeit unvalidated, treatments that promise to reduce patient demand for higher-technology, higher-cost options.[114]

Women may be particularly motivated to seek training in practices such as Therapeutic Touch or reiki because they are looking for a sense of empowerment in male-dominated medical or religious hierarchies.[115] Nursing professor Arlene Miller explains the popularity of Therapeutic Touch among nurses as a "power issue." Because nurses have "always felt a bit abused by medicine," Therapeutic Touch represents what nurses have "uniquely to contribute. They are 'noninvasive,' so it is kind of an antitechnology move also. Nurses can do it without physicians' orders."[116] Because nurses are already essential contributors to the conventional healthcare system, integrating Therapeutic Touch into this system only required recruiting nurses.

Catholic nuns express comparable reasons for embracing reiki. One such nun, "Mary," learned about chakras, the third eye, and nine healing angels—one connected with each energy area—from a group of Franciscan nuns. Her comments point to power struggles between female nuns and male priests.[117] The priests—one in particular "hates what we do"—are invited by church officials to participate in exorcism trainings in another state, but nuns are excluded from this specialized training. The nuns protest by offering their own healing modality. Feeling disempowered by male-dominated medical and religious institutions, some women turn to practices like Therapeutic Touch or reiki for authority to heal without male oversight. It is noteworthy that certain Catholics, even those serious enough about religion to become nuns, embrace practices like reiki in defiance of clerical teachings. In 2009 the United States Conference of Catholic Bishops' Committee on Doctrine singled out reiki as problematic, noting that attempts to "Christianize Reiki by adding a prayer to Christ" do "not affect the essential nature of Reiki" as a religious practice rooted in Buddhism.[118] The bishops' warning highlights broader tendencies among Christian healthcare consumers that have significant theological—as well social, political, and legal—implications.

THE MAINSTREAMING OF HOLISTIC HEALING: IMPLICATIONS

Practices Change Beliefs

Because holistic healing is embodied, participation can shape perception through three interacting processes: (1) awareness of sensory experiences, (2) reinterpretation of experiences through the lens of socially constructed beliefs and values, and (3) cultural associations that remain after subtracting religious language.[119]

The Word-orientation of Christians, combined with health-seeking motives, result in a theological blind spot for how practices can reshape beliefs. Participation not only expresses, but also instills belief; intentions can transform in the course of practice. Thus Christian practitioners of holistic healing sometimes shift beliefs without seeming to notice. For instance, pastor Scott Wyman describes his initiation into reiki as "a very spiritual experience not unlike my experience of baptism, as I felt an increased connection to God and to His healing power," which Wyman identifies with the "Divine or Universal Self. (Bodhicitta, Christ Consciousness, Buddha Nature, etc.)."[120] Christian yogi Brooke Boon, creator of "Holy Yoga," although rejecting traditional yoga, nevertheless came to think of humans as "energetic beings" whose vitality accumulates at "chakras."[121]

Survey research on yoga and mindfulness points to larger patterns in how embodied practices influence religious beliefs.[122] Although many more Americans begin yoga wanting "physical" (54 percent) rather than "spiritual" (8 percent) benefits, most (53 percent) end up exploring "spiritual values."[123] The nature of these values is influenced by the social experiences of yoga practice. The Yoga Alliance certifies half (49 percent) of U.S. yoga teachers; certification requires study of Hindu texts such as the *Bhagavad Gita* and assimilation of "yoga lifestyle" precepts such as ahimsa (nonviolence), dharma (moral law), karma (consequences), and "energy anatomy and physiology (chakras, nadis, etc.)."[124] Whether directly or more subtly, teachers communicate values in the course of instruction. Consequently, most yoga students (62 percent) and teachers (85 percent) change their primary reason for practice over time; the most common change is from seeking "exercise and stress relief" to "spirituality."[125] In one study, among yoga participants with less than one year of yoga exposure, 43 percent identified as Christian, 26 percent as secular, 23 percent as spiritual but not religious (SBNR), and 4 percent as Buddhist; after six years, 28 percent identified as Christian, 27 percent as secular, 31 percent as SBNR, and 9 percent as Buddhist.[126] A majority of MBSR participants (54 percent in one study) report that an eight-week course "deepened their sense of spirituality"; as one MBSR alumnus explains, "I took an 8 week Mindfulness Based Stress Reduction Course two years ago without knowing anything about Buddhism.... That program spurred my curiosity and here I am learning all about the Four Noble Truths."[127] Long-term meditators are statistically less likely to identify as monotheists or religious "nones" and more likely to identify as Buddhist or with "all" religions.[128]

The implications of such changes in religious beliefs, values, and affiliations are not merely personal. As Kabat-Zinn explains of mindfulness practice, meditation on one's present-moment bodily sensations creates an "awareness" of "interconnectedness as the fundamental ground of being."[129] Perceiving that "the infinite number of beings and oneself are not separate, and never were" has a "direct effect" on "how one relates to the rest of the world."[130] Thus individual experiences have profoundly social implications. Those who feel spiritually connected to other people or accountable to a higher power are more likely to become involved in their communities, encourage others—including those outside their usual social networks—to practice holistic healing, and take political or legal action to facilitate or even mandate holistic practices.[131]

Holistic healers often exhibit a missionary zeal to share their practices with others. Buddhist converts gain from meditating a "persuasive worldview" that explains "why suffering happens"—and motivates "going into schools to 'spread the dharma.'"¹³² Many school meditation and yoga programs specifically target "low-income, minority" students perceived as lacking an inner capacity to "self-regulate"—a pattern that might be criticized as "cultural imperialism."¹³³

Holistic healing enthusiasts do not always stop with making favored practices more widely available but may also seek legal and policy changes to require their performance. Goldie Hawn's mission is for MindUP to be "absolutely mandated" in "every school."¹³⁴ The Jois/Sonima/Pure Edge Foundation used arms-length funding to facilitate the "education of members of the legislative and local school boards" and the California "Curriculum Commission to gain support" for "public relations/public policy changes on the state and local levels" that would make training in Jois yoga and mindfulness into requirements for "certification and/or degrees for educators" and an "integrated component of the public education system."¹³⁵ Foundation employees likewise coauthored a resolution passed by New York's legislature establishing a state "Health and Wellness Week."¹³⁶

Consumer Choice

It may seem obvious that government endorsements or requirements to practice holistic healing constrain consumer choice, but coercive pressures are sometimes subtle. Underresourced public schools may feel pressure to accept philanthropic grants that come with strings attached. Schools accepting Lynch Foundation funding must restructure their daily schedule to accommodate two TM sessions of fifteen to twenty minutes each (cutting 150–200 minutes of weekly instructional time).¹³⁷ Schools funded by Jois/Sonima/Pure Edge must accept "mandatory" foundation training in yoga and meditation to ensure "uniformity."[138] Even when parents are asked to sign consent forms—as with TM/Quiet Time—such forms generally frame practices as "non-religious techniques" rather than disclosing not only historic but also ongoing religious associations (for instance, the claim made by TM.org in 2023 that TM leads practitioners to "directly experience the Transcendent").[139] Genuinely "informed consent" requires a level of transparency and voluntarism that is often absent in school-based programs.[140]

The integration of holistic healing into healthcare institutions also influences the choices made by consumers. Patients might infer that services offered by nurses or massage therapists rather than chaplains in hospitals are medical rather than religious.[141] Patients who would object to participating in a practice from another religion might accept the practice as secular because endorsed by a secular medical institution—and potentially experience imperceptibly gradual changes in their own religious beliefs as they participate.

Holistic healing has emerged in the United States as the new religious establishment. Despite the widely heralded separation of church and state in America, therapies premised upon a vitalistic ontology and experiential epistemology and disseminated through social networks are increasingly integrated into mainstream medical and educational institutions. Freedom of choice regarding whether to participate is constrained by supply-side mechanisms of linguistic repackaging and commodification as well as market demand for financially beneficial, socially empowering, and theologically acceptable goods and services. Nevertheless, participation in embodied practices can be religiously transformative in unrecognized ways. The very invisibility of holistic healing's metaphysical foundations and transformative potential contributes to its power. Far from a culturally incoherent or socially and politically insignificant development, the institutional mainstreaming of holistic healing is one of the most powerful engines reshaping public life in twenty-first-century America.

NOTES

1. Robert C. Fuller, *Spiritual but Not Religious: Understanding Unchurched America* (Oxford: Oxford University Press, 2001); Catherine L. Albanese, *A Republic of Mind and Spirit: A Cultural History of American Metaphysical Religion* (New Haven, CT: Yale University Press, 2007).
2. Candy Gunther Brown, *The Healing Gods: Complementary and Alternative Medicine in Christian America* (Oxford: Oxford University Press, 2013).
3. Candy Gunther Brown, *Debating Yoga and Mindfulness in Public Schools: Reforming Secular Education or Reestablishing Religion?* (Chapel Hill: University of North Carolina Press, 2019).
4. Crystal L. Park, Kristen E. Riley, Elena Bedesin, and V. Michelle Stewart, "Why Practice Yoga? Practitioners' Motivations for Adopting and Maintaining Yoga Practice," *Journal of Health Psychology* 21, no. 6 (2016): 887–96; Jeffrey M. Greeson et al., "Changes in Spirituality Partly Explain Health-Related Quality of Life Outcomes After Mindfulness-Based Stress Reduction," *Journal of Behavioral Medicine* 34, no. 6 (2011): 508–18.
5. Michel De Certeau, *The Practice of Everyday Life* (Berkeley: University of California Press, 1984), xi–xxiv; Linda Woodhead, "Tactical and Strategic Religion," in *Everyday Lived Islam in Europe*, ed. Nathal M. Dessing et al. (Farnham, UK: Ashgate, 2014), 9–22.
6. R. Marie Griffith, *Born Again Bodies: Flesh and Spirit in American Christianity* (Berkeley: University of California Press, 2004).
7. See the introduction to this volume; José Casanova, *Public Religions in the Modern World* (Chicago: University of Chicago Press, 1994).
8. Erich Kurt Ledermann, *Philosophy and Medicine* (Brookfield, VT: Gower, 1986).
9. Norman Gevitz, *Other Healers: Unorthodox Medicine in America* (Baltimore: Johns Hopkins University Press, 1988).
10. Ronald L. Numbers, "The Fall and Rise of the American Medical Profession," in *Sickness and Health in America: Readings in the History of*

Medicine and Public Health, ed. Judith Walzer Leavitt and Ronald L. Numbers (Madison: University of Wisconsin Press, 1978), 225–36.
11. James C. Whorton, *Nature Cures: The History of Alternative Medicine in America* (New York: Oxford University Press, 2002).
12. National Center for Complementary and Integrative Health, "Paying for Complementary and Integrative Health Approaches," June 2016, https://www.nccih.nih.gov/health/paying-for-complementary-and-integrative-health-approaches.
13. Whorton, *Nature Cures*.
14. American Hospital Association, "More Hospitals Offering Complementary and Alternative Medicine Services," 2011, https://www.aha.org/system/files/presscenter/pressrel/2011/110907-pr-camsurvey.pdf.
15. Academic Consortium for Integrative Medicine & Health, "Membership," https://imconsortium.org/member-listing/.
16. Casey Ross, Max Blau, and Kate Sheridan, "Medicine with a Side of Mysticism: Top Hospitals Promote Unproven Therapies," *STAT*, March 7, 2017, https://www.statnews.com/2017/03/07/alternative-medicine-hospitals-promote/.
17. Quoted in Ross, Blau, and Sheridan, "Medicine with a Side of Mysticism."
18. AARP, *Complementary and Alternative Medicine: What People 50 and Older Are Using and Discussing with Their Physicians* (Washington, DC: AARP, 2007).
19. David M. Eisenberg et al., "Unconventional Medicine in the United States: Prevalence, Costs, and Patterns of Use," *New England Journal of Medicine* 328, no. 4 (1993): 246–52.
20. Tainya C. Clarke et al., "Trends in the Use of Complementary Health Approaches Among Adults: United States, 2002–2012," *National Health Statistics Reports* 79 (2015): 1–15.
21. Stefanie Syman, *The Subtle Body: The Story of Yoga in America* (New York: Farrar, Straus and Giroux, 2010); Clarke et al., "Trends in the Use of Complementary Health Approaches"; Yoga Journal and Yoga Alliance, with Ipsos Public Affairs, *The 2016 Yoga in America Study* (Boulder, CO: Yoga Journal, 2016).
22. Lindsey I. Black et al., "Use of Complementary Health Approaches Among Children Aged 4–17 Years in the United States: National Health Interview Survey, 2007–2012," *National Health Statistics Reports* 78 (2015): 1–18.
23. Clarke et al., "Trends in the Use of Complementary Health Approaches"; Black et al., "Use of Complementary Health Approaches."
24. *New York Times*, "Poll Finds Meditation, Mysticism, and Yoga Growing in Popularity," November 18, 1976.

25. Maharishi International University, "MIU at a Glance," https://www.miu.edu/about-miu.
26. Aryeh Siegel, "Disabled Army Vet Persuades VA to Abort $8 Million David Lynch Foundation Study on Transcendental Meditation and PTSD," *EINPressWire*, August 1, 2022, https://www.einpresswire.com/article/583527644/disabled-army-vet-persuades-va-to-abort-8-million-david-lynch-foundation-study-on-transcendental-meditation-and-ptsd.
27. UMass Memorial Medical Center, "Center for Mindfulness," https://www.ummhealth.org/umass-memorial-medical-center/services-treatments/center-for-mindfulness.
28. Bethany Butzer et al., "School-Based Yoga Programs in the United States: A Survey," *Advances in Mind-Body Medicine* 29, no. 4 (2015): 18–26.
29. Brown, *Debating Yoga and Mindfulness*.
30. Yoga Ed., "For Schools," https://yogaed.com/yoga-for-schools/#mindful-movement-program.
31. Mindful Schools, "About Us," https://www.mindfulschools.org/about/; MindUP, "Our Mission," https://mindup.org/our-mission/.
32. Pamela E. Jeter et al., "Yoga as a Therapeutic Intervention: A Bibliometric Analysis of Published Research Studies from 1967 to 2013," *Journal of Alternative and Complementary Medicine* 21, no. 10 (2015): 591.
33. Sat Bir S. Khalsa and Bethany Butzer, "Yoga in School Settings: A Research Review," *Annals of the New York Academy of Sciences* 1373 (June 2016): 52 (my emphasis).
34. David Keil, "Negative Experiences in Yoga Practice: What Do Practitioners Report," *Yoga Anatomy*, March 21, 2017, https://www.yoganatomy.com/negative-experiences-in-yoga-practice-survey-results/.
35. Madhav Goyal et al., "Meditation Programs for Psychological Stress and Well-Being: A Systematic Review and Meta-analysis," *JAMA Internal Medicine* 174, no. 3 (2014): 357.
36. Kevin Loria, "7 Ways Meditation Changes Your Brain and Body," *Business Insider*, February 2, 2015, https://www.businessinsider.com/how-meditation-changes-your-brain-2015-1; Tammi R. A. Kral et al., "Absence of Structural Brain Changes from Mindfulness-Based Stress Reduction: Two Combined Randomized Controlled Trials," *Science Advances* 8, no. 20 (2022), https://www.science.org/doi/10.1126/sciadv.abk3316.
37. J. David Creswell et al., "Brief Mindfulness Meditation Training Alters Psychological and Neuroendocrine Responses to Social Evaluative Stress," *Psychoneuroendocrinology* 44 (June 2014): 1–12; Kimberly A.

Schonert-Reichl et al., "Enhancing Cognitive and Social–Emotional Development Through a Simple-to-Administer Mindfulness-Based School Program for Elementary School Children: A Randomized Controlled Trial," *Developmental Psychology* 51, no. 1 (2015): 52–66.
38. Jared R. Lindahl et al., "The Varieties of Contemplative Experience: A Mixed Methods Study of Meditation-Related Challenges in Western Buddhists," *PLOS ONE* 12, no. 5 (2017), https://journals.plos.org/plosone/article?id=10.1371/journal.pone.0176239.
39. Ted J. Kaptchuk, "Acupuncture: Theory, Efficacy, and Practice," *Annals of Internal Medicine* 136, no. 5 (2002): 377.
40. Linda Rosa et al., "A Close Look at Therapeutic Touch," *Journal of the American Medical Association* 279, no. 13 (1998): 1005–10; Gabriel Moss et al., "Assessing the Ability of Reiki Practitioners to Detect Human Energy Fields," *OBM Integrative and Complementary Medicine*, August 4, 2022, https://www.lidsen.com/journals/icm/icm-07-03-033.
41. *Engel v. Vitale*, 370 U.S. 421 (1962): 431.
42. *Malnak v. Yogi*, 440 F. Supp. 1284 (D. N.J. 1977): 1322.
43. David Lynch Foundation, "Quiet Time," https://www.davidlynchfoundation.ca/en/education; *Separation of Hinduism from Our Schools v. Chicago Public Schools et al. 2021*, Case No. 20 C 4540 (2021).
44. *Sedlock v. Baird*, Superior Court of San Diego County, No. 37-2013-00035910-CU-MC-CTL. (2013): 14; *Education for New Generations Charter School v. North Penn School District*, CAB No. 2013-10 (2016).
45. Equal Employment Opportunity Commission, *Compliance Manual on Religious Discrimination*, 2021, https://www.eeoc.gov/laws/guidance/section-12-religious-discrimination#_Toc203359487.
46. *EEOC v. United Health Programs of America, Inc., et al.*, No. 14-CV-3673 (KAM)(JO)(E.D.N.Y.) (2016).
47. Fuller, *Spiritual but Not Religious*; Albanese, *A Republic of Mind and Spirit*.
48. John C. McDowell, *The Gospel According to Star Wars: Faith, Hope, and The Force* (Louisville, KY: Westminster/John Knox Press, 2007), 20.
49. Syman, *The Subtle Body*.
50. Whorton, *Nature Cures*; Anne Harrington, *The Cure Within: A History of Mind-Body Medicine* (New York: W. W. Norton, 2008).
51. Albanese, *A Republic of Mind and Spirit*, 407.
52. Daniel David Palmer, *The Chiropractor's Adjuster: Text-book of the Science, Art and Philosophy of Chiropractic* (Portland, OR: Portland Printing House, 1910), 446, 491–93, 642, 691.
53. Peter Bryner, "Isn't It Time to Abandon Anachronistic Terminology?," *Journal of the Australian Chiropractors' Association* 17, no. 2 (1987): 53–58.

54. Jack Raso, *"Alternative" Healthcare: A Comprehensive Guide* (Amherst, NY: Prometheus, 1994); Glenda Wiese, "Chiropractic History and Trivia," in *Chiropractic Secrets*, ed. Seth Gardner and John S. Mosby (Philadelphia: Hanley and Belfus, 2000), 231–46.
55. William P. McDonald, *How Chiropractors Think and Practice: The Survey of North American Chiropractors* (Ada: Institute for Social Research, Ohio Northern University, 2003); Holly Folk, *The Religion of Chiropractic: Populist Healing from the American Heartland* (Chapel Hill: University of North Carolina Press, 2017).
56. Samuel Hahnemann, *The Homoeopathic Medical Doctrine: Or, "Organon of the Healing Art"* (Dublin: Wakeman, 1833 [1810]), 9, 11, 20, 52; Ross, Blau, and Sheridan, "Medicine with a Side of Mysticism."
57. Jian Kong et al., "Acupuncture De Qi, from Qualitative History to Quantitative Measurement," *Journal of Alternative and Complementary Medicine* 13, no. 10 (2007): 1059–60.
58. Dolores Krieger, *Foundations for Holistic Health Nursing Practices: The Renaissance Nurse* (Philadelphia: Lippincott, 1981), 50.
59. International Association of Reiki Professionals, "All About Reiki," https://iarp.org/learn-about-reiki/.
60. Peggy Jentoft, *Reiki Level One Manual: Reiki Unleashed; Usui Reiki, Contemporary and Traditional* (2006), 31, https://dokumen.tips/documents/reiki-1-peggy-jentoft.html.
61. Kathie Lipinski, "Making Reiki Real," 2004, https://web.archive.org/web/20140108010422/iarp.org/MakingReikiRealArticle.html; Frances Vincen-Brown, "Reiki Therapy," *Experience Festival*, 2010, www.experiencefestival.com/wp/article/reiki-therapy.
62. Jon Kabat-Zinn, *Wherever You Go, There You Are: Mindfulness Meditation in Everyday Life* (New York: Hyperion, 1994), 217–19.
63. See the introduction.
64. Glen Dupreem and Susan Beal, "A Graphic Representation of the Workings of Homeopathy," *American Journal of Homeopathic Medicine* 99, no. 1 (2006): 73; Amit Sood, "Mind-Body Medicine," in *Mayo Clinic Book of Alternative Medicine: Integrating the Best of Natural Therapies with Conventional Medicine*, 2nd ed., ed. Brent A. Bauer (New York: Time Inc., Home Entertainment Books, 2010), 95; Brooke Boon, *Holy Yoga: Exercise for the Christian Body and Soul* (New York: FaithWords, 2007).
65. Gaëtan Sanchez et al., "Decoding Across Sensory Modalities Reveals Common Supramodal Signatures of Conscious Perception," *PNAS* 117, no. 13 (2020): 7437–46.
66. Candy Gunther Brown, *Testing Prayer: Science and Healing* (Cambridge, MA: Harvard University Press, 2012); Brown, *The Healing Gods*.
67. Pamela Miles, *Reiki: A Comprehensive Guide* (New York: Penguin, 2006), 193.

68. R. Alexander Medin, "3 Gurus, 48 Questions: Matching Interviews with Sri T. K. V. Desikachar, Sri B. K. S. Iyengar & Sri K. Pattabhi Jois," *Namarupa*, Fall 2004, 15, 7, 18.
69. Octavia Drughi, "A Deeper Look into Yoga & Spirituality," April 4, 2017, https://www.bookyogaretreats.com/news/yoga-and-spirituality-survey.
70. Maharishi Mahesh Yogi, *Science of Being and Art of Living: Transcendental Meditation* (New York: New American Library, 1968), 19, 68, 158.
71. Richard Hughes Seager, *Buddhism in America* (New York: Columbia University Press, 1999), 225.
72. Yoga Journal and Yoga Alliance, *The 2016 Yoga in America Study*, 28, 29, 31, 32, 38.
73. Jaime Kucinskas, *The Mindful Elite: Mobilizing from the Inside Out* (New York: Oxford University Press, 2018); Michal Pagis, *Inward: Vipassana Meditation and the Embodiment of the Self* (Chicago: University of Chicago Press, 2019).
74. Meredith B. McGuire and Debra Kantor, *Ritual Healing in Suburban America* (New Brunswick, NJ: Rutgers University Press, 1988); Courtney Bender, *The New Metaphysicals: Spirituality and the American Religious Imagination* (Chicago: University of Chicago Press, 2010).
75. Association of Accredited Naturopathic Medical Colleges, "The 6 Principles," September 26, 2008–April 21, 2021, https://web.archive.org/web/20140219211050/https://www.aanmc.org/naturopathic-medicine/the-6-principles.php.
76. John Fetto, "Your Questions Answered," *AdAge*, May 1, 2003, https://adage.com/article/american-demographics/questions-answered/44147.
77. Yoga Journal and Yoga Alliance, *The 2016 Yoga in America Study*, 26, 16.
78. Richard E. Nisbetter and Timothy DeCamp Wilson, "The Halo Effect: Evidence for Unconscious Alteration of Judgments," *Journal of Personality and Social Psychology* 35, no. 4 (1977): 250–56.
79. Margaret Lee Lyles, "My Christian Faith & Reiki," *Reiki for Christians*, http://www.christianreiki.org/my-christian-faith-reiki/.
80. De Certeau, *The Practice of Everyday Life*, xi–xxiv; Woodhead, "Tactical and Strategic Religion."
81. Nurit Zaidman, Ofra Goldstein-Gidoni, and Iris Nehemya, "From Temples to Organizations: The Introduction and Packaging of Spirituality," *Organization* 16, no. 4 (2009): 599, 616; Penelope Gardner-Chloros, *Code-Switching* (New York: Cambridge University Press, 2009); Erving Goffman, *The Presentation of Self in Everyday Life* (Garden City, NY: Doubleday, 1956).
82. "Marcy," quoted in Bender, *The New Metaphysicals*, 42; Jon Kabat-Zinn, "Some Reflections on the Origins of MBSR, Skillful Means and the

Trouble with Maps," *Contemporary Buddhism* 12, no. 1 (2011): 281–306; Daniel Goleman, "Comment," *Inquiring Mind* 2, no. 1 (1985): 7; Goldie Hawn, "How Mindfulness Helps Children Thrive," *Heart-Mind 2013*, The Dalai Lama Center for Peace-Education, June 20, 2013, https://www.youtube.com/watch?v=7pLhwGLYvJU; Kenneth Folk, "The Trojan Horse of Meditation," *Buddhist Geeks*, September 2013, https://web.archive.org/web/20131210035124/www.buddhistgeeks.com/2013/09/bg-296-the-trojan-horse-of-meditation/; Trudy Goodman, Vincent Horn, and Emily Horn, "Stealth Buddhism," *Buddhist Geeks*, August 27, 2014, https://web.archive.org/web/20160405015832/http://www.buddhistgeeks.com/2014/08/bg-331-stealth-buddhism/; Tara Guber, "Tara's Yoga for Kids: One Noble Soul Takes on the Public School System and Wins a Vedic Victory," *Hinduism Today* (Interview), April/May/June 2004, https://www.hinduismtoday.com/magazine/april-may-june-2004/2004-04-tara-s-yoga-for-kids/.

83. Richard Karpel, "The DC 'Yoga Tax' Isn't Really a Yoga Tax," *Yoga Alliance*, July 30, 2014, https://www.yogaalliance.org/the_dc_yoga_tax_isnt_really_a_yoga_tax; "Brief of Amicus Curiae Yoga Alliance in Support of Respondents and Affirmance," Yoga Alliance, October 16, 2014, in *Sedlock v. Baird*, Superior Court of San Diego County, No. 37-2013-00035910-CU-MC-CTL. (2013), 235 Cal. App. 4th 874 (2015), 11, 6.
84. Guber, "Tara's Yoga."
85. Kabat-Zinn, "Some Reflections," 282–83.
86. Ava Wolf and Janet Wing, "How We Got Reiki Into the Hospital," Center for Reiki Research Including Reiki in Hospitals, April 13, 2010–November 7, 2016, https://web.archive.org/web/20100401000000*/https://www.centerforreikiresearch.org/Articles_HowWeGot.aspx.
87. Romans 10:9 (NIV).
88. Brown, *Debating Yoga and Mindfulness*.
89. Wheaton College, "Yoga at Wheaton?," January 2015, https://www.wheaton.edu/media/migrated-images-amp-files/media/files/athletics/Why-Yoga-at-Wheaton.pdf.
90. John 15:5 (NIV); Matthew 7:17, 20 (NIV).
91. Brown, *The Healing Gods*.
92. Albanese, *A Republic of Mind and Spirit*, 510; Brown, *The Healing Gods*.
93. Joel Maxwell, "Nursing's New Age?," *Christianity Today*, February 5, 1996, 98.
94. Email quoted in R. Albert Mohler, "Yahoo, Yoga, and Yours Truly," October 7, 2010, http://www.albertmohler.com/2010/10/07/yahoo-yoga-and-yours-truly/.
95. Brown, *Testing Prayer*.
96. Brown, *The Healing Gods*.

97. Matthew 10:8 (NIV).
98. Kate Bowler, *Blessed: A History of the American Prosperity Gospel* (New York: Oxford University Press, 2013); Actually Free, "Religious Freebies," http://www.actuallyfree.com/free-stuff/religious-freebies/.
99. Ross, Blau, and Sheridan, "Medicine with a Side of Mysticism"; Jeremy Carrette and Richard King, *Selling Spirituality: The Silent Takeover of Religion* (London: Routledge, 2005); Andrea R. Jain, *Selling Yoga: From Counterculture to Pop Culture* (New York: Oxford University Press, 2014); Andrea R. Jain, *Peace Love Yoga: The Politics of Global Spirituality* (New York: Oxford University Press, 2020); Francois Gauthier, *Religion, Modernity, Globalisation: Nation-State to Market* (New York: Routledge, 2020).
100. William L. Rand, "What Is the History of Reiki?," *International Center for Reiki Training*, http://reiki-healing-arts.com/reiki-history.html.
101. Diane Stein, *Essential Reiki Teaching Manual: A Companion Guide for Reiki Healers* (Berkeley, CA: Crossing, 2007).
102. Thumbtack, "How Much Does Reiki Healing Cost?," August 26, 2020, https://www.thumbtack.com/p/reiki-cost.
103. George E. LaMore Jr., "The Secular Selling of a Religion," *Christian Century*, December 10, 1975, 1133; TM.org, "TM Course Fee," https://www.tm.org/course-fee.
104. Jon Kabat-Zinn, "Catalyzing Movement Towards a More Contemplative/Sacred-Appreciating/Non-dualistic Society," The Contemplative Mind in Society: Meeting of the Working Group, Nathan Cummings Foundation & Fetzer Institute, September 29–October 2, 1994, Pocantico, NY, https://web.archive.org/web/20170204171614/http://www.contemplativemind.org/admin/wp-content/uploads/2012/09/kabat-zinn.pdf, 7.
105. UMass Memorial Medical Center, "Center for Mindfulness."
106. David Callahan, *The Givers: Wealth, Power, and Philanthropy in a New Gilded Age* (New York: Knopf, 2017).
107. Urban Zen Foundation, "A Philosophy of Caring by Donna Karan," https://uzit.nyc/.
108. Brown, *Debating Yoga and Mindfulness*.
109. Don Bauder, "Is Yoga a Religion? Courts Say It Is, but Encinitas Schools Have Scrubbed Their Yoga Programs Clean," *San Diego Reader*, April 29, 2015, http://www.sandiegoreader.com/news/2015/apr/29/citylights-yoga-religion/#; Sonia Jones, "A New Online Course Teaches Buddhist Meditation for Free," *Sonima*, January 22, 2016, http://www.sonima.com/videos/study-buddhism/.
110. Frederick M. Hess, ed., *With the Best Intentions: How Philanthropy Is Reshaping K-12 Education* (Cambridge, MA: Harvard Education Press, 2005).

111. Richard K. Payne, "Religion, Self-Help, Science: Three Economies of Western/ized Buddhism," *Journal of Global Buddhism* 20, January (2019): 69–86; Trine Brox and Elizabeth Williams-Oerberg, ed., *Buddhism and Business: Merit, Material Wealth, and Morality in the Global Market Economy* (Honolulu: University of Hawaii Press, 2020).
112. American Hospital Association, "Complementary and Alternative Medicine Services."
113. Frontline, "The Alternative Fix," November 6, 2003, https://www.pbs.org/wgbh/pages/frontline/shows/altmed/etc/synopsis.html.
114. National Center for Complementary and Integrative Health, "Paying for Complementary and Integrative Health Approaches."
115. Anna Fedele and Kim Knibbe, eds., *Secular Societies, Spiritual Selves? The Gendered Triangle of Religion, Secularity and Spirituality* (New York: Routledge, 2020); Linda Woodhead, "Afterword: To the Vagina Triangle and Beyond!," in *Secular Societies, Spiritual Selves? The Gendered Triangle of Religion, Secularity and Spirituality*, ed. Anna Fedele and Kim Knibbe (New York: Routledge, 2020), 233–38.
116. Arlene Miller, "Should Christian Nurses Practice Therapeutic Touch? No," *Journal of Christian Nursing* 4, no. 4 (1987): 19.
117. "Mary," interview by author, April 22, 2010.
118. United States Conference of Catholic Bishops, *Guidelines for Evaluating Reiki as an Alternative Therapy*, March 2009, https://www.usccb.org/resources/evaluation-guidelines-finaltext-2009–03_0.pdf.
119. Brown, *Debating Yoga and Mindfulness*.
120. Scott Wyman, "Christian Minister Uses Reiki," May 23, 2006 –December 24, 2016, https://web.archive.org/web/20161224112729/www.christianreiki.org/info/NunsPriestsMinisters/ChrisitanMinister.htm; Scott Wyman, "Working with Wisdom & Compassion," 2013, www.scottwyman.com/Scott_Wyman/Integrating.html.
121. Boon, *Holy Yoga*, xv, 32.
122. Nancy T. Ammerman, *Sacred Stories, Spiritual Tribes: Finding Religion in Everyday Life* (New York: Oxford University Press, 2013); Meredith B. McGuire, *Lived Religion: Faith and Practice in Everyday Life* (New York: Oxford University Press, 2008).
123. David Keil, "Assessing the Impacts of Yoga Asana—Survey Summary," *Yoga Anatomy*, March 21, 2017, https://www.yoganatomy.com/yoga-asana-survey-results-summary/; David Keil, "What Are the Benefits of Doing a Yoga Practice," *Yoga Anatomy*, March 21, 2017, https://www.yoganatomy.com/benefits-of-yoga-practice-survey-results/.
124. Yoga Journal and Yoga Alliance, *The 2016 Yoga in America Study*, 17, 64; Yoga Alliance, "Spirit of the Standards—RYS 200," July 2016,

https://www.yogaalliance.org/credentialing/standards/200-hour standards.
125. Crystal L. Park et al., "Why Practice Yoga?," *Journal of Health Psychology* 21, no. 6 (2016): 887.
126. Stephen Penman et al., "Yoga in Australia: Results of a National Survey," *International Journal of Yoga* 5, no. 2 (2012): 91–101.
127. Jeffrey M. Greeson et al., "Changes in Spirituality," 512; online comment by "LKH" on Richard K. Payne, "What's Ethics Got to Do with It? The Misguided Debate About Mindfulness and Morality," *Tricycle*, May 14, 2015, https://tricycle.org/trikedaily/whats-ethics-got-do-it/.
128. Dean H. Shapiro, "A Preliminary Study of Long-Term Meditators: Goals, Effects, Religious Orientation, Cognitions," *Journal of Transpersonal Psychology* 24, no. 1 (1992): 23–39.
129. Kabat-Zinn, "Catalyzing Movement," 5.
130. Kabat-Zinn, "Some Reflections," 295.
131. Fetzer Institute, "What Does Spirituality Mean to Us? A Study of Spirituality in the United States," September 2020, 2, https://spiritualitystudy.fetzer.org/sites/default/files/2020-09/What-Does-Spirituality-Mean-To-Us_%20A-Study-of-Spirituality-in-the-United-States.pdf.
132. Tim Lomas et al., "A Religion of Wellbeing? The Appeal of Buddhism to Men in London, United Kingdom," *Psychology of Religion and Spirituality* 6, no. 3 (2014): 204–5.
133. Erica M. S. Sibinga et al., "School-Based Mindfulness Instruction: An RCT," *Pediatrics* 137, no. 1 (2016): 1–8; Tamar Mendelson et al., "Feasibility and Preliminary Outcomes of a School-Based Mindfulness Intervention for Urban Youth," *Journal of Abnormal Child Psychology* 38, no. 7 (2010): 985; Brown, *Debating Yoga and Mindfulness*.
134. Quoted in Marianne Schnall, "Goldie Hawn Talks 'MindUP' and Her Mission to Bring Children Happiness," *Huffington Post*, April 20, 2011, http://www.huffingtonpost.com/marianne-schnall/goldie-hawn-mindup_b_850226.html.
135. Pure Edge Inc. (a.k.a. K. P. Jois USA Foundation, a.k.a. Sonima Foundation), "Tax Filings by Year," *ProPublica 2011–2018*, https://projects.propublica.org/nonprofits/organizations/453182571.
136. Sonima Foundation, "NY State Legislators Pass Resolution Declaring First Week in May 'NY Health and Wellness Week,'" May 9, 2015, https://web.archive.org/web/20160327015942/http://www.sonimafoundation.org/nystate-legislators-pass-resolution-declaring-first-week-in-may-ny-health-and-wellness-week/.
137. David Lynch Foundation, "Frequently Asked Questions," https://www.davidlynchfoundation.org/frequently-asked-questions.html.

138. Andria Shook and Hannah Johnson, *Yoga Leadership and Instruction: Lessons Learned from Charter School Communities* (San Diego, CA: University of San Diego, 2015), 1–2.
139. TM.org, "Transcendental Meditation: The Technique for Inner Peace & Wellness," https://www.tm.org/.
140. Brown, *Debating Yoga and Mindfulness*.
141. Michael H. Cohen, *Healing at the Borderland of Medicine and Religion* (Chapel Hill: University of North Carolina Press, 2006).

4

SPIRITUALIZING THERAPY

How Psychologists Use Spirituality to Counter the Hyperindividualistic Spirit of Therapy

MICHAL PAGIS AND ORLY TAL

Throughout most of human history, religion, spirituality, and psychological therapy were intertwined. When suffering from emotional distress, people turned to spiritual and religious healers who used common shared beliefs and practices as a communal base for healing.[1] With the Enlightenment and its attempt to secularize the public sphere, psychological therapy evolved into a separate value sphere based on a secular, disenchanted ethos.[2] While scholars have long recognized the religious origins of the therapeutic framework, psychology has become an independent, nonreligious source of meaning and practical guidance in different spheres of life—from romance to family life, to work and career—used by people to cope with "the uncertainties that have become inherent in postmodern lives."[3]

The spiritual turn challenges this separation. Spiritual spheres tend to mix religious ideas and practices with therapeutic logic.[4] As Courtney Bender shows, spiritual practitioners, or "new metaphysicals," as she calls them, emphasize body/mind healing and therapy.[5] Similarly, Jaime Kucinskas illustrates how advocates of the contemplative movement used therapy-related institutions and platforms to advance and mainstream mindfulness meditation.[6] Even prayer has been rebranded as a healing practice that incorporates therapeutic dimensions.[7] Likewise, Michal Pagis has shown how in the context of Buddhist meditation practice, therapeutic and spiritual ideas are often intertwined; for example, practitioners of meditation use psychological notions such as regulating emotions, negotiating intimate relations, and self-states to explain their meditation experiences.[8]

In fact, spirituality, as an influential cultural movement that emerged in late modernity,[9] can be defined as the outcome of the integration of the therapeutic and the religious. A prevailing perspective on the rise of spirituality is that the popularization of psychology and its penetration into different spheres of life has entailed a secular penetration into the religious realm, producing the middle ground of "spiritual but not religious." The New Age movement of the 1960s can be seen as an outcome of such penetration, as personal growth movements integrated the psychological with the religious, emphasizing self-improvement, emotions, and happiness.[10] This is why spirituality is frequently described as highly focused on the self and well-being, integrating ideas and logic from Western psychology.[11]

But what happens to the religious when it is penetrated by the therapeutic? In *A Secular Age*, Charles Taylor argues that one of the characterizations of our age is "a shift in framework: certain human struggles, questions, issues, difficulties, problems are moved from a moral/spiritual to a therapeutic register."[12] The influence of the psychological on the spiritual may thus mean a turn away from morality. Indeed, scholars who have written about the "triumph" of the therapeutic have argued that the popularization of psychology is producing a global mindset that emphasizes the individual at the expense of social concern and shared morality.[13] Others have claimed that, while there is a morality behind the therapeutic register, this morality is based on neoliberal capitalist values that advocate individual choice and happiness over social commitments.[14]

This process of the psychologization of religion strengthens the common thesis that spirituality is a privatized version of religion.[15] Just like the "happiness industry" of psychology, spirituality becomes a marketplace where individuals can choose practices and ideas without committing to a specific moral regime.[16] Indeed, critiques of spirituality argue that the intertwining of therapy and religion produces a hyperindividualized, private, psychologized culture.[17] Spiritual practitioners are frequently described as "seekers" who tend to shift from one practice to another, and along with the critique of the therapeutic framework, the individualistic orientation of spiritual seekers is often described as selfish or self-absorbed.[18]

Scholarship on the integration of therapy and religion tends to focus on the influence of the former over the latter: how therapeutic discourse corrodes or corrupts religion, rendering it a hyperindividualistic and subjective matter. Yet this narrative of the triumph of the therapeutic mistakenly assumes a unidirectional influence, neglecting when and how religion influences secular psychology. This influence is visible, for instance, in the recent phenomenon of clinical psychologists, disappointed with the academic and secular versions of "mainstream" psychology, turning to religion to invigorate therapy. Why do these psychologists, who have their own jargon, social status, internal rituals, and accreditations, want to integrate religious ideas and practices into their theory and practice? What do they find in Buddhism and Judaism that cannot be found in Kohut, Winnicott, or humanist and positive psychology? Does the process of spiritualizing psychology only strengthen the hyperindividualistic spirit of our times? Or does it instead contribute something substantial, such as reconnecting psychology to morality and community?

The effort to transform secular psychological therapy by integrating religious ideas and practices reveals an understudied dimension of spirituality as a cultural movement. We name this process *spiritualizing therapy*. We use the notion of "spiritualizing" to denote the picking and choosing of religious elements that are adapted to the therapeutic sphere while leaving out the more institutional and ritualistic elements. The outcome of this process blurs the assumed differentiation between spirituality and the public sphere and represents a challenge to prevailing claims that spirituality is a "private practice."[19] This process is in fact a part of the ongoing deprivatization of religion, as a public, academic, and professional field embraces the spiritual.[20]

We claim that these psychologists look to religion, but they do so in a "spiritual" way to adapt it to psychological discourse. Spiritual milieus differ from the more conservative religious milieus when promoting personal choice and self-authority. Yet, at the same time, spiritual milieus are sites of moral conviction and commitment in the sense that they promote a clear understanding of good and bad that extends beyond notions of personal well-being and includes interpersonal ethics and shared values.[21] As we show in this chapter, in contrast to the claim that spirituality is necessarily hyperindividualistic, our findings illustrate how psychologists turn to spiritual logic and practice to *counter* the hyperindividualistic spirit of contemporary therapy. They turn to the spiritual in an attempt to build a more moral, connected, and communal psychology with a larger vision for humanity.

METHODS AND CASE STUDY

Israel is home to myriad vibrant spiritual circles and groups—including Buddhist meditation, rainbow gatherings, channeling, and the more Jewish-based circles such as Kabbalah teachings, Hassidic groups, and Jewish renewal circles.[22] These spiritual groups tend to offer alternatives to mainstream psychological therapy and up until recently were not considered relevant to the work of professional clinical psychologists. This has recently begun to change with the rise of spirituality-inspired psychology programs receiving recognition and legitimation from being offered as enrichment training at universities and therapy-training institutions.

We focus on two therapeutic communities in Israel that integrate elements from Jewish or Buddhist spiritual traditions into clinical practice. During the years 2018–21 we conducted an ethnographic study of these two groups. The first group of psychologists develops and applies "Jewish psychology" by integrating ideas and practices from Hassidic thought and Kabbalah (Jewish mysticism) into Western mainstream psychodynamic psychotherapy and offering this model to therapists as a two-year continuing education program. The second group integrates the psychoanalytic self-psychology and the teachings of Mahayana Buddhism and applies them in the framework of a seven-year psychoanalytic training program. In both communities most of the therapists were experienced clinicians with private clinics, while some also worked in therapeutic settings in the public and third sectors.[23]

We conducted fieldwork for a duration of eighteen months in the Jewish psychology community and ten months in the psychoanalytic-Buddhist community. In both communities we participated in training programs, courses, workshops, conferences, and retreats. In-depth interviews were conducted with twenty-six certified psychologists and therapists who participate or teach in these programs. All interviews were conducted face-to-face, ranged between one and three hours, and were recorded and transcribed. During the interviews participants were asked to share their interests and motivations to develop, learn, and apply spirituality-inspired psychology, to discuss the ways they apply it in clinical practice alongside the challenges it poses, and to reflect on their personal and professional development as Judaism- or Buddhism-inspired therapists. The field notes and interviews were analyzed using thematic analysis. We read the material multiple times and coded it into what gradually became grounded categories and themes.[24]

THE FAILURES OF MAINSTREAM SECULAR PSYCHOLOGY

The first thing that caught our attention when we spoke with spirituality-inspired psychologists was that their critiques against what they framed as "mainstream" psychology had a strong resonance with the common critiques in the scholarship literature on therapeutic discourse. They spoke against the egocentric spirit of psychology, the lack of connectedness, the absence of morality, and a need for community and a larger vision for society. All these critiques echoed similar claims in the literature that define current therapy-infused spiritualities as individualistic, self-centered, private, and acommunal. Yet, surprisingly, it was to spirituality that these psychologists turned to amend and improve what they saw as the failure of mainstream psychology.

The critiques we encountered resonate with developments in Western psychological thought, including humanistic and positive psychology, that depart from the more conservative psychoanalytical schools and emphasize humanism, positive thinking, and happiness. Yet, even though the psychologists we met criticized the tendency of mainstream psychology to focus on the negative, pathological, or narcissistic, they did not find a solution in humanistic and positive psychology. This was surprising since humanistic and positive psychologies are frequently adopted in spiritual circles. Take, for example, the logic of "positive thinking," or the striving for happiness that has become a central tenet in spiritual milieus. In contrast, the psychologists we studied purposefully stayed away from these popular trends seeing them as highly problematic and superficial.

For example, in one of the classes in the Jewish psychology program, the lecturer distinguished his approach from humanistic psychology when mentioning Victor Frankl (a key figure in humanistic psychology) as an example of a "popular thinker that has influence among the youth . . . who says accurate things . . . but has nothing to say about the drives/passions side of the human being, nothing; a huge part of human experience and he has nothing to say about it, this is why his influence on treatment was minor."

Even though they criticized "mainstream" psychology, our interviewees did not want to radically depart from the mainstream. The psychologists we followed did not become teachers or guides of Buddhism or Judaism. We repeatedly heard arguments against other streams of therapy that took spirituality "too far." Such statements reveal a continuum between religion and secular psychology, a continuum occupied by the middle ground of spirituality. While some spiritual groups locate themselves closer to the religious side, our psychologists remain committed to their existing secular professional training institutions and associations. As one psychologist told us: "We are not trying to produce a Buddhist psychoanalysis, we are trying to create a breakthrough within psychoanalysis, and we are trying to do so using Buddhist philosophy and practice." Likewise in a lecture given in the Judaism-inspired program, the lecturer explained:

"I want to extend, I don't want to cancel. This is why we do not offer training programs for those wanting to become therapists. Here you enter as a psychologist, and you step out as a psychologist.... We want to give enrichment, let's look at the same person from a new perspective and maybe we will see things that you did not see from the previous perspective." In his words and those of others, the training and licensing of therapists remain in the hands of universities and formal institutions. Both programs—the Buddhist and the Jewish—were framed as enrichment and extension for already trained psychotherapists, and not as a substitution for regular clinical psychology training and certification.

The sources that these psychologists rely on can be defined as "religious" or "spiritual" depending on the social context.[25] In the Israeli academic-professional context, both notions—religion and spirituality—carry negative associations representing antiscientific thought.[26] As we were told in interviews, "when you say Jewish Psychology your rating goes down," or "religion, spirituality or God are all considered negative notions in psychoanalysis." Some of the Judaism-inspired psychologists used the notions of "spirituality" and "spiritual" while avoiding the notion of "religion." In the Buddhist sphere, both notions were rarely used.

Yet, in line with the definition of spirituality common to the literature and used in this volume,[27] both spheres selectively adopted elements from Buddhism and Judaism, with an emphasis on the more mystical and embodied dimensions of these religious traditions (e.g., Kabbalah, meditation), while leaving out the more institutional and ritualistic elements. The programs we observed included training with religious figures such as nuns, monks, or rabbis but did not require submission or commitment; the lecturers in these programs encouraged debates, doubts, and dialogue over submission to authority. Moreover, the psychologists we observed did not aim their practice specifically at religious or spiritual people; they adopted spiritual ideas and practices while orienting their therapy to a general audience of potential patients, regardless of their religious beliefs.

In what follows we introduce three themes that represent the critiques raised by our subjects of study against mainstream psychology and the solutions they found in spirituality. First, mainstream psychology assumes an independent, self-relying, and ego-centered individual, while spirituality-inspired psychology challenges this view and brings in moral notions of good will and desire to help others. Second, mainstream psychology emphasizes bounded and atomized individuals, while spirituality-inspired psychology offers ethical work that advances connectedness and oneness. And third, mainstream psychology remains at the level of personal change, while spirituality-inspired psychology promotes a larger vision for humanity.

MORALITY: THE MOTIVATION TO DO GOOD

The first critique raised against mainstream secular psychology was that the psychological person is motivated by self-centered needs and is thus egocentric. This perspective, we were told, denies the possibility of a natural tendency to do good and give to others. The psychologists we spoke with argued against the preoccupation of psychology with a person's own well-being and said that a full and good life, and even self-fulfillment, can take place only when the person shifts from self-absorption to a place of self-extension that includes taking care of others. Such ideas regarding the tendency to do good resonate with humanistic and positive psychology, yet as explained earlier, these approaches were portrayed as marginal to the standard clinical training of therapists in Israel. Take, for example, Oranit, a therapist, who spoke about her experience before joining the Jewish psychology program:

> I was missing the place of the good. The human good as a human motivation. Simple kindness. . . . I thought that it does not make sense that with all the human motivations we learn [in psychology] doing good does not appear as a motivation. Not only is doing good not conceived as a motivation, it is something that one should suspect, always. Always suspect it, otherwise it is not professional, and it all goes back to narcissistic needs.

According to Oranit, the emphasis on narcissistic needs tends to neglect what she sees as a human motivation to do good and be kind. In fact, during her "mainstream" training to become a therapist, she was taught that kindness should always be suspected since it might be rooted in egoistic needs. This emphasis eventually led her to seek spirituality-inspired psychology to integrate the good back into the way she views her patients.

What about the natural desire to give, kindness, compassion, forgiveness, and other such positive qualities? The psychologists we met repeatedly asked. Inspired by Judaism and Buddhism, they emphasized the good traits that human beings share, invoking notions such as "a piece of eternity," "spark," "soul," and a manifestation of "Buddha-nature." They argued that the forces of violence, aggressiveness, jealousy, and hate do not stem from human drives, as Freud claimed, but are secondary phenomena that are born out of discord between the person and the world. As one psychologist told us, "The origin is good, even the bad, even those who do bad, in their origin they are good."

The language of good and bad brings into psychological treatment a morality that is usually absent. In her study on psychology as a dominant cultural force, Eva Illouz argues that psychology as a field of knowledge tends to present itself as amoral and scientific since, "if it wants to address various segments of readership, with differing values and viewpoints, it must be amoral, that is, offer a neutral perspective on problems."[28] Our interviewees supported this claim when referring to mainstream psychology and said, "Modern psychology does not have a morality, in psychology, there is no good or bad." To bring in values and morality they turned to spirituality, where, in contrast to common critiques, they found a shared understanding of moral and social responsibility toward others.

Drawing on kabbalistic and Hassidic ideas, the psychologists who turn to Judaism found a way to integrate the good back into psychology through the idea of the "spark." According to this idea, each person has his or her own unique light, a divine spark, that aspires to express itself in the world. This light, which originates from God, is always good, and the aspiration to express this light is the aspiration of human beings to give, to create, and to love.

Buddhism-inspired psychologists' ideas regarding the moral human being were rooted in self-psychology and the writings of its founder, Heinz Kohut, but received validation and depth through the Buddhist concepts of "Buddha nature" and "interbeing." Assaf, a psychologist participating in the Buddhist program, explained how he understands the concept of Buddha nature: "The Buddhist conception is that there is consciousness that always seeks to evolve, that has power, a power that aspires for good." Likewise, Ehud, a fellow participant in the Buddhist program, contextualized the aspiration for good in the relational field while criticizing mainstream psychology:

> In all the schools [of mainstream psychology] the center is the self, the authentic self, or the self that can live peacefully with inner drives and passions. This perspective does not include the experience of turning outwards as part of the self. It [turning outwards] is not a developmental stage. It is the origin. This is what the human being is. This is what it means to look at a person as a whole, that the other is a part of that person's being.

The orientation toward others that Ehud is referring to is informed by the Buddhist idea of "interbeing." From a Buddhist perspective, all living creatures are connected in a tissue of mutual influence and thus feel a natural responsibility towards each other. The state of interbeing was understood by our Buddhism-inspired interviewees as the essence of humanity, and with it as wisdom that leads to liberation. From this perspective, selflessness is not something that is learned but is instead a deeper truth to be discovered. Michelle, another psychologist, explained how the understanding of these Buddhist concepts offers her "a beautiful way to be beyond personal existence ... in deep and meaningful interactions with your surroundings."

Using notions such as "beautiful," "selfless," and "good," the psychologists we met distinguished between good and bad, making clear that good involves care for others. Yet the integration of morality into their profession did not lead them to be judgmental of patients' actions and thoughts. Such judgment was still considered by them to be highly unprofessional, since it contradicts a basic principle in psychological treatment. Instead, they argued that putting on the spiritual lens enables them to see the good in their patients even when it's deeply hidden. The following example was offered by Ethan, a therapist who integrates Judaism into his work:

> A patient is in a very deep major depression, tried 5–7 different medicines and nothing helps. He can suddenly say to me, "Ethan, under the ruins there is purity." This is the spark that we hang on to, it will be revealed in the end. When? I don't know. . . . But the fact that I have in my head is that the spark is there, and that there is good. It will flourish and grow. It is in prayer, in thinking of him, in talking with him about it, it is in praising him. And then suddenly, again, I didn't say anything, a sentence comes out of him.

This example shows how notions such as "divine spark" and "purity," which hold spiritual connotations, can enter the consulting room. From Ethan's perspective, viewing the patient through a spiritual lens infuses him with faith and hope regarding the healing potential of a patient who is in a difficult and dysfunctional situation. This implicit belief, mystically, seeps into the patient and makes the good flourish and grow.

ETHICS: CONNECTEDNESS AND CONTRACTION

The first theme we presented earlier centered on the natural tendency of the individual to orient herself toward others. The second, interrelated theme focuses on producing an interpersonal sphere that is an enactment of this tendency and allows it to flourish. Mainstream psychology, said our informants, tends to see interpersonal space as composed of atomistic individuals with hard boundaries and distinctions, leaving little room for connectedness, dialogue, and oneness. This emphasis is visible in the psychological clinic, where therapists must keep a clear separation between them and their patients. Here again, the psychologists we studied turned to religious traditions to challenge this distinction—and with it the hierarchical relations between therapist and patient.

Even though according to our informants doing good is a "natural" and "original" tendency of human beings, for this tendency to reveal itself in an interpersonal space there is a need to work on the self. This work on the self can be seen as "ethical work," since it serves the purpose of progressing toward a moral ideal of ego-reduction and self-transcendence.[29] Their work as therapists thus involves deep work on their own self, a spiritual path, that helps them connect to their patient and helps him or her to develop as well.

In the Buddhist context, much of the ethical work on the self is based on meditation practice. An important part of the training program is the opening and closing meditation practice on each studying day in the program and meditation retreats, where the psychologists attempt to cultivate experiences of concentration, compassion, and oneness. They then attempt to take their meditation practice into the consulting room, using their own practice and experiences, since they do not teach meditation to their patients.

Take, for example, the practice of empathy. While in recent years developing empathy has become a common part of mainstream psychotherapy, the psychologists we met in the Buddhist sphere extend and develop this idea using elements from Buddhist thought and practice. They see empathy as the ability to understand a patient's experience "from within," becoming one with the patient. This ability to experience oneness with a patient is not merely conceptual but requires ethical commitment and practice. In their words, to become one with a patient requires the therapist to prioritize the well-being of the other over their own well-being—a state that can be cultivated through Buddhist practice and meditation. Rakefet, a Buddhism-inspired psychologist, gave the following example:

> I have a patient, an executive in a startup company. The company was sold, and she received a lot of money. She left the job, and she is lying on the sofa and talks about herself in such anxiety as if she does not know where she can find food for tomorrow. So, I can give her this interpretation: "You don't have a frame now and it is stressful, so it does not matter that you have 5 million dollars in the bank." And this is an accurate understanding of the situation. But instead, I can be in that anxiety, not to be anxious myself, but be in her anxiety in her feeling of nothingness. And I can . . . listen. Listen, and tell her, "You feel empty, you are empty, you feel that your inner walls are going to fall." And this is the difference, to listen from within her.

For Rakefet and others in her community, the ability to listen to the patient's experience from within and respond to him or her in an accurate and healing manner requires not only attunement to the patient and deep listening but also a state of unity and total immersion with him or her. This empathic response and attitude to the patient's self-needs and psychological deprivations, according to these psychologists, will help the patient reach the good within himself or herself. Later in the talk, Rakefet explained the difference between the mainstream notion that the therapist should put herself on hold and not be judgmental and the unique position that the Buddhist-inspired psychologists aim for an experiential oneness with the patient: "In order to reach such a state, you need ethics. You need to take upon yourself the practice: practice of concentration, practice of humility, practice of compassion, all these things we bring from Buddhism. It offers a very good praxis for bracketing yourself and dwelling in the world of the other from within.... This is ethics, a Levinasian ethics, Buddhist ethics." Interestingly, Rakefet mentioned Emmanuel Levinas and Buddhism side by side, producing connections between our two fields—the Jewish and the Buddhist. Levinas, known for his writings on the phenomenology of entering the experience of another, was deeply inspired by Jewish texts and the Torah. Even though Rakefet refers to Levinas as a humanist philosopher and not as a religious or spiritual source, she chose him over humanist psychologists because of his writings on ethics and morality.

In the Jewish context, the ethical work on the self took place through what the psychologists named the process of *contraction*. This ethical work is based on the kabbalistic theory of contraction (*Tzimzum*), according to which during genesis God contracted himself to make space for the world and for man, and invited man to participate in the creation of the world. Following these spirituality-based relations between God and humans, Judaism-inspired psychologists argue that a central tool for producing an interpersonal space in which the good can be revealed is through contraction, a process where a person reduces and contracts himself to make space for the other. Such contraction is seen as crucial for achieving connection and dialogue and thus is used as a tool in psychological treatment.

The Judaism-inspired psychologists spoke of attempts to contract themselves in the consulting room, sometimes even agreeing to become "the student of the patient," giving up the superior place of "the knower." By staying open to learning from the patient, they enable her "spark" to be revealed and fulfill her desire to give to others. This ethical practice, they argued, produces the connection needed in the consulting room where both the patient and the therapist learn how to make space for each other. Baruch, a psychologist in the Jewish program, summarized this approach when saying: "When I approach a patient, I am not in the role of the one who has the knowledge, that knows what he suffers from.... I know something more general, that this soul came and wants to be revealed, revealed in reality.... And I stand there not as the knower and the doer.... I am a listener. I listen and let him be revealed.... I contract myself and make space for him to be revealed." Spirituality, in these examples, offers psychologists tools in their ethical work to become what they see as better therapists, producing connectedness, dialogue, and an ideal space for the patient that invites connecting to his or her authentic self and inherent kindness. It also produces a humbler place that reduces hierarchy and separation and emphasizes shared humanity.

VISION: A BETTER SOCIAL WORLD FOR HUMANITY AT LARGE

The preceding two themes illustrate how psychologists use religious ideas and practices to counter the individualistic bias that they see as inherent in mainstream psychology and to produce a new kind of spiritual psychology that promotes the good, orientation toward the other, ethics, and connectedness. Yet our informants did not remain in the psychological realm. They also offered a larger vision for themselves, their patients, and humanity at large. They used spirituality to break away from the limits of the personal and psychological and enter the realm of a larger social vision. This social vision is in resonance with the spiritual turn in that it draws from both secular psychology and religion, advocating subjective well-being alongside collective solidarity.

Yet in contrast to the common understanding of the spiritual as a religion of the private self, its purpose is not limited to self-awareness or self-realization.

The leaders of the Jewish program regarded the model of contraction as a general model for society. They criticized what they saw as the competitive spirit of Western culture, which sacralizes the "I." One psychologist went so far as to say: "The idea of contraction is meant to produce a revolution and create a better human society. . . . The person is part of society, he or she needs others, and she has things to give others."

On the micro level, the Judaism-inspired psychologists connected the principle of contraction and one's role in the mission of "repair of the world," *Tikkun Olam*, a Jewish idea that refers to a process in which the work of God has a higher goal that can eventually lead to a better world. This role in the repair of the world provides people with existential meaning and connects them to a mission that is larger than a focus on the self. This mission, they argued, is exactly what is missing from mainstream psychology. One of the lecturers in the Jewish program explained:

> If we take seriously this idea [of contraction] in the context of relations between human beings, this idea of the influence of the person, of partnership, then we are given the role of repair, the belief in repair. We are in a state that a person enters a partnership with God, so he can be a partner in repair, repairing the situation. And this is a very big role, very big, that is on our shoulders. We have great responsibility, capability, faith in us that we can do so much, the making of this space, this space to influence so much.

From the perspective of Jewish spirituality, the act of contraction is not self-deprecation. On the contrary, it allows for the natural tendency to do good to express itself, and it produces a feeling of empowerment as the person is invited to be a part of a world mission. As one psychologist explained, "when I contract myself, I allow the person in front of me to reveal herself, and at the same time when I teach someone to contract, he or she discovers new things about herself." This model, they argued, is first and foremost meant to produce good dialogic psychology. But if it succeeds, there is a message here for society as a whole and a tool for bridging different groups, states, and cultures.

In the Buddhist sphere, the vision for a better society and the role of psychologists in this vision were also raised in a strong and clear voice. As the founder of the Buddhist program proclaimed, he sees the program as producing "a foundation that will encompass the private and the general, the similar and different, the multiple in the oneness, in a universal matrix of total solidarity." The group of Buddhism-inspired psychologists argued that they are answering a real need in the community of psychologists to divert from the "scientific-medical-clinical" understanding of the patient to incorporate spiritual and consciousness-changing content and to step out of personal change into a much larger social change that will benefit human society.

Inspired by the position of Buddhist monks and the model of the *bodhisattvas*, the psychologists saw themselves as "serving leadership" based on the ideal of "life of service." As Rakefet explained: "We did not just pick any stream in Buddhism, we chose Mahayana. The Mahayana is different from the Theravada because the Theravada stops in Nirvana. The enlightened man reached Nirvana. But in the Mahayana, the enlightened man who reached Nirvana returned to the world to help others. The Bodhisattvas, the Bodhisattvas bring healing both to his own suffering and the world." While these may look like big words, these psychologists do not remain at the linguistic level.

The training of the psychoanalytic-Buddhist program holds a strong social orientation, being intentionally situated in one of Israel's most socioeconomically challenged towns, and one that inhabits a mixed population of Jews and Arabs. During the first eighteen months of the program the trainees do not engage in explicit therapy, but rather support the town's residents in need, such as elderly people, children with various challenges and disabilities, kindergarten teachers, and helpers. The goal, as one psychologist put it, is "to learn to be a selfobject from a clean place, not from [the position of] the interpretive therapist."[30] He described the time he spent with a four-year-old girl in her kindergarten, supporting her in her daily routine and interactions with the other children and the teacher.

Led by the notion of "creating a community of therapists that supports a community of residents," the participants in the program offer free-of-charge supervised analyses to the town's residents and, to a lesser extent, the municipality's service professionals, such as educators and social workers. The therapists frequently described their patients as "not the typical audience" that undergoes long-term psychoanalytic treatment, a mix of Jews and Arabs that come from a lower socioeconomic background and challenging life circumstances, some with criminal backgrounds. Their project, they believe, is leading to a deep cultural change, resulting for example in the local language's becoming "gentle": "It becomes spiritual, it becomes emotional. . . . The self of the public becomes a wider self, multidimensional, not racist."

Such claims about a vision for humanity and aspirations to change or repair the world divert from the common understanding of both psychology and spirituality as fields that have little interest in the public sphere. These psychologists, who belong to the elite of Israeli society, find in spirituality a way to integrate a social vision and a mission into their identities as psychologists. They do not aspire solely to help others change themselves and be happy. They aspire to change the world.

SPIRITUALITY, INTERPERSONAL SPACE, AND SOCIAL CHANGE

Our journey among psychologists who are inspired by Buddhism and Judaism illustrates how the influence of spirituality extends beyond the private sphere and enters the prestigious professional world of clinical psychology. This process extends the deprivatization of religion to include the "religion of the heart,"[31] as spirituality is embraced by academic professional institutions. The integration of spirituality and therapy is not limited to marginal New Age groups or the less prestigious alternative spiritual therapy but can be found among mainstream therapists who want to invigorate psychology without radically transforming it.

What does spirituality offer psychologists? Taylor argues that in the "secular age," the shift from the religious register to the therapeutic register leads to the loss of shared morality, as moral questions and problems become framed as questions of mental health and subjective well-being.[32] Illouz seconds this claim, arguing that even when psychology relies on capitalist and liberal values, psychology as an academic and professional field presents itself as scientific and amoral.[33] Spirituality, being a middle ground between religion and secular psychology, includes traces of the religious register and thus holds a potential for a renewal of shared morality. Spiritually diverges from institutionalized religious contexts by emphasizing individual autonomy and self-determination. Yet spiritual settings still foster a distinct grasp of right and wrong that transcends personal interests. These can be used to promote a more communal, social vision for psychology.

What kind of morality does spirituality promote? A morality that extends Durkheim's "cult of the individual" by bringing back nonrational, spiritual elements, and with it collective consciousness and solidarity. This is a morality that fits a world without hierarchical relations, a globalizing world of universal humanity, a world in which one's ethical relation to the other becomes more central than group identifications. In the context we studied, psychologists use spirituality to promote an approach of mutual responsibility and kindness. They use spirituality as tool in ethical work that helps them to produce dialogue, empathy, and oneness. Moreover, they draw on spirituality to advance a general vision for a better social world that incorporates commitments to self-determination side by side social solidarity and community.

The social change that spirituality promotes begins with the micro but aspires to the macro. It starts with the interpersonal and ends with institutions. While we do not know if such a process has an effect on social reality, it is still an important part of the project of spirituality-inspired psychology and, we would like to suggest, of spirituality writ large. Spirituality therefore is not limited to self-enhancement and does not necessarily lead people away from community and shared social visions. In fact, it can become a foundation for projects that aim to change society for the better.

NOTES

1. Stanley W. Jackson, *Care of the Psyche: A History of Psychological Healing* (New Haven, CT: Yale University Press, 1999).
2. Nikolas Rose, *Inventing Our Selves: Psychology, Power, and Personhood* (Cambridge: Cambridge University Press, 1998); Charles Taylor, *A*

Secular Age (Cambridge, MA: Harvard University Press, 2007); Eva Illouz, *Saving the Modern Soul: Therapy, Emotions, and the Culture of Self-Help* (Berkeley: University of California Press, 2008).

3. Illouz, *Saving the Modern Soul*, 6. On the religious origins of the therapeutic framework see Eric Caplan, *Mind Games: American Culture and the Birth of Psychotherapy* (Berkeley: University of California Press, 1998); Eva S. Moskowitz, *In Therapy We Trust: America's Obsession with Self-Fulfilment* (Baltimore: Johns Hopkins University Press, 2001). For Jewish roots, see Andrew R. Heinze, *Jews and the American Soul: Human Nature in the Twentieth Century* (Princeton, NJ: Princeton University Press, 2004).

4. Robert Wuthnow, *After Heaven: Spirituality in America Since the 1950s* (Berkeley: University of California Press, 1998); Paul Heelas and Linda Woodhead, *The Spiritual Revolution: Why Religion Is Giving Way to Spirituality* (Malden, MA: Blackwell, 2005); Galen Watts, *The Spiritual Turn: The Religion of the Heart and the Making of Romantic Liberal Modernity* (Oxford: Oxford University Press, 2022).

5. Courtney Bender, *The New Metaphysicals: Spirituality and the American Religious Imagination* (Chicago: University of Chicago Press, 2010). See also Michal Pagis, "Embodied Therapeutic Culture," in *The Routledge International Handbook of Global Therapeutic Cultures*, ed. Daniel Nehring et al. (New York: Routledge, 2020), 177–90.

6. Jaime Kucinskas, *The Mindful Elite: Mobilizing from the Inside Out* (Oxford: Oxford University Press, 2018).

7. Tanya M. Luhrmann, *When God Talks Back: Understanding the American Evangelical Relationship with God* (New York: Knopf, 2012).

8. Michal Pagis, *Inward: Vipassana Meditation and the Embodiment of the Self* (Chicago: University of Chicago Press, 2019).

9. Watts, *The Spiritual Turn*.

10. James A. Beckford, ed., *New Religious Movements and Rapid Social Change* (London: Sage, 1986); Paul Heelas, *The New Age Movement: The Celebration of the Self and the Sacralization of Modernity* (Oxford: Blackwell, 1999).

11. Heelas and Woodhead, *The Spiritual Revolution*.

12. Taylor, *A Secular Age*, 619.

13. Philip Rieff, *The Triumph of the Therapeutic* (Chicago: University of Chicago Press, 1966); Christopher Lasch, *The Culture of Narcissism: American Life in an Age of Diminishing Expectations* (New York: W. W. Norton, 1980); Ole Jacob Madsen, *The Therapeutic Turn: How Psychology Altered Western Culture* (New York: Routledge, 2014); Daniel Nehring et al., *Transnational Popular Psychology and the Global Self-Help Industry: The Politics of Contemporary Social Change* (London: Palgrave Macmillan, 2016); Daniel Nehring et al., ed., *The*

Routledge International Handbook of Global Therapeutic Cultures (New York: Routledge, 2020).
14. Rose, *Inventing Our Selves*; Micki McGee, *Self-Help, Inc.: Makeover Culture in America* (Oxford: Oxford University Press, 2005); Michal Pagis, "Fashioning Futures: Life Coaching and the Self-Made Identity Paradox," *Sociological Forum* 31, no. 4 (2016): 1083–1103; Edgar Cabanas and Eva Illouz, *Manufacturing Happy Citizens: How the Science and Industry of Happiness Control Our Lives* (Cambridge: Polity Press, 2019).
15. Robert N. Bellah et al., *Habits of the Heart: Individualism and Commitment in American Life* (Berkeley: University of California Press, 1985); Bryan S. Turner, "Religion and Contemporary Sociological Theories," *Current Sociology* 62, no. 6 (2014): 771–88.
16. Wade Clark Roof, *Spiritual Marketplace: Baby Boomers and the Remaking of American Religion* (Princeton, NJ: Princeton University Press, 1999); Jeremy R. Carrette and Richard King, *Selling Spirituality: The Silent Takeover of Religion* (London: Routledge, 2005); Andrea R. Jain, *Peace Love Yoga: The Politics of Global Spirituality* (New York: Oxford University Press, 2020); François Gauthier and Tuomas Martikainen, ed., *The Marketization of Religion* (New York: Routledge, 2020).
17. Turner, "Religion and Contemporary Sociological Theories."
18. For a recent discussion see Jaime Kucinskas and Evan Stewart, "Selfish or Substituting Spirituality? Clarifying the Relationship Between Spiritual Practice and Political Engagement," *American Sociological Review* 87, no. 4 (2022): 584–617.
19. Turner, "Religion and Contemporary Sociological Theories."
20. José Casanova, *Public Religions in the Modern World* (Chicago: University of Chicago Press, 1994).
21. Ammerman, "Spiritual but Not Religious?," 258–78.
22. E.g., Dana Kaplan and Rachel Werczberger, "Jewish New Age and the Middle Class: Jewish Identity Politics in Israel Under Neoliberalism," *Sociology* 51, no. 3 (2017): 575–91; Pagis, *Inward*.
23. The exact names of the communities are excluded for sake of anonymity. The research received the Bar-Ilan University IRB approval and followed ethical guidelines for qualitative research.
24. Kathy Charmaz, *Constructing Grounded Theory: A Practical Guide Through Qualitative Analysis* (London: Sage, 2006).
25. Brian Steensland, Jaime Kucinskas, and Anna Sun, ed., *Situating Spirituality: Context, Practice, and Power* (Oxford: Oxford University Press, 2021).
26. Michal Pagis, Wendy Cadge, and Orly Tal, "Translating Spirituality: Universalism and Particularism in the Diffusion of Spiritual Care from the United States to Israel," *Sociological Forum* 33, no. 3 (2018): 596–618.

27. See the introduction to this volume.
28. Illouz, *Saving the Modern Soul*, 52.
29. Michel Foucault, *Ethics: Subjectivity and Truth (Essential Works of Foucault, 1954–1984, Volume 1)* (New York: New Press, 1994).
30. The "selfobject" is a central concept in self-psychology, referring to the empathic presence that the therapist provides a patient with for the formation of his or her selfhood. See Claudia Kogan, *The Healing Power of Solidarity: A Philosophical, Literary and Psychoanalytic Journey* (Jerusalem: Carmel, 2023): 112 (in Hebrew).
31. Watts, *The Spiritual Turn*.
32. Taylor, *A Secular Age*.
33. Illouz, *Saving the Modern Soul*.

5

THE SPIRITUAL IMPULSE IN SILICON VALLEY

A Content and Discourse Analysis of *Wired* Magazine, 2001–2020

PAUL K. McCLURE AND CHRISTOPHER M. PIEPER

In 1971, twenty years before Sir Tim Berners-Lee helped launch the World Wide Web, an eccentric writer and technologist named Stewart Brand issued these words at the outset of *The Last Whole Earth Catalog*: "We are as gods and might as well get used to it."[1] Obviously cryptic, Brand's words seem even more out of place when viewed from the perspective of secularization theory. Secularization theorists have long predicted that with the unfolding of modernity, science and technology would eventually replace most, if not all, god-talk. Max Weber anticipated a disenchanted world, not one where we viewed ourselves as gods or spoke about a re-enchanted cosmos in religious terms. The secular march would continue, most believed, until the objective terms of science and reason had replaced our religious vocabularies. As Peter Berger then quipped, "a sky empty of angels becomes open to the intervention of the astronomer and, eventually, of the astronaut."[2] Oddly enough, the iconic covers of *Whole Earth Catalog* and its successor, *The Last Whole Earth Catalog*, display some of the first publicly available photographs ever taken of Earth from outer space. So what was Brand's point? Why would a pioneer of the coming digital revolution invoke the gods, or equate himself to one, when writing about the latest technological trends and tools?

Brand's spiritual invocation was not a coincidence but an early signpost for the way Silicon Valley writers appropriate religious and spiritual concepts when writing about emerging digital technologies and related cultural trends. As a bohemian and countercultural icon, Brand's eclecticism not only proved to be a beacon for many innovators of the digital revolution, but his prolific writing and editorial prowess at *Whole Earth* also served as an eventual blueprint for later publications such as *Wired*.[3] Whereas few scholars have explored how elites operating at the nexus of technology and journalism conceive and reconfigure religion and spirituality, doing so bridges an important gap in the literature on technology and the sociology of spirituality. Though many scholars have traditionally conceived of modern science and technology as inherently secularizing forces, many technology journalists embrace alternative narratives or motifs according to which spirituality and technology do not operate in mutually exclusive spheres. While there are potentially many ways to describe and analyze the religious composition of Silicon Valley culture, we recognize *Wired*'s outsized importance as a source for the cultural narratives that emanate from elites in Silicon Valley. Thus, the main question that animates this chapter is this: How do the writers of *Wired* discuss and portray religion and spirituality in their featured articles?

SILICON VALLEY RELIGION AND SPIRITUALITY

To understand how the writers of *Wired* conceive of religion and spirituality, it first helps to grasp some of the surrounding cultural contours that punctuate Silicon Valley's techno-spiritual ethos. Like any print media, technology journalism is a product of a specific social and historical milieu, and the writers at *Wired* are the successors of a stream of thought that stretches back (at least) to the California counterculture of the 1960s. Indeed, scholars have long recognized the presence of fervent spirituality and new religious movements that preceded the rise of the California computer industry. Though science and technology were initially perceived to be disenchanting forces in the eyes of many, Dorien Zandbergen contends that "since the 1960s various processes of 'brokerage' can be traced between New Age spirituality and Silicon Valley 'high tech culture.'"[4] Similarly, Fred Turner and Sam Binkley each highlight the counterculture's role in challenging the presumed sterility of science or the moral vapidity of modern capitalism, seeing instead a logic of reenchantment at work. Turner, for example, points to the rise of virtual communities, which "formed an emotional bulwark against the loneliness of a highly technologized world."[5] And according to Binkley, overlapping networks of writers and journalists in the Bay Area "injected an alternate discourse" that brought new meaning and moral purpose to a consumer culture "yearning for a new cast of lifestyle intellectuals."[6]

One of these "lifestyle intellectuals" was Stewart Brand, who with his associates at *Whole Earth* largely transformed our symbolic understandings of computer technology. As Turner recounts, the computer used to be a symbol of "dehumanization, of centralized bureaucracy and the rationalization of social life," not a portal of expressive individualism or a means to self-improvement.[7] Through his role as editor at *Whole Earth*, Brand provided an emerging bohemian community with the tools and moral language they needed to express themselves. As a charter member of the Merry Pranksters, whom author Tom Wolfe documents in *The Electric Kool-Aid Acid Test*, Brand furthered the notion that one could gain spiritual enlightenment through technology.[8] Alongside Grateful Dead concerts, light shows, and synthetic drugs such as LSD, the personal computer increasingly came to be seen as a tool of reenchantment in an impersonal, rationalized world.[9] Commenting on this symbolic transformation and the unfolding digital revolution, Stef Aupers and Dick Houtman write, "What we are witnessing today is a remarkable convergence of digital technology and spirituality . . . that constitutes a relocation of the sacred to the digital realm, inspired by the desire to overcome the experiences of alienation, suffering, and impotence."[10] The implication here is that the communities, rituals, moral purpose, and sense of meaning or transcendence typically desired within organized religion are increasingly found through social media and other online networks.[11]

Beyond these observations, other demographic and cultural trends in Silicon Valley play a major role in the way writers at *Wired* think about and discuss religious and spiritual issues. For example, compared to many parts of the United States, Silicon Valley has a higher degree of racial, ethnic, and religious diversity. High rates of immigration and intermarriage contribute to a plurality of religious viewpoints, undermining the possibility of a single, dominant religious perspective.[12] As a result, Silicon Valley has been a hotbed for religious pluralism and an attractive space for spiritual entrepreneurs. The sheer variety of perspectives on the West Coast creates a "spiritual marketplace" that inclines individuals to choose among many religious narratives and potentially customize their own belief system.[13]

To see how these cultural trends play out on one organizational level, consider how the company Apple often injects religious and spiritual themes into its promotional advertising. Jaron Lanier, one of the pioneers of virtual reality and a Silicon Valley insider, has observed that Steve Jobs purposefully appropriated popular Hindu gurus to make his products appear more enlightening. As Lanier explains, "Apple exemplifies one strain of influence that is particularly underappreciated: the crossover between countercultural spirituality and tech culture."[14] Walter Isaacson, often considered Jobs's definitive biographer, also highlights Jobs's appreciation of Eastern religions and especially Zen Buddhism.[15] Brett Robinson similarly observes that the architectural design of Apple stores—with their white, clean interiors and translucent glass exteriors—evokes notions of purity and holiness and purposefully seeks to imbue technology with spiritual significance: "In the promotional rhetoric of the Apple computer company, the convergence of the technological and the religious reveals a persistent dialectic at work in the American imagination between rationalism and mysticism."[16] Even the company symbol, an apple, though once associated with the Judeo-Christian account of human origins, is made into an icon for a new generation of believers.[17]

The tendency for engineers and Silicon Valley innovators to step outside the secular realm is not confined merely to Steve Jobs and Apple either. Turner shows that early tech trailblazers were neither conventionally monotheistic nor atheistic but consisted rather of a hodgepodge of spiritually minded hackers, hippies, and new communalists who wanted to gain enlightenment through the material devices they built.[18] Today, their spiritual and moral legacy can perhaps best be witnessed at Burning Man, an annual late-summer event in the Nevada desert where tens of thousands of "Burners" gather and adhere to ten essential principles, including radical inclusion, self-reliance, and self-expression.[19] Culminating with the symbolic burning of a sixty-foot-tall wooden effigy ("the Man"), Burning Man has all the trappings of an emerging belief system and is highly popular among members of the technology industry who see no antithesis between technology and spirituality.

WIRED: ITS ORIGINS, OBJECTIVES, IMPACT, AND READERSHIP

As the nation's most popular monthly magazine to feature current news on technology culture, *Wired* may be considered the unofficial sacred scripture of Silicon Valley. Founded in 1993 by Louis Rossetto and Jane Metcalfe, *Wired* bills itself as the premier technology magazine in the United States. In its earliest issues, journalists frequently solicited the opinions of elite thought leaders in the industry including Nicholas Negroponte, Howard Rheingold, and Kevin Kelly.[20] These visionaries helped give *Wired* a clear identity and voice, thus separating it from other publications that focused more on reviews of the latest technologies.

While recognizing the many different intellectual streams that converge to make *Wired* a distinguished publication, the one most responsible for providing a definitive, if not puzzling, techno-philosophical voice is the late media theorist Marshall McLuhan. A 1993 *Wired* article featuring an interview between Stewart Brand and Camille Paglia in fact declares McLuhan the "patron saint of *Wired* magazine."[21] For the editors at *Wired*, McLuhan's work provides a theoretical basis and vision for how to think about technology. Emerging technologies would not only revolutionize how individuals spend their time and money but also change how people see and interpret the world. Summarizing its objectives and theoretical foundations, Turner writes that "*Wired* aimed to herald the arrival not only of a new era in computing machinery, but a new era in social life."[22]

Since its founding, *Wired* has amassed a wide readership and achieved considerable success. Winning two National Magazine Awards in its first five years, *Wired* quickly grew its readership to more than three hundred thousand individuals per month.[23] Despite having an extensive readership, however, consumers typically fit a narrow demographic profile within the panoply of men's lifestyle magazines.[24] As Turner observes, by the mid-1990s "its readers were 87.9 percent male, 37 years old on average, with an average household income of more than $122,000 per year."[25] Since then *Wired* has experienced changes in ownership, but it has kept its distinctive mission to report on technology and culture. In an age when many magazines have seen drastic reductions in paid readership or have been forced to close or layoff reporters, *Wired* has maintained its position as a major media outlet. According to the Alliance for Audited Media (AAM), *Wired* had a total paid and verified circulation of 892,887 households in 2020, making it one of the country's top 100 consumer magazines and more popular than *Fortune*, *Condé Nast Traveler*, and *Architectural Digest*.[26] Currently owned by Condé Nast Publishing, *Wired* features both online and print versions of its articles and archives nearly all its published content with a digital or print subscription. With an active online readership that reaches more than thirty million people each month, *Wired* is therefore properly considered an authoritative, influential media source that not only reflects the thinking of many elites in the technology industry but also helps frame current debates and shape narratives involving important world issues.[27]

In discussing and analyzing the religious narratives present in *Wired*, we aim to specify how certain schemas pertaining to religion, spirituality, and technology get culturally entrenched. Ultimately, we find evidence for three motifs of this religion-technology relationship: (1) *a conflict motif* that proposes that organized religion and technology are inherently at odds with one another; (2) *a compatibility motif* that seeks to assert the compatibility of organized religion and technology; and (3) *a fulfillment motif* that sees technology and its advances as the natural fulfillment of spiritual beliefs, ideals, and aspirations. This last motif is not only the most common way that *Wired* writers discuss religion and technology; it is also one that reframes that relationship under the banner of spirituality. In subverting traditional understandings of organized religion, writers at *Wired* carve out space for an alternative, techno-spiritual narrative.

DATA AND METHODS

In the course of our analysis we examined issues of *Wired* both for their content and discursive frames from 2001 to 2020.[28] The range of years selected pick up where a substantively related content analysis of *Wired* by Aupers ended.[29] Customary with projects of this nature, practical strategies were used to limit the sample size. Since *Wired* is a monthly publication, we used a random number generator to determine which issues to analyze (1–12, where January=1 and December=12). We then identified and analyzed three issues per year for a total of sixty issues. Since *Wired* publishes many different types of articles—including letters to the editor ("Rants and Raves"), teasers or short reviews ("Start" and "Play"), infographics, interviews, and so forth—we further limited the sample by excluding practically all nonfeature articles. In total, we reviewed close to four hundred articles from the years 2001–2020.

Using this sample, we then scanned articles for general religious or spiritual vocabulary. These included searches for the following: *God, deity, divine, religious, religion, spiritual, spirituality, heaven, hell, church, temple, prayer, faith, holy, Christian, Christianity, Muslim, Islam, Jewish, Judeo-Christian, Jesus, evangelical, supernatural,* and *sacred*. While searching for these words, other secondary terms and phrases were often discovered and documented in the process such as *the Catholic Church, Virgin Mary, Protestant, Old Testament, Tibetan Buddhist doctrine, Hindu, prophet, theological, blasphemy, idolatry, apocalyptic, jihadists, angels, demons, Mennonite, Mormon church, crosses, monks, creationists, fundamentalism, messianic, Nirvana, New Age,* and so forth. In most cases articles could be quickly scanned to determine whether they contained religious or spiritual references, and while some colloquialisms such as *goddammit, holy shit,* and *for God's sake* appeared sporadically, these were excluded from final analysis. Ultimately, more than a hundred articles were found to contain significant religious or spiritual expressions (approximately 28%). These articles were not exclusively focused on religious or spiritual topics, but they contained at least one and usually multiple religious phrases.

Of the more than one hundred articles from 2001 to 2020 that contain religious or spiritual vocabulary, a smaller sample (approximately 44% of that subsample) was then selected and analyzed according to their major discursive frames and motifs. In determining whether an article contains a substantial presence of religious and spiritual motifs, some degree of subjectivity is inevitable. However, the selected articles were revisited multiple times during analysis with assistance and coding provided by additional researchers to verify that religion and spirituality were not incidental. Readers can therefore be confident that the articles included in the discourse analysis represent discernible frames and still support *Wired*'s distinctive objectives to deliver news about technology, culture, and the future.

RELIGIOUS AND SPIRITUAL CONTENT IN *WIRED*

To gain a preliminary understanding of how writers at *Wired* feature religion and spirituality in their writing, we first investigated whether the religious or spiritual terms that were mentioned in their articles were positively or negatively expressed. Distinguishing between positive and negative content requires some inevitable subjectivity, but on the whole, fewer articles (approximately 34%) framed religious or spiritual terms in strictly negative terms, whereas more articles (approximately 62%) contained positive references. In some cases (approximately 5%), we detected a neutral, mixed, or ambivalent frame.

As an example of a negative frame, a *Wired* article entitled, "How Europe Can Stop Worrying and Learn to Love the Future," refers to "the straitjacket of the Catholic church" and conservative Christians in Germany who promote a "crude racist campaign" to prevent Indian immigrants from working in the tech industry.[30] Antiquated or bigoted religious institutions in this case are portrayed as obstructions to the benevolent, technological, and globalizing forces that contribute positively to the world. Likewise, an article about a new videogame in December 2012 discusses a virtual world of "theocratic white supremacists" and "religious nationalism" in obviously negative terms.[31]

Most examples, however, are generally positive and show no antipathy toward religion or spirituality. For instance, Mark Zuckerberg is positively referred to as a "dotcom deity" in the early days of Facebook.[32] Tim O'Reilly, an innovator and "free range proselytizer of the tech revolution," likens himself to the prophet Jeremiah for his ability to predict the future.[33] A professional meteorite hunter named Robert Ward considers his vocation a "spiritual calling" and "God-given directive."[34]

Regardless of whether such (self-) descriptions are used conventionally or appropriated for a more secular audience, they nonetheless reveal the presence and place of spirituality in the minds of many *Wired* writers.

In a few instances, religious terms are ambivalent or unclear. For example, in "Cairo Activists Use Facebook to Rattle Regime," several references are made to Islam and its religious practices, but the Arab Spring was a multilayered social movement with Muslim actors on both sides of the struggle. What does emerge in this article, however, is that while the teachings of Islam may not facilitate Cairo with a clear path toward peace, the tech-savvy activists using Facebook (referenced more than forty times in the article) may now have the digital tools to upend an oppressive regime and change "the dynamics of political dissent."[35]

The Conflict Motif

In *Wired*, some evidence exists to support the prevalence of a conflict motif whereby science and technology confront religion and theology as opposing forces. For example, in "The Crusade Against Evolution," Evan Ratliff monitors the resurgence of antievolutionary arguments, particularly the Intelligent Design movement, and covers its implications for school textbooks and science curricula for the Ohio State Board of Education.[36] While the article generally avoids polemical overtones and provides an evenhanded summary of opposing viewpoints, there is little recognition of alternatives such as theistic evolution. The reader is thus left with a stark binary: Choose between the ultimately misguided position of Intelligent Design or the secular, data-driven theory of evolution. Ratliff reveals his hand toward the end of the article: "In an era when the government is pouring billions into biology, and when stem cells and genetically modified food are front-page news, spending even a small part of the curriculum on bogus criticisms of evolution is arguably more detrimental now than in any time in history."[36]

Although antievolutionists draw the ire among some *Wired* writers, the conflict motif is not confined solely to North American debates between evangelical Christians and their secular enemies. The topic of Islam also surfaces occasionally and serves as a further instance where religion and technology collide. In a wild article entitled "Robots of Arabia," Jim Lewis covers a fascinating conflict involving the moral demands of Islam, the Qatari culture of camel racing, and the developing field of robotics.[37] As the story goes, a group of wealthy Qataris involved in the sport of camel racing had shockingly been coercing smaller, lighter Sudanese boys to compete in their races because they were faster than voluntary, adult competitors. After being made aware of the human rights abuses, the emir of Qatar, Hamad Bin Khalifa Al-Thani, ordered all child jockeys to be replaced with lightweight robots. Then, after a team of Swiss engineers and zoologists built robot jockey prototypes, the camels refused to race because the new robot jockeys didn't resemble their previous human riders. Making matters more complicated, Lewis goes on to explain that Islam also "forbids representations of the human form" since they could be "considered graven images, inducements to idolatry." Reflecting on the peculiar conflict, Lewis writes, "It's a moment created by rampantly *colliding* contexts: Western R&D, international NGO pressures, Arabian traditions, petroleum wealth, and benevolent despotism."[38] In the end, the Swiss engineers were able to satisfy the conflicting demands of the prickly camels and law-abiding Muslims, but the *Wired* story as a whole exemplifies the occasional conflicts that arise between conservative forces of religion and the liberating potential of technology.

The Compatibility Motif

Despite the legacy of secularization theory in the social sciences and its entrenchment in popular culture, other articles in *Wired* support a motif of compatibility, one where organized religious faith exists peacefully in a modern, technological world. For example, prominent scientists such as Francis Collins are occasionally featured and have argued for the reconciliation of science and religion. Further, since advances in modern technology often prompt ethical or religious considerations, *Wired* writers often cover these interactions and feature prominent thinkers who contend that advances in modern technology can move in concert with religious convictions. In "The Remastered Race," for instance, Brian Alexander interviews Ted Peters, a theologian at Pacific Lutheran Theological Seminary, who believes that genetic engineering for humans is a natural extension of God's will. According to Peters, "We are responsible for making the world a better place, and technology is one means whereby we can do it."[39]

Similarly, in a December issue of that same year, Gregg Easterbrook overtly challenges the popularity of the secularization thesis. As he explains, "the pure materialistic view that reigned through the 20th century, holding that everything has a natural explanation, couldn't keep other viewpoints at bay forever. The age-old notion that there is more to existence than meets the eye suddenly looks fresh again."[40] Running the gamut from quantum physics and the Higgs boson "God particle" to new findings in evolutionary biology, Easterbrook's article is remarkable in its extensive coverage of the ideas and people who believe religion, science, and technology are entirely compatible. These sentiments are not isolated to one *Wired* reporter or religious tradition either. In "The Pope's Astrophysicist," Margaret Wertheim pushes back on a materialistic view of the universe while favorably covering the life and thoughts of Father George Coyne, director and senior scientist at the Vatican Observatory.[41] Similarly, an article entitled "Solar, Eclipsed" presents a positive evaluation of "Hinduism's ancient environmental beliefs" and suggests that an ancient religious tradition can exist alongside and even help solve today's most pressing environmental issues.[42]

The Fulfillment Motif

As a departure from these framing strategies, a third motif articulates a narrative where technology is the supreme fulfillment of specific spiritual beliefs, ideals, and practices. Most of the *Wired* articles that bring religion or spirituality prominently into the story not only use this motif but also deploy a particular discourse that undermines organized religion in favor of spirituality. More than half of the articles (52.2%) sampled for their discursive frames from 2001 to 2020 follow the fulfillment motif.

The fulfillment motif distinguishes itself in a few important ways. First, there is often a temporal ordering. By depicting technology as making possible that which organized religion could never achieve by itself, the fulfillment motif suggests that some of the typical ideals of institutional religion (lasting peace on earth, immortality of the soul or body, knowledge of the universe's origins, etc.) can occur only through technological means. Second, whereas the conflict motif views organized religion and technology as bitter enemies, and while the compatibility motif dissolves the tension between the two, this third motif breaks from organized religion by resituating technology as the means to achieve spiritual fulfillment. Third, articles with a fulfillment motif generally spotlight a specific person who, though perhaps inspired by a particular religious tradition in the past, has subsequently abandoned their religious faith in favor of alternative, techno-spiritual solutions.

Wired contributor Brian Alexander follows the fulfillment motif in his article on human cloning. When Alexander interviews an underground scientist referred to as "The Creator," he discovers that the unnamed scientist's motive to clone humans is overtly spiritual. As "The Creator" tells him, "This will be the biggest leap for mankind. . . . It is the central core of Christianity, the resurrection of Jesus, the promise of eternal life!"[43] Despite these spiritual impulses, however, the fulfillment motif is generally inconsistent with traditional religious (or Christian) ideals, and Alexander recognizes as much when he contextualizes the controversy, later stating, "The Catholic Church was (and remains) an especially vociferous opponent of in vitro fertilization." But at the same time, "The Creator" refutes these Catholic objections and considers religious or ethical objections to cloning unwarranted. A structurally similar article from 2017 highlights the pioneering work of Bryan Johnson, an ex-Mormon who left the church to develop a neuroprosthetic device that he believes will allow humans to become telepathic and merge their bodies with AI interfaces.[44]

Departures from the conflict and compatibility motifs are perhaps first evident when *Wired* writers move into trans- or posthumanist territory. Ray Kurzweil, a prolific inventor and author of *The Age of Spiritual Machines* and *The Singularity Is*

Near, is a frequent subject of fascination for *Wired* writers for his bold predictions and belief that humans will one day use technology to transcend and ultimately escape their mortal bodies.[45] In a 2012 *Wired* article, posthumanism is taken up again in an article on Japanese pop culture where James Verini reports on the massive crowds flocking to see a virtual pop star named Hatsune Miku. Verini explains the odd circumstances surrounding Miku and her fans: "Miku is not human. She is a virtual idol, a holographic star. Miku is crowdsourced, ever-evolving, famous software. Not even her fans know, or care, how to taxonomize her. ('She's rather more like a goddess: She has human parts, but she transcends human limitations. She's the great posthuman pop star,' one fansite reads.)"[46] Consequently, the technological innovations that make transhumanism imaginable not only pique the interest of *Wired* writers, but they also subvert organized religious traditions in favor of a techno-spiritual agenda.

A second aspect that supports the fulfillment motif employs what Kevin Kelly calls a "computational metaphor." Describing the universe in mystical terms, Kelly rejects the notion that religion and technology conflict with one another, but at the same time he critiques Judeo-Christian conceptions that portray God as distinct from creation. From Kelly's perspective, the universe is one gigantic computer, and "God Is the Machine."[47] The metaphor of computation, according to Kelly, offers a superior metanarrative to either secularism or what traditional religious dogma can offer. Kelly explains this metaphor's potential: "It is a new universal metaphor. It has more juice in it than previous metaphors: Freud's dream state, Darwin's variety, Marx's progress, or the Age of Aquarius. And it has more power than anything else in science at the moment. In fact the computational metaphor may eclipse mathematics as a form of universal notation."[48]

Kelly's role as former executive editor at *Wired* from 1992 to 1999 has left a visible imprint on the types of stories emerging from Silicon Valley's popular media outlet. For those immersed in the world of software development and coding—or for those seeking to embrace a metanarrative that avoids traditional religious dogmas on the one hand and secularism's hostility to transcendence on the other—the computation metaphor provides a popular third alternative. Kelly explains further: "From this perspective, computation seems almost a theological process. It takes as its fodder the primeval choice between yes or no, the fundamental state of 1 or 0. After stripping away all externalities, all material embellishments, what remains is the purest state of existence: here/not here. Am/not am. In the Old Testament, when Moses asks the Creator, 'Who are you?' the being says, in effect, 'Am.' One bit. One almighty bit. Yes. One. Exist. It is the simplest statement possible."[49] As this passage illustrates, Kelly reinterprets the Old Testament and recasts its meaning so that technology provides the ultimate fulfillment and means to achieve spiritual liberation. The Old Testament God may exist, according to Kelly, but this deity is best understood through the metaphor of computation.

Finally, a third component that appears in connection with the fulfillment motif deals with the logic of reenchantment. Contra Weber, the writers at *Wired* often infuse their articles with a spiritual fervor that views technology as the means to address organized religion's shortcomings. A *Wired* article follows this reenchanting logic when covering the neurologist Oliver Sacks and praises his ability to have "profound mystical feelings which do not have to call on fictitious agencies like angels and demons and deities."[50] In the same October issue, writer Gary Wolf waxes romantically about "Guru David Allen and His Cult of Hyperefficiency." A leader in the life-hacking movement, Allen's advice for how to organize one's personal life contains nothing less than "a spiritual promise" and a litany of self-help, New Age concepts.[51]

Taken together, these articles reveal a narrative that sees technology or, more broadly, technique as the means to fulfill spiritual longing.[52] While many *Wired* writers appropriate spiritual vocabulary in their articles, the best-known spokesperson for this way of thinking is Kevin Kelly, whose presence at *Wired* stretches back to the founding of the magazine and his days with Stewart Brand at *Whole Earth Catalog*. As a result, in contrast to the notions of pure conflict or compatibility, a new fulfillment motif emerges that sees technology as the natural fulfillment of earlier spiritual ideals. From this perspective, technology is not a cold, lifeless tool, as some had thought before the origins of Silicon Valley cyberculture, but an entire way of living and thinking—infused with spiritual potential—that ultimately explains reality and makes life worth living. Kelly summarizes his position and the fulfillment motif more generally in a 2010 interview: "I've actually gone a bit further and come to see technology as an alternative great story, as a different source for understanding where we are in the cosmos. I think technology is something that can give meaning to our lives, particularly in a secular world."[53]

TECHNOLOGY AND SPIRITUAL FULFILLMENT

Most of the digital technology that resides in our homes and workplaces or fills our pockets and purses can trace its origins to Silicon Valley, but what goes less noticed among those interested in technology and social change is how various narratives pertaining to religion and spirituality get culturally embedded. Hoping to shed light on this process, this chapter reveals the prevalence of spirituality in Silicon Valley through the prism of technology reporters at *Wired* magazine. Our project echoes Binkley's ethnography of *Wired*'s predecessor, *Whole Earth Catalog*, where Binkley strives "to bring our understanding of the origins of the postmodern consumer down from the ether of metatheory to the level of actors, innovations, and print media."[54] Likewise, our content and discourse analysis intends to explain more precisely how religion, spirituality, and technology are understood and articulated by some of the leading actors and writers in Silicon Valley. Reaching an estimated thirty million readers each month, *Wired*'s success not only reflects its cultural appeal to technology enthusiasts but also spreads important metanarratives that attempt to explain complex social realities. Some of these narratives, we argue, pertain to the evolving relationships between religion, spirituality, and technology. Indeed, evidence suggests that *Wired* contributors articulate the complex relationships of religion and spirituality to science and technology in multiple ways.

Though both the conflict and compatibility motifs are present in the broader Silicon Valley ethos and in the pages of *Wired*, the most popular narrative involving the religion-technology relationship is expressed through *the fulfillment motif*. In *Wired*, this motif takes an alternative approach, synthesizing elements of the previous two motifs but also subverting their arguments in the process. Aupers's early analysis of *Wired* initially recognized the presence of spirituality and "technoanimism" in what many might otherwise expect to be a thoroughly secular publication.[55] Eventually, these nascent spiritualities found their home beyond the pages of *Wired* too, as Carolyn Chen describes in her book *Work Pray Code: When Work Becomes Religion in Silicon*

Valley. Documenting the lives of Silicon Valley coders and how their lives intersect with spirituality, Chen provides a thorough accounting of techno-utopian work culture. With echoes of the fulfillment motif ringing clearly through the Valley, she concludes, "Techtopia is Silicon Valley's upgraded social 'operating system'—an engineered society where people find their highest *fulfillment* in the utopian workplace."[56] Thus, the fulfillment motif that we find in *Wired* radiates outward in the surrounding Bay Area environment, ultimately getting absorbed by those working in the digital trenches in exactly the way Chen describes.

Where do these ideas originate? For those familiar with the work of Kevin Kelly or his predecessor Stewart Brand, the prevalence of spiritual motifs may not seem so surprising. As Turner has shown, Silicon Valley has long fostered a "digital utopianism" that co-opts spiritual metaphors and subverts traditional religious dogmas.[57] With the fulfillment motif, technology is understood to be the means to fulfill spiritual ideals. The transhumanist movement expressed by Ray Kurzweil exemplifies an attempt to achieve immortality and a Neognostic liberation from the body through technological means.[58] Kevin Kelly's "computational metaphor," which affirms God's existence, reduces the origins of the universe and all material reality to spiritual, informational processes.[59] Further, the frenetic pace of innovation in Silicon Valley derives not solely from a profit motive but also out of a deeper desire to overcome the effects of alienation and disenchantment—in short, a longing to reenchant the world.[60]

So what does it mean for society if the tech sector is increasingly animated by spirituality? Tesla/SpaceX founder Elon Musk acquired social media giant Twitter for approximately $44 billion. Of all the tech leaders in the world, Musk enjoys a singular cult/celebrity following and not coincidentally is distinguished by being the wealthiest human in history. Significantly, unlike his predecessor Jack Dorsey, Musk is also a near-compulsive tweeter, averaging at least a dozen posts per day, many of them with the power to shape markets, political events, and the attitudes of his 120 million followers. Musk represents a new and perhaps unprecedented form of social power, converging unrivaled economic power, technological expertise, and now far-reaching communication capacity. More to the present point, what are the spiritual or religious implications of such a concentrated power? Musk is famously agnostic and holds no traditional religious affiliations. He is, however, highly optimistic regarding the potential of technology (especially his own) to overcome myriad environmental, political, and cultural problems, such as the use of his Starlink satellite internet service to assist Ukraine against the Russian incursion. In this way, he would fit approximately in our fulfillment motif, though in an admittedly less overt spiritual form. Only the most naïve of observers would conclude that such a potent amalgam of social powers in the hands of a techno-utopian will have no large-scale cultural and ideological ripple effects.

The case of Elon Musk is but one useful illustration of the necessity for social scientists of all backgrounds to consider more closely the spiritual facets of technology and its innovators. As postindustrial society continues to concentrate power in the hands of tech companies rather than political or cultural elites as in prior decades, focus must center on places like Silicon Valley and Austin, Texas, in addition to Washington, DC, or Wall Street. This analysis reveals that like all human beings, these engineers, designers, inventors, and coders have complex spiritual identities that will invariably manifest in their creations, affecting the lives of almost everyone else.

In the end, finding the levers that produce cultural change requires understanding how the norms, values, and beliefs traditionally associated with religion interact with the floodwaters released from technological innovation. Over the last few decades, Silicon Valley has arguably become the most important cultural reservoir in the world, impacting not only the residents and writers living in the Bay Area but all those who download new apps on their phones or use Google or Facebook daily. Understanding the complex data humans acquire in life also requires seeking out metanarratives that attempt to explain reality. By locating these narratives and grasping their social implications, scholars can more fully anticipate what role technology plays in producing cultural change, how religion is central to cultural and technological production, and why spirituality is increasingly adopted in the public sphere as an alternative to organized religion. Such anticipations should also provoke new dialogue at the intersection of culture, technology, and religion and challenge assumptions that have placed religion and technology as either eternal enemies or consonant dance partners. At the very least, a different game with a different narrative, one that marches to a new spiritual beat, may be afoot.

NOTES

An earlier, unpublished version of this chapter appears in Paul K. McClure, "Modding My Religion: Exploring the Effects of Digital Technology on Religion and Spirituality" (PhD thesis, Baylor University, 2018). The authors would also like to thank Hunter R. Epperson for his research assistance. This work was partially supported by a Summer Research Grant at the University of Lynchburg.

1. Stewart Brand, *The Last Whole Earth Catalog: Access to Tools* (New York: Random House, 1971).

2. Peter Berger, *The Sacred Canopy: Elements of a Sociological Theory* (Garden City, NY: Anchor, 1969), 112–13.
3. Walter Isaacson, *The Innovators: How a Group of Hackers, Geniuses, and Geeks Created the Digital Revolution* (New York: Simon & Schuster, 2015); Fred Turner, *From Counterculture to Cyberculture: Stewart Brand, the Whole Earth Network, and the Rise of Digital Utopianism* (Chicago: University of Chicago Press, 2008).
4. Dorien Zandbergen, "Silicon Valley New Age: The Co-constitution of the Digital and the Sacred," in *Religions of Modernity: Relocating the Sacred to the Self and the Digital*, ed. Stef Aupers and Dick Houtman (Leiden: Brill, 2010), 163.
5. Fred Turner, "Where the Counterculture Met the New Economy: The WELL and the Origins of Virtual Community," *Technology and Culture* 46, no. 3 (2005): 485.
6. Sam Binkley, "The Seers of Menlo Park: The Discourse of Heroic Consumption in the 'Whole Earth Catalog,'" *Journal of Consumer Culture* 3, no. 3 (2003): 292.
7. Turner, *From Counterculture to Cyberculture*, 2.
8. Tom Wolfe, *The Electric Kool-Aid Acid Test* (New York: Picador, 2008 [1968]).
9. Theodore Roszak, *From Satori to Silicon Valley: San Francisco and the American Counterculture* (San Francisco: Don't Call It Frisco Press, 1986).
10. Stef Aupers and Dick Houtman, "'Reality Sucks': On Alienation and Cybergnosis," *Concilium: International Journal of Theology* 41, no. 1 (2005): 1–11.
11. Tara Isabella Burton, *Strange Rites: New Religions for a Godless World* (New York: PublicAffairs, 2020); Carolyn Chen, *Work Pray Code: When Work Becomes Religion in Silicon Valley* (Princeton, NJ: Princeton University Press, 2022); Craig Detweiler, *iGods: How Technology Shapes Our Spiritual and Social Lives* (Grand Rapids, MI: Brazos Press, 2013).
12. Todd LeRoy Perreira, "Sasana Sakon and the New Asian American: Intermarriage and Identity at a Thai Buddhist Temple in Silicon Valley," in *Asian American Religions: The Making and Remaking of Borders and Boundaries*, ed. Tony Carnes and Fenggang Yang (New York University Press, 2004), 313–37.
13. Wade Clark Roof, *Spiritual Marketplace: Baby Boomers and the Remaking of American Religion* (Princeton, NJ: Princeton University Press, 2001).
14. Jaron Lanier, *Who Owns the Future?* (New York: Simon & Schuster, 2014), 213.
15. Walter Isaacson, *Steve Jobs* (New York: Simon & Schuster, 2011).
16. Brett T. Robinson, *Appletopia: Media Technology and the Religious Imagination of Steve Jobs* (Waco, TX: Baylor University Press, 2013), 68.

17. Andy Crouch, "Steve Jobs: The Secular Prophet," *Wall Street Journal*, October 8, 2011.
18. Turner, "Where the Counterculture Met the New Economy"; Turner, *From Counterculture to Cyberculture*.
19. Lee Gilmore, *Theater in a Crowded Fire: Ritual and Spirituality at Burning Man* (Berkeley: University of California Press, 2010); Fred Turner, "Burning Man at Google: A Cultural Infrastructure for New Media Production," *New Media & Society* 11, nos. 1–2 (2009): 73–79.
20. Nicholas Negroponte, *Being Digital* (New York: Vintage, 1996); Howard Rheingold, *The Virtual Community: Homesteading on the Electronic Frontier* (Cambridge, MA: MIT Press, 2000); Kevin Kelly, *Out of Control: The New Biology of Machines, Social Systems, and the Economic World* (Reading, MA: Basic Books, 1995; Kevin Kelly, *What Technology Wants* (New York: Viking, 2010); Kevin Kelly, *The Inevitable: Understanding the 12 Technological Forces That Will Shape Our Future* (New York: Penguin Books, 2017).
21. Stewart Brand, "Scream of Consciousness," *Wired*, January 1, 1993, https://www.wired.com/1993/01/paglia/.
22. Turner, *From Counterculture to Cyberculture*, 207.
23. Turner, "Where the Counterculture Met the New Economy."
24. Henrik Bødker, "Gadgets and Gurus," *Media History* 23, no. 1 (2017): 67–79.
25. Turner, *From Counterculture to Cyberculture*, 218.
26. AAM, "Total Circulation for Consumer Magazines," 2020, http://abcas3.auditedmedia.com/ecirc/magtitlesearch.asp.
27. *Wired* Press Center, 2019, https://www.wired.com/about/press/.
28. Most analysis for this paper was conducted using *Wired*'s online platform (wired.com) before a paywall was implemented. Hard copies of issues were consulted for years when acquiring articles through online archives was less accessible. For years 2013–2020, issues were accessed and purchased through Zinio (zinio.com), a digital magazine newsstand that carries back issues. Print articles also appear online and contain the same content, though article titles and dates of publication may differ.
29. Stef Aupers, "The Revenge of the Machines: On Modernity, Digital Technology and Animism," *Asian Journal of Social Science* 30, no. 2 (2002): 199–220.
30. Misha Glenny, "How Europe Can Stop Worrying and Learn to Love the Future," *Wired*, February 1, 2001, https://www.wired.com/2001/02/misha/.
31. Chris Suellentrop, "Great Expectations," *Wired*, December 6, 2012, https://www.wired.com/2012/12/ff-bioshock/.

32. Fred Vogelstein, "How Mark Zuckerberg Turned Facebook into the Web's Hottest Platform," *Wired*, September 6, 2007, https://www.wired.com/2007/09/ff-facebook/.
33. Steven Levy, "The Seer," *Wired*, December 21, 2012, https://www.wired.com/2012/12/mf-tim-oreilly-qa/.
34. Joshuah Bearman and Allison Keeley, "Space Invaders," *Wired*, December 17, 2018, https://www.wired.com/story/scramble-claim-worlds-most-coveted-meteorite/.
35. David Wolman, "Cairo Activists Use Facebook to Rattle Regime," *Wired*, October 20, 2008, https://www.wired.com/2008/10/ff-facebook-egypt/.
36. Evan Ratliff, "The Crusade Against Evolution," *Wired*, October 1, 2004, https://www.wired.com/2004/10/evolution-2/.
37. Jim Lewis, "Robots of Arabia," *Wired*, November 1, 2005, https://www.wired.com/2005/11/camel/.
38. Lewis, "Robots of Arabia" (our emphasis).
39. Brian Alexander, "(You)2." *Wired*, February 1, 2001, https://www.wired.com/2001/02/projectx/.
40. Gregg Easterbrook, "The New Convergence," *Wired*, December 1, 2002, https://www.wired.com/2002/12/convergence-3/.
41. Margaret Wertheim, "The Pope's Astrophysicist," *Wired*, December 1, 2002, https://www.wired.com/2002/12/pope-astro/.
42. Charles C. Mann, "Solar, Eclipsed," *Wired*, December 1, 2015, https://www.wired.com/2015/11/climate-change-in-india/.
43. Alexander, "(You)2."
44. John H. Richardson, "Inside the Race to Hack the Human Brain," *Wired*, November 16, 2017, https://www.wired.com/story/inside-the-race-to-build-a-brain-machine-interface/.
45. Ray Kurzweil, *The Age of Spiritual Machines: When Computers Exceed Human Intelligence* (New York: Penguin Books, 2000); Ray Kurzweil, *The Singularity Is Near: When Humans Transcend Biology* (New York: Penguin Books, 2006); Paul Boutin, "Kurzweil's Law," *Wired*, April 1, 2001, https://www.wired.com/2001/04/kurzweil/.
46. James Verini, "How Virtual Pop Star Hatsune Miku Blew Up in Japan," *Wired*, October 19, 2012, https://www.wired.com/2012/10/mf-japan-pop-star-hatsune-miku/.
47. Kevin Kelly, "God Is the Machine," December 1, 2002, https://www.wired.com/2002/12/holytech/.
48. Turner, *From Counterculture to Cyberculture*, 15.
49. Kelly, "God Is the Machine."
50. Steve Silberman, "Oliver Sacks on Earworms, Stevie Wonder and the View from Mescaline Mountain," *Wired*, September 24, 2007, https://www.wired.com/2007/09/ff-musicophilia/.

51. Gary Wolf, "Getting Things Done Guru David Allen and His Cult of Hyperefficiency," *Wired*, September 25, 2007, https://www.wired.com/2007/09/ff-allen/.
52. Jacques Ellul, *The Technological Society*, ed. John Wilkinson (New York: Vintage Books, 1967).
53. Kevin Kelly and Steven Johnson, "Kevin Kelly and Steven Johnson on Where Ideas Come From," *Wired*, September 27, 2010, https://www.wired.com/2010/09/mf-kellyjohnson/.
54. Binkley, "The Seers of Menlo Park," 288.
55. Aupers, "The Revenge of the Machines."
56. Chen, *Work Pray Code*, 196 (our emphasis).
57. Turner, "Where the Counterculture Met the New Economy"; Turner, *From Counterculture to Cyberculture*; Turner, "Burning Man at Google."
58. Kurzweil, *The Age of Spiritual Machines*; Kurzweil, *The Singularity Is Near*.
59. James Gleick, *The Information: A History, a Theory, a Flood* (New York: Vintage, 2012); Kevin Kelly, "Why the Basis of the Universe Isn't Matter or Energy—It's Data," February 28, 2011, *Wired*, https://www.wired.com/2011/02/mf-gleick-qa/.
60. Aupers and Houtman, "Reality Sucks"; Paul Froese, *On Purpose: How We Create the Meaning of Life* (Oxford: Oxford University Press, 2016).

6

LAGGED IDENTITIES AND THE UNDERESTIMATED CIVIC SIGNIFICANCE OF SPIRITUALITY

EVAN STEWART, TIMOTHY DACEY, AND JAIME KUCINSKAS

In *Democracy in America* (1835), Alexis de Tocqueville observed a unique civic spirit fostered by voluntary associations in the United States: "Americans of all ages, all conditions, all minds constantly unite together. Not only do they have commercial and industrial associations to which all belong but also a thousand other kinds, religious, moral, serious, futile, very general and very specialized. . . . I had no notion and I have frequently admired the endless skill with which the inhabitants of the United States manage to set a common aim to the efforts of a great number of men."[1] Tocqueville brings attention to how participation in a voluntary association, whether it be a leisure group, a neighborhood association, or a city council, has long channeled Americans' energy to collective ends, which is a crucial element in democracy. Specifically, these groups cultivate people's ability to engage in what Eliasoph and Lichterman call "civic action": "coordinating action to improve some aspect of common life in society, as they imagine society."[2]

Research in sociology and political science questions whether these conditions for civic action have persisted or changed over time. Political scientist Robert Putnam's groundbreaking study *Bowling Alone* suggests that many American civic groups and activities are in decline. His perennial example of this was declining participation in bowling leagues and, more important, the way that this paralleled other decreases in neighborhood participation, local political engagement, voting, and more. Putnam's prescient work foreshadowed later declines in other kinds of social engagement, including religious affiliation and participation and living alone.[3]

Scholarship on civic decline, however, has drawn criticism for failing to recognize kinds of social activity and civic life that have remained seemingly "invisible," but persistent, even as more publicly recognized activities declined. Civic action doesn't necessarily occur in groups that appear stereotypically "civic," such as formal volunteer organizations.[4] Scholars of racial and economic inequality identify how, among communities with fewer resources, informal childcare among friends and helping neighbors with everyday problems related to poverty are key forms of civic engagement often overlooked by survey data.[5] Such behaviors can have consequences for political involvement. For example, researchers found in one study that as residents in impoverished neighborhoods took responsibility for helping their neighbors make ends meet, their cynicism toward political solutions to local problems, and subsequent political disengagement, increased.[6]

At the heart of these observations is an important lesson about the difference between civic action and the assumptions that scholars and laypeople alike make about which activities "count" as true civic and community-oriented activities. It is necessary to recognize (1) the varied civic behaviors people from different communities do; (2) how people come to recognize certain behaviors as "civic"; and (3) the associated cultural schemas they bundle with "civic," to better understand American public life. How do Americans' normative (and often privileged) assumptions about the civic sphere shape the activities they recognize as substantively civic and good for public life? And how does that affect scholars' portrayals of changing civic culture over time?

In this chapter we investigate the implications of changing religiosity in the United States on civic and political behavior by comparing how people relate religion and spirituality to civic behavior and identities. We explore whether prosocial assumptions about American congregational religion skew reports of civic engagement and therefore might influence the portrayal of such trends in public commentary and research.

To examine these questions, we first review the latest research on spirituality and civic engagement, which is divided between those critical of the growth of a "selfish spirituality," and others who question whether spirituality is emerging as a substitute for religion. In contrast to popular assumptions, the latest survey analyses, based on the 2020 National Religion and Spirituality Survey (NRSS), actually suggest that the majority of spiritual Americans are notably civically engaged.[7] Second, we build on those latest findings by delving deeper into the NRSS data. We replicate, extend, and compare the models used by these previous studies to investigate why narratives of selfish spirituality persist. Our analysis suggests that when surveys ask people about their *identities* as civic people, religious practice is more strongly associated with those identities than spiritual practice. In contrast, when surveys ask about *recent civic behavior*, both religious and spiritual practices are equally associated with such behavior. Third, these findings help us clarify an important point for understanding the underestimated public role of spirituality in the modern United States identified in previous literature: spiritual practice is just as capable of fostering civic behavior as religious practice, but religion gets more acknowledgment and recognition for its ties to

American voluntary life, because religious people associate their religious identities with civic participation more than do spiritual people with their spiritual identities.

AMERICAN NARRATIVES OF "SELFISH SPIRITUALITY"

In 2022 journalist Jane Coaston interviewed Russell Moore, the editor of *Christianity Today* and the former president of the Ethics and Religious Liberty Commission of the Southern Baptist Convention. Coaston noted the "massive interest in spirituality among young people" and inquired, "Why do you think that the church isn't winning more of them over?" Moore responded: "There is a desire for spirituality that often comes along with a suspicion of institutions which can develop itself into all kinds of super-individualized and sometimes commercially exploited kinds of spirituality. So you think of the book *McMindfulness* that's talking about a kind of American Buddhism that wants to take the spiritual practices, but evacuate it of the hard parts of what it means to be a Buddhist. That happens in almost every area of spirituality right now as well."[8] Moore's suspicion of spirituality as a culturally thin, manipulatable, and individualized project reflects a long-standing critique among some Christians of "selfish spirituality"—the claim that spiritual practices foster an individualistic, inward-focused state that disconnects people from engaging in public life in pursuit of the common good.

This argument is not new. In 1908 British Catholic philosopher G. K. Chesterton, for example, argued that the immanent focus of spirituality fostered "introspection, self-isolation, quietism, [and] social indifference," as opposed to the transcendent focus of religion.[9] Max Weber emphasized how Asiatic and

Middle Eastern ascetic practices fostered an "intensive training of the body and spirit" that ultimately encouraged people to distance themselves from the material and larger social world around them.[10] Similar arguments have been echoed by American Christian conservatives suspicious of foreign Asian religions.[11]

Today the assumption that spirituality is more inwardly focused persists, in contrast to the supposedly "outward-focused" nature of religious institutions in the world.[12] Much research undergirds this popular belief, documenting the many prosocial functions of religious congregations. Congregational participation motivates social solidarity and can provide emotional support.[13] In turn, this makes religious institutions a command station for mobilizing volunteer work and other kinds of politically motivated advocacy work.[14] Because it is so well established that local congregations can foster and shape individual and collective religious *and* civic identities, and undergird civic participation, it is reasonable to be concerned that waning participation in religious institutions in favor of spirituality might lead to declining civic engagement as well.[15]

Sociologists of religion have long observed a transition from "dwelling" in religious congregations to individualistic spiritual "seeking" that often comes at the expense of more communal commitments.[16] Other recent case studies on the proliferating spiritual practices outside of congregations raise questions about whether spirituality is inherently an individualist project—where people seek out practices that provide a feeling of close personal fit and therapeutic or pragmatic individualized support, as opposed to a community of strong ties that can be a pillar of larger local communities, in the way religious congregations are often imagined to be.[17]

A related concern among scholars is that the fusion of spirituality with contemporary capitalist modes of production and consumption may negatively impact civic engagement.[18] Carolyn Chen, for example, argues that work has become a new secularized religion among tech employees in Silicon Valley.[19] Tech firms have repackaged religiously inspired spiritual practices (e.g., Hinduism and Buddhism) as a vehicle for employees to find fulfillment and meaning in their lives. As a result, their most valued employees increasingly devote their time to work and its amenities, while neglecting or failing to develop community ties and civic engagement. The selfish spirituality critique importantly shows how possibly exploitative or "greedy" versions of "spirituality" may actually hinder civic engagement, as they encourage people to neglect collective problems or, worse, turn their attention exclusively to worldly issues such as work or earning money.[20]

These scholars raise legitimate concerns that these kinds of spiritual practices do not contribute the same social and cultural capital to civic action as other kinds of practices in formal religious institutions and faith groups. It is also important to consider, however, the wide array of kinds of spiritual practices employed, where and why such practices are used, and the benefits or drawbacks of any particular kind of spiritual practice.[21] Overall, these trends and attendant depictions of spirituality provoke questions about whether spirituality will lead to declining civic and political engagement, which has long been organized through religious congregations.[22]

CIVIC SPIRITUALITY AS A SUBSTITUTE FOR RELIGION

Other recent scholarship investigating the nature of contemporary spirituality reveals some limitations of the selfish spirituality theory, which raise questions about whether concerns of civic decline due to rising spirituality are overstated. When some people distinguish between "spirituality" and "religion," they do so in service of boundary work to distinguish their identities from others. Paul McClure, for example, explains how spiritual but not religious (SBNR) identities are used to differentiate oneself from monotheistic, institutionalized religious perspectives. He concludes that this identity represents a possible budding "third option" between organized religion and secularism.[23] Though the concepts of spirituality and religion each have distinct histories and ideological frameworks, which allow people to invoke them to draw specific symbolic boundaries, these differences do not necessarily mean that religious *practices* and spiritual *practices* provide radically different social goods. Both kinds of practices fall into a theory of lived religious experience that foregrounds meaningful states of practice as a key source of both the religious experience and the spiritual experience. Though people may invoke very different labels (religious and spiritual), each with substantive and unique historical and ideological content, it is possible that both religious and spiritual practices themselves might invoke similar social goods.[24]

Emphasizing these "historically and socially situated symbolic boundaries" that practitioners can tap into throughout their daily lives, Jaime Kucinskas and Evan Stewart examine whether religious practices promote political engagement, and if the individualistic nature of spiritual practices, such as such meditation or yoga, leads to less political engagement.[25] Their study lends important insights relevant to our investigation into the relationships between religion, spirituality, and civic engagement. First, using survey items that asked respondents to report how often they engaged in a set of practices labeled as "spiritual" and how often they engaged in those same practices labeled as "religious," they find that people do indeed distinguish between spiritual and religious practices—respondents reported different clusters of practices under the "religious" label than under the "spiritual" label. Second, using an index of self-reported political behaviors over the past twelve months, including making donations, joining protests, and contacting representatives among others, they find that *both* spiritual and religious practices are equally and positively associated with those activities. Third, their analysis reveals important demographic and cultural differences between spiritual and religious practitioners. Political progressives, respondents of color, and members of the LGBT community were more likely to report spiritual rather than religious practices.

Using different measures from the same NRSS survey data, Brian Steensland, David King, and Barbara Duffy corroborate associations between both religiosity and spirituality and civic engagement.[26] In contrast to measures of religious and spiritual *practice* and political *behaviors* completed in the past twelve months, they used survey items that measured different forms of civic identities. The first set of measures asked respondents whether they thought their spirituality and their religion influenced their civic behavior. The second set of measures inquired about their civic identity rooted in self-assessments of their behavior (if they considered themselves people who participated in their community, such as by staying informed of events, attending community events, knowing their neighbors, interacting with strangers, volunteering, or donating to causes or organizations). They found that people who self-identified as spiritual were more likely to say that their spirituality influenced their civic engagement. In addition, those who thought their spirituality influenced their spiritual engagement were more likely to identify as people involved in the civic activities mentioned earlier. Interestingly, their findings also suggest spiritual identity, as accessed through these measures, was even more strongly tied to self-identified civic identity than religious identity. These new studies suggest that theories of selfish spirituality may be overblown and that spirituality is acting as a substitute for religion, with similar characteristics, for many spiritual people.

A THEORY OF LAGGED CULTURAL IDENTITIES

In seeking to understand why narratives of selfish spirituality persist, even though this previous work finds that many American spiritual practitioners are politically and civically engaged, we pose an alternative theoretical explanation: a theory of *lagged cultural identities*. We suspect that broader cultural narratives about groups of people affect how they view their own identities, describe themselves, and report their behavior. As scholars from the pragmatist school and subsequent work suggests, people learn about what specific social roles mean from those around them.[27] Then, as Erving Goffman depicts, most people seek to enact the roles others expect them to occupy appropriately, taking into account how their perceived audiences may view them.[28] They also use these identities to draw symbolic boundaries that distinguish themselves from others, as is the case with many spiritual but not religious respondents.[29]

Contemporary scholarship on social desirability bias in survey research affirms Goffman's theorizing of people's sensitivity to others' expectations and tendency to conform to social expectations. In answering survey questions, respondents tend to answer questions as they think will be viewed favorably by others, overreporting what they believe to be positive outcomes and underreporting undesirable outcomes. Importantly, this misreporting is not simply deception: it is driven by a genuine desire by respondents to communicate their most salient *identities* to survey researchers, even if their reported behaviors do not always align with those identities. Religious identity is a key example here, where respondents tend to misreport church attendance so that researchers will "accurately" capture the extent to which respondents see themselves as religious people, even if they do not always attend church.[30] Similar issues arise in other socially desirable behaviors such as voting and exercise.[31]

Drawing from a cultural and historical sociological perspective, we suspect that both religious and spiritual practitioners in the United States are subject to biases due to how they understand the identities associated with their practices, rooted in historical cultural lineages of each identity. We suspect that religious Americans have *learned*, through the specific historical and cultural context of the United States, that "religion" is associated with civic life and part of an American civic identity.[32] Thus we expect that they will associate their religiosity with a civic identity, which may incline them to social desirability biases in which they overreport their own civic identities, and possibly behavior.

By contrast, as Watts and Houtman note in the introduction, the sociology of religion has tended to treat spirituality as a "less-than-real" religion with weaker ties to civic behavior. We argue here that a similar process happens among everyday people. As Watts argues, by nature of the cultural lineage of American spirituality, which is grounded in a romantic liberal social imaginary valuing individualism, independence, personal seeking, and authentic self-expression, the "spiritual" may not necessarily *recognize* and *give credit* to spirituality's contributions to their civic engagement. In describing carriers of this romantic liberal tradition, which Watts views as constitutive of the "spiritual turn" in the West, he writes: "We whose vision of the good society finds its roots in the romantic liberal tradition, whose ideals have been shaped by the legacies of the 1960s, and whose identities have been comprehensively constituted by romantic liberal modernity rest largely unaware of our social and institutional debts. As I have repeatedly shown, expressive individualism and the religion of the heart in its various guises encourage this self-understanding, engendering a kind of self-imposed amnesia that obscures from sight the origins of who we are and where we come from."[33] Watts further argues that spiritual carriers of romantic liberal culture tend to separate and distinguish their spiritual cultivation, which they assume is *private*, from their public engagement, even though the former may contribute to skills and motivations which support the latter. Therefore, they miss the influence spirituality plays in fostering their civic selves.

There are also other reasons why reports of civic engagement may vary. People may be members of groups or community organizations that they label as "civic" but that fail to engage in civic action.[34] Or, conversely, an organization's "group style" may promote civic practices even though groups are not thought of as civic organizations. Other organizations that we might assume provide civic skills, such as choral groups, may not effectively transmit those skills in practice.[35] These dynamics can occur for both religious and spiritual groups. Watts observes how some religious congregations behave as "greedy institutions" in that they seek to limit congregants' social activities outside of the specific congregational context, potentially limiting the extent to which they promote civic action in other institutions.[36] And while there are indeed cases where spiritual organizations might also serve as such "greedy institutions," such as Chen's observations of spirituality in the workplace, this research emphasizes how the "greediness" of either religious or spiritual groups is not due to the inherent nature of either religion or spirituality itself, but rather a function of specific group and organizational dynamics.[37]

This work suggests that researchers need to distinguish between the characteristics of a social group that actually foster civic action and the characteristics of a group that would lead people to label that group a "civic" organization.[38] Groups that appear civically minded, such as nonprofit organizations, may neither necessarily nor successfully cultivate a group style of civic action among their members. Conversely, groups that we would not necessarily consider to be civically engaged, such as corporations, may impart such a group style. In either case, Eliasoph and Lichterman remind us that group form does not necessarily align with group function.[39] People may be engaged with civic action without labeling it as such, or they may *recognize and name* civic action without necessarily practicing it in a substantive way. We suspect that a similar issue is at play with religion and spirituality.

Table 6.1 summarizes our theoretical argument and attendant hypotheses. In light of the research detailed earlier, while both religion and spirituality may be *actually* associated with civic behaviors (hypotheses 1a and 2a), we suspect that the religious will be more likely to explicitly link their religiosity with their civic behavior in survey responses because religiosity is typically recognized in the popular American imagination as associated with civic engagement in the public sphere (hypotheses 1b and 1c). By contrast, because spirituality is typically associated with the private sphere, we expect spiritual practitioners to be more inclined to report civic identities with weaker associations with spirituality (hypothesis 2b).

Table 6.1 How Lagged Spiritual and Religious Practices May Affect Civic Reports

	Civic behaviors (What people do)	Civic identities (What people imagine defines a public person)	Hypotheses
Religious practice	**Positively associated**	**Recognized** in the public imagination	1a: Frequent religious practitioners will report more frequent civic behaviors than nonfrequent practitioners. 1b: Frequent religious practitioners will report stronger civic identities than nonfrequent practitioners and spiritual practitioners. 1c: Frequent religious practitioners will report a stronger religio-civic identity than nonfrequent practitioners and spiritual practitioners.
Spiritual practice	**Positively associated**	**Less recognized** in the public imagination	2a: Frequent spiritual practitioners will report more frequent civic behaviors than nonfrequent spiritual practitioners. 2b: Frequent spiritual practitioners will report weaker civic identities than nonfrequent religious practitioners.

METHOD

Data

We use the 2020 National Religion and Spirituality Survey (NRSS) conducted by NORC's AmeriSpeak Panel service. The NRSS used a general population sample of U.S. adults over the age of eighteen. A total of 3,609 respondents completed the survey (an interview completion rate of 28 percent).

Measures

Our two main independent variables for this study are the frequency of Religious and Spiritual Practices. Questions included the following prompt: "Some people consider the following activities to be [religious/spiritual] activities. How often do you engage in the following as [religious/ spiritual] activities?" Activities included prayer, yoga, martial arts, or other physical activity, meditation, study of religious text, Tarot cards or fortune telling, reading, attending religious service, attending other religious or spiritual groups, art (e.g., singing, painting, listening to music), being in nature, writing, honoring or communicating with ancestors, offering or donation, acts of service, acts of protest, and teaching in a religious or spiritual setting. Respondents indicated their frequency of practice on a five-point scale including "daily, weekly, monthly, less than once a month, or never." In keeping with Kucinskas and Stewart, we created two mean-standardized scales from these items: a spirituality scale composed of Tarot, yoga, nature, honoring ancestors, art, writing, meditation, and fasting from the spirituality battery, and a religion scale composed of reading, teaching, making offerings, attending religious and spiritual events, prayer, and study of texts from the religion battery. We then test the relationship between each of these scales and multiple dependent variables that move from behavior-focused reports to identity-focused indicators.[40]

Our first dependent variable is *past civic behavior*.[41] This included a battery of activities that asked respondents, "During the past 12 months, have you done any of the following or not?" Activities included attending a meeting to talk about political or social concerns; calling, writing, or visiting a government official to express your views on a public issue; giving money to a candidate, campaign, or organization concerned with a political or social issue; joining a protest march, rally, or demonstration; and signing a petition on the internet or on paper about a political or social issue. Respondents indicated yes or no, yielding a count scale of total activities reported.

Our second dependent variable is *general civic identity*.[42] Respondents were given a general set of questions about civic behaviors and norms and asked, "How well do the following statements describe you?" Prompts included invoking positive community change, staying informed, attending community events, knowing neighbors, interacting with strangers, volunteering, and donating. Respondents indicated "not at all, slightly, moderately, or very well." We note here that this scale represents a "hybrid" measure that falls between behavior-focused and identity-focused measures: it asks about behaviors but invites respondents to report a general sense of fit to these descriptions of a civic person rather than asking them to report discrete past activities.

Our third and fourth dependent variables measure whether respondents explicitly link *religion and civic behavior* and whether they link *spirituality and civic behavior*. NRSS survey questions asked respondents to state whether their religion or their spirituality influenced their political views, political activity (such as voting, volunteering for political campaigns or issues, or donating to candidates or political organizations), civic engagement (such as volunteering in my community or donating to charity), and holding politicians accountable. Respondents reported each explicit link on a five-point Likert-type scale that included "strongly agree, somewhat agree, neither agree nor disagree, somewhat disagree, strongly disagree."

In addition to each of these core measures, we also include a set of standard demographic control variables used by Kucinskas and Stewart.[43] These include partisanship, belief in god/a higher power, sexuality, gender, age, race, household income, education, marital status, and religious identification.

Analysis

Our analysis replicates and extends previous research by using a set of independent variables identified by one previous study and a set of dependent variables identified in another.[44] Our aim is to take a variety of outcome measures related to civic engagement and examine whether self-reported religious and spiritual practices are associated differently with each of those outcomes in a comparative light. First, we examine the relationship between reported spiritual/religious behaviors and reported civic behaviors in the past twelve months using OLS regressions and controlling for standard demographic characteristics.[45] This model is essentially a replication of Kucinskas and Stewart to establish a baseline set of estimates.[46]

Second, we test whether those religious and spiritual behavior reports are associated with respondents' salient sense of civic identities, as Steensland and colleagues' findings suggest.[47] Here we use their outcome measures for a general civic identity, as well as their perceived and reported link between spirituality and civic identity and religion and civic identity. We move beyond their original models by using respondents' reports of their *specific* spiritual and religious behaviors as opposed to general reports of spiritual or religious salience.[48]

Our theoretical expectations in table 6.1 posit that both spiritual and religious practices will be positively associated with civic behavior reports, but they may be differentially associated with whether respondents recognize and report a connection between religious, spiritual, and civic identities. If religious practice is associated with a civic identity but spiritual practice is not, that would indicate some evidence of a lagged cultural identity at work.

Because each of our dependent variables uses a different response scale, we use mean-centered measures to compare rates of change in units of one standard deviation from the mean to make each set of models comparable and test our theory.[49] After we estimate each model, we use Wald tests for the equality of coefficients to test whether the religious and spiritual practice scales are estimated to have an equivalent estimated association with each outcome. After testing whether we can observe a significant and substantive difference in the association between religious and spiritual practice on each outcome, we then visualize the coefficient estimates for each model to compare differences across model specification.

RESULTS

The main results of these analyses are presented in table 6.2, and we visualize the differences in the estimated religious and spiritual practice relationships in figure 6.1.

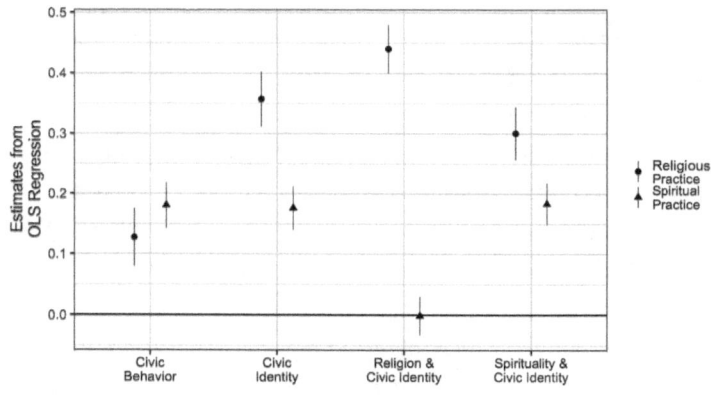

FIGURE 6.1 Estimated Relationships Between Practice, Political Behavior, and Civic Identities

Figure 6.1 shows the most important findings for our analysis. When our outcome measure focuses on specific reports of civic behaviors, both religious and spiritual practice have a comparable, positive association with the outcome. When our outcome measures explicitly focus on *civic identity*, however, we observe differential associations between religious practice and civic identities. Religious practice was more strongly associated with reports of a general civic identity (hypothesis 1b). It was also more strongly associated with agreement that one's religion shaped their civic identities (hypothesis 1c), and surprisingly, it was also more strongly associated with agreement that *spirituality* shaped one's civic identity.

Table 6.2 reports full regression results. When we estimate a model with the outcome variable for actual reports of past political behavior in the last twelve months, rather than self-reported civic identities, our results replicate Kucinskas and Stewart's finding that the religious and spiritual practice scales have essentially equal positive relationships with political behavior:

the spiritual/behavior relationship is even estimated to be a little stronger than the religious/behavior relationship.[50] This affirms our hypotheses 1a and 2a. A supplemental Wald test confirmed that these estimated relationships were not significantly different from each other in magnitude ($\beta_{Relig} = 0.13$, $\beta_{Spir} = 0.18$, $F = 2.19$, $p = .14$).

But in the identity-focused outcomes in table 6.2, the estimated relationship between religious practice and each outcome measure was stronger than the estimated relationship between spiritual practice and each outcome measure. Supplemental Wald tests for significantly different coefficient estimates confirmed this (Civic Identity $\beta_{Relig} = 0.36$, $\beta_{Spir} = 0.18$, $F = 27.79$, $p < .001$); Spirituality & Civic Identity $\beta_{Relig} = 0.30$, $\beta_{Spir} = 0.18$, $F = 12.49$, $p < .001$); Religion and Civic Identity $\beta_{Relig} = 0.44$, $\beta_{Spir} = -0.001$, $F = 214.60$, $p < .001$]). These findings support our theory that lagged cultural identities may be present, as more frequent spiritual practitioners are not necessarily as likely to report stronger civic identities as more frequent religious practitioners. As we expected in hypotheses 1b, 1c, and 2b, religious practice is more closely tied to self-identified civic identities and religio-civic identities, while spiritual practice was more weakly associated with civic and spiritual-civic identities.

Examining table 6.2 in detail yields some additional important findings that lend further context to our understanding of American civic engagement. First, our explanatory variables for the civic behavior model produce a weaker model fit than the identity variables, with a higher BIC and lower adjusted R-squared values. This suggests that our models are better at explaining variation in respondents' identities as a civic people, rather than their actual patterns in civic behaviors reported. Second, we observe differences in the demographic correlates of reported civic behaviors (model 1) and civic identities (model 2).

Table 6.2 Regression Model Results

	Civic behavior	Civic identity	Spirituality and civic identity	Religion and civic identity
Religious practice	**0.128 (0.024)***	**0.357 (0.023)***	**0.301 (0.022)***	**0.440 (0.020)***
Spiritual practice	**0.181 (0.019)***	**0.177 (0.018)***	**0.184 (0.018)***	-0.001 (0.016)
Republican partisanship	-0.050 (0.010)***	-0.051 (0.009)***	0.006 (0.009)	0.051 (0.008)***
Belief in God	-0.060 (0.019)**	-0.025 (0.018)	0.139 (0.017)***	0.084 (0.016)***
Gay/Lesbian/Bisexual	0.295 (0.073)***	0.033 (0.069)	0.202 (0.067)**	0.017 (0.061)
No sexuality disclosed	0.232 (0.093)*	0.097 (0.088)	-0.198 (0.085)*	-0.087 (0.077)
Age	0.121 (0.020)***	0.116 (0.019)***	0.094 (0.019)***	0.016 (0.017)
Income	0.078 (0.019)***	0.028 (0.018)	0.003 (0.018)	-0.033 (0.016)*
Black	-0.171 (0.061)**	-0.005 (0.058)	-0.074 (0.056)	-0.055 (0.051)
Other race	-0.081 (0.129)	0.049 (0.122)	-0.175 (0.118)	-0.065 (0.108)
Hispanic	-0.067 (0.051)	-0.036 (0.048)	-0.098 (0.047)*	-0.067 (0.042)
2+ Race ID	0.077 (0.095)	0.205 (0.090)*	-0.051 (0.087)	-0.097 (0.079)
Asian	-0.260 (0.095)**	-0.169 (0.091)+	-0.115 (0.088)	-0.093 (0.080)
Midwest	-0.068 (0.055)	-0.003 (0.052)	-0.053 (0.051)	0.047 (0.046)
South	-0.077 (0.051)	0.052 (0.048)	0.002 (0.047)	0.081 (0.043)+
West	-0.040 (0.054)	-0.015 (0.051)	0.019 (0.049)	0.083 (0.045)+
High school diploma	0.209 (0.063)***	0.014 (0.060)	0.172 (0.058)**	0.149 (0.052)**
Some college	0.341 (0.063)***	0.043 (0.060)	0.127 (0.058)*	0.090 (0.053)+
BA+	0.555 (0.066)***	0.270 (0.062)***	0.180 (0.060)**	0.131 (0.055)*
Widowed	0.021 (0.085)	0.124 (0.081)	-0.102 (0.079)	-0.131 (0.071)+
Divorced	0.018 (0.058)	0.040 (0.055)	0.020 (0.053)	-0.074 (0.048)

(continued)

	Civic behavior	Civic identity	Spirituality and civic identity	Religion and civic identity
Separated	0.047 (0.113)	0.010 (0.108)	-0.124 (0.104)	-0.040 (0.095)
Never married	0.064 (0.048)	-0.027 (0.046)	-0.046 (0.044)	0.008 (0.040)
Living with partner	0.093 (0.064)	-0.018 (0.061)	-0.136 (0.059)*	-0.077 (0.054)
Male	-0.040 (0.035)	0.031 (0.033)	-0.036 (0.032)	-0.039 (0.029)
Catholic	-0.022 (0.057)	0.177 (0.054)**	-0.150 (0.052)**	-0.084 (0.047)+
Other Christian	-0.057 (0.049)	0.019 (0.046)	-0.034 (0.045)	-0.154 (0.041)***
Other religion	0.166 (0.067)*	0.034 (0.063)	-0.031 (0.061)	-0.349 (0.056)***
Atheist/agnostic	0.435 (0.080)***	0.218 (0.076)**	-0.074 (0.073)	-0.486 (0.066)***
Nothing in particular	0.165 (0.063)**	0.075 (0.060)	-0.076 (0.058)	-0.394 (0.053)***
Intercept	0.040 (0.124)	0.091 (0.118)	-0.584 (0.114)***	-0.430 (0.103)***
Number of observations	2,970	2,970	2,970	2,970
R^2	0.174	0.25	0.314	0.434
R^2 adjusted	0.165	0.242	0.307	0.429
AIC	8,745.9	8,441.2	8,245.5	7,671.2
BIC	8,937.8	8,633.1	8,437.3	7,863.1
Log-likelihood	-4,340.972	-4,188.591	-4,090.729	-3,803.602
F	20.621	32.586	44.806	75.237
RMSE	0.9	0.86	0.83	0.75

Notes: Two-tailed tests of significance, standardized coefficients reported with standard errors in parentheses. +p<.10, *p<.05, **p<.01, ***p<.001.

We find that some differences in reported civic behaviors across religious groups do not persist in terms of civic identities and vice versa. Catholics, for example, report stronger civic *identities* than Protestants (p<.01), even though the two groups are not significantly different in terms of their actual reported political behavior. Yet, interestingly in model 4, Protestants express marginally higher agreement that religion influences their civic identities than Catholics and significantly higher agreement with this statement than every other religious group (p<.001). These findings suggest that the explicit cultural claim to an association between religiosity and civic identities may be conceptually tied to Christian denominations in the United States, even when other groups are more civically engaged or civically self-identified. Model 3, in contrast, shows that there are few significant differences between religious groups' average rate of agreement that spirituality influences their civic lives (with the exception of Catholics versus Protestants).

In taking into account other sociodemographic factors, we observe a much clearer education gradient for reported civic and political behaviors, where each level of additional education is significantly and positively associated with additional behaviors reported. In contrast, only the difference between college completers and those with less than a high school diploma is significantly associated with reporting a higher civic identity.

Just as gay, lesbian, and bisexual respondents report significantly higher past political behaviors and higher rates of spiritual practice than heterosexual-identified respondents, they also report stronger agreement that spirituality influences their civic identities. LGB and heterosexual respondents are not significantly different in their agreement that religion shapes their civic identities. In this way, the spirituality/civic identity link and the religion/civic identity link may operate differently for different social and demographic groups, providing multiple routes to the conceptualization of an engaged, civic self that do not necessarily have to move through formal religious institutions.

These results also raise the question of how closely related civic identities and behaviors are in the general population. We estimate supplemental models in table 6.3 to test this question, using our civic-identity outcome measures as independent variables predicting reports of civic behavior in the past twelve months. These models include all the independent variables from table 6.2. We find general civic identities (model 1) are positively associated with behavioral reports, even net of controls for claiming religious and/or spiritual civic identities (model 4).

We also find that a self-reported link between spirituality and civic identity is positively associated with actual civic behavior. This affirms Steensland and colleagues' argument that some spiritual people not only perceive a link with civic behavior but also consistently report additional past civic behavior.

Claiming that religion influences one's civic behavior (model 3) is at first associated with civic behaviors, but at only half the magnitude of reporting a general civic identity. However, its relationship is fully attenuated once we control for all predictors in model 4. This suggests that the religious are particularly likely to *believe* that their religion influences their civic behavior, but such a belief is not associated with higher rates of reported civic practices in a robust manner across models when controls are included.

WHY LAGGED IDENTITIES MATTER

Our results indicate an important pattern that supports a theory of lagged cultural identities. Although reports of spiritual and

Table 6.3 Civic Identities and Civic Behavior

	Model 1	Model 2	Model 3	Model 4
Civic identity	0.281 (0.019)***			0.255 (0.019)***
Self-reported link spirituality and civic identity		0.219 (0.020)***		0.172 (0.024)***
Self-reported link religion and civic identity			0.149 (0.022)***	0.011 (0.026)
Controls	X	X	X	X
Number of observations	2,970	2,970	2,970	2,970
R^2	0.233	0.207	0.187	0.255
R^2 adjusted	0.225	0.199	0.178	0.246
AIC	8,527.6	8,625.3	8,701.6	8,446.3
BIC	8,725.5	8,823.1	8,899.5	8,656.2
Log-likelihood	−4,230.820	−4,279.633	−4,317.823	−4,188.143
F	28.783	24.787	21.752	30.402
RMSE	0.89	0.9	0.91	0.88

Notes: Two-tailed tests of significance, standardized coefficients reported with standard errors in parentheses. +p<.10, *p<.05, **p<.01, ***p<.001. Models include all independent variables from table 7.2 as controls.

religious practices are equally, positively associated with political behaviors in our data, we find that respondents do not afford them equal *credit* in fostering civic life. Instead, religious practice is more closely associated with the *perception* that one is a civic person and that religion and spirituality influence civic identity. While spiritual practice is associated with civic behavior reports, it is not as strongly associated with respondents' civic identities. We suspect this is due to the long-standing association of spirituality with the private sphere and religiosity with active public engagement in the United States.[51] When we ask people to reflect on themselves as civic people, frequent religious practitioners not only report a stronger religio-civic identity but a spiritual and religious identity as well, as compared to spiritual practitioners and nonpractitioners.

To be clear, we do still find support for the conclusion, from Steensland and colleagues, that some spiritual practitioners do agree that their spirituality influences their civic identity, and that those beliefs are significantly associated with actual civic practices.[52] In contrast, religio-civic beliefs were not as strongly associated with actual civic behavior reports as the spiritual-civic belief measure.

These findings remind us that researchers of civic and political engagement must carefully parse identities from behaviors, recognizing that normative considerations of civic engagement may skew reports of identities more than behavioral measures. Our results point to the necessity of taking social desirability bias seriously as a potential feature, not simply a bug or a source of measurement error, in our analyses.

As the editors argue in the introduction, spirituality is perfectly capable of providing similar benefits for civic life as religious practice. This insight has likely been obscured, however, by congregational religion's prominent historical role in fostering American civic identity, which, we suspect, can distort Americans' reports of their civic identities by inflating the extent to which people who see themselves as religious see themselves as people engaged in civic action and deflating the extent to which people who see themselves as spiritual *also* see themselves as engaged in civic action. Part of the reason that the narrative of selfish spirituality is so widespread is likely that people continue to hold normative, binary understandings of what constitutes public and personal identities and continue to assign religious identities to the public and relegate spiritual identities to the private.[53] Our results suggest that respondents associate religiosity with their own images of their civic selves more strongly than spirituality. This may help explain social desirability biases that contribute to religious overreports of civic behavior documented in past research. It can additionally help us understand present and future underreporting of civic behavior by spiritual practitioners.

In evaluating changing religious and spiritual behavior, scholars should remember one of the most important lessons conveyed in the civic engagement literature in works such as *Democracy in America* (1835), *Bowling Alone* (2000), and more recent accounts of civic group styles,[54] namely that an incredibly wide variety of activities can provide the experience and skills necessary to cultivate civic engagement in public life. Yet one of the challenges of studying civic and recreational activity—bowling leagues, for example—is that taste in leisure activities changes over time, so there is a good chance that social science is not currently measuring the most popular emergent leisure activities that may be providing the same kind of framework in the Tocquevillean sense for civic engagement. The activities that are transmitting civic skills may not necessarily be the activities that show up in established measures in survey data or time use. For example, secularized spiritual values, ideas, or practices may be integrated into business practices (like mindful pauses or emails at work, or leadership training at McKinsey & Co.), activism, self-help groups, or virtual communities. Indeed, Watts traces the role of spirituality in secular civic associations such as the Toastmasters and substance abuse recovery groups.[55] For the civic engagement literature, our results suggest that a clearer emphasis on different kinds of activities may be warranted to challenge or change the narrative of simple civic decline in the United States. In line with prior research in spirituality, our findings show how spiritual practice likely reproduces the social and cultural benefits often assumed to be conferred by religious practice, although in more subtle and perhaps more unconscious ways.

It is important to note that we do not necessarily focus *explicitly* on behaviors in real time, or over time. Nor can we tie our theoretical mechanism, lagged cultural identities, directly to respondents' narratives of civic behavior given our measures at hand. Future longitudinal research employing time diary studies, experience sampling methods, other behavioral trace data, and in-depth interview data will be necessary to validate our theory and findings. Much remains to be understood about *how* spiritual practitioners connect their practices invoking the sacred to civic life. For us to better understand how spirituality can contribute to civil society in the United States, future research needs to acknowledge spiritual practitioners' unique blind spots due to the romantic liberal culture of which they are a part—and take care to investigate the peripheral and lagging conscious and unconscious effects of spiritual activity. Precise and multifaceted measurement strategies rooted in practices and behavior, such as what we have modeled here, are necessary to parse through such reporting distortions and blind spots.

Despite these limitations, the findings in this chapter teach us about contemporary Americans' normative assumptions about who counts as a civic person. Among Americans, it seems that a cultural lag exists for some spiritual *and* religious practitioners who, perhaps unconsciously, continue to bundle religiosity and civic engagement together more so than spirituality and civic participation. This continues, even though the people we examined *doing* civic behavior were as likely to report spiritual practice as religious practice.

NOTES

1. Alexis de Tocqueville, *Democracy in America* (London: Penguin Classics, 2003 [1835]), 596.
2. Paul Lichterman and Nina Eliasoph, "Civic Action," *American Journal of Sociology* 120, no. 3 (2014): 809.
3. Michael Hout and Claude S. Fischer, "Why More Americans Have No Religious Preference: Politics and Generations," *American Sociological Review* 67, no. 2 (2002): 165–90; Michael Hout and Claude S. Fischer, "Explaining Why More Americans Have No Religious Preference: Political Backlash and Generational Succession, 1987–2012," *Sociological Science* 1, October (2014): 423–47; Eric Klinenberg, *Going Solo: The Extraordinary Rise and Surprising Appeal of Living Alone* (New York: Penguin, 2013).
4. Lichterman and Eliasoph, "Civic Action," 2014.
5. Matthew Desmond and Adam Travis, "Political Consequences of Survival Strategies Among the Urban Poor," *American Sociological Review* 83, no. 5 (2018): 869–96; Patricia Hill Collins, "The New Politics of Community," *American Sociological Review* 75, no. 1 (2010): 7–30.
6. Desmond and Travis, "Political Consequences," 2018.
7. Jaime Kucinskas and Evan Stewart, "Selfish or Substituting Spirituality? Clarifying the Relationship Between Spiritual Practice and Political Engagement," *American Sociological Review* 87, no. 4 (2022): 584–617; Brian Steensland, David P. King, and Barbara J. Duffy, "The Discursive and Practical Influence of Spirituality on Civic Engagement," *Journal for the Scientific Study of Religion* 61, no. 2 (2022): 389–407.

8. "Transcript: Ezra Klein Show with Russell Moore," *New York Times*, August 23, 2022.
9. Thomas A. Tweed, *The American Encounter with Buddhism, 1844–1912: Victorian Culture and the Limits of Dissent* (Chapel Hill: University of North Carolina Press, 2000).
10. Max Weber, *The Religion of India* (New York: Free Press, 1958), 331.
11. Tweed, *The American Encounter with Buddhism*.
12. Courtney Bender and Omar McRoberts, "Mapping a Field: Why and How to Study Spirituality," *Social Science Research Council Working Papers*, October 2012, https://tif.ssrc.org/wp-content/uploads/2010/05/Why-and-How-to-Study-Spirituality.pdf.
13. Katie E. Corcoran, "Emotion, Religion, and Civic Engagement: A Multilevel Analysis of US Congregations," *Sociology of Religion* 81, no. 1 (2020): 20–44; Mary Pattillo-McCoy, "Church Culture as a Strategy of Action in the Black Community," *American Sociological Review* 63, no. 6 (1998): 767–84.
14. Brad R. Fulton, "Religious Organizations: Cross-cutting the Nonprofit Sector," in *The Nonprofit Sector*, 3rd ed., ed. Walter W. Powell and Patricia Bromley (Stanford, CA: Stanford University Press, 2020), 579–98; Brad R. Fulton, "Trends in Addressing Social Needs: A Longitudinal Study of Congregation-Based Service Provision and Political Participation," *Religions* 7, no. 5 (2016): 5; Paul Lichterman, *Elusive Togetherness: Church Groups Trying to Bridge America's Divisions* (Princeton, NJ: Princeton University Press, 2005); Aldon D. Morris, *The Origins of the Civil Rights Movement* (New York: Simon & Schuster, 1986); Nathan R. Todd and Jaclyn D. Houston, "Examining Patterns of Political, Social Service, and Collaborative Involvement of Religious Congregations: A Latent Class and Transition Analysis," *American Journal of Community Psychology* 51, no. 3–4 (2013): 422–38.
15. Paul Lichterman, "Religion and the Construction of Civic Identity," *American Sociological Review* 73, no. 1 (2008): 83–104.
16. Robert N. Bellah et al., *Habits of the Heart: Individualism and Commitment in /American Life* (Berkeley: University of California Press, 1985); Richard Madsen, "The Archipelago of Faith: Religious Individualism and Faith Community in America Today," *American Journal of Sociology* 114, no. 5 (2009): 1263–1301; Wade Clark Roof et al., "American Spirituality," *Religion and American Culture* 9, no. 2 (1999): 131–57; Christian Smith and Melinda Lundquist Denton, *Soul Searching: The Religious and Spiritual Lives of American Teenagers* (Oxford: Oxford University Press, 2009); Robert Wuthnow, *The Restructuring of American Religion* (Princeton, NJ: Princeton University Press, 1988); John O'Brien, "Individualism as a Discursive Strategy of Action:

Autonomy, Agency, and Reflexivity Among Religious Americans," *Sociological Theory* 33, no. 2 (2015): 173–99.
17. Carolyn Chen, *Work Pray Code: When Work Becomes Religion in Silicon Valley* (Princeton, NJ: Princeton University Press, 2022); Galen Watts, *The Spiritual Turn: The Religion of the Heart and the Making of Romantic Liberal Modernity* (Oxford: Oxford University Press, 2022); Jaime Kucinskas, *The Mindful Elite: Mobilizing from the Inside Out* (New York: Oxford University Press, 2019).
18. Kathryn Lofton, *Oprah: The Gospel of an Icon* (Berkeley: University of California Press, 2011); Kathryn Lofton, *Consuming Religion* (Chicago: University of Chicago Press, 2017); Watts, *The Spiritual Turn*.
19. Chen, *Work Pray Code*.
20. Lewis A. Coser, *Greedy Institutions: Patterns of Undivided Commitment* (New York: Macmillan, 1974); Watts, *The Spiritual Turn*.
21. Steensland, King, and Duffy, "The Discursive and Practical Influence."
22. Ruth Braunstein, Todd N. Fuist, and Rhys H. Williams, ed., *Religion and Progressive Activism: New Stories about Faith and Politics* (New York: New York University Press, 2017); Kraig Beyerlein and John R. Hipp, "From Pews to Participation: The Effect of Congregation Activity and Context on Bridging Civic Engagement," *Social Problems* 53, no. 1 (2006): 97–117; Paul Lichterman, *Elusive Togetherness: Church Groups Trying to Bridge America's Divisions* (Princeton, NJ: Princeton University Press, 2005); Robert D. Putnam and David E. Campbell, *American Grace: How Religion Divides and Unites Us* (New York: Simon & Schuster, 2010); Christian Smith, *American Evangelicalism: Embattled and Thriving* (Chicago: University of Chicago Press, 1998); Andrew L. Whitehead and Samuel L. Perry, *Taking America Back for God: Christian Nationalism in the United States* (Oxford: Oxford University Press, 2020); Richard L. Wood and Mark R. Warren, "A Different Face of Faith-Based Politics: Social Capital and Community Organizing in the Public Arena," *International Journal of Sociology and Social Policy* 22, no. 9–10, (2002): 6–54; Robert Wuthnow and John H. Evans, *The Quiet Hand of God: Faith-Based Activism and the Public Role of Mainline Protestantism* (Berkeley: University of California Press, 2002).
23. Paul K. McClure, "Something Besides Monotheism: Sociotheological Boundary Work Among the Spiritual, but Not Religious," *Poetics* 62 (June (2017): 63.
24. Nancy T. Ammerman, *Studying Lived Religion: Contexts and Practices* (New York: New York University Press, 2021).
25. Kucinskas and Stewart, "Selfish or Substituting Spirituality?," 4.
26. Steensland, King, and Duffy, "The Discursive and Practical Influence."
27. Erving Goffman, *The Presentation of Self in Everyday Life* (Garden City, NY: Anchor Books, 1956); George H. Mead, *Mind, Self, and Society:*

From the Standpoint of a Social Behaviorist (Chicago: University of Chicago Press, 1934).
28. Goffman, *The Presentation of Self in Everyday Life*.
29. Michèle Lamont and Virág Molnár, "The Study of Boundaries in the Social Sciences," *Annual Review of Sociology* 28 (2002): 167–95; McClure, "Something Besides Monotheism."
30. C. Kirk Hadaway and Penny Long Marler, "Did You Really Go to Church This Week? Behind the Poll Data," *The Christian Century*, May 6 (1998): 472–75; C. Kirk Hadaway, Penny Long Marler, and Mark Chaves, "What the Polls Don't Show: A Closer Look at U.S. Church Attendance," *American Sociological Review* 58, no. 6 (1993): 741–52.
31. Stephen Ansolabehere and Eitan Hersh, "Validation: What Big Data Reveal about Survey Misreporting and the Real Electorate," *Political Analysis* 20, no. 4 (2012): 437–59; Philip S. Brenner and John DeLamater, "Lies, Damned Lies, and Survey Self-Reports? Identity as a Cause of Measurement Bias," *Social Psychology Quarterly* 79, no. 4 (2016): 333–54.
32. Robert N. Bellah, "Civil Religion in America," *Daedalus* 134, no. 4 (2005): 40–55; Penny Edgell, Joseph Gerteis, and Douglas Hartmann, "Atheists as 'Other': Moral Boundaries and Cultural Membership in American Society," *American Sociological Review* 71, no. 2 (2006): 211–34; Watts, *The Spiritual Turn*.
33. Watts, *The Spiritual Turn*, 223.
34. Lichterman and Eliasoph, "Civic Action."
35. Matthew Baggetta and Ricardo Bello-Gomez, "Can You Sing Your Way to Good Citizenship? Recreational Association Structures and Member Political Participation," *Social Problems* (advance access), 2023, https://doi.org/10.1093/socpro/spado27.
36. Watts, *The Spiritual Turn*, 184; Coser, *Greedy Institutions*.
37. Chen, *Work Pray Code*.
38. Jeffrey C. Alexander and Philip Smith, "The Discourse of American Civil Society: A New Proposal for Cultural Studies," *Theory and Society* 22, no. 2 (1993): 151–207.
39. Lichterman and Eliasoph, "Civic Action."
40. Kucinskas and Stewart, "Selfish or Substituting Spirituality?" Readers may note that fasting at first appears more appropriate to include in the religious rather than the spiritual practices scale. We include it in the spiritual practice scale in keeping with the measurement approach in Kucinskas and Stewart, "Selfish or Substituting Spirituality?" Their PCA analysis found that the fasting measure was more closely correlated with the spiritual practices rather than religious practices.
41. Kucinskas and Stewart, "Selfish or Substituting Spirituality?"

42. This is the same outcome variable used in Steensland, King, and Duffy, "The Discursive and Practical Influence."
43. Kucinskas and Stewart, "Selfish or Substituting Spirituality?," used this outcome variable.
44. Kucinskas and Stewart, "Selfish or Substituting Spirituality?"; Steensland, King, and Duffy, "The Discursive and Practical Influence."
45. Data from the NRSS 2020 are publicly available at the Association of Religion Data Archives: https://doi.org/10.17605/OSF.IO/GNHEF. Data collection was funded by the Fetzer Institute and Hattaway Communications.
46. Kucinskas and Stewart, "Selfish or Substituting Spirituality?"
47. Steensland, King, and Duffy, "The Discursive and Practical Influence."
48. David P. King, Barbara J. Duffy, and Brian Steensland, "The Role of Spiritual Practices in the Multidimensional Impact of Religion and Spirituality on Giving and Volunteering," *Nonprofit and Voluntary Sector Quarterly*, January 23, 2024, https://journals.sagepub.com/doi/10.1177/08997640231221533.
49. John Fox, *Applied Regression Analysis and Generalized Linear Models*, 3rd ed. (Thousand Oaks, CA: Sage, 2016).
50. Kucinskas and Stewart, "Selfish or Substituting Spirituality?"
51. Watts, *The Spiritual Turn*; Tocqueville, *Democracy in America*.
52. See Steensland, King, and Duffy, "The Discursive and Practical Influence."
53. Alexander and Smith, "The Discourse of American Civil Society"; Watts, *The Spiritual Turn*.
54. Lichterman and Eliasoph, "Civic Action."
55. Watts, *The Spiritual Turn*.

7

WHEN THE SPIRITUAL IS POLITICAL

Self-Realization and the Quest for Social Justice

GALEN WATTS

The search for authenticity, nearly everywhere we find it in modern times, is bound up with a radical rejection of things as they are.

—Marshall Berman

Something fascinating is afoot. Spirituality—widely assumed by scholars to be privatized and thus apolitical—is increasingly trumpeted by factions of the twenty-first century left; in the same breath, progressive activists, scholars, and professionals denounce the oppressive social and cultural structures that pervade modern societies—such as sexism, racism, and homophobia—while championing the need for self-realization, personal transformation, and spiritual awakening. More and more, calls for social justice are couched in the sociological language of structures, systems, and ideology critique *as well as* the therapeutic-cum-religious language of healing, learning, and growth, while spiritual practices like yoga and mindfulness meditation are regularly boasted as essential tools in the activist toolkit.

How do we make sense of these developments? From where do they come? In what ways might they challenge the academic consensus that spirituality is politically insignificant? And what do they tell us about progressive politics in twenty-first century liberal democracies? I will explore these questions, using the methods and tools of cultural sociology, by critically examining the dominant view among sociologists that "spirituality" is privatized. Most scholars have failed to appreciate the *implicit political vision* that increasingly animates talk of "spirituality" on the left. This vision holds that the spiritual quest for self-realization requires that the norms and ideas which oppress us from *within* be identified, questioned, and unlearned, while the social, political, and economic institutions which oppress us from *without* be toppled or dismantled. Or, put another way: the task of creating a socially just world demands both personal renewal and societal reform, both a consciousness-shift and policy change, both moral purification and institutional change—for only then shall we be truly liberated.

The origins of this political vision date back to the 1960s. It flows out of the romantic expressivism that animated the New Age, the New Left, and the liberation movements of this era. This cultural logic holds that mainstream social institutions and cultural norms are deeply oppressive, for they stifle, corrupt, and potentially stigmatize the benevolent authentic self that resides at the core of every individual. It goes without saying that this cultural critique is potentially quite radical. And yet, as many have pointed out, the general approach to politics espoused by members of the New Age movement was to focus narrowly on the individual; New Agers largely saw the spiritual path as one of personal transformation rather than institutional reform, and hence many continue to view "spirituality" without "religion" as lacking political significance. However, during and in the wake of the 1960s, many progressive scholars and activists adapted the discourse of spirituality for their own emancipatory purposes. In the process they produced *a new kind of politics*, one that sees the *spiritual quest for self-realization* and the *political quest for social justice* as two sides of the same coin and thus demands *both* inner *and* outer transformation. Although it has taken a number of years, this political vision has gradually moved from the cultural margins to the center. Indeed, seen through a discourse analysis of best-selling books, academic tracts, journal articles, websites, and op-eds, this political imaginary has not only increasingly become common sense among progressive activists and scholars but now finds institutional support across a variety of primary and secondary institutions. In a word, the spiritual has gone political.

SPIRITUALITY: PRIVATE/PERSONAL OR PUBLIC/POLITICAL?

As Linda Woodhead observes, the consensus among scholars is that spirituality is privatized and thus apolitical.[1] However, within this consensus there exist roughly two schools of thought. One camp, following the logic of secularization theory, contends that spirituality is apolitical, first because it is not "real" religion, and second, because it remains excluded from and disinterested in the "public sphere." On this view, spirituality remains ineffectual and impotent owing to its limited scope and ambitions; far removed from the levers of state power, and more concerned with intimate relations and self-esteem than the heady world of electoral politics and civic engagement, spirituality is interpreted as a mere consumer preference with little public or political significance.[2] Aptly illustrating this view, Bryan Turner contends,

"The growth of post-institutional, post-Christian spirituality appears to be the perfect counterpart to the erosion of citizenship and the emergence of the passive subject." He thus concludes, "spirituality does not have the socially transformative potentialities of organised religions."[3]

The other camp, taking a more critical perspective, argues that spirituality is apolitical because it is quietist or accommodationist. On this view, spirituality fails to be properly "political" because it endorses personal solutions to what proponents view as structural, that is, public problems, encouraging political quietism rather than resistance.[4] According to this school, then, spirituality is politically consequential only in the sense that it preserves the status quo—thus, it is not really "political" at all. Exemplifying this perspective, Jeremy Carrette and Richard King contend, "Privatised spirituality emerges here as the new cultural Prozac bringing transitory feelings of ecstatic happiness and thoughts of self-affirmation, but never addressing sufficiently the underlying problem of social isolation and injustice."[5]

Admittedly, there is some truth in both these views. Spirituality is rarely explicitly mobilized at the level of electoral politics or among groups in civil society.[6] There are no "spiritual but not religious" political parties, citizens and politicians tend not to couch their public addresses in the language of spirituality,[7] and there are few, if any, interest groups lobbying on the basis of spiritual demands. Moreover, as a stand-alone discourse, spirituality is unabashedly individualistic, focused, as it is, on *self-realization* and *personal* transformation.[8] So it makes sense to think of spirituality as what José Casanova would call a "private religion," if by that we mean a form of religion that does not seek to mobilize publicly against competing religious and secular movements or institutionalize itself in the form of a political party.[9] Yet the claim that it lacks public or political significance warrants scrutiny.

For one, as Anna Fedele and Kim Knibbe point out, the distinction between public and private has historically been both value-laden and deeply gendered, with the private/personal sphere associated with domesticity, passivity, and femininity and therefore devalued, while the public/political sphere was associated with productivity, activity, and masculinity, and therefore esteemed.[10] Now, I do not think that the distinction between public and private is per se gendered in this way—that is, one can reasonably make a distinction between the "personal/private" and the "political/public" without thereby valuing one over the other. However, it cannot be denied that many of the claims proffered from within these two schools of thought subtly, if unwittingly, reify this gendered binary.[11] For another, I fear that owing to the assumptions animating these two accounts, much of importance has been obscured. Consider: while those in the first camp may be right that spirituality is "private" in that it does not seek to engage in "politics" as conceived within liberal or civic republican political theory, whereby the political/public is associated with the state, while the personal/private is associated with the family and the market,[12] these scholars mistake their analytical categories for social reality. For it is one thing to contend that spirituality is privatized in that it finds a natural home in the "private sphere," as one defines it, and quite another to conclude that it therefore lacks "socially transformative potentialities."

Part of the problem, as Dick Houtman and I note in the introduction, stems from an erroneous conception of spirituality: many in the first camp assume that spirituality lacks cultural coherence and institutional support. Invocations of "spirituality," on this view, lack any stable cultural core, or shared underlying logic. But as the chapters in this volume demonstrate, this is just plain wrong; not only is spirituality a coherent discourse, but it also finds support in many "public" institutions (e.g., education, the arts, corporations, etc.), even if not the state.

But there is more to it than this. Accepting the liberal distinction between private/personal and public/political spheres, this school of thought tends to conceive of religions that primarily concern themselves with personal life as lacking political significance.[13] Indeed, this explains why spiritual practitioners are commonly charged with being narcissistic, selfish, and politically disengaged.[14] Needless to say, this view mistakenly assumes that a concern with personal life precludes a lack of concern for public life.[15] And in so doing, it fails to appreciate that the discourse of spirituality is increasingly tethered to a broad political imaginary that views self-transformation as a necessary, if not sufficient, condition for realizing a socially just world. Furthermore, it neglects the fact that what takes place within the "private/personal" sphere can have enormous implications for the "public/political sphere"—what is most important, it can lead to a radical redrawing of the boundary that separates them.

This insight lies at the core of José Casanova's *Public Religions in the Modern World*. In this work he theorizes what he calls the "deprivatization of modern religion," a process he contends comes in three forms: first, when religions enter civil society to force the public to reflect upon what constitutes public morality (e.g., conservative Protestant mobilization against abortion); second, when religions enter the public sphere to contest the functionalist and instrumentalist logics institutionalized within the two major societal systems of the state and the economy (e.g., the Roman Catholic Church's criticisms of free-market capitalism); and third, when religions insist on making public what liberal societies have deemed private moral issues (e.g., religious appeals to the "common good"). So, for Casanova, what it means for a religion to "go public"—and therefore, "get political"—is, in effect, for it *to contest the boundaries between the public and private* as institutionalized in modern liberal societies.

The reason this is noteworthy is that, while it might be true that spirituality is not "public" in the same way, say, American conservative evangelicalism is, I nevertheless believe we are increasingly seeing a form of spirituality that, taking inspiration from (or better yet, synthesizing with) second-wave feminism and other liberationist discourses, functions to *politicize* the *personal*—and thus could arguably qualify as a kind of "public religion."[16] Of course, whether or not spirituality is in the process of "deprivatizing," as Casanova defines it, is less interesting than the fact that by identifying the sources of individual and societal oppression as *both* within *and* without, the type of spirituality that we increasingly see championed on the political left offers justification for quite radical personal *and* structural reform—and is therefore anything but politically insignificant.

Among those in the second camp, the assumptions are rather different. Proponents of this view do not accept, either analytically or normatively, the liberal distinction between public and private; indeed, it is precisely owing to their skepticism of this distinction that they charge spirituality with lacking political significance. Thus, from within this school of thought, to be properly "political" is to speak in terms of structures and systems, not individuals. Indeed, to prescribe personal transformation is in effect to "blame the victim," or to treat the symptoms rather than the causes of injustice. Proponents interpret the focus on personal life—emotional processes, thought and behavioral patterns, self-development—typical of spirituality as less socially transformative than conservative, a form of legitimation for the status quo. The problem with this account is that it mistakenly assumes that attention to the personal precludes attention to the institutional, or that talk of the "spiritual" cannot be reconciled with talk of social structures. That is, as a result of narrowly focusing on the rhetoric of personal transformation and self-realization typical of spiritual discourse, advocates of this school have thereby ignored the growing extent to which these ideals are increasingly tied to a broader political imaginary wherein the spiritual and the structural are conceived as necessary allies in the fight for social justice. And in doing so, they significantly underestimate the socially transformative, and thus politically consequential, potential of spirituality today.

THE EXPRESSIVE REVOLUTION AND THE BIRTH OF A NEW KIND OF PROGRESSIVE POLITICS

It is a near truism that the 1960s was a period of tremendous cultural and social upheaval. Myriad movements were spawned, social experimentation flourished, and the spirit of utopianism reigned, particularly among the young. Scholars have struggled to produce a comprehensive account of what took place at this time, given the sheer diversity of cultural innovation produced. However, most would agree that beneath the dizzying array of "experiments in living" born during this era lay a shared, if inchoate, cultural logic—what we might call, following Charles Taylor, romantic expressivism.[17]

Precisely when this logic found its first articulation will forever remain a mystery, but it is scholarly convention to trace it back to Jean-Jacques Rousseau. In *The Social Contract*, Rousseau put into words what would later become a rallying cry of revolutionaries around the world; positing a radical disjunction between his true inner self and the outer world of social norms and cultural conventions, he proclaimed, "Man is born free, but is everywhere in chains." With this proclamation, Rousseau basically invented the romantic view of identity, which holds that who we *really* are is *presocial*, that our essential core predates the process of socialization.[18] Of course, an important corollary of this view is that humans are fundamentally good. As Irving Babbitt explains in *Rousseau and Romanticism*, "Evil, says Rousseau, foreign to man's constitution, is introduced into it from without. . . . Instead of the old dualism between good and evil in the breast of the individual, a new dualism is thus set up between artificial and corrupt society and 'nature.'"[19] It also follows from romantic expressivism that what is right or true for one individual may not be so for another—given that each of us has a unique authentic self within us, we may well have our own (inner) truths. Indeed, it is for just this reason that, from within this cultural logic, society must necessarily be the source of ignorance, moral corruption, and oppression: for if goodness and truth reside within us, then any lack of these in our lives, it naturally follows, must be the result of the distorting, alienating, and corrupting forces of our social environment.

This cultural logic became commonsense among 1960s youth, inspiring the radicalism of the counterculture, and animating many, if not most, of the social movements of the era.[20] Indeed, it is for this reason that Talcott Parsons labeled this great swelling up of Rousseauvian fervor the "Expressive Revolution."[21] Armed with a romantic expressivist logic, students and progressive activists experienced the *doxa* of their societies as alienating and oppressive. And in response, they rose up, vehemently criticizing almost every mainstream institution—from the Christian churches, to the school, to the nuclear family, to the capitalist corporation—for stifling and repressing their authentic selves.[22]

Amid this uproar the New Age movement emerged, eventually establishing itself as the religious (or rather "spiritual") wing of the counterculture.

New Agers freely borrowed from humanistic psychological discourse; as natural bricoleurs, they culled from both "secular" or "religious" sources. But what they popularized, above all else was a conception of spirituality that derived its logic from Rousseau's expressivism. Indeed, in almost every respect, New Agers typified the countercultural type, embracing the expressivist critique of mainstream society along with a romantic conception of identity.[23] The New Age rejection of "religion" was premised on wholly romantic presuppositions: religions were institutional by-products of society and thus oppressive, while "spirituality" was a personal by-product of Nature and thus liberating.[24] Moreover, the ultimate goal of life, New Agers declared, was for each person to find and follow their own truth and to realize their true self.[25] In fact, this was, in a nutshell, what it meant to be "spiritual." Importantly, New Agers thus willingly endorsed the same critique proffered by liberationists and political radicals of the period: they too diagnosed the social and cultural structures of society as fundamentally corrupting, alienating, and at odds with human flourishing. They too decried the state of the modern industrial world. And they too saw the need for social transformation. Hence the need for a "New Age."[26]

Yet most New Agers were decidedly inward-looking. While they might have been revolutionaries in spirit, their model of social change was narrowly individualistic.[27] *Personal transformation alone will produce societal reform*—this was their credo. And it derived, primarily, from placing an extreme emphasis on the power of individual consciousness: it was an earnest belief among many New Agers that the outer world is a mere reflection of the inner world, such that to the extent that one changes the latter, the former will naturally follow. Indeed, in some iterations of New Age thought, the existence of an "outer world" was actually denied, for it was assumed that we are creators of our own reality by means of our thought processes. So it became commonplace for those identified with the New Age movement to turn away from "politics" toward the "personal" and preoccupy themselves with identifying unhealthy habits, unconscious beliefs, and instinctual emotional responses that were preventing them from realizing their true spiritual selves.

No doubt this was often quite hard work. The most devoted New Agers removed themselves from society, set up communes, and adopted extremely alternative (sometimes ascetic) lifestyles. Even those who did not take it this far often took the task of self-inquiry very seriously, engaging in long and painstaking forms of therapy of the post-Freudian variety. Paradoxically, then, to realize one's authentic self-demanded intense discipline, effort, and work—and lots of them.[28] But despite their utopianism, the presumption among most New Agers was that the task could be completed without policy or structural reform.

It is this accommodationist legacy that continues to shape academic thought about spirituality. And, admittedly, not entirely without warrant. In the wake of the 1960s, as spirituality migrated beyond the quixotic borderlands of New Age communes and West Coast retreat centers, infiltrating, via popular culture, literature, and film, mainstream Western culture, it was this inward-facing strand of spirituality that often found wide resonance with Western publics. Moreover, in the 1980s and 1990s, as the market for books, workshops, and business seminars on spirituality grew, New Age gurus such as Deepak Chopra and Wayne Dwyer often reframed the spiritual path to cohere with the logic of consumer capitalism.[29] Spirituality in the 1980s therefore became unabashedly world-affirming: the quest for self-realization could now comfortably take place within mainstream society as it was; to achieve "authenticity" was reduced to being "nice," getting along with one's colleagues, and having a positive attitude; and self-development was increasingly oriented toward achieving material success. Furthermore, the expressivist critique of mainstream society earlier championed by political radicals and commune dwellers was significantly tamed; the primary sources of oppression in society, the discourse of spirituality now held, were not systemic sexism, racism, or homophobia, but parents.

At the same time, despite these processes of domestication, spirituality always remained the preserve of those with left-of-center sympathies.[30] It was rarely a force for social conservatism. But the fact is that the spiritual quest for self-realization often remained a private matter—primarily concerned with acclimating people to whatever circumstances they found themselves in (be it, the home, the office, or the market). Yet despite this quietist legacy, the New Age movement also birthed a strand of spirituality that was decidedly more outward-looking. Or perhaps it is more accurate to say that members of the various liberation movements that emerged during this period, who shared with New Agers a commitment to romantic expressivism, adapted the discourse of spirituality for their own political purposes. For these activists and scholars, the quest for self-realization and the quest for social justice were one and the same, for a truly just society, they argued, would be one where every individual is able to be their authentic self. Moreover, the "authentic self" championed by this group, far from being conceived as a merely "nice" and congenial individual, was one that had rid itself of all unconscious biases, oppressive beliefs, and residual prejudices—an almost saintly figure. Among this group, the language of "spirituality" became critical to discussing the inner work required in the fight against oppression—work that was, in their view, necessary (but not sufficient) to achieving social justice.

SPIRITUALITY AND THE INNER WORK OF SOCIAL JUSTICE

Feminism and the Politics of Authenticity

When activist and writer Carol Hanisch coined the feminist slogan the "personal is political" she had multiple meanings in mind.[31] First, she sought to draw attention to those issues which liberal states at the time deemed "private" that, in her view, ought to be open to "public" (state) scrutiny and regulation—for instance, domestic violence and workplace discrimination. In this way, Hanisch was committed to *politicizing the personal*—expanding those areas of social life that she thought should be subject to state, or legislative, intervention. However, her slogan also sought to *personalize the political* by conceiving of the oppressive structures of society as having colonized and corrupted the subjectivities of modern women. Crucially, this political move derived from a romantic expressivist logic: for Hanisch, along with many other feminists of the time,[32] the authentic self within each and every modern woman was stifled and distorted as a result of growing up in a patriarchal and sexist society. Thus, realizing a truly just world required not merely changing the patriarchal structures responsible for this but also recovering from the traumas already inflicted—that is, it required what Hanisch called "political therapy."[33]

Now, it merits mentioning that many feminists of the period challenged this expressivist logic; some did so from a Marxist perspective, while others took a more classically liberal view. But I think it fair to say that romantic expressivism remained an important, even dominant, strand of feminist thought. Indeed, we can see this in the scholarly literature of that period.[34]

In a well-known critique of the work of Catherine MacKinnon, who questioned the need for authenticity-talk in feminist politics, legal scholar Ruth Colker wrote in the pages of the *Boston University Law Review*, "I believe that we have an authentic self because assuming that we do *not* have an authentic self makes no sense to me. For example, through our feminist work, we try to peel away social influences that limit our authenticity or freedom. If we are successful in our attempt to peel away those influences, what would be left? It only makes sense for me to assume that what would be left would be our authentic selves."[35] Colker's position was by no means exceptional. Moreover, it aptly illuminates the logic of expressivism as it was adapted by feminists: feminism as a political project presupposes the existence of an authentic self. In fact, it requires it:

> Society has strongly influenced our gender, as well as our larger personhood. We need to struggle against limiting forces in our lives to move toward authenticity, which, in terms of our feminist work, means struggling against the forces of patriarchy. Our glimpses of our authentic selves can provide us with the strength and direction necessary to struggle against the brokenness and subordination in our lives. Without a sense of our authentic selves, we would have no basis for selecting priorities in our feminist struggles.[36]

As Colker's example makes clear, for many post-1960s feminists, feminism entailed a "politics of authenticity."[37] The goal was to create a world where women could be their true selves. To achieve this, feminists in the 1960s and 1970s theorized that certain tools would be necessary; one was the practice of consciousness-raising.[38]

According to Katie Sarachild, who introduced the practice in a paper presented at the First National Women's Liberation Conference in 1973, consciousness-raising serves to help women identify and challenge the "male supremacist Establishment and its forces of discrimination" as they pervade the modern female consciousness—that is, to identify the "political" dimensions of their "personal" problems.[39] Or, following Colker, we might say that a central purpose of this practice is to help feminists distinguish between their authentic self, and the polluting forces of society. Indeed, this inner work is considered crucial to the feminist project.

Now, it is important to keep in mind that among almost all second-wave feminists consciousness-raising was seen as only one among many necessary resources in the fight against injustice. As Colker observed, "Our journey toward authenticity . . . requires more than discovering our inner selves. We also need to work to create a world in which we can freely *experience* our authentic selves."[40] What this requires, she argued, is dismantling, or at least significantly reforming, the institutions, laws, and policies that were stifling the self-realization of women in society. The reason for this is that the source of feminist oppression, Colker averred, was in *society*, not the self. But given that women had been *socialized* into a patriarchal and sexist society—leaving their authentic selves distorted and hindered—romantic expressivist feminists like Colker held that an interest in the institutional could never be divorced from a preoccupation with the personal. Indeed, the two were seen as necessarily bound together.

Nor was she alone. In the opening pages of her book *Revolution from Within*, feminist activist and journalist Gloria Steinem writes, "I, who had spent the previous dozen years working on external barriers to women's equality, had to admit there were internal ones too." Steinem goes on to suggest that feminists need to take the inner barriers to emancipation just as seriously the outer ones. Indeed, for her, "self-esteem"—how women feel about themselves—is a *political* problem, not merely a *personal* one. Moreover, this flows directly out of a romantic expressivist logic. She writes, "somewhere within each of us, buried at varying depths depending on the age and degree of neglect or abuse, shame or coercion we endured, there is a resistant, daydreaming, rebellious, creative, unique child—a true self who is waiting." For Steinem, a chief aspect of the feminist project is to uncover this "unique and true self"—what requires both institutional change *and* self-work.[41]

What of the discourse of spirituality? Where does it enter the picture? No doubt, much feminist activism in the 1960s was avowedly secular, in some cases even antireligious. Yet there always remained a strand of feminism that enthusiastically embraced the language of spirituality, especially when discussing the imperative of *inner work*—that is, the work of distinguishing the parts of one's self that are by-products of society from those that are authentically one's own, and the work of unlearning the former while recovering the latter. For proponents of this strand, the feminist project itself was often seen as "spiritual" in nature. For instance, according to Colker, "the search for authenticity can be a dynamic, feminist-spiritual journey. We can try to create a space of inner peace where we can catch a glimpse of ourselves removed from patriarchy and the other limiting influences of modern society. In this state of inner peace, we can attempt to discover our selves behind and beyond our selves—what I call our 'authentic' selves."[42]

Similarly, Steinem writes in *Revolution from Within*, "any religion in which God looks suspiciously like the ruling class is very different from spirituality that honors the godliness in each of us." She then adds, "all religions still have within them some tradition of listening to an inner voice and therefore acknowledging the sacred worth of each individual and of nature."[43] Thus expressivist feminists like Colker and Steinem adapted the discourse of spirituality in order to speak about the inner work they believed was required by the feminist project, thereby helping to pioneer a trend in feminist thought that has grown increasingly prominent.

Self-Recovery in Black Radical Thought

Some might argue that this preoccupation with inner spiritual work has always been the preserve of privileged white feminists. But this overlooks recent developments within black feminist thought. While it is true that the civil rights movement largely eschewed the language of expressivism, in its wake there emerged a strand of black political thought which, as Clovis Semmes reports, "suggested the need to be free of a slave mentality and White cultural corporation domination." Moreover, in order to do this, the logic went, "one had to understand, and to truly tap into, one's innate but unused capabilities for self-control and personal elevation."[44] For instance, in their 1968 book *Black Rage* William H. Grier and Price M. Cobbs shed light on the myriad psychological wounds inflicted on blacks owing to the history of slavery in America.[45] Semmes therefore concludes that, within a specific strand of black radical thought, there has always been an "important relationship between progressive politics and personal transformation."[46]

We see this clearly in the work of the late black feminist scholar and activist bell hooks. In her *Sisters of the Yam: Black Women and Self-Recovery*, hooks writes, "Those of us committed to the feminist movement, to black liberation struggle, need to work for self-actualization." In fact, she urges her readers to "see self-actualization as part of our efforts to resist white supremacy and sexist oppression."[47] Then, anticipating backlash from her fellow black feminists, hooks writes,

> often when I tell black folks that I believe the realm of mental health, of psychic well-being, is an important arena for black liberation struggle, they reject the idea that any "therapy"—be it in a self-help program or a professional therapeutic setting—could be a location for political praxis. This should be no surprise. Traditional therapy, mainstream psychoanalytic practices, often do not consider "race" an important issue, and as a result do not adequately address the mental-health dilemmas of black people. Yet these dilemmas are very real. They persist in our daily life and they undermine our capacity to live fully and joyously. They even prevent us from participating in organized collective struggle aimed at ending domination and transforming society. In traditional southern black folk life, there was full recognition that the needs of the spirit had to be addressed if individuals were to be fully self-actualized.[48]

From within hooks's expressivist framework, the quest for emancipation requires attention to both the inner and the outer—and this is especially so for members of marginalized communities who have been scarred and traumatized by the oppressive structures of society, by systemic racism, sexism, and heterosexism. On the one hand, then, hooks asks her fellow black feminists to decolonize their minds, which she defines as "breaking with the ways our reality is defined and shaped by the dominant culture." On the other, she contends that "working to build communities of resistance that are particularly focused on social and political concerns is always necessary." Thus hooks seeks, in her words, to "politicize movements for self-recovery,"[49] not by reducing the political to the personal but rather by attending to both. In other words, for hooks the politics of authenticity demands radical structural reform—the dismantling of racial hierarchies, and a comprehensive antiracist platform implemented across society—but it also requires that people of color who have internalized these oppressive ideas struggle to unlearn them.

Furthermore, it is notable that hooks, like Colker and Steinem, invokes the language of spirituality when discussing the inner work she views as a prerequisite for collective emancipation. She writes, "the spiritual and the religious are not necessarily one and the same. My intent is to share the insight that cultivating spiritual life can enhance the self-recovery process and enable the healing of wounds." In fact, she makes crystal clear her commitment to spirituality in the closing pages of *Sisters of the Yam*: "Living a life in the spirit, a life where our habits of being enable us to hear inner voices, to comprehend reality with both our hearts and our minds, puts us in touch with divine essence. Practicing the art of living is one way we sustain contact with our 'higher self.'"[50]

Privilege and the "Spiritual" Task of Oppressors

We have seen that from within the progressive imagination bequeathed to us by the Expressive Revolution of the 1960s, the quest for social justice has increasingly been conceived as a quest for self-realization—for the just society is one where all members of society are able to be their authentic selves. In turn, according to feminists like Colker, Steinem, and hooks, the cultural and social structures of patriarchy, sexism, and racism must be reconstructed or dismantled. Equally, it is imperative for members of marginalized and stigmatized communities that have internalized oppressive social and cultural structures to engage in processes of consciousness-raising and self-work (frequently couched in the language of spirituality) in order to unlearn these habits of feeling and thought, thereby freeing their true selves. However, it is not only the disadvantaged that must engage in inner work, for the privileged are equally caught up in webs of domination and inauthenticity.

We see this clearly in the work of Robin DiAngelo. A diversity trainer and best-selling author of *White Fragility*, DiAngelo focuses less on the inner work required of the marginalized than on that demanded of the *privileged*. Adopting the expressivist critique of society popularized in the 1960s, she argues, "racism is infused in every part of our society, our beings, and our perspectives."[51] What is more, "Since all individuals who live within a racist system are enmeshed in its relations," DiAngelo reasons, "this means that all are responsible for either perpetuating or transforming that system."[52] It follows, she contends, that white people have a dual moral responsibility: to "work on our own internalized oppression—the ways in which we impose limitations on ourselves based on the societal messages we receive about the inferiority of the lower status groups we belong to" as well as "the internalized dominance that results from being socialized in a racist society—the ways in which we consciously or unconsciously believe that we are more important, more valuable, more intelligent, and more deserving than people of color."[53]

It is useful to make explicit the logic of DiAngelo's arguments, since they have been subject to innumerable misinterpretations.[54] Critics have assumed that in her work DiAngelo indicts "white people" while raising up "black people." But this misconstrues the expressivism at the core of her thinking. For DiAngelo, "whiteness" and "blackness" are social and cultural constructs, and thus not who anyone *truly* is. Rather, it is the *socialization* process that her work attacks, the process whereby particular cultural judgements about "whiteness" and "blackness" are internalized by individuals, for she views *this* as the primary source of oppression. The reason this matters is that it follows from within DiAngelo's expressivist schema that being privileged is not actually in anyone's interest, for it serves to "maintain a state of *false* consciousness," and thus keep the privileged person both ignorant and inauthentic.[55] Or put another way: prejudice, internalized dominance, and racist beliefs, for DiAngelo, harm the (white) individual who harbors them, since they prohibit that person from realizing their authentic self. Finally, despite what some have suggested, DiAngelo is adamant that her politics are not merely inward looking. Rather, she views the quest for racial justice as taking place along two fronts: first, in efforts to combat "institutionalized racism" and second, at the personal level, in the form of "anti-racist education."[56]

Of course, DiAngelo rarely adopts the language of spirituality when discussing the inner work she prescribes. Yet it should not be difficult to see that it easily lends itself to it. For just as expressivist feminists like Colker, Steinem, and hooks have held that the process of unlearning requires painstaking and prolonged self-work, so too does DiAngelo maintain that this process "cannot be addressed from an intellectual place; it must be an experiential, long-term process."[57] And indeed, this explains why many others inspired by her work have freely adopted a more explicitly spiritual approach.

In his book *Stay Woke*, African American activist and writer Justin Michael Williams instructs readers how to use "spiritual" practices to challenge the limiting beliefs and/or unlearn the discriminatory ideas they've internalized. Similarly, in *Do Better: Spiritual Activism for Fighting and Healing from White Supremacy*, antiracist educator Rachel Ricketts outlines a spiritual program to root out the inner pathologies produced by living in a systemically racist society. Legal scholar and writer Ronda V. Magee likewise offers counsel to the disadvantaged and the privileged seeking self-realization in her *The Inner Work of Racial Justice*—a book that, like Ricketts's, explicitly champions spiritual practices such as meditation in accomplishing this task. In fact, it has become commonplace today to read of the emancipatory implications of spiritual practices such as mindfulness and yoga.[58] For instance, Deborah Orr remarks, "feminist scholars have theorized that yoga techniques can help women access unoccupied subjective sites from which to mount resistance to oppressive discourses by enabling them to develop forms of self-acceptance."[59] Indeed, an example of this literature is the academic textbook *Social Justice, Inner Work & Contemplative Practice*, in which contributor Sheryl Petty contends, "the intersection of *inner work* and *social justice* can lead to the natural unfolding of joy, compassion, clarity, and all the positive qualities, and can also wake up fundamental parts of our humanity that have been deadened."[60] Another example, found in the same volume, is Gale Young's description of her harrowing and painful "journey into owning my own Whiteness":

> For the first time I had empathy for myself and could, with a wider heart, invite in more perspectives of others' experiences. I

let myself feel my fear and could begin to see and understand others' fear. I could practice the courage to witness the harm done to me by others by oppressive, unjust laws and practices. I could own the harm I unknowingly passed on to others. I was able to "sit with" these awful and powerful feelings time and time again, and still do. I needed the help of my therapist and meditation practice to do so.[61]

As this example makes clear, increasingly, spiritual practices are mobilized in the interest of realizing not just the authentic self, but also a more just world.

Purifying the Soul for the Sake of Social Justice

As should be clear, the spiritual quest for self-realization as it is articulated within the contemporary progressive imaginary is incredibly morally demanding. Because the authentic self is conceived as fundamentally benevolent—and thus antiracist, antisexist, and antiheterosexist in nature—the spiritual task of self-realization demands intense work on one's self in order realize a form of subjectivity that is free of prejudices, implicit biases, ill will, or internalized dominance. Those who are committed to spirituality, on this view, must work tirelessly to purge themselves of all traces of internalized dominance, internalized oppression, and any other remnant of the polluting process of socialization. However, because the source of oppression is said to derive from *society*, rather than *self*, from within this political imaginary, inner work is widely considered necessary yet insufficient to realize a just world. Indeed, hearts must change, but so too must the structures that surround them.

MAPPING THE PROGRESSIVE IMAGINARY

In the 1960s and '70s, New Agers, in romantic expressivist fashion, rejected modern institutions but prescribed as a remedy quietism: rather than join these institutions, they instead retreated from them. But in the ensuing years, many members of the liberationist movements of this period entered the primary and secondary institutions of modern liberal societies and set to work disseminating the type of romantic expressivism they had crafted. As a result, this political vision has not only steadily gained traction among contemporary progressives, but it is increasingly making its way into key primary and secondary institutions—leading to changes at both the *spiritual* (personal) and *structural* (institutional) levels.

Consider first the personal: as Foucault has taught us, to the extent that particular discourses and technologies of the self become institutionalized within specific fields, they can have significant social consequences. So it is noteworthy that one increasingly finds within the corporate and educational worlds novel diversity training seminars and workshops like those of DiAngelo that function to disseminate this political vision.[62] In these trainings, employees learn how to interrogate and identify the stereotypes, implicit biases, and prejudices they have unwittingly internalized. They are taught how to deconstruct their own oppressor and oppressed identities and to uncover the authentic, unbiased, and virtuous self that lies beneath these social constructs. Furthermore, participants who belong to minority groups learn not only how to heal from the psychological wounds inflicted on them from living in an unjust society, but also how to identify the slights and harms (sometimes called "microaggressions") that function to stifle their self-realization.

Similar developments are also taking place within healthcare. For instance, in 2018 the American Psychological Association released its official guidelines for psychological practice with boys and men. In the guidelines, the association maintains that boys are oppressed by a "dominant ideology of masculinity." And we have increasingly seen in public discourse denunciations of "toxic masculinity," which is said to stunt the cognitive, intellectual, and emotional growth of boys and men.[63] In these developments, it is not difficult to detect the logic of expressivism: the implicit claim is that in order for boys and men to realize their true (nontoxic) selves, they must unlearn the oppressive ideas they have been socialized into. Furthermore, the American Medical Association and the Association of American Medical Colleges recently released a report titled, "Advancing Health Equity: A Guide to Language, Narrative and Concepts," which lays out a long list of terms and phrases that these professional associations contend are harmful and thus should be retired. The report reads, "Our responsibility is to develop and embody critical consciousness and to be aware of how our choices of words reinforce dominant narratives, and when they open possibilities for moving toward equity." In short, the increasing attention to self-work within the corporate, educational, and healthcare fields is evidence, I believe, of the growing prevalence of this progressive imaginary.

Nevertheless, some might doubt that a discourse so focused on the *personal* (self-work) can be publicly or politically significant. However, this view underestimates the radical character of the politics of authenticity—which seeks, in its progressive guise, to redraw the boundary between public and private. As I have made clear, it is increasingly accepted among progressives that the quest for self-realization requires *both* inner *and* outer change, and the reason for this is that ostensibly "personal" issues such as self-esteem and self-image are, on this view, considered "political"—the result of oppressive social structural forces. So while inner work is prescribed as a solution, so too is institutional reform. Indeed, for many progressives today, the task of successful self-realization is made impossible by the continued existence of racist, sexist, and heterosexist discourses and ideologies.

This helps to explain why we have seen significant institutional changes co-occur alongside the rise of these individualistic discourses. For instance, it has become the norm for corporations, educational institutions, arts organizations, and even governments to produce and enforce antiracist policies.[64] Moreover, across a variety of institutional fields there have been widespread efforts to increase the diversity and inclusion of minorities—be they racial, sexual, gendered, or otherwise. In education and media, there have recently been significant sanctions brought against those who are seen to uphold the unjust status quo, be it through the language they use or the particular views they publicly express, a practice that is often called by its critics "cancel culture."[65]

Leaving aside positive or negative judgments, what is clear is that these sanctions follow naturally from the progressive politics of authenticity—to the extent that particular words, narratives, or tropes reify and reaffirm discriminatory beliefs, they are said to cause harm. For it is commonly believed that individuals can only realize their true selves in institutional spaces which have been purged of the oppressive forces of sexism, racism, and heterosexism. In short, the rise of discourses on self-work have actually been coterminous with a rise in institutional changes (at times, even at the level of the state). And this is not coincidental, for both of these flow naturally out of the broad romantic expressivist vision that has made inroads on the political left.

Of course, discourses of self-work have both secular and spiritual renditions. For some progressive activists, to speak of the inner work of racial or social justice need not entail a spiritual dimension. Indeed, for some, talk of spirituality may be entirely anathema. But as the examples I listed earlier suggest, it would be mistaken to discount the attraction of spirituality to contemporary progressives. For while the discourse of spirituality may be "personal," it is increasingly tethered to a broad vision which is expressly "political," and thus focused on institutional change. Accordingly, scholars who have narrowly focused on the rhetoric of self-realization and personal transformation have failed to appreciate the political vision that animates these concepts. At its most basic, this is a vision that aspires to a world where all individuals can be their authentic selves; and in doing so it sees both inner and outer work as necessary to get the job done.

NOTES

1. Linda Woodhead, "New Forms of Public Religion: Spirituality in Global Civil Society," in *Religion Beyond Its Private Role in Modern Society*, ed. Wim Hofstee and Arie van der Kooij (Danvers: Brill, 2013), 29–54.
2. Robert N. Bellah et al., *Habits of the Heart: Individualism and Commitment in American Life* (Berkeley: University of California Press, 1985); David Voas and Alasdair Crockett, "Religion in Britain: Neither Believing nor Belonging," *Sociology* 39, no. 1 (2005): 11–28; Steve Bruce, "Secularization and the Impotence of Individualized Religion," *Hedgehog Review* 8 (Spring–Summer 2006): 35–45; Steve Bruce, *Secular Beats Spiritual: The Westernization of the Easternization of the West* (Oxford: Oxford University Press, 2017).
3. Bryan S. Turner, *Religion and Modern Society: Citizenship, Secularization and the State* (Cambridge: Cambridge University Press, 2013), 177, 208.
4. Véronique Altglas, *From Yoga to Kabbalah: Religious Exoticism and the Logics of Bricolage* (Oxford: Oxford University Press, 2014); Jeremy

Carrette and Richard King, *Selling Spirituality: The Silent Takeover of Religion* (London: Routledge, 2005); Craig Martin, *Capitalizing Religion: Ideology and the Opiate of the Bourgeoisie* (London: Bloomsbury, 2014); James Dennis LoRusso, *Spirituality, Corporate Culture, and American Business: The Neoliberal Ethic and the Spirit of Global Capital* (New York: Bloomsbury, 2017); Slavoj Žižek, "From Western Marxism to Western Buddhism," *Cabinet Magazine*, no. 2 (2001), https://www.cabinetmagazine.org/issues/2/zizek.php.
5. Carrette and King, *Selling Spirituality*, 77.
6. There are exceptions. See Gordon Lynch, *The New Spirituality: An Introduction to Progressive Belief in the Twenty-first Century* (London: I. B. Tauris, 2007); Anna Clot-Garrell and Mar Griera, "Beyond Narcissism: Toward an Analysis of the Public, Political and Collective Forms of Contemporary Spirituality," *Religions* 10, no. 579 (2019): 1–15. However, these exceptions prove the rule.
7. An interesting exception to this is the case of Marianne Williamson, although even she refrained from speaking in the language of spirituality in public addresses. See Galen Watts, "Marianne Williamson and the Religion of Spirituality," *The Conversation*, October 6, 2019, https://theconversation.com/marianne-williamson-and-the-religion-of-spirituality-123399.
8. Jaime Kucinskas, *The Mindful Elite: Mobilizing from the Inside Out* (New York: Oxford University Press, 2018). Of course, this is not to deny that some forms of individualism are more individualistic (or less relational) than others. See Paul Heelas and Linda Woodhead, *The Spiritual Revolution: Why Religion Is Giving Way to Spirituality* (Malden, MA: Blackwell, 2005).
9. José Casanova, *Public Religions in the Modern World* (Chicago: University of Chicago Press, 1994), 61. Indeed, this is precisely the argument I advance in Galen Watts, *The Spiritual Turn: The Religion of the Heart and the Making of Romantic Liberal Modernity* (Oxford: Oxford University Press, 2022).
10. Anna Fedele and Kim Knibbe, "Introduction: Spirituality, the Third Category in a Gendered Triangle," in *Secular Societies, Spiritual Selves? The Gendered Triangle of Religion, Secularity and Spirituality*, ed. Anna Fedele and Kim Knibbe (New York: Routledge, 2020), 1–29.
11. Linda Woodhead, "Real Religion and Fuzzy Spirituality? Taking Sides in the Sociology of Religion," in *Religions of Modernity: Relocating the Sacred to the Self and the Digital*, ed. Dick Houtman and Stef Aupers (Danvers: Brill, 2010), 31–48.
12. Ruth Gavison, "Feminism and the Public/Private Distinction," *Stanford Law Review* 4, no. 1 (1992): 5.

13. Linda Woodhead, "New Forms of Public Religion: Spirituality in Global Civil Society," in *Religion Beyond Its Private Role in Modern Society*, ed. Wim Hofstee and Arie van der Kooij (Danvers: Brill, 2013), 29–54; Anna Fedele and Kim Knibbe, "Introduction: Spirituality, the Third Category in a Gendered Triangle," in Fedele and Knibbe, *Secular Societies, Spiritual Selves?*, 1–29; Sharday Mosurinjohn and Galen Watts, "Religious Studies and the Spiritual Turn," *Method & Theory in the Study of Religion* 33, no. 5 (2021): 482–504.
14. Christopher Lasch, *The Culture of Narcissism: American Life in an Age of Diminishing Expectations* (London: W. W. Norton, 1979); Lillian Daniel, *When "Spiritual but Not Religious" Is Not Enough: Seeing God in Surprising Places, Even the Church* (New York: Jericho Books, 2013).
15. Paul Lichterman, *The Search for Political Community: American Activists Reinventing Commitment* (Cambridge: Cambridge University Press, 1996); Siobhan Chandler, "Private Religion in the Public Sphere," in *Religions of Modernity: Relocating the Sacred to the Self and the Digital*, ed. Stef Aupers and Dick Houtman (Leiden: Brill, 2010), 69–88; Joantine Berghuijs, Jos Pieper, and Cok Bakker, "New Spirituality and Social Engagement," *Journal for the Scientific Study of Religion* 52, no. 4 (2013): 775–92; Jaime Kucinskas and Evan Stewart, "Selfish or Substituting Spirituality? Clarifying the Relationship Between Spiritual Practice and Political Engagement," *American Sociological Review* 87, no. 4 (2022): 584–617.
16. Casanova explicitly denies the possibility that spirituality could be deemed a "public religion," seeing it as the quintessential "religion of the private self" (*Public Religions*, 52). Yet, like many others, he radically underestimates both its cultural coherence and institutional support, and thus fails to appreciate the potentially radical character of its implicit cultural critique.
17. Charles Taylor, *Sources of the Self: The Making of the Modern Identity* (Cambridge, MA: Harvard University Press, 1989).
18. Francis Fukuyama, *Identity: The Demand for Dignity and the Politics of Resentment* (New York: Farrar, Straus and Giroux, 2018).
19. Irving Babbitt, *Rousseau and Romanticism* (Boston: Houghton Mifflin Company, 1919), 130.
20. Colin Campbell, *The Easternization of the West: A Thematic Account of Cultural Change in the Modern Era* (Boulder, CO: Paradigm Publishers, 2007), 188.
21. Talcott Parsons, "Religion in Postindustrial America: The Problem of Secularization," *Social Research* 51, no. 1 (1984): 493–525.
22. Berman, *The Politics of Authenticity*; Luc Boltanski and Eve Chiapello, *The New Spirit of Capitalism* (New York: Atheneum, 1970).

23. Wouter J. Hanegraaff, *New Age Religion and Western Culture: Esotericism in the Mirror of Secular Thought* (New York: Brill, 1996).
24. Anna Fedele, "'God Wants Spiritual Fruits Not Religious Nuts': Spirituality as Middle Way Between Religion and Secularism at the Marian Shrine of Fátima," in Fedele and Knibbe, *Secular Societies, Spiritual Selves?*, 166–83.
25. Campbell, *The Easternization of the West*, 130.
26. Mark Satin, *New Age Politics, Healing Self and Society: The Emerging New Alternative to Marxism and Liberalism* (London: Whitecap Books/Fairweather Press, 1978).
27. Guy Redden, "Religion, Cultural Studies and New Age Sacralization of Everyday Life," *European Journal of Cultural Studies* 14, no. 6 (2011), 660.
28. Paul Heelas, *The New Age Movement: The Celebration of the Self and the Sacralization of Modernity* (Oxford: Blackwell, 1996).
29. Paul Heelas, *Spiritualities of Life: New Age Romanticism and Consumptive Capitalism* (Malden, MA: Blackwell, 2008).
30. See Lynch, *The New Spirituality*; Watts, *The Spiritual Turn*.
31. Carol Hanisch, "The Personal Is Political," *Notes from the Second Year: Women's Liberation*, 1970, https://webhome.cs.uvic.ca/~mserra/AttachedFiles/PersonalPolitical.pdf.
32. See Betty Friedan, *The Feminine Mystique* (New York: Dell, 1963).
33. Hanisch, "The Personal Is Political."
34. Katharine T. Bartlett, "Feminist Legal Methods," *Harvard Law Review* 103, no. 4 (1990): 829–88; Sue Bruley, "Consciousness-Raising in Clapham: Women's Liberation as 'Lived Experience' in South London in the 1970s," *Women's History Review* 22, no. 5 (2013): 717–38.
35. Ruth Colker, "Feminism, Sexuality, and Self: A Preliminary Inquiry Into the Politics of Authenticity," *Boston University Law Review* 68 (1988): 221.
36. Colker, "Feminism, Sexuality, and Self," 220.
37. Berman, *The Politics of Authenticity*.
38. Bartlett, "Feminist Legal Methods."
39. Katie Sarachild, "Consciousness-Raising: A Radical Weapon," 1973, https://www.rapereliefshelter.bc.ca/wp-content/uploads/2021/03/Feminist-Revolution-Consciousness-Raising-A-Radical-Weapon-Kathie-Sarachild.pdf, 147.
40. Colker, "Feminism, Sexuality, and Self," 220.
41. Gloria Steinem, *Revolution from Within: A Book of Self-Esteem* (Boston: Little, Brown and Company, 1992), 3, 80, 154.
42. Colker, "Feminism, Sexuality, and Self," 219–20.
43. Steinem, *Revolution from Within*, 303, 313.

44. Cass Sunstein, "What the Civil Rights Movement Was and Wasn't (with Notes on Martin Luther King, Jr. and Malcolm X)," in *Reassessing the Sixties: Debating the Political and Cultural Legacy*, ed. Stephen Macedo (New York: W. W. Norton, 1997), 253–82; Clovis E. Semmes, "Entrepreneur of Health: Dick Gregory, Black Consciousness, and the Human Potential Movement," *Journal of African American Studies* 16, no. 3 (2012): 538.
45. William H. Grier and Price M. Cobbs, *Black Rage* (New York: Basic Books, 1968).
46. Semmes, "Entrepreneur of Health," 548.
47. bell hooks, *Sisters of the Yam: Black Women and Self-Recovery* (New York: Routledge, 2015), 13.
48. hooks, *Sisters of the Yam*, 25.
49. hooks, *Sisters of the Yam*, 10, 173, 14.
50. hooks, *Sisters of the Yam*, 198, 199.
51. Robin J. DiAngelo, "My Class Didn't Trump My Race: Using Oppression to Face Privilege," *Multicultural Perspectives* 8, no. 1 (2006): 55.
52. Robin J. DiAngelo, "White Fragility," *International Journal of Critical Pedagogy* 3, no. 3 (2011): 67.
53. DiAngelo, "My Class Didn't Trump My Race," 53.
54. See, for example, John McWhorter, "The Dehumanizing Condescension of *White Fragility*," *The Atlantic*, July 15, 2020; Jonathan Chait, "Is the Anti-Racism Training Industry Just Peddling White Supremacy?," *New York*, July 16, 2020.
55. Robin J. DiAngelo, "Heterosexism: Addressing Internalized Dominance," *Journal of Progressive Human Services* 8, no. 1 (1997): 14.
56. DiAngelo, "White Fragility," 67.
57. DiAngelo, "Heterosexism," 10.
58. There is also a growing literature that takes critical aim at the forms of mindfulness mediation which are seen as corrupted and therefore non-emancipatory. See, e.g., Ronald E. Pursuer, *McMindfulness: How Mindfulness Became the New Capitalist Spirituality* (London: Repeater Books, 2019). However, this critique simply strengthens my point, which is that progressives presume that these practices *ought* to be emancipatory.
59. Deborah Orr, "The Uses of Mindfulness in Anti-oppressive Pedagogies: Philosophy and Praxis," *Canadian Journal of Education* 27, no. 4 (2002): 493.
60. Sheryl Petty, "Waking Up to All of Ourselves: Inner Work, Social Justice, & Systems Change," *Initiative for Contemplation Equity & Action* 1, no. 1 (2017): 9. Petty makes sure to add, "Such a practice is not engaged as a panacea; it is engaged to transform and transmute, as alchemy, to unleash our inherent wisdom and liberatory capacity."

61. Gale Young, "Becoming a White Foot-Soldier—Evolving Into Humanity: The Dangerous Intersections of the Personal, Professional, Political and Spiritual," *Initiative for Contemplation Equity & Action* 1, no. 1 (2017): 37.
62. Nora Zelevansky, "The Big Business of Unconscious Bias," *New York Times*, November 20, 2019; Bridget Read, "Doing the Work at Work: What Are Companies Desperate for Diversity Consultants Actually Buying?," *The Cut*, May 26, 2021.
63. Maya Salam, "What Is Toxic Masculinity?," *New York Times*, January 22, 2019; Michael Carley, "What Is Toxic Masculinity?," *The Good Men Project*, April 5, 2018, https://goodmenproject.com/ethics-values/what-is-toxic-masculinity-dg/.
64. Gillian Friedman, "Here's What Companies Are Promising to Do to Fight Racism," *New York Times*, August 23, 2020; Gayle Markovitz and Samantha Sault, "What Companies Are Doing to Fight Systemic Racism," World Economic Forum, June 24, 2020, https://www.weforum.org/agenda/2020/06/companies-fighting-systemic-racism-business-community-black-lives-matter/. Consider, for instance, the following message on the official website of the Province of Ontario: "As one of the province's largest employers, the Ontario Public Service (OPS) has the responsibility to lead by example in advancing racial equity. It's our responsibility to build a diverse, inclusive, accessible and respectful workplace where every employee has a voice and the opportunity to fully contribute. We must *speak truth to power* by acknowledging that racism exists in the workplace, which is a reflection of our society and our history" (Ontario Public Service, "Message from the Secretary of the Cabinet," https://www.ontario.ca/page/ontario-public-service-anti-racism-policy#section-0).
65. David Acevedo, "Tracking Cancel Culture in Higher Education," National Association of Scholars, October 15, 2021; Marc Tracy, "Two Journalists Exit New York Times After Criticism of Past Behavior," *New York Times*, February 5, 2021.

8

A STARTLING ALLIANCE?

Spirituality, Populism, and Antivaccination Protest

DICK HOUTMAN AND STEF AUPERS

At the heart of modernity lies an intimate connection between political power and scientific reason. Animated by a "gardening" ambition, modern states rely on scientific knowledge to impose order on society and to justify their authority. In doing so they treat modern science as epistemically superior to all other types of understandings of the world, as basically constituting the only type of "real" knowledge.[1] The rise of the modern state has thus been coterminous with the rise of modern science—and what is more, their synchronous triumphs have depended upon the devaluation and profanation of alternative ways of knowing, such as those pertaining to religion.[2]

Although strikingly resilient, this marriage of state power and science has never been uncontested.[3] In the 1960s and 1970s it was targeted on an unprecedented scale by young, well-educated, and politically progressive adherents of the "counterculture." Those concerned railed against what they saw as an overly rationalized, technocratic society, pointing their arrows at the state-science nexus. They critiqued science for acting as the willing handmaiden of an allegedly oppressive "system," uncritically serving the latter's interests and endowing it with misplaced legitimacy.

The countercultural spirit is exemplified by Horkheimer and Adorno's *Dialectic of Enlightenment*, which accuses reason of betraying its Enlightenment promise of paving the way to freedom and emancipation.[4]

Intriguingly, however, contestations of the state-science nexus have in recent decades shifted from the political left to the right, with climate skepticism and vaccine hesitation as the principal new markers.[5] This shift became abundantly clear when the COVID-19 pandemic caught the West by surprise. As a response to the crisis, connections between state power and expert knowledge reached unprecedented highs, fanning protests that took shape as interconnected political and science-related populisms.[6] The countries where populist parties had been most successful were indeed those where vaccine hesitancy reached its highest peaks and it was the populist right, more than any other political group, that carried the torch of antivaccination protest.[7]

Yet it is clear that these protests did not remain confined to the populist right, but boasted a motley crew of far-right political activists, conspiracy theorists, and adherents of spirituality.[8] Survey research does indeed highlight that spirituality is an even more important predictor of vaccine skepticism and low faith in science than rightist political leanings.[9] This led the spiritual but not religious to march alongside the populist right against state-led vaccination programs during the COVID-19 crisis. This alliance is puzzling. After all, spiritual seekers have long been advocates of the progressive political ideals that animated the 1960s–1970s counterculture in which spirituality emerged.[10] So how to account for this startling alliance with the populist right? And how can such spiritual public engagement be reconciled with spirituality's received reputation of privatism and quietism in the first place?[11]

We explain in what follows that antivaccination protests by the spiritual but not religious are not politically but religiously motivated. Our argument proceeds in three steps. First, we discuss how the anti-institutional counterculture of the 1960s and 1970s evolved in multiple and divergent directions, giving rise not only to the "spiritual turn" in religion and the new left in politics but also to the populist right that played such a major role in the recent COVID-19 protests. Second, we discuss how spirituality and rightist populism, despite their shared anti-institutionalism, give rise to strikingly different motives to oppose state-led vaccination programs. Spiritual adherents, we argue, understand such government policies as nothing less than an assault on the sacred, which motivates them to overcome privatism and quietism for religious rather than political reasons. Third and finally, we elaborate on the significance of the cultural-sociological principle that motives cannot simply be inferred from acts, and on why this is important to the study of spiritual and nonspiritual contestations of the state-science nexus.

COUNTERCULTURAL ANTI-INSTITUTIONALISM AND ITS DIRECTIONS

Countercultural Anti-Institutionalism

In the 1960s and 1970s, protests against the modern marriage of state power and science were carried by predominantly young, well-educated, and politically progressive sympathizers of the counterculture. Countercultural youth dismissed the modern understanding of science as strictly neutral and objective, instead seeing it as a state ideology that protected, safeguarded, and legitimized the "system" and its vested interests. They thus understood science as a manifestation and foundational legitimation of "the technocracy," a term used to refer to "the regime of experts—or of those who can employ the experts." As Theodore Roszak summarizes the issue: "It will be enough to define the technocracy as that society in which those who govern justify themselves by appeal to technical experts who, in turn, justify themselves by appeal to scientific forms of knowledge. And beyond the authority of science, there is no appeal." The counterculture critiqued this technocracy as an extreme and dismal manifestation of modernity, "entangled in the scientific worldview of the Western tradition," basically "the mature product of technological progress and the scientific ethos."[12] Its protest was driven by discontents with an overly rationalized and dehumanizing order that exercised stifling control over human lives, stood in the way of personal freedom and authenticity, and was utterly devoid of meaning.[13] At the heart of the counterculture we thus find a dismissive attitude vis-à-vis modern society and its rationalized institutions, an anti-institutionalism that also explains the countercultural fascination with nonrationalized and nonalienating mythical fantasy worlds. It is neither coincidental that Tolkien's *Lord of the Rings* was "absolutely the favorite book of every hippie," as Warren Hinckle observes, nor that "power to the imagination" quickly became the rallying cry of the counterculture.[14]

Its emphasis on personal authenticity and cultural imagination makes the counterculture profoundly romantic: it "pushed Romantic individualism to ever more extreme lengths in contradistinction to the bureaucratic and bourgeois individualism of the instrumental enclave."[15] At the beginning of the 1980s Bernice Martin moreover observed that there were hardly any signs of a withering away of countercultural romanticism: "If [the counter-culture] ever was truly a counter-culture, it had certainly ceased to be so by the mid-1970s because its most characteristic methods and messages had been appropriated by mainstream culture."[16] Almost twenty years later British historian Arthur Marwick could make the same observation, pointing out the lasting cultural influence and significance of the logic of the counter-culture in the West: "The consequences of what happened in the sixties were long-lasting: the sixties cultural revolution . . . established the enduring cultural values and social behaviour for the rest of the century."[17]

And indeed, a host of students of social and cultural change have highlighted and documented the infiltration of countercultural anti-institutionalism into a wide range of social realms. Unsurprisingly, this infiltration occurred most emphatically in those social realms that were critiqued as particularly suffocating and alienating back in the 1960s: those of work and consumption, but also, and more important for our discussion in this chapter, those of religion and politics.[18]

The Spiritual Turn

Arguably more than anything else, the counterculture sparked the pervasive shift that constitutes the general backdrop of this volume: that from Christianity in its traditional organizational, ritual, and doctrinal forms to a basically mystical, Eastern-style spirituality.[19] The latter understands the sacred as a universal spirit or life force that precedes, permeates, and connects all that exists—human society, nature, and the cosmos as a whole. While the self is consequently conceived as basically a knot in an omnipresent field of spiritual energy, the course of Western civilization is understood as having increasingly disconnected the self from this spiritual field due to the processes sociologists traditionally identify with "modernization" (i.e., industrialization, rationalization, urbanization, and the like) and the rationalized institutions these give rise to.

Spirituality's anti-institutionalism thus stems from its understanding of social institutions and institutionalized belief systems as stifling personal spirituality. Conformity to established religious authorities like priesthoods or doctrines (or indeed to any other, nonreligious forms of authority) is here seen as the principal cause of suffering and unhappiness.[20] This is why spirituality has always been susceptible to conspiracy thinking, and dismissive of the traditional types of religious organization in the West—seen as incompatible with spiritual ideals of personal authenticity, religiously inclusive "perennialism," and spiritual "seekership."[21] This is also why spirituality initially found its home in a "cultic milieu" that "continually [gives] birth to new cults, absorbing the debris of the dead ones and creating new generations of cult-prone individuals."[22] Historian of religion Wouter Hanegraaff, a keen observer of esotericism and the New Age movement, demonstrates sharp insight into the sociological implications of this spiritual focus on individual authenticity: "Individualism functions as an in-built defense mechanism against social organization and institutionalization: as soon as any group of people involved with New Age ideas begins to take up 'cultic' characteristics, this very fact already distances them from the basic individualism of New Age spirituality."[23]

This is why spiritual seekers identify least with the most institutionalized, organized, and doctrinal religions. Particularly disliked are those that traditionally dominated the West, especially Catholicism, with its church-based hierarchy of authority, and orthodox strains of Protestantism, with their emphasis on literal belief in the Bible as God's revealed Word. Spiritual seekers are much more sympathetic to Eastern-style religions that foreground the significance of personal experiential contact with the sacred. The favorite is without a doubt Buddhism, precisely because of its—in Western eyes—marked emphasis on meditation and experience and virtual absence of a need to believe in anything whatsoever. Philip Mellor indeed demonstrates that native British Buddhists list "authoritarianism, institutionalism, dogmatism, triumphalism, ritualism and formalism" as the principal shortcomings of Christian religion.[24] Positing a sacred realm that can be neither captured in human-made institutions nor reduced to religious doctrines, spirituality understands institutions as dismal barriers between the self and the sacred. With anti-institutionalism thus situated at its heart, spirituality's experiential inwardness encourages not so much political protest and revolt, but rather institutional disengagement and withdrawal—hence its traditionally foregrounded privatism and political quietism.

Redemptive Politics, Left and Right

Yet, the counterculture also engendered major political transformations. Central to these is a "new-leftist" politics that emphasizes liberation from oppressive, conformity-demanding systems of authority ("the system"), and from cultural narratives like traditional Christian doctrines about gender, sexuality, marriage, and the like, which force individuals into a conformity defined by social roles that force them to become what they are not.[25]

Much like spirituality as its quietist and inward-looking counterpart, this new left in politics foregrounds anti-institutionalism and liberation from oppressive social forces. The cultural engine of new-leftist politics was—and still is—the identity politics of new social movements like the gay liberation movement, second wave feminism, the civil rights movement in the United States, and its principal contemporary offshoots, the LGBTQ+ and Black Lives Matter movements.[26] Unlike the economic class struggle of the old left, this new left thus engages in a struggle for cultural liberation, aimed at expanding opportunities for freedom, self-expression, and personal authenticity, especially for sexual and ethnic minority groups that have traditionally been denied the right to "be themselves."

The rise of this new left introduced a notorious rift with the old class-centered socialist and communist left. It is indeed telling how the countercultural protesters in Paris in May 1968 were quickly turned off by the "hallmark of the socialist and communist parties of the Old Left," i.e., its authoritarian leadership and bureaucratic organization, seen as "simply [reproducing] the unfreedom found in the larger society (not to mention the Soviet Union)."[27]

From the 1980s onward a similar bifurcation occurred on the political right due to the rise and electoral success of new right-wing populism.[28] Observers have typically interpreted this populism as a hostile and dismissive response to the new-leftist political quest for a more culturally inclusive society, a sort of "counter-revolutionary conservative backlash" informed by an "authoritarian reflex," a "counter-revolution" against the culturally progressive "silent revolution" sparked by the new social movements and new-leftist political parties since the 1960s.[29] As Pippa Norris and Ronald Inglehart put it: "[This] authoritarian reflex [entails] a defensive reaction strongest among socially conservative groups feeling threatened by the rapid processes of economic, social, and cultural change, rejecting unconventional social mores and moral norms, and finding reassurance from a collective community of like-minded people, where transgressive strongman leaders express socially incorrect views while defending traditional values and beliefs."[30]

Here, too, cultural identity issues have become central to politics, even though unlike the counterculture and the new left this new populist right does not advocate for the rights of formerly excluded minority groups, but rather celebrates national identity and the alleged virtues of "ordinary" ("hard-working," "tax-paying," "law-abiding," and so on) citizens. Examples of political parties hawking such discourse can nowadays be found all over Western Europe, with some of the best known and most electorally successful ones being Alternatives for Germany, the UK Independence Party, the Party for Freedom and Forum for Democracy (the Netherlands), the True Finns (Finland), the People's Party (Switzerland, Denmark), the Progress Party (Norway), Flemish Interest (Belgium), National Front (France), Lega Nord (Italy), and Golden Dawn (Greece). Examples elsewhere in the West are the Republican Party under Donald Trump, the People's Party of Canada, Australia's One Nation Party, and New Zealand First. Yet these parties' marked differences with the counterculture and the new left easily obscure a similarity that has all too often been overlooked. For despite right-wing populism's nationalist defense of a historically rooted and ethnically defined nation, with all the xenophobia and longing for cultural homogeneity this entails, its markedly anti-institutional style also betrays an indebtedness to the counterculture, whether leftist or rightist political partisans like it or not.[31]

More than that, it can even be argued that back in the 1960s and 1970s the counterculture, the new left, and the new social movements were themselves profoundly populist, critiquing "the system" in the name of "ordinary citizens" and accusing mainstream parties of "adapting" or "selling out" to the political establishment.[32] For populism is a form of politics that divides the world "into two homogeneous and antagonistic groups, 'the pure people' versus 'the corrupt elite,'" while proposing that government "should be an expression of the *volonté générale* (general will) of the people." This applies to the new left as much as the new right, even though it is obvious that their respective notions of "the people" differ profoundly—respectively "an active, self-confident, well-educated, progressive people" and "the hard-working . . . law-abiding citizen, who, in silence but with growing anger, sees his world being 'perverted' by progressives, criminals, and aliens."[33]

There is indeed nothing *intrinsically* "right-wing" or "exclusionary" about populism, since it entails not much more than a political style that "challenges the legitimate authority of 'the establishment'" in the name of "the people," conceived as "the only legitimate source of political and moral authority in a democracy." As "a style of rhetoric" or "thin-centered ideology,"[34] it can effortlessly be combined with either rightist "exclusivist" or leftist "inclusivist" political agendas. Indeed, leftist populism boasts a rich history in South America (e.g., Argentina's Peronist tradition, or the late Hugo Chávez, Venezuelan president from 1999 until his death in 2013), while at the end of the nineteenth century the People's Party in the United States waged a leftist-populist fight against exploitative economic elites in the name of economic justice.[35] Moreover, in contemporary Europe parties like Italy's Five Star Movement, Spain's Podemos, Syriza in Greece, the Socialist Party in the Netherlands, and the Left Party in Germany stand out as no less populist than their right-wing counterparts.[36]

Whether left- or right-wing, populism entails a politics that critiques the establishment and political elites in the name of what Paul Taggart calls a "heartland"—an imagined, ideal place "in which . . . a virtuous and unified population resides."[37] Of course, such a heartland exists only in the cultural imagination as a sort of blueprint of what society should ideally be like.[38] As "a state of mind in experience, in thought, or in practice, [that] is oriented towards objects which do not exist in the actual situation" it features a markedly utopian edge in the classical Mannheimian sense.[39] As a product of the cultural imagination, the populist heartland provides a yardstick to identify the shortcomings and injustices of actually existing society as much as a blueprint for its dreamed-of utopian successor.

One of the intriguing ironies of twentieth-century history, in short, is the way today's populist right has come to appropriate the proverbial creed of the leftist-progressive counterculture of the 1960s, "power to the imagination." Much like the counterculture, the new left and the new social movements, the populist right relocates politics from the state and the political system to the bosom of society. Equally dismayed with "bureaucrats and managers [who] have developed a cult of expertise that shuts out ordinary people from participation in collective decision making,"[40] right-wing populism engenders a shift away from "system-following" to "system-challenging" politics. Margaret Canovan characterizes the latter as "redemptive" rather than "pragmatic:" "Pragmatically, democracy means institutions: institutions not just to limit power, but also to constitute it and make it effective. But in redemptive democracy (as in redemptive politics more generally) there is a strong anti-institutional impulse: the romantic impulse to directness, spontaneity and the overcoming of alienation."[41] The COVID-19 pandemic demonstrated powerfully how the populist right has become a principal carrier of this type of anti-institutional politics, contesting as it did the state-science nexus—or more specifically, the state-led attempts at curbing the crisis through vaccination programs, social distancing, masking requirements, and the like.[42]

ANTIVACCINATION PROTEST: A STARTLING ALLIANCE?

Contemporary Contestations of the State-Science Nexus

Yet the spiritual but not religious also played an active role in antivaccination rallies and protests, often side by side with this populist right. This is at first sight odd and puzzling, given that these spiritual seekers continue to boast a marked affinity with the principal ideals of new-leftist politics, "self-actualization and moral self-determination" as much as "post-materialist values, environmentalism, [and] sympathy for social minorities such as homosexuals and migrants."[43] The progressive "moral individualism" this entails foregrounds the right to cultural inclusion despite cultural otherness—an individualism through which those concerned set themselves apart from their conservative religious counterparts.[44] Now whereas among the public at large such a progressive political profile typically evoked support for vaccinations during the COVID-19 crisis,[45] many spiritual folks failed to join the ranks, engaging in antivaccination protest instead. So here a leftist-progressive political profile coincided with *opposition to* rather than *support for* vaccination programs. How to explain this?

Spiritual Understandings of Nature and the Body

The heart of the matter is that spirituality understands society and its institutions as a principal source of alienation and suffering. So here the socialized self—the sort of person society's predefined structures, roles, and functions attempt to mold one into—is understood as "false" and "unreal," precisely because it is externally imposed rather than representing who one "really" is, or who one is "by nature." What is needed, therefore, is to do away with this "fake" self and replace it with its "real" counterpart, allegedly situated in the deeper layers of consciousness. This spiritual self is precisely seen as "real," "authentic," and "pure," because it precedes and transcends society rather than being its socialized product. It is conceived as part and parcel of a spiritual force that permeates all of the world and the universe and that connects "everything," not least body and mind.

It is neither new nor surprising that this spiritual tenet that "everything is connected" gives rise to opposition to vaccinations (and to biomedicine and modern science more generally). For the long-standing tradition of Western esotericism of which spirituality is an offshoot has always been critical of both mind-body dualism (often attributed to René Descartes, 1595–1650) and the modern reductionist approach to health it helped institutionalize.[46] Dismissing such dualism, spirituality embraces an alternative concept of health, which conceives of body, mind, and spirit as intimately connected and ultimately inseparable:

> It is . . . radically different from the traditional Western model, which typically envisages illness and disease as caused by natural forces that invade or attack the body either from within (such as cancer) or without (as in the case of germs and viruses). In either case these have to be countered, that is, beaten off or overcome in some way, through skilled human intervention. This may be by means of drugs, in particular antibiotics, or through the use of vaccines, surgical intervention, or such techniques as chemotherapy. In all cases scientific knowledge and technological skill combine to produce the "weapons" needed in this "war" against "a natural enemy." The [holistic] model could not be more different. Here nature is regarded as the cure rather than as the source

of disease, the assumption being that if an individual is ill, then this will be because he or she is not properly "adjusted" to the natural flow of energies that exist within and around him or her.[47]

The dissemination of this logic of holistic healing in the West has popularized a wide range of therapies relying on natural resources (herbs, oils, crystals, sound, light, color), patients' own natural healing abilities, and "non-invasive, hands-on manipulative techniques such as massage."[48] Emphasizing wholeness and connectedness, holistic healing's understanding of health, healing, and health care considers an isolated treatment of distinct illnesses, symptoms, or body parts as futile and senseless, as indeed more "symptom relief" than proper "health care." Dutch general practitioners who double as holistic healers, for instance, deny that modern biomedicine can actually "cure" their patients. They may use Western medicine in instances where they need to prevent their patients from dying, to be sure, but nonetheless distinguish sharply between such "death prevention" and veritable "healthcare." For these doctors, seeking refuge in biomedicine entails no more than a sort of emergency response to years of preventative neglect, including neglect of all sorts of nonphysical problems that could and should have been treated holistically much earlier on. While alternative health practitioners thus see biomedical interventions as tragically inevitable in such situations, they still understand them as unnatural and as failing to make a genuine contribution to the health of their patients.[49]

The spiritually inclined, in short, consider holistic healthcare superior to its modern dualist and reductionist counterpart and dismiss as "unnatural" modern medicine's refusal to treat humans as wholes. For in a spiritual understanding nature, including who one is "by nature" as a person, entails a powerful spiritual force that needs to be defended against invasions by the nonnatural, the artificial, the man-made, and the technological. This "lay theory of immunity" sacralizes the natural immune system and makes it central to the attainment and preservation of health.[50] It leads spiritual antivaxxers to see chemical vaccines as doing more harm than good: the acquisition of immunity and recovery from disease are in their view natural processes that cannot and should not be technologically short-circuited. Attempting to nonetheless do so amounts to damaging the self-healing powers of the human body, which motivates spiritual resistance to vaccination to defend the natural body against chemical intruders.

Sacred and Profane in Spirituality

Spirituality in effect downplays not only "revealed" religious truths but also "proven" and reproducible scientific facts, obtained through rigorous experimental research methods. In doing so it dismisses both of the epistemologies that have vied for supremacy in the West for centuries: religious dogma and scientific reason. While these two are obviously far from identical, they nonetheless both assume that truth can be validated "from the outside," as it were, and that it is as such universally binding to all.[51] According to their spiritual counterpart, on the other hand, "truth" can never be externally validated but can "only be found by personal, inner revelation, insight or 'enlightenment'" and can as such "only be personally experienced."[52]

Personal experiences here take on spiritual significance, precisely because they are conceived as emanations of the sacred force that lies within. What feels good and what feels bad reveals who one "really" or "at deepest" is, and as such provides spiritual guidance. "The embodied experience of the self is ... seen as a more valid source of revelation about the divine than external teachings from scriptures or prophets," as Gordon Lynch puts it.[53] This detracts not only from the authority of traditional religion, however, but also accounts for the "inherent irreconcilability of the *intuitive epistemology* of a spiritual belief system with science."[54] When it comes to the question of getting vaccinated or not, spirituality spurs its adherents to prioritize not expert advice but their personal experiences and "the wisdom of their own body."

This experiential epistemology does much to sustain and reinforce the ontological spiritual notion of the human body as a natural, self-healing whole. After all, why accept the infusion of chemicals into one's natural, healthy body when *it feels* artificial, unnatural, and plainly wrong to do so? Spiritual epistemology and spiritual ontology thus reinforce each other, in the process consolidating and deepening critiques of biomedicine and vaccination programs. For those who are spiritually engaged vaccinations *are* wrong because they *feel* wrong, and they *feel* wrong because they *are* wrong. During the coronavirus crisis the spiritual but not religious could not stop expressing their trust in the self-healing powers of their own bodies ("My body is strong, healthy, and able to cope with viruses like COVID-19") and distrust of vaccinations ("Vaccinations are unnecessary, and perhaps even poisonous"). In the words of one spiritual advocate: "This isn't hippy stuff, it's the truth. The body can find its own solutions, its own intelligence, if we let it do that."[55]

Given these spiritual understandings of health, nature, and biomedicine, it ceases to be surprising that politically progressive spiritual seekers marched alongside the populist right against COVID-19 vaccination campaigns. The spiritually inclined did not do so because they held far-rightist political ideas, but did so *in spite* of their leftist-progressive ones—political profiles that among nonspiritual groups tended to predict support for vaccination programs.[56] Spiritual protests against state-led vaccination programs were not politically motivated but directed against the modern scientific denial of the status of the human body as a "self-healing natural whole" and against state-led initiatives to open it up to "artificial" chemicals. This is perfectly consistent with Emile Durkheim's *The Elementary Forms of Religious Life*, where he conceptualizes religion as a group-based "unified system of beliefs and practices relative to sacred things, that is to say, things set apart and forbidden."[57] Central to this understanding of religion are collectively held beliefs about what is "sacred," that is, what is so special and important that it needs to be set apart, venerated, and protected from pollution and desecration by the "profane"—the vulgar, the everyday, and the mundane.[58] During the COVID-19 crisis this logic gave rise to a deeply felt urge in spiritual circles to defend the sacredness of the natural body against its desecration by an invasion of chemicals by Pfizer, BioNTech, and Moderna. The social and political pressures of getting vaccinated that marked public responses to the COVID-19 crisis thus launched spirituality despite itself into the public sphere, upending its traditional academic portrayal as quintessentially privatized and "challenging [its] peaceful/apolitical stereotype."[59]

MEANING, MOTIVES, AND MODERN MEDICINE

"Meaning," Jack Douglas and Frances Waksler observe, "is not inherent in the act."[60] What people do says very little about what drives their acts, because motives cannot be inferred from acts.[61] Home insulation may be motivated by either frugality or concerns about sustainability and climate change, just like studying hard can be motivated either by instrumental ambitions of attaining a well-paid, high-status job or expressive desires for personal and intellectual growth. Likewise, the meaning of protesting against government-backed vaccination programs cannot be inferred from the act itself either. For such protests may be motivated by either right-wing populist suspicions about a state trying to increase its control over the population or by spiritual indignations about the desecration of what is considered sacred: nature and the human body. As Mar Griera and colleagues have observed, the mere fact that spiritual seekers engaged in antivaccination protests alongside the populist right during the recent COVID-19 pandemic cannot be taken as evidence that they identify politically with the populist right.[62]

Although it stands out as the progressive counterpart of conservative Christianity, the type of spirituality discussed in this volume shares a marked vaccine hesitancy with the latter.[63] High regional incidences of *either* traditional Christianity *or* spirituality tend to lead to high rates of vaccine hesitancy.[64] In a country like the Netherlands, where both groups are present in significant numbers, orthodox Protestant vaccine hesitancy is most prevalent in the "Bible Belt," which runs from the southwest of the country to its northeast. This is the area where vaccine campaigns are traditionally least successful and where as a consequence occasional outbreaks of infectious diseases like poliomyelitis, measles, rubella, and mumps occur.[65] Vaccination rates, however, also tend to be low in progressive, cosmopolitan university towns like Amsterdam and Utrecht owing to concentrations of the spiritual but not religious.[66] Needless to say, smaller and more markedly spiritual hotspots in other countries—like Glastonbury (United Kingdom), Findhorn (Scotland), Byron Bay (Australia), and

Sedona (Arizona)—stand out even more empathically as antivaxx hotspots with correspondingly low vaccination rates.[67]

Even though the vaccine hesitancies of orthodox Protestants and spiritual seekers are both religiously rather than politically motivated, their motives are once again profoundly different, informed as they are by contrasting understandings of the sacred. Orthodox Protestant dualism leads its adherents to submit to an omnipotent God who sovereignly decides in matters of life and death.[68] In this understanding, getting oneself or one's children vaccinated amounts to a refusal to accept the sovereignty of God. Spirituality's holism, on the other hand, leads its adherents to put their trust in their spiritually connected, natural, self-healing bodies. In this alternative religious understanding, getting vaccinated means distrusting or denying nature's sacred healing forces. In terms of worldview-informed motives, in short, vaccine-hesitant spiritual groups differ as much from orthodox religious groups as they do from right-wing populists.

The principle that worldview-informed motives cannot simply be inferred from the acts they give rise to is vital in the study of contestations of the state-science nexus. For much research in this area remains confined to the behavioral surface of what people do (or don't do). Yet to reach beyond the surface of mere behavior, attention is needed to *why* people do what they do: what ideals they cherish, celebrate, and aim for, as expressed in their motives, themselves informed by religious, spiritual, or political worldviews.[69] Doing so is all the more important because antivaccination protests, distrust in scientific experts, and related phenomena all raise questions about the empirical validity of the received sociological wisdom that religion will more or less inevitably give way to science as its superior and legitimate successor. If, again with Durkheim, one dismisses the notion that religion necessarily entails belief in supernatural powers, this hypothesis may in fact be part and parcel of a new, basically "secular" religion of scientism, vying to wrest authority from its "truly" religious predecessor.[70] Today's contestations of the state-science nexus suggest that this power grab has been remarkably less smooth than sociologists have traditionally expected, predicted, and hoped for, which raises the question of whether the received sociological account is empirically valid at all. The alternative is important enough to consider: that next to traditional Christian religion, modern science has also lost much of its former authority. If such a dual decline has indeed occurred, it is quite likely that it is intimately bound up with the dissemination of spirituality, at odds with religious belief and scientific reason alike.

NOTES

The authors thank the participants of the publication workshop in Leuven in April 2022 for their helpful suggestions and comments. Special thanks are due to Franz Höllinger, who shared some of his unpublished survey findings about politics, spirituality, and vaccination hesitancy with us.

1. Zygmunt Bauman, *Legislators and Interpreters: On Modernity, Postmodernity and Intellectuals* (Cambridge: Polity, 1987); Zygmunt Bauman, *Intimations of Postmodernity* (London: Routledge, 1992), vii–xvii; Stephen Toulmin, *Cosmopolis: The Hidden Agenda of Modernity* (Chicago: University of Chicago Press, 1990).
2. Steven Seidman, *Contested Knowledge: Social Theory in the Postmodern Era* (Cambridge, MA: Blackwell, 1994), 19–53.
3. Dick Houtman, Stef Aupers, and Rudi Laermans, "Introduction: A Cultural Sociology of the Authority of Science," in *Science Under Siege: Contesting the Secular Religion of Scientism*, ed. Dick Houtman, Stef Aupers, and Rudi Laermans (New York: Palgrave Macmillan, 2021), 1–34.
4. Max Horkheimer and Theodor W. Adorno, *Dialectic of Enlightenment: Philosophical Fragments*, ed. Gunzelin Schmid Noerr and Edmund Jephcott (Stanford, CA: Stanford University Press, 2002 [1944]).

5. Gordon Gauchat, "Politicization of Science in the Public Sphere: A Study of Public Trust in the United States, 1974 to 2010," *American Sociological Review* 77, no. 2 (2012): 167–87; Bastiaan T. Rutjens et al., "Science Skepticism Across 24 Countries," *Social Psychological and Personality Science* 13, no. 1 (2022): 102–17.
6. Marta Tomasi, "Populism, Politics, and Science in the Midst of the Pandemic," *Tecnoscienza* 12, no. 2 (2021): 145–54.
7. Jonathan Kennedy, "Populist Politics and Vaccine Hesitancy in Western Europe: An Analysis of National-level Data," *European Journal of Public Health* 29, no. 3 (2019): 512–16.
8. Mar Griera et al., "Conspirituality in COVID-19 Times: A Mixed-Method Study of Anti-Vaccine Movements in Spain," *Journal for the Academic Study of Religion* 35, no. 2 (2022): 193.
9. Rutjens et al., "Science Skepticism"; Bastiaan T. Rutjens and Romy van der Lee, "Spiritual Skepticism? Heterogeneous Science Skepticism in the Netherlands," *Public Understanding of Science* 29, no. 3 (2020): 335–52; Bastiaan T. Rutjens, Natalia Zarzeczna, and Romy van der Lee, "Science Rejection in Greece: Spirituality Predicts Vaccine Scepticism and Low Faith in Science in a Greek Sample," *Public Understanding of Science* 31, no. 4 (2022): 428–36.
10. Galen Watts and Dick Houtman, introduction to this volume; Franz Höllinger, "Does the Counter-Cultural Character of New Age Persist? Investigating Social and Political Attitudes of New Age Followers," *Journal of Contemporary Religion* 19, no. 3 (2004): 289–309; Frans Höllinger, "Value Orientations and Social Attitudes in the Holistic Milieu," *British Journal of Sociology* 68, no. 2 (2017): 293–313; Gordon Lynch, *The New Spirituality: An Introduction to Progressive Belief in the Twenty-first Century* (London: I. B. Taurus, 2007).
11. Thomas Luckmann, *The Invisible Religion: The Problem of Religion in Modern Society* (New York: Macmillan, 1967); Anton C. Zijderveld, *The Abstract Society: A Cultural Analysis of Our Time* (York: Doubleday, 1970).
12. Theodore Roszak, *The Making of a Counter Culture: Reflections on the Technocratic Society and Its Youthful Opposition* (New York: Doubleday, 1969), 7, 8.
13. Zijderveld, *Abstract Society*, 71–72.
14. Warren Hinckle, quoted in Robert S. Ellwood, *The Sixties Spiritual Awakening: American Religion Moving from Modern to Postmodern* (New Brunswick, NJ: Rutgers University Press, 1994), 201.
15. Bernice Martin, *A Sociology of Contemporary Cultural Change* (Oxford: Blackwell, 1981), 21; see also Colin Campbell, *The Easternization of the West: A Thematic Account of Cultural Change in the Modern Era* (Boulder, CO: Paradigm, 2007), 184–249.

16. Martin, *Cultural Change*, 16.
17. Arthur Marwick, *The Sixties: Cultural Revolution in Britain, France, Italy, and the United States, c. 1958-c. 1974* (New York: Oxford University Press, 1998), 806.
18. Dick Houtman, *Op jacht naar de echte werkelijkheid: Dromen over authenticiteit in een wereld zonder fundamenten* (The Hunt for Real Reality: Dreams of Authenticity in a World without Foundations) (Amsterdam: Pallas Publications, 2008). On work: Luc Boltanski and Eve Chiapello, *The New Spirit of Capitalism*, ed. Gregory Elliott (London: Verso, 2005); Kobe De Keere, "From a Self-Made to an Already-Made Man: A Historical Content Analysis of Professional Advice Literature," *Acta Sociologica* 57, no. 4 (2014): 311–24; Paul Heelas, "The Sacralization of the Self and New Age Capitalism," in *Social Change in Contemporary Britain*, ed. Nicholas Abercrombie and Alan Warde (Cambridge: Polity Press, 1992), 139–66. On consumption: Thomas Frank, *The Conquest of Cool: Business Culture, Counter Culture, and the Rise of Hip Consumerism* (Chicago: University of Chicago Press, 1998; James H. Gilmore and B. Joseph Pine, *Authenticity: What Consumers Really Want* (Cambridge, MA: Harvard Business Press, 2007); Joseph Heath and Andrew Potter, *Nation of Rebels: Why Counterculture Became Consumer Culture* (New York: Harper Collins, 2004). On religion: Watts and Houtman, introduction; Campbell, *The Easternization of the West*; Lynch, *The New Spirituality*; Stef Aupers and Dick Houtman, eds., *Religions of Modernity: Relocating the Sacred to the Self and the Digital* (Leiden: Brill, 2010); Galen Watts, *The Spiritual Turn: The Religion of the Heart and the Making of Romantic Liberal Modernity* (Oxford: Oxford University Press, 2022). On politics: Ronald Inglehart, *The Silent Revolution: Changing Values and Political Styles Among Western Publics* (Princeton, NJ: Princeton University Press, 1977); Dick Houtman, Peter Achterberg, and Anton Derks, *Farewell to the Leftist Working Class* (New Brunswick, NJ: Transaction, 2008).
19. Watts and Houtman, introduction; Campbell, *The Easternization of the West*; Paul Heelas and Linda Woodhead, *The Spiritual Revolution: Why Religion Is Giving Way to Spirituality* (Oxford: Blackwell, 2005).
20. Anna Halafoff, Andres Singleton, and Ruth Fitzpatrick, "Spiritual Complexity in Australia: Wellbeing and Risks," *Social Compass* 70, no. 2 (2023): 254–55.
21. Egil Asprem and Asbjørn Dyrendal, "Conspirituality Reconsidered: How Surprising and How New is the Confluence of Spirituality and Conspiracy Theory?," *Journal of Contemporary Religion* 30, no. 3 (2015): 367–82.

22. Colin Campbell, "The Cult, the Cultic Milieu and Secularisation," *A Sociological Yearbook of Religion in Britain* 5 (1972): 121–22. See, however, Campbell's chapter in this volume.
23. Wouter J. Hanegraaff, "New Age Religion," in *Religion in the Modern World*, ed. Linda Woodhead et al. (London: Routledge, 2002), 259. See also Watts and Houtman, introduction.
24. Philip A. Mellor, "Protestant Buddhism? The Cultural Translation of Buddhism in England," *Religion* 21, no. 1 (1991): 77.
25. Inglehart, *Silent Revolution*; Zijderveld, *Abstract Society*.
26. Ronald Inglehart, *Culture Shift in Advanced Industrial Society* (Princeton, NJ: Princeton University Press, 1990): 371–92; Hanspeter Kriesi, "New Social Movements and the New Class in the Netherlands," *American Journal of Sociology* 94, no. 5 (1989): 1078–1116; Claus Offe, "New Social Movements: Challenging the Boundaries of Institutional Politics," *Social Research* 52, no. 4 (1985): 817–68; Watts, *Spiritual Turn*, 61–80.
27. Leonard Williams, "Ideological Parallels Between the New Left and the New Right," *Social Science Journal* 24, no. 3 (1987): 318.
28. Dick Houtman and Peter Achterberg, "Two Lefts and Two Rights: Class Voting and Cultural Voting in the Netherlands, 2002," *Sociologie* 1, no. 1 (2010): 61–76.
29. Houtman, Achterberg, and Derks, *Farewell*; Piero Ignazi, "The Silent Counter-Revolution: Hypotheses on the Emergence of Extreme Right-Wing Parties in Europe," *European Journal of Political Research* 22, no. 1 (1992): 3–34; Pippa Norris and Ronald Inglehart, *Cultural Backlash: Trump, Brexit, and Authoritarian Populism* (Cambridge: Cambridge University Press, 2019), 16.
30. Norris and Inglehart, *Cultural Backlash*, 16.
31. That said, the history of how exactly the counterculture has contributed to the rise of the populist right has to the best of our knowledge not yet been written. To successfully do so, what needs to be foregrounded is not how the new left and new right differ from each other but rather what they have in common.
32. Cas Mudde, "The Populist Zeitgeist," *Government and Opposition* 39, no. 4 (2004): 548, 543, 557.
33. Norris and Inglehart, *Cultural Backlash*, 5.
34. Norris and Inglehart, *Cultural Backlash*, 4; Cas Mudde, "The Populist Zeitgeist," 544.
35. Thomas Frank, *The People, No: A Brief History of Anti-Populism* (New York: Metropolitan, 2020).
36. Norris and Inglehart, *Cultural Backlash*, 3–31.
37. Paul Taggart, *Populism* (Buckingham, UK: Open University Press, 2000), 95.

38. Mudde, "The Populist Zeitgeist," 557.
39. Karl Mannheim, *Ideology and Utopia: An Introduction to the Sociology of Knowledge*, ed. Louis Wirth and Edward Shils (San Diego: Harcourt, Brace, Jovanovich, 1985 [1936]), 173.
40. Williams, "Parallels," 320.
41. Margaret Canovan, "Trust the People! Populism and the Two Faces of Democracy," *Political Studies* 47, no. 1 (1999): 2–16, 10.
42. Kennedy, "Hesitancy"; Tomasi, "Populism."
43. Höllinger, "Value Orientations," 309; see also Höllinger, "Counter-Cultural."
44. Dick Houtman and Peter Mascini, "Why Do Churches Become Empty, While New Age Grows? Secularization and Religious Change in the Netherlands," *Journal for the Scientific Study of Religion* 41, no. 3 (2002): 455–73; Dick Houtman and Stef Aupers, "The Spiritual Turn and the Decline of Tradition: The Spread of Post-Christian Spirituality in 14 Western Countries, 1981–2000," *Journal for the Scientific Study of Religion* 46, no. 3 (2007): 305–20; Lynch, *The New Spirituality*.
45. Rutjens et al., "Science Skepticism."
46. Hanegraaff, *New Age Religion and Western Culture*.
47. Campbell, *The Easternization of the West*, 102–3.
48. Campbell, *The Easternization of the West*, 103. See also Candy Gunther Brown's chapter in this volume.
49. Nadine Raaphorst and Dick Houtman, "A Necessary Evil That Does Not 'Really' Cure Disease: The Domestication of Biomedicine by Dutch Holistic General Practitioners," *Health: An Interdisciplinary Journal for the Social Study of Health, Illness and Medicine* 20, no. 3 (2016): 242–57.
50. Eva Dubé et al., quoted in Anna Halafoff et al., "Selling (Con)spirituality and COVID-19 in Australia: Convictions, Complexity and Countering Dis/misinformation," *Journal for the Academic Study of Religion* 35, no. 2 (2022): 155.
51. Ernest Gellner, *Postmodernism, Reason and Religion* (London: Routledge, 1992); Houtman, Aupers, and Laermans, "Introduction."
52. Hanegraaff, *New Age Religion and Western Culture*, 519.
53. Lynch, *The New Spirituality*, 55.
54. Rutjens et al., "Science Skepticism," 114 (emphasis in original). See also Rutjens and Van der Lee, "Spiritual Skepticism."
55. Quoted in Jules Evans, "Make Love, Not Vaccines: Why Are New Age Hippies So Anti-Vax?," https://www.philosophyforlife.org/blog/make-love-not-vaccines-why-are-new-age-hippies-so-anti-vax.
56. Rutjens et al., "Science Rejection"; Franz Höllinger, personal communication.

57. Emile Durkheim, *The Elementary Forms of Religious Life* (New York: Free Press, 1995 [1912]), 44.
58. In Durkheim's account, group-based ceremonial ritual practices are key in venerating the sacred, reaffirming its exceptional status, and setting it apart from the realm of the profane.
59. Halafoff, Singleton, and Fitzpatrick, "Complexity," 256.
60. Jack D. Douglas and Frances C. Waksler, *The Sociology of Deviance: An Introduction* (Boston: Little, Brown, and Company, 1982), 24.
61. Colin Campbell, *The Myth of Social Action* (Cambridge: Cambridge University Press, 1986); Willem de Koster, *On the Meaning of Meaning* (Rotterdam: Erasmus University, 2022).
62. Griera et al., "Conspirituality." See also Jaron Harambam's chapter in this volume.
63. Lynch, *The New Spirituality*.
64. Jason P. Martens and Bastiaan T. Rutjens, "Spirituality and Religiosity Contribute to Ongoing COVID-19 Vaccination Rates: Comparing 195 Regions Around the World," *Vaccine: X*, no. 12 (2022): 100241.
65. Wilhelmina L. M. Ruijs et al., "Religious Subgroups Influencing Vaccination Coverage in the Dutch Bible Belt: An Ecological Study," *BMC Public Health* 11 (2011), article 102.
66. Josje Ten Kate, Willem de Koster, and Jeroen van der Waal, "'Following Your Gut' or 'Questioning the Scientific Evidence': Understanding Vaccine Skepticism Among More-Educated Dutch Parents," *Journal of Health and Social Behavior* 62, no. 1 (2021): 96.
67. Evans, "Make Love, Not Vaccines."
68. Dick Houtman, Anneke Pons, and Rudi Laermans, "Religion and Solidarity: The Vicissitudes of Protestantism," in *Shifting Solidarities: Trends and Developments in European Societies*, ed. Ine van Hoyweghen, Valeria Pulignano, and Gert Meyers (London: Palgrave MacMillan, 2020), 229–49.
69. Harambam, this volume; De Koster, *Meaning*.
70. David Bloor, *Science and Social Imagery* (Chicago: University of Chicago Press, 1976), 46–54; Houtman, Aupers, and Laermans, "Introduction"; Seidman, *Contested Knowledge*, 19–53.

9

CONSPIRITUALITY

An (Un)happy Marriage of Conspiracy Theories and Spirituality?

JARON HARAMBAM

Whoever witnessed one of the many anti-COVID-19 policy protests held throughout the Netherlands between 2020 and 2022 years saw a remarkable sight: right-wing sympathizers holding the Dutch national flag, walking hand in hand with a variety of spiritual groups carrying yellow umbrellas with red hearts and positive slogans painted on them.[1] They, and several others, carried signs reading "The Media is the Virus" and "COVID-1984." While the flags expressed a nationalism that is rarely publicly displayed in the modestly patriotic Netherlands, the yellow umbrellas reflected a bottom-up and newly developed symbol of "Loving, Peaceful and Positive Resistance" by two women (one of them a person of color) who came up with the idea in February 2021 after being aggressively dispersed by police water cannons.

The contrast between these two public symbols is striking. Yet their bearers all shout in unison: "Love, Freedom, No Dictatorship." This chant became the motto of the Dutch coronavirus resistance movement, heard throughout the country. At protests against government mandates, one found young men with jeans, bomber jackets, black army boots, and shaved heads marching next to fifty-year-old female hippies wearing colorful clothes and bead necklaces while giving out group hugs. There were people shouting angrily about how the government is lying, while others gave away flowers to riot police officers. The coronavirus demonstrations in the Netherlands were, like many of their international counterparts, a true hodgepodge of individuals, social backgrounds, political leanings, and worldviews.[2]

This unusual sight confused many in the Dutch media: How do these radically different groups come together so easily? What unites right-wing nationalists, urban yoga hipsters, and leftist spiritual tree huggers? How do their (seemingly) different worldviews collide into one master narrative of distrusting public authorities and resisting "dictatorial" policies? Is their shared dissatisfaction with the governmental approach to the COVID-19 pandemic enough to bridge such great ideological differences? Quickly, Dutch journalists found the answer: the common denominator across all these circles was a penchant for conspiracy theories.[3]

Both left-leaning spiritual seekers and angry populist-right protesters (and many in between) held strong convictions that the reality about the pandemic presented to them by media, politicians, and scientists was a scam organized by technocratic global elites to force the public into obedience. For these dissenters, the COVID-19 pandemic was nothing more than a massive plot to fool ordinary people into permitting the government to take away their civil liberties, roll out new surveillance technologies, destroy small businesses, and enforce mandatory vaccinations. It was the perfect story to legitimize the "Great Reset"—the radical reconfiguration of our economic and societal global order introduced in June 2020 by Klaus Schwab, founder and executive chairman of the World Economic Forum (WEF). Schwab's plea to seize this "rare but narrow window of opportunity to reset our world" quickly garnered popularity among world leaders and suspicious notoriety in conspiracy circles for its covert ambition to restructure the world in nefarious ways.[4]

This gradual recognition that conspiracy theories serve as the central thread connecting these varied and seemingly contrasting groups was not unique to the Netherlands, but rather present all over the Western world. From Italy to the United States, and from France to Australia, journalists expressed confusion, unease, and surprise about this startling alliance of "soft positive female spirituality" and "hard negative male conspiracy theories." In *Wired* magazine, a journalist with ties to the holistic milieu wrote that while she knew she needed to "monitor the spread of online disinformation and conspiracy theories," she "never expected to find them at [her] yoga class."[5] While a *Guardian* article remarked that on Instagram "wellness advocates used to talk about Bali retreats and cooking with coconut oil. But now they [are] posting links about 5G, Bill Gates or more coded but no less strange messages that 'we' shouldn't trust 'them.'"[6]

What happened? Should we be surprised that spiritual adherents were suddenly expressing conspiratorial worldviews? And were these left-leaning spiritual progressives suddenly turning into conspiratorial militant right-wing activists, as these journalists supposed?

Despite the apparent novelty of these developments, scholars studying spirituality have previously pointed out that certain central characteristics of the spiritual worldview, movements, and practices share affinities with what has come to be known as "conspiracy culture." For instance, Colin Campbell's original conceptualization of the "cultic milieu" emphasized spirituality's cultural kinship with certain kinds of deviant belief systems, ranging from (pseudo)scientific narratives, political ideologies, and esoteric beliefs and practices.[7] What they all share, Campbell argued, is a common opposition and distrust of dominant societal or culturally mainstream discourses. Similarly, Christopher Partridge speaks of "occulture" as a mélange of "hidden, rejected and oppositional" beliefs and practices that are explained by conspiratorial understandings.[8] In the previous chapter in this volume Dick Houtman and Stef Aupers emphasize how spiritual and populist groups share a marked anti-institutionalism that challenges the cultural mainstream. Interestingly, these affinities have also been picked up on from the other side—by those studying conspiracy theories. For example, in the early 2000s political scientist Michael Barkun and historian Nicholas Goodrick-Clarke wrote about the popularity of various esoteric ideas, supernatural beliefs, and occult epistemologies in U.S. millennialist movements and Aryan Nazi cults.[9]

Of course, the affinities are not hard to miss: contemporary conspiracy culture is rife with websites that discuss New World Order theories alongside spiritual awakening narratives—all while selling nutritional supplements used to maximize natural health potential.[10] Or take the many Instagram celebrities, yoga coaches, and wellness influencers urging their followers to resist vaccinations, to focus on nutritious organic food and building up their immune systems, and break free from the shackles of the corporate medical-health industry.[11] And what of the "QAnon Shaman" who became (in)famous in the 2021 insurrection on Capitol Hill and turned out to be a nature-loving, organic food–eating practitioner of yoga and meditation?[12] Spirituality, in short, is often a key feature of contemporary conspiracy culture.[13]

Not surprisingly, there exists a neologism to capture this cultural confluence. In an influential article, Charlotte Ward and David Voas coined the term "conspirituality" to describe what they saw as a "rapidly growing web movement expressing an ideology fueled by political disillusionment and alternative spiritual worldviews."[14] Prescient and insightful, Ward and Voas's analysis has inspired a growing body of research and popular commentary, which exploded in the wake of the COVID-19 pandemic.[15] Indeed, many simply take as fact Ward and Voas's assumption that the coalition of spirituality and conspiracy culture is a frictionless, tension-free endeavor.

Yet this assumption is not warranted. Over the course of my ongoing ethnographic research in the (Dutch) conspiracy milieu, I have encountered many instances of cultural conflict between these two elements.[16] Given the peculiarity of this blend of seemingly opposed ideologies and cultural groups, it perhaps makes sense to highlight their affinities. However, my hunch is that the tendency to foreground affinities over conflicts derives in part from their methodological approach. Ward and Voas's analysis was not based on empirical data but rather armchair theorizing. By contrast, an empirically grounded cultural sociological approach may be necessary to bring to light the tensions that exist on the ground. In fact, in support of this claim, Griera and colleagues found in their recent study of the Spanish antivaccine movement that Twitter analyses show clear confluences of far-right conspiracist with spiritual ideologies, while ethnographic fieldwork reveals far more complexity.[17] Thus, like in any other social configuration, there are always both affinities *and* conflicts—also in conspirituality.

In this chapter I explore how conspiracy theories and spirituality go together and draw from similar cultural understandings of the world, but also how this confluence creates frictions and disputes in both milieux. To do so, I draw on ten years of research into the many different worlds of (Dutch) conspiracy theorists and present empirical examples of such converging and contentious engagements between the spiritual and the conspiratorial.

But to situate these better, I start with a theoretical overview of the history of this confluence of spirituality and conspiracy theories and continue with more contemporary manifestations in the digital "post-truth" age. The underlying methodological argument is that a cultural sociological approach to the topic of conspirituality yields more comprehensive insights in both their affinities and conflicts because it stays close to the lived experiences of actual people and their ideas and practices.

HISTORICAL BEDFELLOWS OR A NEW HYBRID SYSTEM OF BELIEF?

Both "spirituality" and "conspiracy culture" are complex and diffuse signifiers. They are both container concepts that encompass various ideologies, beliefs, practices, and people that have historically been united by their opposition to the cultural mainstream. Now, as Colin Campbell notes in this volume, given the popularity and increasing public presence of spirituality, the extent to which it remains opposed to the cultural mainstream remains open to debate. Yet it remains the case that both conspiracy theories and spirituality are understood *by their adherents* as being opposed to certain dominant religious, political, and scientific orthodoxies and authorities. Moreover, the social and cultural worlds in which spiritual and conspiratorial ideas and practices flourish are similarly diverse and fluid, taking the form of loose networks more than neatly bounded communities. Hence, I have used Campbell's original notion of a cultic "milieu" in my own work on conspiracy culture to describe this relatively stable yet dynamic subculture.[18]

However, to think about the affinities and conflicts between spirituality and conspiracy culture, it is necessary to provide some working definitions of each. As Watts and Houtman explain in the introduction herein, spirituality can be conceived as a third-way mystical tradition in which the divine is seen as an omnipresent and immanent life-force, with religious truths attained through personal experience rather than exegesis, and salvation necessitating the pursuit of authenticity instead of conformity to social norms. Spirituality is found in various domains of contemporary life, from the workplace to social media, and includes all kinds of practices associated with (westernized) Eastern cultural forms such as yoga and meditation, reiki and acupuncture, and the healing power of natural food.

Conspiracy theories, on the other hand, are generally seen as explanations of social events that point to hidden and nefarious actions by particular groups of people.[19] These ideas embody a wide array of topics, ranging from the mundane to the supernatural. But whether we speak about concerns about the rise of "Orwellian" totalitarian governments, strong anti-institutional distrust directed against mainstream media, QAnon inspired notions of satanic pedophile networks, beliefs in the existence of extraterrestrial beings, or ideological resistance to Big Corporations, they all come together in the conspiratorial worldview that opaque global power bastions covertly work together to put humanity into submission. And since conspiracy theories go against the explanations that mainstream epistemic authorities offer (science, media, and politics), they serve as countervailing understandings of reality. That said, they are more than epistemic beliefs alone, since conspiracy theories blossom in various (online) subcultural communities and shape their practices and identities.[20] People find meaning and community in those oppositional understandings of reality. They create new symbols, rituals, and ways of living that go against the grain of mainstream society. Moreover, these ideas circulate in (online) networks where entrepreneurship, algorithms, and social cohesion spur their popularity. Conspiracy culture is thus broader than mere beliefs alone, but the central unifying factor is indeed the conviction that an elite cabal controls and shapes the world for their own benefit.[21]

From these descriptions it may seem odd that spirituality and conspiracy culture go together so easily. The former is much more concerned with the *inner world*, while the latter contrasts by focusing on the *outer world*. This is indeed the argument of Ward and Voas as they introduce the concept of conspirituality. They note that conspiracy theory is "male-dominated, often conservative, generally pessimistic, and typically concerned with current affairs," while spirituality is "predominantly female, liberal, self-consciously optimistic, and largely focused on the self and personal relationships."[22] Yet despite these cultural differences conspiracy theories and spirituality find common ground, Ward and Voas contend, in the shared belief that a paradigm shift or a radical societal awakening will counter the looming totalitarian New World Order.

Furthermore, there is actually much historical affinity between spirituality and conspiracy culture. Asprem and Dyrendal, for example, argue that "conspiracism and esoterism are joined at the hip," while stressing the "historical continuity between the occultist milieu of the nineteenth century and the cultic milieu of the second half of the twentieth century."[23] But also in cultural terms, there is much similarity; in addition to the shared opposition to dominant orthodoxies, both spirituality and conspiracy culture conceptualize the world in holistic terms (all consciousness is one—everything is connected), both disavow mainstream ontologies (reality is alienating illusion—nothing is what it seems), both distrust and reject modern institutions for corrupting our minds (the system imposes suffocating societal roles—trust no one), and both prioritize the self as the ultimate epistemological source (find truth by looking deep down in yourself—do your own research).

Additionally, these affinities are not merely ideological but play out in social life. Ward and Voas propose as key examples of conspirituality the British conspiracy theorist David Icke, the American documentary series *Zeitgeist*, and the Australian *Nexus Magazine*. David Icke is a genuine conspiracy theorist celebrity who enjoys worldwide popularity through his many books, YouTube videos, and performances in large event halls. In his work, Icke weaves together everyday conspiracy theories about media, the scientific establishment and global leaders into an overarching narrative that holds we are ruled by an alien race of shape-shifting reptiles. But he also fuses these ideas with belief in a radical awakening of humanity that would reinstall original spiritual gifts and higher consciousness.[24] The *Zeitgeist* documentary series, which became known worldwide between 2007 and 2011, chronicles conspiracy theories about the mystical origins of Christianity, 9/11, and the financial system, and has been viewed more than 400 million times. The documentary argues for a radically different socioeconomic system, in which sustainability, technological innovation, and care for people and nature stand central. The series became so popular that a global social movement to achieve those goals emerged.[25] Last, *Nexus Magazine*, which dates to the 1980s, publishes alternative news and articles about geopolitics, surveillance, and conspiracy theories as well as alternative medicine, the supernatural, and UFOs. What all these examples have in common, Ward and Voas argue, is that they temper the political cynicism of conspiracy thinking with spiritual optimism and the belief in the coming of a new, better world.[26]

This everyday mixing of spiritual and conspiratorial elements was present in my own fieldwork. Many of the (Dutch) conspiracy websites I examined have categories such as "Consciousness," "Health," and "Spiritual," next to "Politics," "Corona," and "Propaganda." And at the many physical places where conspiracy theorists meet each other (e.g., film screenings, demonstrations, and social meetups), it was clear that various forms of spirituality merge effortlessly with conspiracy theories.[27] At such places, one finds stalls with books on personal growth, self-help, and alternative healing. There are brochures for reincarnation therapy courses and other workshops helping people to find their spiritual path. And in the coffee breaks people speak of the importance of waking up from the Matrix that "they" have built around us. Spirituality is a staple ingredient of conspiracy culture—present and past.

NETWORKED CONSPIRITUALITY IN THE SOCIAL MEDIA AGE

What is perhaps new and surprising about conspirituality is how the internet and its specific affordances have enabled its dissemination and popularization. Ward and Voas note how "the web is central to its [conspirituality's] importation of political and spiritual ideology into the mainstream," because "as websites became easier to access and build, transmission and adoption were facilitated. The virtual social networks created by web users make it possible to spread ideas very widely and very quickly."[28] Indeed, this is even more the case now given that the ubiquity and specific participatory affordances of social media platforms have not only created the infrastructures to reach massive audiences and unite different groups but have also fostered the emergence of online cultures characterized by a distrust of mainstream epistemic authorities, personal seekership, and dedication to "doing one's own research" to find spiritual and political truths.[29]

This platformization of conspirituality has multiple dimensions. A first aspect to consider is how the business models and the algorithmic systems of social media platforms easily funnel "innocuous" people toward more and more extreme conspiratorial content simply because it "sells."[30] Keeping people hooked on social media platforms is key to their profit and survival, and controversial content like conspiracy theories accomplishes this well.[31]

But even more generally, social media platforms use filtering and recommendation algorithms that suggest items that have been liked/consumed before by like-minded people. This easily leads to feedback loops, with people interested in spirituality and related matters (like health, nutrition, or mindfulness) soon ending up with all kinds of conspiracy theories in their feeds, simply because of the political economy of social media platforms.[32]

But it is important to note that technology and media exposure alone cannot explain the confluence of spirituality and conspiracy theories online—what would imply a return to simplistic media effects theories.[33] Assuming that people are ignorant and manipulable cultural dupes does not reflect how social media use actually works. For in fact people actively consume and create online content on the basis of their own worldviews and interests. And following social media logics, they also do so to share with others and to create a following, which often becomes a business model. Indeed, contemporary scholars stress the way spiritual gurus, yoga teachers, and wellness advocates actively propagate conspiratorial content through their own social media channels.[34]

This can take many forms. Some literally provide a platform to conspiracy theorists by inviting them on their YouTube channel, as Kundalini yoga teacher Guru Jagat did to talk about "facts that aren't factual and truths that aren't true."[35] Alternatively, they co-opt conspiratorial language about "evil forces at work" in podcasts about health and lifestyle.[36] Still others, like Dutch top model Doutzen Kroes, who, inspired by her sister and nutritional power food coach Rens Kroes and her fellow spiritual friends, posts inspirational quotes from spiritual handbooks combined with calls to "do your own research" and to "remain vigilant about what *they* want you to believe."[37]

Halafoff and her colleagues report on the way the Australian wellness movement participated in the online show of conspiracy theorist Fanos Panayides and the New Earth Project's (NEP) online platforms. These platforms are run by British conspiritualist Sacha Stone, who strives to "empower a conscious humanity to reclaim its sovereign birthright."[38] Or consider how yoga influencer Stephanie Birch used conspiracy theory hashtags such as "#greatawakening" on her Instagram while posting that "we are experiencing a spiritual warfare against mastery manipulating puppets that go back years."[39] These social media practices are often packaged in "soft feminine aesthetics" that "make conspiracy theories beautiful" and more attractive to women.[40] And this has seeped deep into the conspiracy world, giving rise to the term "pastel Q-Anon," since as female influencers use pastel colors and similar forms of aesthetic branding to mainstream dark conspiracy theories to their audiences.[41] The point is that these "spiritual influencers" utilize the cultures and affordances of social media platforms, also called "micro-celebrity branding techniques,"[42] to reach and bring together the spiritually and conspiratorially minded, thus enabling networked conspirituality.

Many journalists and scholars emphasize the economic gains these spiritual influences garner by reaching larger audiences and making conspiratorial thinking more mainstream. Guerin contends, "yoga entrepreneurs have become adept at seizing the opportunities the pandemic has presented and preying on the vulnerabilities of their audiences."[43] And in her insightful study of what Baker calls "alt.health influencers," she speaks about how they "monetise their audiences by appealing to alternative health and wellness modalities instead of conventional medical practices."[44] Similarly, Halafoff and colleagues show how Australian conspiritualists sell various goods and services online while taking advantage of their celebrity status as online influencers.[45] They advertise and sell nutritional supplements, spiritual books, yoga retreats, and consciousness festivals while promoting conspiratorial thought and fostering distrust of mainstream authorities. Following the key social media business logic of engagement and traffic, the more followers they have, and the more interactions with influencers' contents, the more they earn from platforms.[46] Bridging different worlds, as conspirituality influencers do, has become a business model.

Finally, there is now a Netflix for conspirituality: the online media platform Gaia. For about ten euros per month, customers can enjoy "over 8,000 informative, consciousness-expanding and enlightening films, original shows, yoga and meditation classes, and more that you won't find anywhere else."[47] Gaia embodies a professionalized and mass-produced form of conspirituality: its website is well designed, its content can be viewed on all kinds of devices, and it deploys filtering and recommendation algorithms. Their motto is "Watch, Transform, Belong," illustrating how the platform promises a sense of community. Furthermore, the website boasts "exclusive, original series on topics you won't find in the mainstream media—the nature of the universe, ancient wisdom, the unexplained, alternative healing, and more." It describes itself as "a member-supported media network of truth seekers and believers empowering an evolution of consciousness." On the main page, there is a customer review section, replete with testimonies of how formative Gaia has been in their spiritual journey toward radical awakening. The fusion of spirituality and conspiracy theories is clear as the light of day.

Despite these technological and commercial features, it remains clear that the substantive elective affinities between the spiritual and the conspiratorial worlds are the main drivers of (networked) conspirituality. These mostly revolve around their (strategic) opposition toward mainstream epistemic authorities, the preference for "softer" epistemologies (such as perennial knowledge, intuition, and experience), and their focus on personal discovery and societal awakening. Yet this fusion of spirituality with conspiracy theories also creates frictions and fissures, and clear resistance from both parties.

CONSPIRITUALITY SUPERSTAR DAVID ICKE INSPIRES AND IRRITATES

If anyone personifies conspirituality, it is David Icke. As mentioned earlier, Icke is a true conspiracy theory celebrity: he has been around since the early 1990s and has since built an entire emporium around his controversial conspiratorial ideas. He has a multimedia website boasting articles, books, videos, and an e-commerce shop. His website is visited over one million times per month by a diverse audience (in terms of age and sex) from all over the world (although dominated by the Anglo-Saxon countries).[48] But he is also very much a performer. Next to conveying his ideas in various media forms, he enjoys taking center stage. Literally: he frequently does hourlong shows in stadiums and theaters around the world, during which he takes his audience on a compelling tour through his ideas. And he has charisma, too; he makes jokes in a working-class East Midlands English dialect but is dead serious at times as well.[49]

Icke is most famous—or infamous—for his "reptilian thesis": the idea that the world's elites are shapeshifting reptilian-human hybrids that pass as humans yet originate from other domains of our universe. Although outlandish, his theories actually start rather mundane, by stressing the corruption and dogmatism of our modern institutions—media, science, politics, religion, and so on—and how they manipulate "us" and "program our minds" into acquiescence.[50] Icke integrates all these institutions into a single pyramid with a network of secret societies and powerful families at its top, sometimes called "Illuminati bloodlines" and at other times the "Rothschild Zionists." But, as Icke explains, "there is this other-dimensional, non-human, level to look at"—the supernatural and ancient history explaining where we are now. This is how we get to the "reptilian thesis" through which Icke gained his fame and notoriety.[51] According to Icke, these alien races have infiltrated our human bloodlines and undermined our potential to reach higher consciousness.

Icke's ideas are great exemplars of today's "super conspiracy theories," that is, "conspiratorial constructs in which multiple conspiracies are believed to be linked together hierarchically."[52] Icke brings the heavens and the earths together in one overarching conspiracy theory about institutional corruption, pervasive mind control, multidimensional universes, and shapeshifting reptilian races. This is quite an accomplishment: being able to convincingly bring so many different ideas together in one master narrative of deceit is a narratological feat. Indeed, as Lewis and Kahn rightfully note, "Icke's greatest strength is his totalizing ambition to weave numerous sub-theories into an extraordinary narrative that is both all-inclusive and all-accounting."[53]

But he is also known for his "synthesis" of seemingly different or even "antithetical" ideas: he brings together New Age teachings with apocalyptic conspiracy theories about a coming totalitarian New World Order.[54] Icke sketches a pristine image of a forgotten past when people still lived in harmony with the natural world and were connected to higher levels of consciousness. But he then argues that "the road to tyranny began when these reptilians arrived here and changed our DNA so that we can no longer access the world beyond our five senses: 'they want to lock humanity in that prison.'" He anticipates salvation from all the misery and subjugation extra-terrestrial elites have imposed on humans by means of a radical awakening of humanity that will bring back the spiritual powers we once had. But to get there, Icke maintains, we need to "get off our knees" and revolt against their domination; we need to "free our minds from the programming of a lifetime [and] remove the barriers of belief and perception that keep us from enlightenment."[55]

Similar to many people in the field of spirituality, Icke eclectically draws on a multitude of epistemic sources to support his arguments and persuade his audience.[56] His claims to truth are a hodgepodge of epistemological strategies: he draws on his own personal experience, talks effortlessly about all kinds of perennial narratives in ancient cultures, uses technological imagery, and references to science fiction to help people believe, yet also draws on both natural science and critical social theory to support his super conspiracy theory. This eclectic use of epistemologies, moving from the visceral to the cerebral, is also common in the spiritual milieu. Scholars of spirituality practically all emphasize how both leaders and followers deploy several epistemologies to express and support their views. They all "pick-and-mix" from established epistemic authorities and various kinds of heterodox knowledge.[57] In late modernity, where no single institution has a monopoly on truth, and where people remain wary of mainstream institutions and their truth claims, deploying a diverse range of epistemic strategies is a winning formula.

But Icke's fusion of conspiratorial and spiritual thought is not just ideational; it is visible in his audience too. Many scholars highlight how he is able to bring together a diverse range of people.[58] As Lewis and Kahn argue, "Icke appeals equally to bohemian hipsters and right-wing reactionary fanatics [who] are just as likely to be sitting next to a 60-something UFO buff, a Nuwaubian, a Posadist, a Raëlian, or New Age earth goddess."[59] His fan base is strikingly diverse: from new religious movements to political anarchists, alternative healers, and far-right militants—a radical assortment of societal classes, generations and subcultures come together in his audience.[60] All of them, however, share a discontent with our current societal order, and more precisely with the way our primary institutions (e.g., science, politics, religion, media, etc.) work.

Icke is not without critics, even among those who actually buy his books and visit his shows. Over the course of my fieldwork—which included attending a 2011 performance of his in Amsterdam—I found out that his fanaticism and radical activism are often met with resistance, because many do not see militancy as the way forward.[61] To give some examples of what my interlocuters had to say about him: "Well, David Icke for example, a very intelligent man who has really done his homework, so with 80 percent of what he is saying, I think yes, fine, feels good, I get it. But at a certain point he completely tips the scales and goes way too far, way too fanatic. That's all based on fear (Julie, a twenty-eight-year-old therapeutic counselor)."[62]

Or in the words of Robert, a posh middle-aged man who works for an international fruit trading company and enjoyed Icke's performance in Amsterdam until the militancy took over:

> I had that with David Icke at the end of his show, that's really a pep talk, like, "Yeah, let's fight, let's go into resistance!" I don't agree with that, that's not the way to go, to stand up and "get off your knees." Those are powerful terms . . . it's a shame people are so easily lured into resistance, you'll hear that as the audience applauds and whistles when David calls for resistance, revolt and mutiny, well, that's exactly what *not* to do, it only works negatively. It generates counter-effects.[63]

Like Robert, many of my interlocutors spoke of the adverse effects Icke's aggressive attitude generates, how fighting and resistance only generates more bloodshed. Instead, they argue that there must be another way than radical activism to bring about change:

> David Icke, I've followed him for five years or so, but he is always in such a fighter's mood. That doesn't generate good responses. I don't agree with fighting, that only provokes counter fighting, provokes resistance. The same counts for ArgusEyes6 [a Dutch conspiracy website], also in a fighter's mood. Barricade work. Barricades never worked, well, maybe, but they incite so much resistance. I think there are other ways and entrances (Lucy, a 46-year-old haptonomic therapist).[64]

This attitude is especially common among spiritually minded conspiracy theorists, who largely oppose the activist strategies of protest, resistance, and confrontation that are popular among many others. Activism, these people contend, is based on negative emotions like aggression and fear which should be avoided. As Julie and Lucy continue:

> It's to turn fanatic, push matters over the edge and end up in frenzy. But instead of informing yourself, being aware about things, you're basing your decisions on fear. Basically, you have two choices: either you go along with that fear or you go along with what happens if your consciousness opens. Someone like David Icke, for example, he drags you into fear. (Julie)[65]

> Fear is our biggest enemy. It destroys our own judgment, our feelings and discriminatory capacities so that we will comply with the arbitrary whims of others. (Lucy)

While these people may share with the more radical or activist conspiracy theorists the importance of "awakening" to understand what is really going on under the surface of society, they strongly reject the idea that convincing others of one's truth by screaming louder than the rest and by standing on the barricades is the way to go. They believe instead that real change can only occur by finding the good within oneself, and by being a living example for others.[66] Steven, a thirty-two-year-old consultant in the green energy industry, who refers to himself as a "dreamer of a better world," explains: "And one wonders, couldn't it make sense that whatever you see happening "outside," is actually a reflection of what happens inside? In the end, the revolution that is going on now, truly is an inner revolution."[67] Tellingly, the influential 1980s New Age bestseller *The Aquarian Conspiracy*, written by Marilyn Ferguson, already develops the argument that "real" revolutions are not built on political protest and activism, but rather on personal change and "inner discoveries." A new age of peace and stability, she claims, can emerge only when individuals exemplify a better world. Many of my interlocutors agree:[68]

> If you're imposing things, you're not doing it right. If you really believe in something, you become what you believe, you'll radiate and don't need to say anything at all. (Julie)

> If I make sure to raise my frequency by being honest, treating people well, and by loving, the rest will vibrate along. I don't need to interfere with other people's lives! (Pauline)

> I don't think resistance is the right way to go, what I do instead is to apply it to myself. And if other people notice it, ask about it, feel touched by it, then it will have an effect, not by imposing it on people. I think that will have much more effect than pushing. To inspire others instead of terrifying them. (Robert)

What all these spiritual seekers are saying is that "the hard and negative male side of conspirituality," as Ward and Voas call it, does not merge easily with "the soft feminine side of spirituality."[69] Put even more strongly, these radically different ideas about how to position oneself and act in the world create marked frictions and divisions in the conspiratorial milieu, with the radical militancy and activism of some conspiritualists dismissed by many others. This appears even more true now that various far-right conspiracy theorists have appropriated the culture of the holistic milieu while taking the stage of social media and (world) politics. And the same counts for spiritual resistance to the antiscientific tendencies of their counterparts during the COVID-19 pandemic.

CONSPIRITUALITY CONTESTED FROM BOTH SIDES

The tensions between the spiritual and the conspiratorial worlds have been tolerated by each side for a long time, which explains why Ward and Voas conceptualized their confluence as unproblematic and fictionless. However, with the rise of Trump and the QAnon movement in the United States over the last decade and the COVID-19 pandemic, which shook virtually all societies to the core, this lenient attitude has started to become problematic.

Jonathan Ong, for example, presents fascinating digital ethnographic research done among fifteen online spiritual influencers who practice "various forms of resistance against dangerous disinformation and white supremacy within alternative spiritual, or 'woo woo,' communities."[70] He shows how and why these "progressive spiritual influencers took actions against the collision of mystical teachings with far-right (QAnon) conspiracy theory, protesting specifically against the legitimation of antiscientific, antidemocratic, and anti-institutional discourse by "hijacking" popular spiritual discourse about "resisting fear," "raising consciousness," and "radical awakening." Their resistance takes many forms, from "educational content that calls out the spiritual hijacking of esoteric beliefs" to explicitly "correcting dangerous conspiracy theory and medical disinformation."[71] Ong warns that while these spiritual vocabularies may sound "well-meaning," they "could be intentionally repurposed to promote insidious political agendas without believers being fully aware what they have gotten into." Whether this suggestion of guilelessness actually holds is an open question, but fears of spiritual seekers being lured into extremist positions are certainly real.

Cécile Guerin speaks about spiritual teachers who actively opposed the incorporation of conspiracy theories in the holistic milieu.[72] She points to cult survivor and yoga teacher Matthew Remski, who "lists figures in the wellness industry who have shared conspiracy theories and aims at exposing 'faux-progressive wellness utopianism.'" Or consider Seane Corn, cofounder of Off the Mat and Into the World, a California-based "community bridging the tools of yoga with sustainable and conscious activism."[73] Since the start of the pandemic Corn experienced increased paranoia and hostility in her yoga and wellness community that went far beyond the "antivaxx stuff" she was used to: "I felt like I had a responsibility to speak up as a member of the community. I hoped that by interjecting, I would help some of the students that were getting drawn into this rhetoric." Finally, Halafoff and colleagues show how "prominent influencers in the wellness industry in Australia, such as Sarah Wilson, made public statements challenging conspiracist views and encouraging members of wellness communities to be vaccinated for the public good."[74]

And then there are the various testimonies of journalists in the Netherlands about how the popularity of conspiratorial thought in people's spiritual circles has caused severe discomfort and conflict.[75] These reporters have written about their unease with the amount of disinformation about the pandemic that was shared in their social circles, and about how people they had been doing yoga or spiritual trainings with for years suddenly pushed them away because they followed government guidelines. I myself got many emails from people about how their "smart, sensitive and spiritual loved ones seemed brainwashed by conspiracy theories." As a response to the surge of conspirituality in the Netherlands during the pandemic, various spiritual practitioners, from yoga teachers to reiki coaches, grouped together on Facebook. As one member states: "having that uncanny feeling that something is wrong is one thing, but believing that governments are colluding internationally is quite another. It felt like people I've worked with and befriended for years suddenly turned right-wing, where I kept being left."[76] Stine Jensen, a Dutch philosopher, yoga teacher, and author of the book *Go East: A Philosopher's Journey through the World of Yoga, Mindfulness and Spirituality*, expressed a similar discomfort in a major Dutch newspaper, pointing out how spiritual people have now come to be put on a par with extremists and are "forced to actively disassociate from fascism," while the connections between the two are actually far from evidenced by empirical data.[77] The key point is that the fact of conspirituality has engendered a real divide within the holistic milieu.

Interestingly, disapproval of the confluence of spirituality and conspiracy theories is also expressed by hard-core conspiracy theorists. Their criticism and unease come from a strong disapproval of "soft epistemologies" that allegedly erode their credibility in public debates. While spiritual people endorse following intuition, experience, and feelings, critical conspiracy theorists reject these sources of knowledge in lieu of positivist epistemologies. Aiming to decipher the "real" truth, they insist on facts, evidence, and the scientific method.[78] Think, for example, of the 9/11 Truth Movement, whose members analyze videos and boast complicated mathematical calculations to argue that planes cannot possibly have caused the collapse of the Twin Towers. Or Flat Earthers, who perform all kinds of experiments with lenses, binoculars, and geometric slats to establish that Earth is actually flat. This positivistic stance clearly conflicts with spiritual seekers' disposition to follow their intuition and feelings rather than rely on rationality or science.[79] For spiritual folk, real knowledge is not something rational but first and foremost something deeply emotional, while hardcore conspiracy buffs get irritated by such "woo-woo" epistemologies.

These conflicts are not merely ideological but also relate to credibility in public debates. Tired of hearing spiritual people say that "things don't feel right" or that "the facts don't resonate with them," positivist conspiracy theorists understand that if they and their alternative visions of reality are to be believed, they need to produce solid evidence and hard facts.[80] This conflict often becomes manifest in projects that conspiracy theorists and spiritual people set up collaboratively. For example, for years I have been following the online media platform Café Weltschmerz, which publishes videos that feature "discussions and perspectives that are not present (enough) in the regular media." Their mission is to "use citizen journalism as a means of change. . . . Our interviewers are autonomous cross-thinkers and experts in their field."[81] The platform is run by volunteers from all walks of life, both hardcore conspiracy theorists and more spiritually minded individuals. Yet few of their broadcasts cover topics that appeal to spiritual audiences, much to the chagrin of their spiritually inclined volunteers. In their conversations with me, the producers indicate that they frequently bring up the desirability of expanding the number of spiritual programs yet consistently receive no for an answer, because such programs are seen by its owners to undermine the credibility of the media platform.

SHARED AFFINITIES AND BOUNDARY WORK

In recent years the affinities between the worlds of spirituality and conspiracy theories have become apparent. Commentators witnessed QAnon-related conspiracy theories packaged in soft pastel colors thriving on the Instagram feeds of domestic housewives and spiritual women alike.[82] During the COVID-19 crisis, many supporters of holistic philosophies of life, alternative medicine, yoga, reiki, and mindfulness distrusted and contested the official narratives and measures taken to contain the pandemic.[83] The notion that mainstream epistemic authorities cannot be trusted, so that "doing one's own research," "waking up," and "following one's inner-knowing" become necessary, is fundamental to a conspiratorial worldview that finds considerable resonance in the holistic milieu.

For many this is an (unpleasant) surprise.[84] However, those who have studied both spirituality and conspiracy theories will be less shocked, since there are longstanding historical and intellectual affinities between spiritual groups and ideologies and their conspiratorial counterparts.[85] According to Ward and Voas, the evolution of these historical affinities has produced conspirituality, a unified movement that combines the pessimistic elements of conspiracy thinking with the spiritual belief in salvation through radical human awakening.[86] And given the very public character of this alliance during the COVID-19 pandemic, many in academia and the popular press simply accepted Ward and Voas's analysis without qualifications.[87]

But should we conceptualize "conspirituality" as a unified movement? Or is it rather a pragmatic synthesis of distinct ideologies? In this chapter I have tried to show that although conspiracy theorists and spiritual seekers share a distrust of societal institutions and a do-it-yourself epistemology in common, there are also many frictions and conflicts when they meet and interact. The emphasis on facts, evidence, and scientific calculation of conspiracy theorists clashes with the spiritual prioritization of feelings, resonances, and intuitions as guides to true knowledge. And while the spiritually inclined tend to reject the militant activism of conspiracy theorists as a way to attain a better world, the more positivist conspiracy theorists fear that their credibility is undermined when "softer" spiritual epistemologies take over.[88]

It makes more sense, therefore, to conceptualize the confluence of the spiritual and the conspiratorial as resulting from an elective affinity in the classical Weberian sense. Because there surely exists an overlap between these two cultural worlds, talk of "conspirituality" is useful, if also somewhat misleading. We should beware of essentializing conspirituality as a unified and stable movement, and instead stay sensitive to the everchanging and porous boundaries between the two cultural forms. One way to do so is by drawing on the great work of Thomas Gieryn and Michèle Lamont and Virág Molnár, who direct attention to the practical work that needs to be done to maintain or dissolve (cultural) boundaries.[89] This invites sociological studies of conspirituality that address how and why different people try to erect, blur, or bridge boundaries between the spiritual and the conspiracy world—be they real conspirituality buffs or those who oppose their confluence. Given the cultural and political stakes, I hope to have demonstrated that such a perspective sheds much-needed light on the internal complexity attending conspirituality.

NOTES

1. Jaron Harambam, "Distrusting Consensus: How a Uniform Corona Pandemic Narrative Fostered Suspicion and Conspiracy Theories," *Journal of Digital Social Research* 5, no. 3 (2023): 109–39.
2. Harambam, "Distrusting Consensus."
3. Anne Corré, "Waar spiritualiteit en samenzwering elkaar ontmoeten" (Where Spirituality and Conspiracy Meet), *NRC Handelsblad*, May 5, 2021; Rosa van Gool and Coen van de Ven, "Wij zijn het nieuwe nieuws" (We Are the New News), *De Groene Amsterdammer*, September 14,

2021; Doortje Smithuijsen, "De opkomst van 'wellnessrechts': Yogales als broeinest van complottheorieën" (The Rise of the "Wellness Right": Yoga Class as Hotbed of Conspiracy Theories), *Vrij Nederland*, April 7, 2021.
4. Naomi Klein, "The Great Reset Conspiracy Smoothie," *Intercept*, December 8, 2020, https://theintercept.com/2020/12/08/great-reset-conspiracy/.
5. Cécile Guerin, "The Yoga World Is Riddled with Anti-vaxxers and QAnon Believers," *Wired*, January 28, 2021.
6. Brigid Delaney, " 'Evil Forces': How Covid-19 Paranoia United the Wellness Industry and Rightwing Conspiracy Theorists," *Guardian*, June 8, 2020.
7. Colin Campbell, "The Cult, the Cultic Milieu and Secularisation," *A Sociological Yearbook of Religion in Britain* 5 (1972): 119–36. For an updated rethinking of this concept, see Campbell's chapter in this volume.
8. Christopher Partridge, *The Re-enchantment of the West*, vol. 2, *Alternative Spiritualities, Sacralization, Popular Culture and Occulture* (London: T&T Clark, 2006).
9. Michael Barkun, *A Culture of Conspiracy: Apocalyptic Visions in Contemporary America* (Berkeley: University of California Press, 2006); Nicholas Goodrick-Clarke, *The Occult Roots of Nazism: Secret Aryan Cults and Their Influence on Nazi Ideology* (New York: New York University Press, 2003).
10. Delaney, "Evil Forces."
11. Guerin, "The Yoga World."
12. Julie Gerstein, "The US Fur-Wearing, Face-painted 'QAnon Shaman' Has Asked Trump for a Presidential Pardon," *Business Insider*, January 15, 2021.
13. Jaron Harambam, *Contemporary Conspiracy Culture: Truth and Knowledge in an Era of Epistemic Instability* (London: Routledge, 2020).
14. Charlotte Ward and David Voas, "The Emergence of Conspirituality," *Journal of Contemporary Religion* 26, no. 1 (2011): 103–21.
15. Egil Asprem and Asbjorn Dyrendal, "Conspirituality Reconsidered: How Surprising and How New Is the Confluence of Spirituality and Conspiracy Theory?," *Journal of Contemporary Religion* 30, no. 3 (2015): 367–82; David G. Robertson, "Conspiracy Theories and the Study of Alternative and Emergent Religions," *Nova Religio: The Journal of Alternative and Emergent Religions* 19, no. 2 (2015): 5–16; Beth Singler, *The Indigo Children: New Age Experimentation with Self and Science* (London: Routledge, 2017); Julian Walker, Matthew Remski and Derek Beres, *Conspirituality: How New Age Conspiracy Theories Became a Public Threat* (Toronto: Random House Canada, 2023); Mar Griera et al., "Conspirituality in COVID-19 Times: A Mixed-Method Study

of Antivaccine Movements in Spain," *Journal for the Academic Study of Religion* 35, no. 2 (2022): 192–217; Anna Halafoff et al., "Selling (Con)spirituality and COVID-19 in Australia: Convictions, Complexity and Countering Dis/misinformation," *Journal for the Academic Study of Religion* 35, no. 2 (2022): 141–67; Stephanie A. Baker, "Alt.Health Influencers: How Wellness Culture and Web Culture Have Been Weaponised to Promote Conspiracy Theories and Far-right Extremism During the COVID-19 Pandemic," *European Journal of Cultural Studies* 25, no. 1 (2022): 3–24.
16. Harambam, *Contemporary Conspiracy Culture*.
17. Griera et al., "Conspirituality in COVID-19 Times."
18. Campbell, "The Cult, the Cultic Milieu and Secularization"; Harambam, *Contemporary Conspiracy Culture*.
19. Karen M. Douglas et al., "Understanding Conspiracy Theories," *Political Psychology* 40, no. 1 (2019): 3–35.
20. Gina Husting and Martin Orr, "Dangerous Machinery: 'Conspiracy Theorist as a Transpersonal Strategy of Exclusion," *Symbolic Interaction* 30, no. 2 (2007): 127–50; Mathijs Pelkmans and Rhys Machold, "Conspiracy Theories and Their Truth Trajectories," *Focaal*, no. 59 (2011): 66–80.
21. Husting and Orr, "Dangerous Machinery"; Pelkmans and Machold, "Conspiracy Theories."
22. Ward and Voas, "Conspirituality," 104.
23. Asprem and Dyrendal, "Conspirituality Reconsidered."
24. Jaron Harambam and Stef Aupers, "From the Unbelievable to the Undeniable: Epistemological Pluralism, Or How Conspiracy Theorists Legitimate Their Extraordinary Truth Claims," *European Journal of Cultural Studies* 24, no. 4 (2021): 990–1008.
25. Harambam, *Contemporary Conspiracy Culture*, 46–47.
26. Ward and Voas, "Conspirituality," 108.
27. Harambam, *Contemporary Conspiracy Culture*.
28. Ward and Voas, "Conspirituality," 116.
29. Baker, "Alt.Health Influencers"; Halafoff et al., "Selling (Con)spirituality."
30. Zeynep Tufekci, "YouTube, the Great Radicalizer," *New York Times*, March 10, 2018; Rebecca Lewis, "'This Is What the News Won't Show You': YouTube Creators and the Reactionary Politics of Micro-Celebrity," *Television & New Media* 21, no. 2 (2020): 201–17.
31. Emma Llansó et al., "Artificial Intelligence, Content Moderation, and Freedom of Expression," Transatlantic Working Group on Content Moderation Online and Freedom of Expression, 2020, https://www.ivir.nl/publicaties/download/AI-Llanso-Van-Hoboken-Feb-2020

.pdf; Katja Valaskivi, "Circulation of Conspiracy Theories in the Attention Factory," *Popular Communication* 20, no. 3 (2022): 162–77.
32. Christian Fuchs, *Social Media: A Critical Introduction* (London: Sage, 2021); José van Dijck, Thomas Poell and Martijn de Waal, *The Platform Society: Public Values in a Connective World* (New York: Oxford University Press, 2018).
33. Simone Tosoni, "Misinformation, Social Media and the Pandemic Crisis: Challenging the Return to a Powerful Media Effects Paradigm," *Technoscienza* 12, no. 2 (2021): 174–92.
34. Baker, "Alt.Health Influencers"; Delaney, "Evil Forces"; Guerin, "The Yoga World."
35. Guerin, "The Yoga World."
36. Delaney, "Evil Forces."
37. Van Gool and Van de Ven, "Wij zijn het nieuwe nieuws"; Jaron Harambam, "The Proliferation of Alternative Media: How Corona Conspiracy Theories in The Netherlands Fostered New Social Movements," in *Covid Conspiracy Theories in Global Perspective*, ed. Michael Butter and Peter Knight (London: Routledge, 2022), 252–68.
38. Halafoff et al., "Selling (Con)spirituality," 148.
39. Guerin, "The Yoga World."
40. Kaitlyn Tiffany, "The Women Making Conspiracy Theories Beautiful," *Atlantic*, August 15, 2020.
41. Marc-André Argentino, "Pastel Q-Anon," *Global Network on Extremism and Technology*, March 17, 2021, https://gnet-research.org/2021/03/17/pastel-qanon/; Mia Bloom and Sophia Moskalenko, *Pastels and Pedophiles: Inside the Mind of QAnon* (Stanford, CA: Stanford University Press, 2021).
42. Baker, "Alt.Health Influencers"; Lewis, "This Is What the News Won't Show You."
43. Guerin, "The Yoga World."
44. Baker, "Alt.Health Influencers," 6.
45. Halafoff et al., "Selling (Con)spirituality."
46. Fuchs, "Social Media."
47. https://www.gaia.com.
48. https://www.similarweb.com/website/davidicke.com/#traffic.
49. Harambam and Aupers, "From the Unbelievable to the Undeniable."
50. Harambam and Aupers, "From the Unbelievable to the Undeniable," 995.
51. Barkun, *A Culture of Conspiracy*, 105.
52. Barkun, *A Culture of Conspiracy*, 6.
53. Tyson Lewis and Richard Kahn, "The Reptoid Hypothesis: Utopian and Dystopian Representational Motifs in David Icke's Alien Conspiracy Theory," *Utopian Studies* 16, no. 1 (2005): 50.

54. Barkun, *A Culture of Conspiracy*; Ward and Voas, "Conspirituality."
55. Harambam and Aupers, "From the Unbelievable to the Undeniable," 995.
56. Harambam and Aupers, "From the Unbelievable to the Undeniable," 995.
57. Colin Campbell, *Easternization of the West: A Thematic Account of Cultural Change in the Modern Era* (Boulder, CO: Paradigm Publishers, 2007); Wouter Hanegraaff, *New Age Religion and Western Culture: Esotericism in the Mirror of Secular Thought* (New York: State University of New York Press, 1997); Partridge, *The Re-enchantment of the West*.
58. Barkun, *A Culture of Conspiracy*; Ward and Voas, "Conspirituality."
59. Lewis and Kahn, "The Reptoid Hypothesis," 46.
60. Harambam and Aupers, "From the Unbelievable to the Undeniable."
61. Jaron Harambam and Stef Aupers. "'I Am Not a Conspiracy Theorist': Relational Identifications in the Dutch Conspiracy Milieu," *Cultural Sociology* 11, no. 1 (2017): 113–29.
62. Harambam and Aupers, "I Am Not a Conspiracy Theorist," 121.
63. Harambam and Aupers, "I Am Not a Conspiracy Theorist," 121.
64. Harambam and Aupers, "I Am Not a Conspiracy Theorist," 121.
65. Harambam and Aupers, "I Am Not a Conspiracy Theorist," 122.
66. Watts calls this "methodological individualism." See Galen Watts, "The Religion of the Heart: 'Spirituality' in Late Modernity," *American Journal of Cultural Sociology* 10, no. 1 (2022): 1–33.
67. Harambam and Aupers, "I Am Not a Conspiracy Theorist," 122.
68. Harambam and Aupers, "I Am Not a Conspiracy Theorist," 122.
69. Ward and Voas, "Conspirituality."
70. Aleena Chia et al., "Everything Is Connected: Networked Spirituality in the New Age," *AoIR Selected Papers of Internet Research* (2021): 4–5, https://doi.org/10.5210/spir.v2021i0.12093.
71. Chia et al., "Everything Is Connected," 4–5.
72. Guerin, "The Yoga World."
73. https://www.offthematintotheworld.org/.
74. Halafoff et al., "Selling (Con)spirituality," 148.
75. Corré, "Waar spiritualiteit en samenzwering elkaar ontmoeten"; Van Gool and Van de Ven, "Wij zijn het nieuwe nieuws"; Smithuijsen, "De opkomst van 'wellnessrechts.'"
76. Corré, "Waar spiritualiteit en samenzwering elkaar ontmoeten."
77. Stine Jensen, "'Yoga' is niet synoniem met radicaal-rechtse denkbeelden," *NRC Handelsblad*, March 31, 2021.
78. Harambam, *Contemporary Conspiracy Culture*, 170.
79. Harambam, *Contemporary Conspiracy Culture*, 171.
80. Harambam, *Contemporary Conspiracy Culture*, 177–79.
81. Harambam, "The Proliferation of Alternative Media."

82. Argentino, "Pastel Q-Anon"; Tiffany, "The Women Making Conspiracy Theories Beautiful."
83. Baker, "Alt.Health Influencers"; Harambam, "The Proliferation of Alternative Media."
84. Delaney, "Evil Forces"; Guerin, "The Yoga World."
85. Asprem and Dyrendal, "Conspirituality Reconsidered"; Stef Aupers and Jaron Harambam, "Rational Enchantments: Conspiracy Theory Between Secular Skepticism and Spiritual Salvation," in *Handbook of Conspiracy Theory and Contemporary Religion*, ed. Asbjørn Dyrendal, David G. Robertson and Egil Asprem (Leiden: Brill, 2018), 48–69.
86. Ward and Voas, "Conspirituality."
87. Delaney, "Evil Forces"; Guerin, "The Yoga World."
88. Harambam and Aupers, "I Am Not a Conspiracy Theorist."
89. Thomas F. Gieryn, *Cultural Boundaries of Science: Credibility on the Line* (Chicago: University of Chicago Press, 1999); Michèle Lamont and Virág Molnár, "The Study of Boundaries in the Social Sciences," *Annual Review of Sociology* 28: 167–95.

BIBLIOGRAPHY

AARP. *Complementary and Alternative Medicine: What People 50 and Older Are Using and Discussing with Their Physicians*. Washington, DC: AARP, 2007.
Academic Consortium for Integrative Medicine & Health. "Membership." 2023. https://imconsortium.org/member-listing/.
Acevedo, David. "Tracking Cancel Culture in Higher Education." *National Association of Scholars*. October 15, 2021. https://www.nas.org/blogs/article/tracking-cancel-culture-in-higher-education.
Actually Free. "Religious Freebies." http://www.actuallyfree.com/free-stuff/religious-freebies/.
Addley, Esther. "Study Shows that 60% of Britons Believe in Conspiracy Theories." *Guardian*, November 23, 2018.
Adler, Margot. *Drawing Down the Moon: Witches, Druids, Goddess-Worshippers and Other Pagans in America Today*. Rev. ed. London: Penguin, 1986.
Albanese, Catherine L. *A Republic of Mind and Spirit: A Cultural History of American Metaphysical Religion*. New Haven, CT: Yale University Press, 2007.
Alexander, Brian. "(You)2." *Wired*, February 1, 2001. https://www.wired.com/2001/02/projectx/.
Alexander, Jeffrey C. *The Meanings of Social Life: A Cultural Sociology*. Oxford: Oxford University Press, 2003.
Alexander, Jeffrey C., and Philip Smith. "The Discourse of American Civil Society: A New Proposal for Cultural Studies." *Theory and Society* 22, no. 2 (1993): 151–207.
———. "The Strong Program: Origins, Achievements, and Prospects." In *Handbook of Cultural Sociology*, ed. John R. Hall, Laura Grindstaff, and Ming-Cheng Lo, 13–24. London: Routledge, 2010.

Alliance for Audited Media. "Total Circulation for Consumer Magazines." 2020. http://abcas3.auditedmedia.com/ecirc/magtitlesearch.asp.

Altglas, Véronique. *From Yoga to Kabbalah: Religious Exoticism and the Logics of Bricolage*. Oxford: Oxford University Press, 2014.

———. "Spirituality and Discipline: Not a Contradiction in Terms." In Altglas and Wood, *Bringing Back the Social into the Sociology of Religion*, 79–107.

Altglas, Véronique, and Matthew Wood. *Bringing Back the Social Into the Sociology of Religion: Critical Approaches*. Boston: Brill, 2018.

American Hospital Association. "More Hospitals Offering Complementary and Alternative Medicine Services." 2011. https://www.aha.org/system/files/presscenter/pressrel/2011/110907-pr-camsurvey.pdf.

Ammerman, Nancy T. *Sacred Stories, Spiritual Tribes: Finding Religion in Everyday Life*. Oxford: Oxford University Press, 2014.

———. "Spiritual but Not Religious? Beyond Binary Choices in the Study of Religion." *Journal for the Scientific Study of Religion* 52, no. 2 (2013): 258–78.

———. *Studying Lived Religion: Contexts and Practices*. New York: New York University Press, 2021.

Ansolabehere, Stephen, and Eitan Hersh. "Validation: What Big Data Reveal about Survey Misreporting and the Real Electorate." *Political Analysis* 20, no. 4 (2012): 437–59.

Arat, Alp. " 'What It Means to Be Truly Human': The Postsecular Hack of Mindfulness." *Social Compass* 64, no. 2 (2017): 167–79.

Argentino, Marc-André. "Pastel Q-Anon." *Global Network on Extremism and Technology*. March 17, 2021. https://gnet-research.org/2021/03/17/pastel-qanon/.

Asprem, Egil, and Asbjørn Dyrendal. "Conspirituality Reconsidered: How Surprising and How New is the Confluence of Spirituality and Conspiracy Theory?" *Journal of Contemporary Religion* 30, no. 3 (2015): 367–82.

Association of Accredited Naturopathic Medical Colleges. "The 6 Principles." September 26, 2008–April 21, 2021. https://web.archive.org/web/20140219211050/https://www.aanmc.org/*naturopathic*-medicine/the-6-principles.php.

Aupers, Stef. "The Revenge of the Machines: On Modernity, Digital Technology and Animism." *Asian Journal of Social Science 30*, no. 2 (2002): 199–220.

Aupers, Stef, and Dick Houtman. "Beyond the Spiritual Supermarket: The Social and Public Significance of New Age Spirituality." *Journal of Contemporary Religion* 21, no. 2 (2006): 201–22.

———. " 'Reality Sucks': On Alienation and Cybergnosis." *Concilium: International Journal of Theology 41*, no. 1 (2005): 1–11.

———, eds. *Religions of Modernity: Relocating the Sacred to the Self and the Digital*. Leiden: Brill, 2010.

Aupers, Stef, and Jaron Harambam. "Rational Enchantments: Conspiracy Theory Between Secular Skepticism and Spiritual Salvation." In *Handbook of Conspiracy Theory and Contemporary Religion*, ed. Asbjørn Dyrendal, David G. Robertson, and Egil Asprem, 48–69. Leiden: Brill, 2018.

Babbitt, Irving. *Rousseau and Romanticism*. Boston: Houghton Mifflin Company, 1919.

Baggetta, Matthew, and Ricardo Bello-Gomez. "Can You Sing Your Way to Good Citizenship? Recreational Association Structures and Member Political Participation." *Social Problems* (advance access). 2023. https://doi.org/10.1093/socpro/spado27.

Baker, Stephanie Alice. "Alt.Health Influencers: How Wellness Culture and Web Culture Have Been Weaponised to Promote Conspiracy Theories and Far-Right Extremism During the COVID-19 Pandemic." *European Journal of Cultural Studies* 25, no. 1 (2022): 3–24.

Barkun, Michael. *A Culture of Conspiracy: Apocalyptic Visions in Contemporary America*. Berkeley: University of California Press, 2006.

Barrows, Henry, ed. *The World's Parliament of Religions (Two Volumes)*. Chicago: The Parliament Publishing Company, 1893.

Bartlett, Katharine T. "Feminist Legal Methods." *Harvard Law Review* 103, no. 4 (1990): 829–88.

Bauder, Don. "Is Yoga a Religion? Courts Say It Is, but Encinitas Schools Have Scrubbed Their Yoga Programs Clean." *San Diego Reader*, April 29, 2015. http://www.sandiegoreader.com/news/2015/apr/29/citylights-yoga-religion/#.

Bauman, Zygmunt. *Intimations of Postmodernity*. London: Routledge, 1992.

———. *Legislators and Interpreters: On Modernity, Postmodernity and Intellectuals*. Cambridge: Polity, 1987.

Bearman, Joshuah, and Allison Keeley. "Space Invaders." *Wired*, December 17, 2018. https://www.wired.com/story/scramble-claim-worlds-most-coveted-meteorite/.

Beckford, James A., ed. *New Religious Movements and Rapid Social Change*. London: Sage, 1986.

Bell, Daniel. "The Return of the Sacred: The Argument About the Future of Religion." *Zygon* 13, no. 3 (1978): 187–208.

Bell, Emma, and Scott Taylor. "The Elevation of Work: Pastoral Power and the New Age Work Ethic." *Organization* 10, no. 2 (2003): 329–49.

Bellah, Robert N. "Civil Religion in America." *Daedalus* 134, no. 4 (2005): 40–55.

———. "Flaws in the Protestant Code: Theological Roots of American Individualism." In *The Robert Bellah Reader*, ed. Robert Bellah and Steven M. Tipton, 225–45. Durham, NC: Duke University Press, 2006.

Bellah, Robert N., Richard Madsen, William M. Sullivan, Ann Swidler, and Steven M. Tipton. *Habits of the Heart: Individualism and Commitment in American Life*. Berkeley: University of California Press, 1985.

Bender, Courtney. *The New Metaphysicals: Spirituality and the American Religious Imagination*. Chicago: University of Chicago Press, 2010.

Bender, Courtney, Wendy Cadge, Peggy Levitt, and David Smilde. "Introduction: Religion on the Edge: De-centering and Re-centering." In *Religion on the Edge: De-centering and Re-centering the Sociology of Religion*, ed. Courtney Bender, Wendy Cadge, Peggy Levitt, and David Smilde, 1–20. Oxford: Oxford University Press, 2013.

Bender, Courtney, and Omar McRoberts. "Mapping a Field: Why and How to Study Spirituality." *Social Science Research Council Working Papers*. October 2012. https://tif.ssrc.org/wp-content/uploads/2010/05/Why-and-How-to-Study-Spirituality.pdf.

Beres, Derek, Matthew Remski, and Julian Walker. "Russell Brand's Man Stans." Conspirituality Podcast Series, October 19, 2023. https://podcasts.apple.com/gb/podcast/176-russell-brands-man-stans/id1515827446.

Berger, Helen A. *Solitary Pagans: Contemporary Witches, Wiccans, and Others Who Practice Alone*. Columbia: University of South Carolina Press, 2019.

———. "The 'Sonnenrad' Used in Shooters' Manifestos: A Spiritual Symbol of Hate." *The Conversation*, May 27, 2022. https://theconversation.com/the-sonnenrad-used-in-shooters-manifestos-a-spiritual-symbol-of-hate-183319.

Berger, Helen A., Evan A. Leach, and Leigh S. Shaffer. *Voices from the Pagan Census: A National Survey of Witches and Neo-pagans in the United States*. Columbia: University of South Carolina Press, 2003.

Berger, Peter L. *The Sacred Canopy: Elements of a Sociological Theory of Religion*. Garden City, NY: Anchor, 1969.

Berghuijs, Joantine, Jos Pieper, and Cok Bakker. "Being 'Spiritual' and Being 'Religious' in Europe: Diverging Life Orientations." *Journal of Contemporary Religion* 28, no. 1 (2013): 15–23.

———. "New Spirituality and Social Engagement." *Journal for the Scientific Study of Religion* 52, no. 4 (2013): 775–92.

Berman, Marshall. *The Politics of Authenticity: Radical Individualism and the Emergence of Modern Society*. New York: Atheneum, 1970.

Berman, Morris. *The Re-enchantment of the World*. Ithaca, NY: Cornell University Press, 1981.

Besant, Annie. *Mysticism*. London: Theosophical Publishing Society, 1914.

Beyerlein, Kraig, and John R. Hipp. "From Pews to Participation: The Effect of Congregation Activity and Context on Bridging Civic Engagement." *Social Problems* 53, no. 1 (2006): 97–117.

Binkley, Sam. "Psychological Life as Enterprise: Social Practice and the Government of Neo-liberal Interiority." *History of the Human Sciences* 24, no. 3 (2011): 83–102.

———. "The Seers of Menlo Park: The Discourse of Heroic Consumption in the 'Whole Earth Catalog.'" *Journal of Consumer Culture* 3, no. 3 (2003): 283–313.

Black, Lindsey I., Tainya C. Clarke, Patricia M. Barnes, Barbara J. Stussman, and Richard L. Nahin. "Use of Complementary Health Approaches Among Children Aged 4–17 Years in the United States: National Health Interview Survey, 2007–2012." *National Health Statistics Reports* 78 (2015): 1–18.

Bloom, Mia, and Sophia Moskalenko. *Pastels and Pedophiles: Inside the Mind of QAnon*. Stanford, CA: Stanford University Press, 2021.

Bloor, David. *Science and Social Imagery*. Chicago: University of Chicago Press, 1976.

Bødker, Henrik. "Gadgets and Gurus: Wired Magazine and Innovation as a Masculine Lifestyle." *Media History* 23, no. 1 (2017): 67–79.

Boltanski, Luc, and Eve Chiapello. *The New Spirit of Capitalism*. London: Verso, 2005.

Boon, Brooke. *Holy Yoga: Exercise for the Christian Body and Soul*. New York: FaithWords, 2007.

Boutin, Paul. "Kurzweil's Law." *Wired*, April 1, 2001. https://www.wired.com/2001/04/kurzweil/.

Bowler, Kate. *Blessed: A History of the American Prosperity Gospel*. Oxford: Oxford University Press, 2013.

Brand, Stewart. *The Last Whole Earth Catalog: Access to Tools*. New York: Random House, 1971.

———. "Scream of Consciousness." *Wired*, January 1, 1993. https://www.wired.com/1993/01/paglia/.

Brasher, Brenda. *Godly Women: Fundamentalism and Female Power*. New Brunswick, NJ: Rutgers University Press, 1998.

Braunstein, Ruth, Todd N. Fuist, and Rhys H. Williams, eds. *Religion and Progressive Activism: New Stories About Faith and Politics*. New York: New York University Press, 2017.

Brenner, Philip S., and John DeLamater. "Lies, Damned Lies, and Survey Self-Reports? Identity as a Cause of Measurement Bias." *Social Psychology Quarterly* 79, no. 4 (2016): 333–54.

———. "Social Desirability Bias in Self-Reports of Physical Activity: Is an Exercise Identity the Culprit?" *Social Indicators Research* 117, no. 2 (2014): 489–504.

Brooks, David. "The Age of Aquarius, All Over Again!" *New York Times*, June 10, 2019.

Brown, Callum G. *The Death of Christian Britain: Understanding Secularisation, 1800–2000.* 2nd ed. London: Routledge, 2009.
Brown, Candy Gunther. *Debating Yoga and Mindfulness in Public Schools: Reforming Secular Education or Reestablishing Religion?* Chapel Hill: University of North Carolina Press, 2019.
———. *The Healing Gods: Complementary and Alternative Medicine in Christian America.* Oxford: Oxford University Press, 2013.
———. *Testing Prayer: Science and Healing.* Cambridge, MA: Harvard University Press, 2012.
Brox, Trine, and Elizabeth Williams-Oerberg, ed. *Buddhism and Business: Merit, Material Wealth, and Morality in the Global Market Economy.* Honolulu: University of Hawaii Press, 2020.
Bruce, Steve. *God Is Dead.* Malden, MA: Blackwell, 2002.
———. *Secular Beats Spiritual: The Westernization of the Easternization of the West.* Oxford: Oxford University Press, 2017.
———. *Secularisation: In Defence of an Unfashionable Theory.* Oxford: Oxford University Press, 2011.
———. "Secularization and the Impotence of Individualized Religion," *Hedgehog Review* 8 (Spring/Summer 2006): 35–45.
Bruley, Sue. "Consciousness-Raising in Clapham: Women's Liberation as 'Lived Experience' in South London in the 1970s," *Women's History Review* 22, no. 5 (2013): 717–38.
Bryner, Peter. "Isn't It Time to Abandon Anachronistic Terminology?" *Journal of the Australian Chiropractors' Association* 17, no. 2 (1987): 53–58.
Bullivant, Stephen. *Nonverts: The Making of Ex-Christian America.* New York: Oxford University Press, 2022.
Burton, Tara Isabella. *Strange Rites: New Religions for a Godless Age.* New York: PublicAffairs, 2020.
Butt, Riazat. "Half of Britons Do Not Believe in Evolution, Survey Finds." *Guardian*, February 1, 2009.
Butzer, Bethany, Marina Ebert, Shirley Telles, and Sat Bir S. Khalsa. "School-Based Yoga Programs in the United States: A Survey." *Advances in Mind-Body Medicine* 29, no. 4 (2015): 18–26.
Cabanas, Edgar, and Eva Illouz. *Manufacturing Happy Citizens: How the Science and Industry of Happiness Control Our Lives.* Cambridge: Polity Press, 2019.
Callahan, David. *The Givers: Wealth, Power, and Philanthropy in a New Gilded Age.* New York: Knopf, 2017.
Campbell, Colin. "The Cult, the Cultic Milieu and Secularisation." *A Sociological Yearbook of Religion in Britain* 5 (1972): 119–36.
———. *The Easternization of the West: A Thematic Account of Cultural Change in the Modern Era.* Boulder, CO: Paradigm Publishers, 2007.

———. "Half-Belief and the Paradox of Ritual Instrumental Activism: A Theory of Modern Superstition." *British Journal of Sociology* 47, no. 1 (1996): 151–65.
———. *Has Sociology Progressed? Reflections of an Accidental Academic.* Cham, Switzerland: Palgrave Macmillan, 2019.
———. *The Myth of Social Action.* Cambridge: Cambridge University Press, 1986
———. "The Secret Religion of the Educated Classes." *Sociological Analysis* 39, no. 2 (1978): 146–56.
Canovan, Margaret. "Trust the People! Populism and the Two Faces of Democracy." *Political Studies* 47, no. 1 (1999): 2–16.
Caplan, Eric. *Mind Games: American Culture and the Birth of Psychotherapy.* Berkeley: University of California Press, 1998.
Carley, Michael. "What Is Toxic Masculinity?" *The Good Men Project.* April 5, 2018. https://goodmenproject.com/ethics-values/what-is-toxic-masculinity-dg/.
Carrette, Jeremy R., and Richard King. *Selling Spirituality: The Silent Takeover of Religion.* London: Routledge, 2005.
Casanova, José. *Public Religions in the Modern World.* Chicago: University of Chicago Press, 1994.
Chait, Jonathan. "Is the Anti-Racism Training Industry Just Peddling White Supremacy?" *New York.* July 16, 2020. https://nymag.com/intelligencer/2020/07/antiracism-training-white-fragility-robin-diangelo-ibram-kendi.html.
Chandler, Siobhan. "Private Religion in the Public Sphere." In Aupers and Houtman, *Religions of Modernity*, 69–88.
Charmaz, Kathy. *Constructing Grounded Theory: A Practical Guide Through Qualitative Analysis.* London: Sage, 2006.
Chaves, Mark. "Secularization as Declining Religious Authority." *Social Forces* 72, no. 3 (1994): 749–74.
Chen, Carolyn. *Work Pray Code: When Work Becomes Religion in Silicon Valley.* Princeton, NJ: Princeton University Press, 2022.
Chesterton, G. K. *Orthodoxy.* 1908. London: Fontana, 1961.
Chia, Aleena, Jonathan Corpus Ong, Hugh Davies, and Mack Hagood. "Everything is Connected: Networked Spirituality in the New Age." *AoIR Selected Papers of Internet Research*, 2021. https://doi.org/10.5210/spir.v2021i0.12093.
Clarke, Tainya C., Lindsey I. Black, Barbara J. Stussman, Patricia M. Barnes, and Richard L. Nahin. "Trends in the Use of Complementary Health Approaches Among Adults: United States, 2002–2012." *National Health Statistics Reports* 79 (2015): 1–15.
Clot-Garrell, Anna, and Mar Griera. "Beyond Narcissism: Toward an Analysis of the Public, Political and Collective Forms of Contemporary Spirituality." *Religions* 10, no. 579 (2019): 1–15.

Cohen, Michael H. *Healing at the Borderland of Medicine and Religion*. Chapel Hill: University of North Carolina Press, 2006.

Coleman, Simon. *The Globalisation of Charismatic Christianity: Spreading the Gospel of Prosperity*. Cambridge: Cambridge University Press, 2000.

Colker, Ruth. "Feminism, Sexuality, and Self: A Preliminary Inquiry Into the Politics of Authenticity." *Boston University Law Review* 68 (1988): 217–64.

Collins, Randall. "The Classical Tradition in Sociology of Religion." In *The SAGE Handbook of the Sociology of Religion*, ed. James A. Beckford and N. J. Demerath III, 19–38. Los Angeles: Sage, 2007.

Comaroff, Jean. "The Politics of Conviction: Faith on the Neo-liberal Frontier." *Social Analysis* 53, no. 1 (2009): 17–38.

Corcoran, Katie E. "Emotion, Religion, and Civic Engagement: A Multilevel Analysis of US Congregations." *Sociology of Religion* 81, no. 1 (2020): 20–44.

Corré, Anne. "Waar spiritualiteit en samenzwering elkaar ontmoeten" (Where Spirituality and Conspiracy Meet). *NRC Handelsblad*, May 5, 2021.

Cortois, Liza, Stef Aupers, and Dick Houtman. "The Naked Truth: Mindfulness and the Purification of Religion." *Journal of Contemporary Religion* 33, no. 2 (2018): 303–17.

Coser, Lewis A. *Greedy Institutions: Patterns of Undivided Commitment*. New York: Macmillan, 1974.

Cox, Harvey. *Fire from Heaven: The Rise of Pentecostal Spirituality and the Reshaping of Religion in the Twenty-first Century*. New York: Addison-Wesley, 1995.

Creswell, J. David, Laura E. Pacilio, Emily K. Lindsay, and Kirk Warren Brown. "Brief Mindfulness Meditation Training Alters Psychological and Neuroendocrine Responses to Social Evaluative Stress." *Psychoneuroendocrinology* 44 (June 2014): 1–12.

Crockett, Alasdair, and David Voas. "Generations of Decline: Religious Change in 20th-Century Britain." *Journal for the Scientific Study of Religion* 45, no. 4 (2006): 567–84.

Crouch, Andy. "Steve Jobs: The Secular Prophet." *Wall Street Journal*, October 8, 2011.

Daniel, Lillian. *When "Spiritual but Not Religious" Is Not Enough: Seeing God in Surprising Places, Even the Church*. New York: Jericho Books, 2013.

David Lynch Foundation. "Frequently Asked Questions." 2023. https://www.davidlynchfoundation.org/frequently-asked-questions.html.

Davies, Owen. *Cunning-Folk: Popular Magic in English History*. London: Bloomsbury, 2003.

Davies, Owen, and Willem de Blécourt. "Introduction: Beyond the Witch Trials." In *Beyond the Witch Trials: Witchcraft and Magic in Enlightenment*

Europe, ed. Owen Davies and Willem de Blécourt, 1–8. Manchester: Manchester University Press, 2004.

Davies, Stephen. "The Cultic Milieu and the Rise of the Violent Fringe." American Institute for Economic Research (AIER). August 7, 2019. https://www.aier.org/article/the-cultic-milieu-and-the-rise-of-violent-fringe/.

Day, Abby. *The Religious Lives of Older Laywomen: The Last Active Anglican Generation*. Oxford: Oxford University Press, 2017.

De Certeau, Michel. *The Practice of Everyday Life*. Berkeley: University of California Press, 1984.

De Keere, Kobe. "From a Self-Made to an Already-Made Man: A Historical Content Analysis of Professional Advice Literature." *Acta Sociologica* 57, no. 4 (2014): 311–24.

De Koster, Willem. *On the Meaning of Meaning*. Rotterdam: Erasmus University, 2022.

Delaney, Brigid. "'Evil Forces': How Covid-19 Paranoia United the Wellness Industry and Rightwing Conspiracy Theorists." *Guardian*, June 8, 2020.

Desmond, Matthew, and Adam Travis. "Political Consequences of Survival Strategies Among the Urban Poor." *American Sociological Review* 83, no. 5 (2018): 869–96.

Detweiler, Craig. *iGods: How Technology Shapes Our Spiritual and Social Lives*. Grand Rapids, MI: Brazos Press, 2013.

DiAngelo, Robin J. "Heterosexism: Addressing Internalized Dominance." *Journal of Progressive Human Services* 8, no. 1 (1997): 5–21.

———. "My Class Didn't Trump My Race: Using Oppression to Face Privilege." *Multicultural Perspectives* 8, no. 1 (2006): 51–56.

———. "White Fragility." *International Journal of Critical Pedagogy* 3, no. 3 (2011): 54–70.

Douglas, Jack D., and Frances C. Waksler. *The Sociology of Deviance: An Introduction*. Boston: Little, Brown, and Company, 1982.

Douglas, Karen M., Joseph E. Uscinski, Robbie M. Sutton, Aleksandra Cichocka, Nefes Turkay, Chee Siang Ang, and Farzin Deravi. "Understanding Conspiracy Theories." *Political Psychology* 40, no. 1 (2019): 3–35.

Drescher, Elizabeth. *Choosing Our Religion: The Spiritual Lives of America's Nones*. Oxford: Oxford University Press, 2016.

Drughi, Octavia. "A Deeper Look into Yoga & Spirituality." April 4, 2017. https://www.bookyogaretreats.com/news/yoga-and-spirituality-survey.

Dupreem, Glen, and Susan Beal. "A Graphic Representation of the Workings of Homeopathy." *American Journal of Homeopathic Medicine* 99, no. 1 (2006): 73–77.

Durkheim, Emile. *The Elementary Forms of Religious Life*. Ed. Karen E. Fields. 1912. New York: Free Press, 1995.

E&T Editorial Staff. "UFOS Hovering in the Mind of the British Public, Survey Reveals." *E&T Engineering and Technology*. March 22, 2021. https://eandt.theiet.org/content/articles/2021/03/ufos-hovering-in-the-minds-of-the-british-public-according-to-survey/.

Easterbrook, Gregg. "The New Convergence." *Wired*, December 1, 2002. https://www.wired.com/2002/12/convergence-3/.

Edgell, Penny, Joseph Gerteis, and Douglas Hartmann. "Atheists as 'Other': Moral Boundaries and Cultural Membership in American Society." *American Sociological Review* 71, no. 2 (2006): 211–34.

Education for New Generations Charter School v. North Penn School District, CAB No. 2013-10 (2016).

Edwards, Charlotte. "Flat-Earthers Ridiculed on Social Media After Space-X Launch Footage Captures Curvature of Our Planet." *Sun*, June 1, 2020.

EEOC v. United Health Programs of America, Inc., et al., No. 14-CV-3673 (KAM)(JO)(E.D.N.Y.) (2016).

Eisenberg, David M., Ronald C. Kessler, Cindy Foster, Frances E. Norlock, David R. Calkins, and Thomas L. Delbanco. "Unconventional Medicine in the United States: Prevalence, Costs, and Patterns of Use." *New England Journal of Medicine* 328, no. 4 (1993): 246–52.

Eliasoph, Nina. "'Close to Home': The Work of Avoiding Politics." *Theory and Society* 26, no. 5 (1997): 605–47.

Ellul, Jacques. *The Technological Society*. New York: Vintage Books, 1967.

Ellwood, Robert S. *The Sixties Spiritual Awakening: American Religion Moving from Modern to Postmodern*. New Brunswick, NJ: Rutgers University Press, 1994.

Engel v. Vitale, 370 U.S. 421 (1962).

Equal Employment Opportunity Commission. *Best Practices of Private Sector Employers*. 2008. https://www.eeoc.gov/best-practices-private-sector-employers.

———. *Compliance Manual on Religious Discrimination*. 2021. https://www.eeoc.gov/laws/guidance/section-12-religious-discrimination#_Toc203 359487.

Erjavec, Karmen, and Zala Volčič. "Management Through Spiritual Self-help Discourse in Post-socialist Slovenia." *Discourse and Communication* 3, no. 2 (2009): 123–43.

Estés, Clarissa Pinkola. *Women Who Run with the Wolves: Myths and Stories of the Wild Woman Archetype*. New York: Ballantine, 1992.

Evans, Jules. "Make Love, Not Vaccines: Why Are New Age Hippies So Anti-Vax?" https://www.philosophyforlife.org/blog/make-love-not-vaccines-why-are-new-age-hippies-so-anti-vax, 2021.

Faith Survey. "UK Religion Survey 2017." https://faithsurvey.co.uk/uk-religion-survey.html.

Fedele, Anna. "'God Wants Spiritual Fruits Not Religious Nuts': Spirituality as Middle Way between Religion and Secularism at the Marian Shrine of Fátima." In Fedele and Knibbe, *Secular Societies, Spiritual Selves?*, 166–83.
Fedele, Anna, and Kim Knibbe, eds. *Secular Societies, Spiritual Selves? The Gendered Triangle of Religion, Secularity and Spirituality.* New York: Routledge, 2020.
Feldt, Laura. "Harry Potter and Contemporary Magic: Fantasy Literature, Popular Culture, and the Representation of Religion." *Journal of Contemporary Religion* 31, no. 1 (2016): 101–14.
Fetto, John. "Your Questions Answered." *AdAge*, May 1, 2003. https://adage.com/article/american-demographics/questions-answered/44147.
Fetzer Institute. *What Does Spirituality Mean to Us? A Study of Spirituality in the United States.* September 2020. https://spiritualitystudy.fetzer.org/sites/default/files/2020-09/What-Does-Spirituality-Mean-To-Us_%20A-Study-of-Spirituality-in-the-United-States.pdf.
Folk, Holly. *The Religion of Chiropractic: Populist Healing from the American Heartland.* Chapel Hill: University of North Carolina Press, 2017.
Folk, Kenneth. "The Trojan Horse of Meditation." *Buddhist Geeks*, September 2013. https://web.archive.org/web/20131210035124/www.buddhistgeeks.com/2013/09/bg-296-the-trojan-horse-of-meditation/.
Foucault, Michel. *Ethics: Subjectivity and Truth.* New York: New Press, 1994.
Fox, John. *Applied Regression Analysis and Generalized Linear Models.* 3rd ed. Thousand Oaks, CA: Sage, 2016.
Frank, Thomas. *The Conquest of Cool: Business Culture, Counter Culture, and the Rise of Hip Consumerism.* Chicago: University of Chicago Press, 1998.
———. *The People, No: A Brief History of Anti-Populism.* New York: Metropolitan, 2020.
Friedan, Betty. *The Feminine Mystique.* New York: Dell, 1963.
Friedman, Gillian. "Here's What Companies Are Promising to Do to Fight Racism." *New York Times*, August 23, 2020.
Froese, Paul. *On Purpose: How We Create the Meaning of Life.* New York: Oxford University Press, 2016.
Frontline. "The Alternative Fix." November 6, 2003. https://www.pbs.org/wgbh/pages/frontline/shows/altmed/etc/synopsis.html.
Fuchs, Christian. *Social Media: A Critical Introduction.* London: Sage, 2021.
Fukuyama, Francis. *Identity: The Demand for Dignity and the Politics of Resentment.* New York: Farrar, Straus and Giroux, 2018.
Fuller, Robert C. *Spiritual but Not Religious: Understanding Unchurched America.* Oxford: Oxford University Press, 2001.
Fulton, Brad R. "Religious Organizations: Cross-cutting the Nonprofit Sector." In *The Nonprofit Sector*, ed. Walter W. Powell and Patricia Bromley, 579–98. Stanford, CA: Stanford University Press, 2020.

———. "Trends in Addressing Social Needs: A Longitudinal Study of Congregation-Based Service Provision and Political Participation." *Religions* 7, no. 5 (2016): 51.
Gaddini, Katie. *The Struggle to Stay: Why Single Evangelical Women are Leaving the Church*. New York: Columbia University Press, 2022.
Gardner-Chloros, Penelope. *Code-Switching*. New York: Cambridge University Press, 2009.
Garrett, William R. "Maligned Mysticism: The Maledicted Career of Troeltsch's Third Type." *Sociological Analysis* 36, no. 3 (1975): 205–23.
Gauchat, Gordon. "Politicization of Science in the Public Sphere: A Study of Public Trust in the United States, 1974 to 2010." *American Sociological Review* 77, no. 2 (2012): 167–87.
Gauthier, François. *Religion, Modernity, Globalisation: Nation-State to Market*. New York: Routledge, 2020.
Gauthier, François, and Tuomas Martikainen, ed. *The Marketization of Religion*. New York: Routledge, 2020.
Gavison, Ruth. "Feminism and the Public/Private Distinction," *Stanford Law Review* 45, no. 1 (1992): 1–45.
Gellner, Ernest. *Postmodernism, Reason and Religion*. London: Routledge, 1992.
Gerstein, Julie. "The US Fur-Wearing, Face-Painted 'QAnon Shaman' Has Asked Trump for a Presidential Pardon." *Business Insider*, January 15, 2021.
Gevitz, Norman. *Other Healers: Unorthodox Medicine in America*. Baltimore: Johns Hopkins University Press, 1988.
Gilmore, James H., and B. Joseph Pine. *Authenticity: What Consumers Really Want*. Cambridge, MA: Harvard Business Press, 2007.
Gilmore, Lee. *Theater in a Crowded Fire: Ritual and Spirituality at Burning Man*. Berkeley: University of California Press, 2010.
Gleick, James. *The Information: A History, a Theory, a Flood*. New York: Vintage, 2012.
Glendinning, Tony, and Steve Bruce. "New Ways of Believing or Belonging: Is Religion Giving Way to Spirituality?" *British Journal of Sociology* 57, no. 3 (2006): 399–414.
Glenny, Misha. "How Europe Can Stop Worrying and Learn to Love the Future." *Wired*, February 1, 2001. https://www.wired.com/2001/02/misha/.
Godrej, Farah. "The Neoliberal Yogi and the Politics of Yoga." *Political Theory* 45, no. 6 (2017): 772–800.
Goffman, Erving. *The Presentation of Self in Everyday Life*. Garden City, NY: Doubleday, 1956.
Goleman, Daniel. "Comment." *Inquiring Mind* 2, no. 1 (1985): 7.
Goodman, Trudy, Vincent Horn, and Emily Horn. "Stealth Buddhism." *Buddhist Geeks*, August 27, 2014. https://web.archive.org

/web/20160405015832/http://www.buddhistgeeks.com/2014/08/bg-331-stealth-buddhism/.
Goodrick-Clarke, Nicholas. *The Occult Roots of Nazism: Secret Aryan Cults and Their Influence on Nazi Ideology*. New York: New York University Press, 1992.
Goyal, Madhav, Sonal Singh, Erica M. S. Sibinga, Neda F. Gould, Anastasia Rowland-Seymour, Ritu Sharma, Zackary Berger, et al. "Meditation Programs for Psychological Stress and Well-Being: A Systematic Review and Meta-analysis." *JAMA Internal Medicine* 174, no. 3 (2014): 357–68.
Greeson, Jeffrey M., Daniel M. Webber, Moria J. Smoski, Jeffrey G. Brantley, Andrew G. Ekblad, Edward C. Suarez, and Ruth Quillian Wolever. "Changes in Spirituality Partly Explain Health-Related Quality of Life Outcomes After Mindfulness-Based Stress Reduction." *Journal of Behavioral Medicine* 34, no. 6 (2011): 508–18.
Grier, William H., and Price M. Cobbs. *Black Rage*. New York: Basic Books, 1968.
Griera, Mar, Jordi Morales i Gras, Anna Clot-Garrell, and Rafael Cazarín. "Conspirituality in COVID-19 Times: A Mixed-Method Study of Anti-Vaccine Movements in Spain." *Journal for the Academic Study of Religion* 35, no. 2 (2022), 192–217.
Griffith, R. Marie. *Born Again Bodies: Flesh and Spirit in American Christianity*. Berkeley: University of California Press, 2004.
———. *God's Daughters: Evangelical Women and the Power of Submission*. Berkeley: University of California Press, 1997.
Grogan, Jessica. *Encountering America: Humanistic Psychology, Sixties Culture & the Shaping of the Modern Self*. New York: HarperCollins, 2013.
Guber, Tara. "Tara's Yoga for Kids: One Noble Soul Takes on the Public School System and Wins a Vedic Victory." *Hinduism Today* (Interview), April/May/June 2004. http://www.hinduismtoday.com/modules/smartsection/item.php?itemid=1328.
Guerin, Cécile. "The Yoga World Is Riddled with Anti-vaxxers and QAnon Believers." *Wired*, January 28, 2021.
Hadaway, C. Kirk, and Penny Long Marler. "Did You Really Go to Church This Week? Behind the Poll Data." *The Christian Century*, May 6, 1998, 472–75.
Hadaway, C. Kirk, Penny Long Marler, and Mark Chaves. "What the Polls Don't Show: A Closer Look at U.S. Church Attendance." *American Sociological Review* 58, no. 6 (1993): 741–52.
Hahnemann, Samuel. *The Homoeopathic Medical Doctrine: Or, "Organon of the Healing Art."* 5th ed. Dublin: Wakeman, 1833 [1810].
Halafoff, Anna, Anna Marriott, Ruth Fitzpatrick, and Enqi Weng. "Selling (Con)spirituality and COVID-19 in Australia: Convictions,

Complexity and Countering Dis/misinformation." *Journal for the Academic Study of Religion* 35, no. 2 (2022): 166–88.

Halafoff, Anna, Andres Singleton, and Ruth Fitzpatrick. "Spiritual Complexity in Australia: Wellbeing and Risks." *Social Compass* 70, no. 2 (2023), 243–62.

Hanegraaff, Wouter J. "New Age Religion." In *Religion in the Modern World*, ed. Linda Woodhead, Paul Fletcher, Hiroko Kawanami, and David Smith, 249–63. London: Routledge, 2002.

———. *New Age Religion and Western Culture: Esotericism in the Mirror of Secular Thought*. Leiden: Brill, 1996.

Hanisch, Carol. "The Personal Is Political." *Notes from the Second Year: Women's Liberation*, 1970. https://webhome.cs.uvic.ca/~mserra/AttachedFiles/PersonalPolitical.pdf.

Harambam, Jaron. *Contemporary Conspiracy Culture: Truth and Knowledge in an Era of Epistemic Instability*. London: Routledge, 2020.

———. "Distrusting Consensus: How a Uniform Corona Pandemic Narrative Fostered Suspicion and Conspiracy Theories." *Journal of Digital Social Research* 5, no. 3 (2023): 109–39.

———. "The Proliferation of Alternative Media: How Corona Conspiracy Theories in The Netherlands Fostered New Social Movements." In *Covid Conspiracy Theories in Global Perspective*, ed. Michael Butter and Peter Knight, 252–68. London: Routledge, 2022.

Harambam, Jaron, and Stef Aupers. "From the Unbelievable to the Undeniable: Epistemological Pluralism, Or How Conspiracy Theorists Legitimate Their Extraordinary Truth Claims." *European Journal of Cultural Studies* 24, no. 4 (2021): 990–1008.

———. "'I Am Not a Conspiracy Theorist': Relational Identifications in the Dutch Conspiracy Milieu." *Cultural Sociology* 11, no. 1 (2017): 113–29.

Harrington, Anne. *The Cure Within: A History of Mind-Body Medicine*. New York: Norton, 2008.

Harris, Ruth. *Guru to the World: The Life and Legacy of Vivekananda*. Cambridge, MA: Belknap Press, 2022.

Harvey, Graham. *What Do Pagans Believe?* London: Granta, 2007.

Hawn, Goldie. "How Mindfulness Helps Children Thrive." *Heart-Mind 2013*. The Dalai Lama Center for Peace-Education, June 20, 2013. https://www.youtube.com/watch?v=7pLhwGLYvJU.

Heath, Joseph, and Andrew Potter. *Nation of Rebels: Why Counterculture Became Consumer Culture*. New York: HarperCollins, 2004.

Heelas, Paul. "The Limits of Consumption and the Post-modern 'Religion' of the New Age." In *The Authority of the Consumer*, ed. Russell Keat, Nigel Whiteley, and Nicolas Abercrombie, 94–105. London: Routledge, 1994.

———. *The New Age Movement: The Celebration of the Self and the Sacralization of Modernity*. Oxford: Blackwell, 1996.

———. "The Sacralization of the Self and New Age Capitalism." In *Social Change in Contemporary Britain*, ed. Nicholas Abercrombie and Alan Warde, 139–66. Cambridge: Polity Press, 1992.

———. *Spiritualities of Life: New Age Romanticism and Consumptive Capitalism*. Malden, MA: Blackwell, 2008.

Heelas, Paul, and Linda Woodhead. *The Spiritual Revolution: Why Religion Is Giving Way to Spirituality*. Malden, MA: Blackwell, 2005.

Heinze, Andrew R. *Jews and the American Soul: Human Nature in the Twentieth Century*. Princeton, NJ: Princeton University Press, 2004.

Hervieu-Léger, Danièle. "Religion and Modernity in the French Context: For a New Approach to Secularization." *Sociological Analysis* 51, Special Presidential Issue (1990): S15–S25.

Hess, Frederick M., ed. *With the Best Intentions: How Philanthropy Is Reshaping K-12 Education*. Cambridge, MA: Harvard Education Press, 2005.

Hill Collins, Patricia. "The New Politics of Community." *American Sociological Review* 75, no. 1 (2010): 7–30.

Höllinger, Franz. "Does the Counter-Cultural Character of New Age Persist? Investigating Social and Political Attitudes of New Age Followers." *Journal of Contemporary Religion* 19, no. 3 (2004): 289–309.

———. "Value Orientations and Social Attitudes in the Holistic Milieu." *British Journal of Sociology* 68, no. 2 (2017): 293–313.

hooks, bell. *Sisters of the Yam: Black Women and Self-recovery*. New York: Routledge, 2015.

Horkheimer, Max, and Theodor W. Adorno. *Dialectic of Enlightenment: Philosophical Fragments*. Ed. Gunzelin Schmid Noerr and Edmund Jephcott. 1944. Stanford, CA: Stanford University Press, 2002.

Hout, Michael, and Claude S. Fischer. "Explaining Why More Americans Have No Religious Preference: Political Backlash and Generational Succession, 1987–2012." *Sociological Science* 1 (October 2014): 423–47.

———. "Why More Americans Have No Religious Preference: Politics and Generations." *American Sociological Review* 67, no. 2 (2002): 165–90.

Houtman, Dick. *Op jacht naar de echte werkelijkheid: Dromen over authenticiteit in een wereld zonder fundamenten* (The Hunt for Real Reality: Dreams of Authenticity in a World Without Foundations). Amsterdam: Pallas Publications, 2008.

Houtman, Dick, and Peter Achterberg. "Two Lefts and Two Rights: Class Voting and Cultural Voting in the Netherlands, 2002." *Sociologie* 1, no. 1 (2010): 61–76.

Houtman, Dick, Peter Achterberg, and Anton Derks. *Farewell to the Leftist Working Class*. New Brunswick, NJ: Transaction, 2008.

Houtman, Dick, and Stef Aupers. "Religions of Modernity: Relocating the Sacred to the Self and the Digital." In Aupers and Houtman, *Religions of Modernity*, 1–30.

———. "The Spiritual Turn and the Decline of Tradition: The Spread of Post-Christian Spirituality in 14 Western Countries, 1981–2000." *Journal for the Scientific Study of Religion* 46, no. 3 (2007): 305–20.

Houtman, Dick, Stef Aupers, and Rudi Laermans. "Introduction: A Cultural Sociology of the Authority of Science." In *Science Under Siege: Contesting the Secular Religion of Scientism*, ed. Dick Houtman, Stef Aupers, and Rudi Laermans, 1–34. New York: Palgrave Macmillan, 2021.

Houtman, Dick, Paul Heelas, and Peter Achterberg. "Counting Spirituality? Survey Methodology After the Spiritual Turn." *Annual Review of the Sociology of Religion: New Methods in the Sociology of Religion* (2012): 25–44.

Houtman, Dick, and Peter Mascini. "Why Do Churches Become Empty, While New Age Grows? Secularization and Religious Change in the Netherlands." *Journal for the Scientific Study of Religion* 41, no. 3 (2002): 455–73.

Houtman, Dick, Anneke Pons, and Rudi Laermans. "Religion and Solidarity: The Vicissitudes of Protestantism." In *Shifting Solidarities: Trends and Developments in European Societies*, ed. Ine van Hoyweghen, Valeria Pulignano, and Gert Meyers, 229–49. London: Palgrave MacMillan, 2020.

Humanists U.K. "Religion and Belief: Some Surveys and Statistics." n.d. https://humanists.uk/campaigns/religion-and-belief-some-surveys-and-statistics/.

Huss, Boaz. "Spirituality: The Emergence of a New Cultural Category and Its Challenge to the Religious and the Secular." *Journal of Contemporary Religion* 29, no. 1 (2014): 47–60.

Husting, Ginna, and Martin Orr. "Dangerous Machinery: 'Conspiracy Theorist' as a Transpersonal Strategy of Exclusion." *Symbolic Interaction* 30, no. 2 (2007): 127–50.

Hutton, Ronald. *The Triumph of the Moon: A History of Modern Pagan Witchcraft*. Oxford: Oxford Paperbacks, 1995.

Ignazi, Piero. "The Silent Counter-Revolution: Hypotheses on the Emergence of Extreme Right-Wing Parties in Europe." *European Journal of Political Research* 22, no. 1 (1992): 3–34.

Illouz, Eva. *Cold Intimacies: The Making of Emotional Capitalism*. Cambridge: Polity, 2007.

———. *Saving the Modern Soul: Therapy, Emotions, and the Culture of Self-Help*. Berkeley: University of California Press, 2008.

Inglehart, Ronald. *Culture Shift in Advanced Industrial Society*. Princeton, NJ: Princeton University Press, 1990.

———. *The Silent Revolution: Changing Values and Political Styles Among Western Publics*. Princeton, NJ: Princeton University Press, 1977.

International Association of Reiki Professionals. "All About Reiki." 2012. https://iarp.org/learn-about-reiki/.
Isaacson, Walter. *The Innovators: How a Group of Hackers, Geniuses, and Geeks Created the Digital Revolution*. New York: Simon & Schuster, 2015.
———. *Steve Jobs*. New York: Simon & Schuster, 2011.
Ivakhiv, Adrian. *Reclaiming Sacred Ground: Pilgrims and Politics at Glastonbury and Sedona*. Bloomington: Indiana University Press, 2001.
Jackson, Paul. "Cultic Milieus and the Extreme Right." Open Democracy. May 9, 2019. https://www.opendemocracy.net/en/cultic-milieus-and-extreme-right/.
Jackson, Stanley W. *Care of the Psyche: A History of Psychological Healing*. New Haven, CT: Yale University Press, 1999.
Jain, Andrea R. *Peace Love Yoga: The Politics of Global Spirituality*. Oxford: Oxford University Press, 2020.
———. *Selling Yoga: From Counterculture to Pop Culture*. New York: Oxford University Press, 2014.
Jensen, Stine. "'Yoga' is niet synoniem met radicaal-rechtse denkbeelden" (Yoga is Not Synonymous with Radical-Right Ideas). *NRC Handelsblad*, March 31, 2021.
Jentoft, Peggy. *Reiki Level One Manual: Reiki Unleashed; Usui Reiki, Contemporary and Traditional*, 2006. https://web.archive.org/web/2016*/pjentoft.com/REIKIONE.pdf.
Jeter, Pamela E., Jeremiah Slutsky, Nilkamal Singh, and Sat Bir S. Khalsa. "Yoga as a Therapeutic Intervention: A Bibliometric Analysis of Published Research Studies from 1967 to 2013." *Journal of Alternative and Complementary Medicine* 21, no. 10 (2015): 586–92.
Jones, Sonia. "A New Online Course Teaches Buddhist Meditation for Free." *Sonima*, January 22, 2016. http://www.sonima.com/videos/study-buddhism/.
Jordan, William. "8% of Britons Believe Horoscopes Can Predict the Future." July 3, 2015. https://yougov.co.uk/politics/articles/12731-8-of-Britons-believe-horoscopes-predict-the-future.
Kabat-Zinn, Jon. "Catalyzing Movement Towards a More Contemplative / Sacred-Appreciating / Non-dualistic Society." The Contemplative Mind in Society: Meeting of the Working Group. Nathan Cummings Foundation & Fetzer Institute, September 29-October 2, 1994, Pocantico, NY. https://web.archive.org/web/20170204171614/http://www.contemplativemind.org/admin/wp-content/uploads/2012/09/kabat-zinn.pdf.
———. "Some Reflections on the Origins of MBSR, Skillful Means and the Trouble with Maps." *Contemporary Buddhism* 12, no. 1 (2011): 281–306.
———. *Wherever You Go, There You Are: Mindfulness Meditation in Everyday Life*. New York: Hyperion, 1994.

Kaplan, Dana, and Rachel Werczberger. "Jewish New Age and the Middle Class: Jewish Identity Politics in Israel Under Neoliberalism." *Sociology* 51, no. 3 (2017): 575–91.

Kaplan, Jeffrey, and Heléne Lööw, ed. *The Cultic Milieu: Oppositional Subcultures in an Age of Globalization*. Walnut Creek, CA: Rowman & Littlefield, 2002.

Kaptchuk, Ted J. "Acupuncture: Theory, Efficacy, and Practice." *Annals of Internal Medicine* 136, no. 5 (2002): 374–83.

Karpel, Richard. "The DC 'Yoga Tax' Isn't Really a Yoga Tax." *Yoga Alliance*, July 30, 2014. https://www.yogaalliance.org/the_dc_yoga_tax_isnt_really_a_yoga_tax.

Kasselstrand, Isabella, Phil Zuckerman, and Ryan T. Cragun. *Beyond Doubt: The Secularization of Society*. New York: New York University Press, 2023.

Katz, Roberta, Sarah Ogilvie, Jane Shaw, and Linda Woodhead. *Gen Z, Explained: The Art of Living in a Digital Age*. Chicago: University of Chicago Press, 2021.

Keil, David. "Assessing the Impacts of Yoga Asana—Survey Summary." *Yoga Anatomy*, March 21, 2017. https://www.yoganatomy.com/yoga-asana-survey-results-summary/.

———. "Negative Experiences in Yoga Practice: What Do Practitioners Report." *Yoga Anatomy*, March 21, 2017. https://www.yoganatomy.com/negative-experiences-in-yoga-practice-survey-results/.

———. "What Are the Benefits of Doing a Yoga Practice." *Yoga Anatomy*, March 21, 2017. https://www.yoganatomy.com/benefits-of-yoga-practice-survey-results/.

Kelly, Kevin. "God Is the Machine." *Wired*, December 1, 2002. https://www.wired.com/2002/12/holytech/.

———. *The Inevitable: Understanding the 12 Technological Forces That Will Shape Our Future*. New York: Penguin, 2017.

———. *Out of Control: The New Biology of Machines, Social Systems, & the Economic World*. Reading, MA: Basic Books, 1995.

———. *What Technology Wants*. New York: Viking, 2010.

———. "Why the Basis of the Universe Isn't Matter or Energy—It's Data." *Wired*, February 8, 2011. https://www.wired.com/2011/02/mf_gleick_qa/.

Kelly, Kevin, and Steven Johnson. "Kevin Kelly and Steven Johnson on Where Ideas Come From." *Wired*, September 27, 2010. https://www.wired.com/2010/09/mf-kellyjohnson/.

Kennedy, Jonathan. "Populist Politics and Vaccine Hesitancy in Western Europe: An Analysis of National-level Data." *European Journal of Public Health* 29, no. 3 (2019): 512–16.

Khalsa, Sat Bir S., and Bethany Butzer. "Yoga in School Settings: A Research Review." *Annals of the New York Academy of Sciences* 1373 (June 2016): 45–55.

King, David, P., Barbara J. Duffy, and Brian Steensland. "The Role of Spiritual Practices in the Multidimensional Impact of Religion and Spirituality on Giving and Volunteering." *Nonprofit and Voluntary Sector Quarterly*, January 23, 2024. https://journals.sagepub.com/doi/10.1177/08997640231221533.

Klein, Naomi. "The Great Reset Conspiracy Smoothie." *Intercept*, December 8, 2020. https://theintercept.com/2020/12/08/great-reset-conspiracy/.

Klinenberg, Eric. *Going Solo: The Extraordinary Rise and Surprising Appeal of Living Alone*. New York: Penguin, 2013.

Kogan, Claudia. *The Healing Power of Solidarity: A Philosophical, Literary and Psychoanalytic Journey*. (In Hebrew.) Jerusalem: Carmel, 2023.

Kong, Jian, Randy Gollub, Tao Huang, Ginger Polich, Vitaly Napadow, Kathleen Hui, Mark Vangel, Bruce Rosen, and Ted J. Kaptchuk. "Acupuncture De Qi, from Qualitative History to Quantitative Measurement." *Journal of Alternative and Complementary Medicine* 13, no. 10 (2007): 1059–70.

Kopf, David. *The Brahmo Samaj and the Shaping of the Modern Indian Mind*. Princeton, NJ: Princeton University Press, 1979.

———. *British Orientalism and the Bengal Renaissance: The Dynamics of Indian Modernization, 1773–1835*. Berkeley: University of California Press, 1969.

Kral, Tammi R. A., Kaley Davis, Cole Korponay, Matthew J. Hirshberg, Rachel Hoel, Lawrence Y. Tello, Robin I. Goldman, Melissa A. Rosenkranz, Antoine Lutz, and Richard J. Davidson. "Absence of Structural Brain Changes from Mindfulness-based Stress Reduction: Two Combined Randomized Controlled Trials." *Science Advances* 8, no. 20 (2022). https://www.science.org/doi/10.1126/sciadv.abk3316.

Krieger, Dolores. *Foundations for Holistic Health Nursing Practices: The Renaissance Nurse*. Philadelphia: Lippincott, 1981.

Kriesi, Hanspeter. "New Social Movements and the New Class in the Netherlands." *American Journal of Sociology* 94, no. 5 (1989): 1078–16.

Kucinskas, Jaime. *The Mindful Elite: Mobilizing from the Inside Out*. New York: Oxford University Press, 2018.

Kucinskas, Jaime, and Evan Stewart. "Selfish or Substituting Spirituality? Clarifying the Relationship Between Spiritual Practice and Political Engagement." *American Sociological Review* 87, no. 4 (2022): 584–617.

Kürti, László. "Neo-Shamanism, Psychic Phenomena and Media Trickery." In *The Cultic Milieu: Oppositional Subcultures in an Age of Globalization*, ed. Jeffrey Kaplan and Heléne Lööw, 110–37. Walnut Creek, CA: Rowman & Littlefield, 2002.

Kurzweil, Ray. *The Age of Spiritual Machines: When Computers Exceed Human Intelligence*. New York: Penguin, 2000.

———. *The Singularity Is Near: When Humans Transcend Biology*. New York: Penguin, 2006.

Lago, Mary. *Imperfect Encounter: The Letters of William Rothenstein and Rabindranath Tagore*. Cambridge, MA: Harvard University Press, 1972.

Lamont, Michèle, and Virág Molnár. "The Study of Boundaries in the Social Sciences." *Annual Review of Sociology* 28 (2002): 167–95.

LaMore, George E., Jr. "The Secular Selling of a Religion." *Christian Century*, December 10, 1975, 1133.

Lanier, Jaron. *Who Owns the Future?* New York: Simon & Schuster, 2014.

Lasch, Christopher. *The Culture of Narcissism: American Life in an Age of Diminishing Expectations*. New York: W. W. Norton, 1979.

Lau, Kimberley J. *New Age Capitalism: Making Money East of Eden*. Philadelphia: University of Pennsylvania Press, 2000.

Ledermann, Erich Kurt. *Philosophy and Medicine*. Brookfield, VT: Gower, 1986.

Lee, Lois. *Recognizing the Non-religious: Reimagining the Secular*. Oxford: Oxford University Press, 2015.

Levy, Steven. "The Seer." *Wired*, December 21, 2012. https://www.wired.com/2012/12/mf-tim-oreilly-qa/.

Lewis, James R., and J. Gordon Melton, ed. *Perspectives on the New Age*. Albany: State University of New York Press, 1992.

Lewis, Jim. "Robots of Arabia." *Wired*, November 1, 2005. https://www.wired.com/2005/11/camel/.

Lewis, Rebecca. "'This Is What the News Won't Show You': YouTube Creators and the Reactionary Politics of Micro-celebrity." *Television & New Media* 21, no. 2 (2020): 201–17.

Lewis, Tyson, and Richard Kahn. "The Reptoid Hypothesis: Utopian and Dystopian Representational Motifs in David Icke's Alien Conspiracy Theory." *Utopian Studies* 16, no. 1 (2005): 45–74.

Lichterman, Paul. *Elusive Togetherness: Church Groups Trying to Bridge America's Divisions*. Princeton, NJ: Princeton University Press, 2005.

———. "Religion and the Construction of Civic Identity." *American Sociological Review* 73, no. 1 (2008): 83–104.

———. *The Search for Political Community: American Activists Reinventing Commitment*. Cambridge: Cambridge University Press, 1996.

Lichterman, Paul, and Nina Eliasoph. "Civic Action." *American Journal of Sociology* 120, no. 3 (2014): 798–863.

Lindahl, Jared R., Nathan E. Fisher, David J. Cooper, Rochelle K. Rosen, and Willoughby B. Britton. "The Varieties of Contemplative Experience: A Mixed Methods Study of Meditation-Related Challenges in Western Buddhists." *PLOS ONE* 12, no. 5 (2017): 30176239.

Lipinski, Kathie. "Making Reiki Real." 2004. https://web.archive.org/web/20140108010422/iarp.org/MakingReikiRealArticle.html.

Lipka, Michael, and Claire Gecewicz. "More Americans Now Say They're Spiritual but Not Religious." *Pew Research Center*, September 6, 2017.

https://www.pewresearch.org/fact-tank/2017/09/06/more-americans-now-say-theyre-spiritual-but-not-religious/.

Llansó, Emma, Joris van Hoboken, Paddy Leerssen, and Jaron Harambam. "Artificial Intelligence, Content Moderation, and Freedom of Expression." Transatlantic Working Group on Content Moderation Online and Freedom of Expression, 2020. https://www.ivir.nl/publicaties/download/AI-Llanso-Van-Hoboken-Feb-2020.pdf.

Lofton, Kathryn. *Consuming Religion*. Chicago: University of Chicago Press, 2017.

——. *Oprah: The Gospel of an Icon*. Berkeley: University of California Press, 2011.

Lomas, Tim, Tina Cartwright, Tudi Edginton and Damien Ridge. "A Religion of Wellbeing? The Appeal of Buddhism to Men in London, United Kingdom." *Psychology of Religion and Spirituality* 6, no. 3 (2014): 198–207.

Loria, Kevin. "7 Ways Meditation Changes Your Brain and Body." *Business Insider*, February 2, 2015. https://www.businessinsider.com/how-meditation-changes-your-brain-2015-1.

LoRusso, James Dennis. *Spirituality, Corporate Culture, and American Business: The Neoliberal Ethic and the Spirit of Global Capital*. New York: Bloomsbury, 2017.

——. "Towards Radical Subjects: Workplace Spirituality as Neoliberal Governance in American Business." In *Spirituality, Organization and Neoliberalism: Understanding Lived Experiences*, ed. Emma Bell, Sorin Gog, Anca Simionca, and Scott Taylor, 1–26. Cheltenham, UK: Edward Elgar, 2020.

Luckmann, Thomas. *The Invisible Religion: The Problem of Religion in Modern Society*. New York: Macmillan, 1967.

Luhrmann, Tanya M. *When God Talks Back: Understanding the American Evangelical Relationship with God*. New York: Knopf, 2012.

Lyles, Margaret Lee. "My Christian Faith & Reiki." *Reiki for Christians*, February 26, 2013. http://www.christianreiki.org/my-christian-faith-reiki/.

Lynch, Gordon. *The New Spirituality: An Introduction to Progressive Belief in the Twenty-First Century*. London: I. B. Tauris, 2007.

Lyon, David. *Jesus in Disneyland: Religion in Postmodern Times*. Malden, MA: Polity Press, 2000.

Madsen, Ole Jacob. *The Therapeutic Turn: How Psychology Altered Western Culture*. New York: Routledge, 2014.

Madsen, Richard. "The Archipelago of Faith: Religious Individualism and Faith Community in America Today." *American Journal of Sociology* 114, no. 5 (2009): 1263–1301.

Maharishi International University. "MIU at a Glance." https://www.miu.edu/about-miu.

Maharishi Mahesh Yogi. *Science of Being and Art of Living: Transcendental Meditation*. 1963. New York: New American Library, 1968.

Malnak v. Yogi, 440 F. Supp. 1284 (D. N.J. 1977), 592 F.2d 197 (3d Cir. 1979).

Mann, Charles C. "Solar, Eclipsed." *Wired*, December 1, 2015. https://www.wired.com/2015/11/climate-change-in-india/.

Mannheim, Karl. *Ideology and Utopia: An Introduction to the Sociology of Knowledge*. 1936. San Diego: Harcourt, Brace, Jovanovich, 1985.

Markovitz, Gayle, and Samantha Sault. "What Companies Are Doing to Fight Systemic Racism." *World Economic Forum* June 24, 2020. https://www.weforum.org/agenda/2020/06/companies-fighting-systemic-racism-business-community-black-lives-matter/.

Marler, Penny Long, and C. Kirk Hadaway. "'Being Religious' or 'Being Spiritual' in America: A Zero-Sum Proposition?" *Journal for the Scientific Study of Religion* 41, no. 1 (2002): 289–300.

Martens, Jason P., and Bastiaan T. Rutjens. "Spirituality and Religiosity Contribute to Ongoing COVID-19 Vaccination Rates: Comparing 195 Regions Around the World." *Vaccine: X*, no. 12 (2022): 100241.

Martí, Gerardo. *American Blindspot: Race, Class, Religion, and the Trump Presidency*. Lanham, MD: Rowman & Littlefield, 2019.

Martin, Bernice. *A Sociology of Contemporary Cultural Change*. Oxford: Blackwell, 1981.

Martin, Craig. *Capitalizing Religion: Ideology and the Opiate of the Bourgeoisie*. London: Bloomsbury, 2014.

Martin, David. *Pentecostalism: The World Their Parish*. Oxford: Blackwell, 2002.

Marwick, Arthur. *The Sixties: Cultural Revolution in Britain, France, Italy, and the United States, c. 1958–c. 1974*. New York: Oxford University Press, 1998.

"Mary." Interview by Candy Gunther Brown, April 22, 2010.

Maxwell, Joe. "Nursing's New Age?" *Christianity Today*, February 5, 1996, 96–99.

McClure, Paul K. "Modding My Religion: Exploring the Effects of Digital Technology on Religion and Spirituality." PhD thesis, Baylor University, 2018.

———. "Something Besides Monotheism: Sociotheological Boundary Work Among the Spiritual, but Not Religious." *Poetics* 62 (June 2017): 53–65.

McDonald, William P. *How Chiropractors Think and Practice: The Survey of North American Chiropractors*. Ada: Institute for Social Research, Ohio Northern University, 2003.

McDowell, John C. *The Gospel According to Star Wars: Faith, Hope, and The Force*. Louisville, KY: Westminster John Knox, 2007.

McGee, Micki. *Self-Help, Inc.: Makeover Culture in America*. Oxford: Oxford University Press, 2005.

McGuire, Meredith B. *Lived Religion: Faith and Practice in Everyday Life.* Oxford: Oxford University Press, 2008.
McGuire, Meredith B., and Debra Kantor. *Ritual Healing in Suburban America.* New Brunswick, NJ: Rutgers University Press, 1988.
McKellar, Peter. *A Textbook of Human Psychology.* London: Cohen & West, 1952.
McLuhan, Marshall. *Understanding Media: The Extensions of Man.* Cambridge, MA: MIT Press, 1964.
McWhorter, John. "The Dehumanizing Condescension of *White Fragility.*" *The Atlantic,* July 15, 2020.
Mead, George H. *Mind, Self, and Society: From the Standpoint of a Social Behaviorist.* Chicago: University of Chicago Press, 1934.
Medin, R. Alexander. "3 Gurus, 48 Questions: Matching Interviews with Sri T. K. V. Desikachar, Sri B. K. S. Iyengar & Sri K. Pattabhi Jois." *Namarupa,* Fall 2004, 6–18.
Mellor, Philip A. "Protestant Buddhism? The Cultural Translation of Buddhism in England." *Religion* 21, no. 1 (1991): 73–92.
Mendelson, Tamar, Mark T. Greenberg, Jacinda K. Dariotis, Laura Feagans Gould, Brittany L. Rhoades, and Philip J. Leaf. "Feasibility and Preliminary Outcomes of a School-Based Mindfulness Intervention for Urban Youth." *Journal of Abnormal Child Psychology* 38, no. 7 (2010): 985–94.
Miles, Pamela. *Reiki: A Comprehensive Guide.* New York: Penguin, 2006.
Miller, Arlene. "Should Christian Nurses Practice Therapeutic Touch? No." *Journal of Christian Nursing* 4, no. 4 (1987): 15–19, 29–30.
Mindful Schools. "About Us." 2023. https://www.mindfulschools.org/about/.
MindUP. "Our Mission." 2023. https://mindup.org/our-mission/.
Mohler, R. Albert. "Yahoo, Yoga, and Yours Truly." October 7, 2010. http://www.albertmohler.com/2010/10/07/yahoo-yoga-and-yours-truly/.
Moore, J. Stuart. *Chiropractic in America: The History of a Medical Alternative.* Baltimore: Johns Hopkins University Press, 1993.
Morris, Aldon D. *The Origins of the Civil Rights Movement.* New York: Simon & Schuster, 1986.
Moskowitz, Eva S. *In Therapy We Trust: Americas Obsession with Self-Fulfilment.* Baltimore: Johns Hopkins University Press, 2001.
Moss, Gabriel, Gi-Ming Wang, Bethanny Bristol, Hasina Momotaz, Ming Li, and Richard Lee. "Assessing the Ability of Reiki Practitioners to Detect Human Energy Fields." *OBM Integrative and Complementary Medicine,* August 4, 2022. https://www.lidsen.com/journals/icm/icm-07-03-033.
Mosurinjohn, Sharday, and Galen Watts. "Religious Studies and the Spiritual Turn." *Method & Theory in the Study of Religion* 33, no. 5 (2021): 482–504.

Mudde, Cas. "The Populist Zeitgeist." *Government and Opposition* 39, no. 4 (2004): 541–63.

Nadesan, Majia Holmer. "The Discourses of Corporate Spiritualism and Evangelical Capitalism." *Management Communication Quarterly* 13, no. 1 (1999): 3–42.

National Center for Complementary and Integrative Health. "Paying for Complementary and Integrative Health Approaches." June 2016. https://www.nccih.nih.gov/health/paying-for-complementary-and-integrative-health-approaches.

———. "Timeline." 2023. https://www.nccih.nih.gov/about/nccih-timeline.

Negroponte, Nicholas. *Being Digital*. New York: Vintage, 1996.

Nehring, Daniel, Emmanuel Alvarado, Eric C. Hendriks, and Dylan Kerrigan. *Transnational Popular Psychology and the Global Self-help Industry: The Politics of Contemporary Social Change*. London: Palgrave Macmillan, 2016.

Nehring, Daniel, Ole Jacob Madsen, Edgar Cabanas, China Mills, and Dylan Kerrigan, ed. *The Routledge International Handbook of Global Therapeutic Cultures*. New York: Routledge, 2020.

Nethercot, Arthur Hobart. *The First Five Lives of Annie Besant*. London: R. Hart-Davis, 1961.

Nisbetter, Richard E., and Timothy DeCamp Wilson. "The Halo Effect: Evidence for Unconscious Alteration of Judgments." *Journal of Personality and Social Psychology* 35, no. 4 (1977): 250–56.

Norris, Pippa. *Democratic Deficit: Critical Citizens Revisited*. New York: Cambridge University Press, 2011.

Norris, Pippa, and Ronald Inglehart. *Cultural Backlash: Trump, Brexit, and Authoritarian Populism*, Cambridge: Cambridge University Press, 2019.

Numbers, Ronald L. "The Fall and Rise of the American Medical Profession." In *Sickness and Health in America: Readings in the History of Medicine and Public Health*, ed. Judith Walzer Leavitt and Ronald L. Numbers, 225–36. Madison: University of Wisconsin Press, 1978.

O'Brien, John. "Individualism as a Discursive Strategy of Action: Autonomy, Agency, and Reflexivity Among Religious Americans." *Sociological Theory* 33, no. 2 (2015): 173–99.

Offe, Claus. "New Social Movements: Challenging the Boundaries of Institutional Politics." *Social Research* 52, no. 4 (1985): 817–68.

Ontario Public Service. "Message from the Secretary of the Cabinet." 2023. https://www.ontario.ca/page/ontario-public-service-anti-racism-policy#section-0.

Orr, Deborah. "The Uses of Mindfulness in Anti-Oppressive Pedagogies: Philosophy and Praxis." *Canadian Journal of Education* 27, no. 4 (2002): 477–90.

Owen, Alex. *The Darkened Room: Women, Power and Spiritualism in Late Victorian England*. London: Virago Press, 1989.
———. *The Place of Enchantment: British Occultism and the Culture of the Modern*. Chicago: University of Chicago Press, 2004.
Pagis, Michal. "Embodied Therapeutic Culture." In *The Routledge International Handbook of Global Therapeutic Cultures*, ed. Daniel Nehring et al., 177–90. New York: Routledge, 2020.
———. "Fashioning Futures: Life Coaching and the Self-made Identity Paradox." *Sociological Forum* 31, no. 4 (2016): 1083–1103.
———. *Inward: Vipassana Meditation and the Embodiment of the Self*. Chicago: University of Chicago Press, 2019.
Pagis, Michal, Wendy Cadge, and Orly Tal. "Translating Spirituality: Universalism and Particularism in the Diffusion of Spiritual Care from the United States to Israel." *Sociological Forum* 33, no. 3 (2018): 596–618.
Palmer, Daniel David. *The Chiropractor's Adjuster: Text-book of the Science, Art and Philosophy of Chiropractic*. Portland, OR: Portland Printing House, 1910.
Park, Crystal L., Kristen E. Riley, Elena Bedesin, and V. Michelle Stewart. "Why Practice Yoga? Practitioners' Motivations for Adopting and Maintaining Yoga Practice." *Journal of Health Psychology* 21, no. 6 (2016): 887–96.
Parsons, Talcott. "Religion in Postindustrial America: The Problem of Secularization." *Social Research* 51, no. 1 (1984): 493–525.
Parsons, Talcott, and Gerald M. Platt. *The American University*. Cambridge, MA: Harvard University Press, 1973.
Parsons, William B., and Robert C. Fuller. "Spiritual but Not Religious: A Brief Introduction." In *Being Spiritual but Not Religious: Past, Present, Future(s)*, ed. William B. Parsons, 15–29. New York: Routledge, 2018.
Partridge, Christopher. *The Re-enchantment of the West*. 2 vols. New York: T&T Clark, 2005–6.
Pattillo-McCoy, Mary. "Church Culture as a Strategy of Action in the Black Community." *American Sociological Review* 63, no. 6 (1998): 767–84.
Payne, Richard K. "Religion, Self-Help, Science: Three Economies of Western/ized Buddhism." *Journal of Global Buddhism* 20 (January 2019): 69–86.
———. "What's Ethics Got to Do with It? The Misguided Debate about Mindfulness and Morality." *Tricycle*, May 14, 2015. https://tricycle.org/trikedaily/whats-ethics-got-do-it/.
Pearson, Joanne. *Wicca and the Christian Heritage: Ritual, Sex and Magic*. New York: Routledge, 2007.
Pelkmans, Mathijs, and Rhys Machold. "Conspiracy Theories and Their Truth Trajectories." *Focaal*, no. 59 (2011): 66–80.

Penman, Stephen, Marc Cohen, Philip Stevens, and Sue Jackson. "Yoga in Australia: Results of a National Survey." *International Journal of Yoga* 5, no. 2 (2012): 91–101.

Perreira, Todd LeRoy. "Sasana Sakon and the New Asian American: Intermarriage and Identity at a Thai Buddhist Temple in Silicon Valley." In *Asian American Religions: The Making and Remaking of Borders and Boundaries*, ed. Tony Carnes and Fenggang Yang, 313–37. New York: New York University Press.

Perry, Samuel L. "(Why) Is the Sociology of Religion Marginalized? Results from a Survey Experiment." *American Sociologist* 54, no. 3 (2023): 1–27.

Petersen, Jesper Aagaard. "The Black Helicopter: A Lecture in Hyperreality, Or Why Academese Matters." May 19, 2010. https://jespaa.wordpress.com/2010/05/19/a-lecture-in-hyperreality-or-why-academese-matters/.

Petty, Sheryl. "Waking Up to All of Ourselves: Inner Work, Social Justice, & Systems Change." *Initiative for Contemplation Equity & Action* 1, no. 1 (2017): 1–14.

Pew Research Center. "Being Christian in Western Europe." May 29, 2018. https://www.pewforum.org/2018/05/29/being-christian-in-western-europe/.

"Poll Finds Meditation, Mysticism, and Yoga Growing in Popularity." *New York Times*, November 18, 1976.

Pollack, Detlef, and Gert Pickel. "Religious Individualization or Secularization? Testing Hypotheses of Religious Change—The Case of Eastern and Western Germany." *British Journal of Sociology* 58, no. 4 (2007): 603–32.

Porterfield, Amanda. *The Transformation of American Religion: The Story of a Late-Twentieth-Century Awakening*. Oxford: Oxford University Press, 2001.

Possamai, Adam. "Alternative Spiritualities and the Cultural Logic of Late Capitalism." *Culture and Religion* 4, no. 1 (2003): 31–45.

——. "Popular and Lived Religions." *Current Sociology* 63, no. 6 (2015): 781–99.

——. "Producing and Consuming New Age Spirituality: The Cultic Milieu and the Network Paradigm." In *The Handbook of New Age*, ed. Daren Kemp and James R. Lewis, 151–66. Leiden: Brill, 2007.

Price, H. H. *Belief: The Gifford Lectures*. London: Allen & Unwin, 1969.

Prochaska, Frank. *Christianity and Social Service in Modern Britain*. New York: Oxford University Press, 2006.

Pure Edge Inc. (a.k.a. K. P. Jois USA Foundation, a.k.a. Sonima Foundation). "Tax Filings by Year." *ProPublica 2011–2018*. https://projects.propublica.org/nonprofits/organizations/453182571.

Purser, Ronald E. "Critical Perspectives on Corporate Mindfulness." *Journal of Management, Spirituality & Religion* 15, no. 2 (2018): 105–8.

———. *McMindfulness: How Mindfulness Became the New Capitalist Spirituality.* London: Repeater Books, 2019.

Putnam, Robert D. *Bowling Alone: The Collapse and Revival of American Community.* New York: Simon & Schuster, 2000.

Putnam, Robert D., and David E. Campbell. *American Grace: How Religion Divides and- Unites Us.* New York: Simon & Schuster, 2010.

Raaphorst, Nadine, and Dick Houtman. "A Necessary Evil That Does Not 'Really' Cure Disease: The Domestication of Biomedicine by Dutch Holistic General Practitioners." *Health: An Interdisciplinary Journal for the Social Study of Health, Illness and Medicine* 20, no. 3 (2016): 242–57.

Rand, William L. "What Is the History of Reiki?" 2015. International Center for Reiki Training, http://reiki-healing-arts.com/reiki-history.html.

Raso, Jack. *"Alternative" Healthcare: A Comprehensive Guide.* Amherst, NY: Prometheus, 1994.

Ratliff, Evan. "The Crusade Against Evolution." *Wired*, October 1, 2004. https://www.wired.com/2004/10/evolution-2/.

Read, Bridget. "Doing the Work at Work: What Are Companies Desperate for Diversity Consultants Actually Buying?" *The Cut*, May 26, 2021.

Redden, Guy. "Religion, Cultural Studies and New Age Sacralization of Everyday Life." *European Journal of Cultural Studies* 14, no. 6 (2011): 649–63.

Rennison, Susan Joy. "Spiritual Evolution in the Cultic Milieu." April 22, 2013. https://susanrennison.co.uk/Spiritual_Evolution_Cultic_Milieu_v2013.pdf.

Reveley, James. "Neoliberal Meditations: How Mindfulness Training Medicalizes Education and Responsibilizes Young People." *Policy Futures in Education* 14, no. 4 (2016): 497–511.

Rheingold, Howard. *The Virtual Community: Homesteading on the Electronic Frontier.* Cambridge, MA: MIT Press, 2000.

Richardson, John H. "Inside the Race to Hack the Human Brain." *Wired*, November 16, 2017. https://www.wired.com/story/inside-the-race-to-build-a-brain-machine-interface/.

Rieff, Philip. *The Triumph of the Therapeutic.* Chicago: University of Chicago Press, 1966.

Riis, Ole, and Linda Woodhead. *A Sociology of Religious Emotion.* Oxford: Oxford University Press, 2010.

Rimke, Heidi Marie. "Governing Citizens Through Self-help Literature." *Cultural Studies* 14, no. 1 (2000): 61–78.

Robertson, David G. "Conspiracy Theories and the Study of Alternative and Emergent Religions." *Nova Religio: The Journal of Alternative and Emergent Religions* 19, no. 2 (2015): 5–16.

———. *UFOs, Conspiracy Theories and the New Age: Millennial Conspiracism.* London: Bloomsbury, 2016.

Robinson, Brett T. *Appletopia: Media Technology and the Religious Imagination of Steve Jobs*. Waco, TX: Baylor University Press, 2013.
Roof, Wade Clark, Anne E. Patrick, Ronald L. Grimes, and Bill J. Leonard. "American Spirituality." *Religion and American Culture* 9, no. 2 (1999): 131–57.
———. *A Generation of Seekers: The Spiritual Journeys of the Baby Boom Generation*. San Francisco: Harper, 1993.
———. *Spiritual Marketplace: Baby Boomers and the Remaking of American Religion*. Princeton, NJ: Princeton University Press, 2001.
Rosa, Linda, Emily Rosa, Larry Sarner, and Stephen Barrett. "A Close Look at Therapeutic Touch." *Journal of the American Medical Association* 279, no. 13 (1998): 1005–10.
Rose, Nikolas S. *Governing the Soul: The Shaping of the Private Self*. New York: Free Association Books, 1989.
———. *Inventing Our Selves: Psychology, Power, and Personhood*. Cambridge: Cambridge University Press, 1998.
Ross, Casey, Max Blau, and Kate Sheridan. "Medicine with a Side of Mysticism: Top Hospitals Promote Unproven Therapies." *STAT*, March 7, 2017. https://www.statnews.com/2017/03/07/alternative-medicine-hospitals-promote/.
Roszak, Theodore. *From Satori to Silicon Valley: San Francisco and the American Counterculture*. San Francisco: Don't Call It Frisco Press, 1986.
———. *The Making of a Counter Culture: Reflections on the Technocratic Society and Its Youthful Opposition*. New York: Doubleday, 1969.
Rountree, Kathryn. *Embracing the Witch and the Goddess: Feminist Ritual-Makers in New Zealand*. New York: Taylor & Francis, 2004.
Ruijs, Wilhelmina L. M., Jeannine L. A. Hautvast, Koos van der Velden, Sjoerd de Vos, Hans Knippenberg, and Marlies E. J. L. Hulscher. "Religious Subgroups Influencing Vaccination Coverage in the Dutch Bible Belt: An Ecological Study." *BMC Public Health* 11, article 102 (2011). https://bmcpublichealth.biomedcentral.com/articles/10.1186/1471-2458-11-102.
Rutjens, Bastiaan T., Nikhil Sengupta, Romy van der Lee, Guido M. van Koningsbruggen, Jason P. Martens, Andre Rabelo, and Robbie M. Sutton. "Science Skepticism Across 24 Countries." *Social Psychological and Personality Science* 13, no. 1 (2022): 102–17.
Rutjens, Bastiaan T., and Romy van der Lee. "Spiritual Skepticism? Heterogeneous Science Skepticism in the Netherlands." *Public Understanding of Science* 29, no. 3 (2020): 335–52.
Rutjens, Bastiaan T., Natalia Zarzeczna, and Romy van der Lee. "Science Rejection in Greece: Spirituality Predicts Vaccine Scepticism and Low Faith in Science in a Greek Sample." *Public Understanding of Science* 31, no. 4 (2022): 428–36.

Salam, Maya. "What Is Toxic Masculinity?" *New York Times*, January 22, 2019.

Salomonsen, Jone. *Enchanted Feminism: Ritual Constructions of Gender, Agency and Divinity Among the Reclaiming Witches of San Francisco.* London: Routledge, 2001.

Sanchez, Gaëtan, Thomas Hartmann, Marco Fuscà, Gianpaolo Demarchi, and Nathan Weisz. "Decoding Across Sensory Modalities Reveals Common Supramodal Signatures of Conscious Perception." *PNAS* 117, no. 13 (2020): 7437–46.

Sarachild, Katie. "Consciousness-Raising: A Radical Weapon." 1973. https://www.rapereliefshelter.bc.ca/wp-content/uploads/2021/03/Feminist-Revolution-Consciousness-Raising-A-Radical-Weapon-Kathie-Sarachild.pdf, 144–50.

Satin, Mark. *New Age Politics, Healing Self and Society: The Emerging New Alternative to Marxism and Liberalism.* London: Whitecap Books/Fairweather Press, 1973.

Scherer, Jochen. " 'Truth Is What's True for Me?': Reassessing the Knowledge Claims of New Age Spirituality." PhD thesis, Bangor University, 2011.

Schmidt, Leigh Eric. *Restless Souls: The Making of American Spirituality.* Berkeley: University of California Press, 2012.

Schnall, Marianne. "Goldie Hawn Talks 'MindUP' and Her Mission to Bring Children Happiness." *Huffington Post*, April 20, 2011. http://www.huffingtonpost.com/marianne-schnall/goldie-hawn-mindup_b_850226.html.

Schonert-Reichl, Kimberly A., Eva Oberle, Molly Stewart Lawlor, David Abbott, Kimberly Thomson, Tim F. Oberlander, and Adele Diamond. "Enhancing Cognitive and Social–Emotional Development Through a Simple-to-Administer Mindfulness-Based School Program for Elementary School Children: A Randomized Controlled Trial." *Developmental Psychology* 51, no. 1 (2015): 52–66.

Seager, Richard Hughes. *Buddhism in America.* New York: Columbia University Press, 1999.

———. *The Dawn of Religious Pluralism: Voices from the World's Parliament of Religions.* La Salle, IL: Open Court, 1993. f

Seddon, Philip. *The New Age: An Assessment.* Bramcote, UK: Grove Books, 1990.

Sedlock v. Baird, Superior Court of San Diego County, No. 37–2013–00035910-CU-MC-CTL. (2013), 235 Cal. App. 4th 874 (2015).

Seidman, Steven. *Contested Knowledge: Social Theory in the Postmodern Era.* Cambridge, MA: Blackwell, 1994.

Semmes, Clovis E. "Entrepreneur of Health: Dick Gregory, Black Consciousness, and the Human Potential Movement." *Journal of African American Studies* 16, no. 3 (2012): 537–49.

Separation of Hinduism from Our Schools v. Chicago Public Schools et al. 2021, Case No. 20 C 4540 (2021).

Shapiro, Dean H. "A Preliminary Study of Long-Term Meditators: Goals, Effects, Religious Orientation, Cognitions." *Journal of Transpersonal Psychology* 24, no. 1 (1992): 23–39.

Shaw, Jane. *Pioneers of Modern Spirituality: The Neglected Anglican Innovators of a "Spiritual but Not Religious" Age*. London: Darton, Longman and Todd, 2017.

Sheldrake, Philip. *Spirituality: A Brief History*. Chichester, UK: Wiley-Blackwell, 2013.

Shook, Andria, and Hannah Johnson. *Yoga Leadership and Instruction: Lessons Learned from Charter School Communities*. San Diego: University of San Diego, 2015.

Shropshire, Kitty. "The Radical Right in the Cultic Milieu." Center for the Analysis of the Radical Right. August 21, 2020. https://www.radicalrightanalysis.com/2020/08/21/the-radical-right-in-the-cultic-milieu/.

Sibinga, Erica M. S., Lindsey Webb, Sharon R. Ghazarian, and Jonathan M. Ellen. "School-Based Mindfulness Instruction: An RCT." *Pediatrics* 137, no. 1 (2016): 1–8.

Siegel, Aryeh. "Disabled Army Vet Persuades VA to Abort $8 Million David Lynch Foundation Study on Transcendental Meditation and PTSD." *EINPressWire*. August 1, 2022. https://www.einpresswire.com/article/583527644/disabled-army-vet-persuades-va-to-abort-8-million-david-lynch-foundation-study-on-transcendental-meditation-and-ptsd.

Silberman, Steve. "Oliver Sacks on Earworms, Stevie Wonder and the View from Mescaline Mountain." *Wired*, September 24, 2007. https://www.wired.com/2007/09/ff-musicophilia/.

Singler, Beth. *The Indigo Children: New Age Experimentation with Self and Science*. London: Routledge, 2017.

Smith, Christian. *American Evangelicalism: Embattled and Thriving*. Chicago: University of Chicago Press, 1998.

Smith, Christian, and Melinda Lundquist Denton. *Soul Searching: The Religious and Spiritual Lives of American Teenagers*. Oxford: Oxford University Press, 2009.

Smithuijsen, Doortje. "De opkomst van 'wellnessrechts': Yogales als broeinest van complottheorieën" (The Rise of the 'Wellness Right': Yoga Class as a Hotbed for Conspiracy Theories). *Vrij Nederland*, April 7, 2021.

Sointu, Eeva. *In Search of Wellbeing: Reflecting on the Use of Alternative and Complementary Medicines*. Unpublished PhD thesis. Lancaster, UK: Department of Sociology, Lancaster University, 2005.

Sointu, Eeva, and Linda Woodhead. "Holistic Spirituality, Gender, and Expressive Selfhood." *Journal for the Scientific Study of Religion* 47, no. 2 (2008): 259–76.

Somin, Ilya. "The Growth of the Cultic Milieu and the Spread of Harmful Ideas." *Reason*, July 8, 2019. https://reason.com/volokh/2019/08/07/the-growth-of-the-cultic-milieu-and-the-spread-of-harmful-ideas/.
Sonima Foundation. "NY State Legislators Pass Resolution Declaring First Week in May 'NY Health and Wellness Week.'" May 9, 2015. https://web.archive.org/web/20160327015942/http://www.sonimafoundation.org/nystate-legislators-pass-resolution-declaring-first-week-in-may-ny-health-and-wellness-week/.
Sood, Amit. "Mind-Body Medicine." In *Mayo Clinic Book of Alternative Medicine: Integrating the Best of Natural Therapies with Conventional Medicine*, 2nd ed., ed. Brent A. Bauer, 94–117. New York: Time Inc. Home Entertainment Books, 2010.
Starhawk. *The Spiral Dance: A Rebirth of the Ancient Religion of the Great Goddess*. San Francisco: Harper, 1999.
Steensland, Brian, David P. King, and Barbara J. Duffy. "The Discursive and Practical Influence of Spirituality on Civic Engagement." *Journal for the Scientific Study of Religion* 61, no. 2 (2022): 389–407.
Steensland, Brian, Jaime Kucinskas, and Anna Sun, ed. *Situating Spirituality: Context, Practice, and Power*. Oxford: Oxford University Press, 2021.
Steensland, Brian, Lauren Chism Schmidt, and Xiaoyun Wang. "Spirituality: What Does It Mean and to Whom?" *Journal for the Scientific Study of Religion* 57, no. 3 (2018): 450–72.
Stein, Diane. *Essential Reiki Teaching Manual: A Companion Guide for Reiki Healers*. Berkeley, CA: Crossing, 2007.
Steinem, Gloria. *Revolution from Within: A Book of Self-Esteem*. Boston: Little, Brown and Company, 1992.
Stolz, Jörg. "Secularization Theories in the Twenty-First Century: Ideas, Evidence, and Problems (Presidential Address)." *Social Compass* 67, no. 2 (2020): 282–308.
Strhan, Anna. *Aliens and Strangers? The Struggle for Coherence in the Everyday Lives of Evangelicals*. Oxford: Oxford University Press, 2015.
Stringer, Martin. *Contemporary Western Ethnography and the Definition of Religion*. New York: Continuum, 2008.
Stronged. "Campbell, Colin. The Cult, The Cultic Milieu and Secularization. A Sociological Yearbook of Religion in Britain, SCM Press London, 1972." *Honoured*, March 11, 2013. https://honoured.wordpress.com/2013/03/11/campbell-colin-the-cult-the-cultic-milieu-and-secularization-a-sociological-yearbook-of-religion-in-britain-scm-press-london-1972/.
Suellentrop, Chris. "Great Expectations." *Wired*, December 6, 2012. https://www.wired.com/2012/12/ff-bioshock/.
Sunstein, Cass. "What the Civil Rights Movement Was and Wasn't (with Notes on Martin Luther King, Jr. and Malcolm X)." In *Reassessing the*

Sixties: Debating the Political and Cultural Legacy, ed. Stephen Macedo, 253–82. New York: Norton, 1997.

Sutcliffe, Steven J. *Children of the New Age: A History of Spiritual Practices*. London: Routledge, 2003.

——. "New Age, World Religions and Elementary Forms." In *New Age Spirituality: Rethinking Religion*, ed. Steven J. Sutcliffe and Ingvild Saelid Gilhus, 17–34. London: Routledge, 2014.

Syman, Stefanie. *The Subtle Body: The Story of Yoga in America*. New York: Farrar, Straus and Giroux, 2010.

Taggart, Paul. *Populism*. Buckingham, UK: Open University Press, 2000.

Taylor, Charles. *A Secular Age*. Cambridge, MA: Harvard University Press, 2007.

——. *Sources of the Self: The Making of the Modern Identity*. Cambridge, MA: Harvard University Press, 1989.

Ten Kate, Josje, Willem de Koster, and Jeroen van der Waal. "'Following Your Gut' or 'Questioning the Scientific Evidence': Understanding Vaccine Skepticism Among More-Educated Dutch Parents." *Journal of Health and Social Behavior* 62, no. 1 (2021): 85–99.

Thiessen, Joel. *The Meaning of Sunday: The Practice of Belief in a Secular Age*. London: McGill-Queen's University Press, 2015.

Thiessen, Joel, and Sarah Wilkins-Laflamme. *None of the Above: Nonreligious Identity in the US and Canada*. New York: New York University Press, 2020.

Thumbtack. "How Much Does Reiki Healing Cost?" August 26, 2020. https://www.thumbtack.com/p/reiki-cost.

Tiffany, Kaitlyn. "The Women Making Conspiracy Theories Beautiful." *Atlantic*, August 15, 2020.

Tipton, Steven M. *Getting Saved from the Sixties*. Berkeley: University of California Press, 1982.

TM.org. "TM Course Fee." 2023. https://www.tm.org/course-fee.

——. "Transcendental Meditation: The Technique for Inner Peace & Wellness." https://www.tm.org/.

Tobias, Andrada. "Steps on Life Change and Spiritual Transformation: The Project of the Self." *Studia UBB Sociologia* 61, no. 2 (2016): 125–44.

Tocqueville, Alexis de. *Democracy in America*. 1835. London: Penguin, 2003.

Todd, Nathan R., and Jaclyn D. Houston. "Examining Patterns of Political, Social Service, and Collaborative Involvement of Religious Congregations: A Latent Class and Transition Analysis." *American Journal of Community Psychology* 51, no. 3–4 (2013): 422–38.

Tomasi, Marta. "Populism, Politics, and Science in the Midst of the Pandemic." *Tecnoscienza* 12, no. 2 (2021): 145–54.

Tosoni, Simone. "Misinformation, Social Media and the Pandemic Crisis: Challenging the Return to a Powerful Media Effects Paradigm." *Tecnoscienza* 12, no. 2 (2021): 174–91.

Toulmin, Stephen. *Cosmopolis: The Hidden Agenda of Modernity*. Chicago: University of Chicago Press, 1990.
Tracy, Marc. "Two Journalists Exit New York Times After Criticism of Past Behavior." *New York Times*, February 5, 2021.
"Transcript: Ezra Klein Show with Russell Moore." *New York Times*, August 23, 2022.
Troeltsch, Ernst. *The Social Teachings of the Christian Churches*. 1912. 2 vols. Louisville, KY: Westminster/John Knox Press, 1992.
Tromp, Paul, Anna Pless, and Dick Houtman. "A Smaller Pie with a Different Taste: The Evolution of the Western-European Religious Landscape." *Review of Religious Research* 64, no. 1 (2022): 127–44.
———. "Do 'Spiritual' Self-identifications Signify Affinity with New Age Religion? Survey Evidence from the Netherlands." *Journal of Contemporary Religion*, February 28, 2024. https://www.tandfonline.com/doi/full/10.1080/13537903.2024.2315809.
Tschannen, Oliver. "The Secularization Paradigm: A Systematization." *Journal for the Scientific Study of Religion* 30, no. 4 (1991): 396–415.
Tufekci, Zeynep. "YouTube, the Great Radicalizer." *New York Times*, March 10, 2018.
Tumber, Catherine. *American Feminism and the Birth of New Age Spirituality: Searching for the Higher Self, 1875–1915*. Lanham, MD: Rowman & Littlefield, 2002.
Turner, Bryan S. "Religion and Contemporary Sociological Theories." *Current Sociology* 62, no. 6 (2014): 771–88.
———. *Religion and Modern Society: Citizenship, Secularization and the State*. Cambridge: Cambridge University Press, 2013.
Turner, Fred. "Burning Man at Google: A Cultural Infrastructure for New Media Production." *New Media & Society* 11, no. 1–2 (2009): 73–94.
———. *From Counterculture to Cyberculture: Stewart Brand, the Whole Earth Network, and the Rise of Digital Utopianism*. Chicago: University of Chicago Press, 2008.
———. "Where the Counterculture Met the New Economy: The WELL and the Origins of Virtual Community." *Technology and Culture* 46, no. 3 (2005): 485–512.
Tweed, Thomas A. *The American Encounter with Buddhism, 1844–1912: Victorian Culture and the Limits of Dissent*. Chapel Hill: University of North Carolina Press, 2000.
UMass Memorial Medical Center. "Center for Mindfulness." 2023. https://www.ummhealth.org/umass-memorial-medical-center/services-treatments/center-for-mindfulness.
Underhill, Evelyn. *Mysticism: The Nature and Development of Spiritual Consciousness*. 1910. 12th ed. Oxford: One World, 1993.

United States Conference of Catholic Bishops. *Guidelines for Evaluating Reiki as an Alternative Therapy.* March 2009. https://www.usccb.org/resources/evaluation-guidelines-finaltext-2009-03_0.pdf.

University of Cambridge. Research. "Elvis Is Alive and the Moon Landings Were Faked: The (Conspiracy) Theory of Everything." October 25, 2016, https://www.cam.ac.uk/research/features/elvis-is-alive-and-the-moon-landings-were-faked-the-conspiracy-theory-of-everything.

Urban Zen Foundation. "A Philosophy of Caring by Donna Karan." https://uzit.nyc/.

Valaskivi, Katja. "Circulation of Conspiracy Theories in the Attention Factory." *Popular Communication* 20, no. 3 (2022): 162–77.

Van der Veer, Peter. "Spirituality in Modern Society." *Social Research* 76, no. 4 (2009): 1097–1120.

Van Dijck, José, Thomas Poell, and Martijn de Waal. *The Platform Society: Public Values in a Connective World.* New York: Oxford University Press, 2018.

Van Gool, Rosa, and Coen Van de Ven. "Wij zijn het nieuwe nieuws" (We Are the New News). *De Groene Amsterdammer,* September 14, 2020.

Verini, James. "How Virtual Pop Star Hatsune Miku Blew Up in Japan." *Wired,* October 19, 2012. https://www.wired.com/2012/10/mf-japan-pop-star-hatsune-miku/.

Versluis, Arthur. *American Gurus: From Transcendentalism to New Age Religion.* Oxford: Oxford University Press, 2014.

Vincen-Brown, Frances. "Reiki Therapy." Experience Festival. 2010. www.experiencefestival.com/wp/article/reiki-therapy.

Vincett, Giselle. "Quagans: Fusing Quakerism with Contemporary Paganism." *Quaker Studies* 13, no. 2 (2009): 220–37.

Vivekananda. "Hinduism." In *The World's Parliament of Religions,* ed. Henry Barrows, 2:968–78. Chicago: Parliament Publishing Company, 1893.

Voas, David. "The Rise and Fall of Fuzzy Fidelity in Europe." *European Sociological Review* 25, no. 2 (2009): 155–68.

Voas, David, and Mark Chaves. "Is the United States a Counterexample to the Secularization Thesis?" *American Journal of Sociology* 121, no. 5 (2016): 1517–56.

Voas, David, and Alasdair Crockett. "Religion in Britain: Neither Believing nor Belonging." *Sociology* 39, no. 1 (2005): 11–28.

Vogelstein, Fred. "How Mark Zuckerberg Turned Facebook Into the Web's Hottest Platform." *Wired,* September 6, 2007. https://www.wired.com/2007/09/ff-facebook/.

Waldersee, Victoria. "Which Science-Based Conspiracy Theories Do Britons Believe?" 2019. https://yougov.co.uk/politics/articles/22839-which-science-based-conspiracy-theories-do-britons.

Ward, Charlotte, and David Voas. "The Emergence of Conspirituality." *Journal of Contemporary Religion* 26, no. 1 (2011): 103–21.
Warren, Rick. *The Purpose Driven Life: What on Earth Am I Here For?* Grand Rapids, MI: Zondervan, 2002.
Watts, Galen. "Are You a Neoliberal Subject? On the Uses and Abuses of a Concept." *European Journal of Social Theory* 25, no. 3 (2022): 458–76.
———. "Marianne Williamson and the Religion of Spirituality." *The Conversation*. October 6, 2019. https://theconversation.com/marianne-williamson-and-the-religion-of-spirituality-123399.
———. "Missing the Forest for the Trees: 'Spiritual' Religion in a Secular Age." *Toronto Journal of Theology* 34, no. 2 (2018): 243–56.
———. "The Religion of the Heart: 'Spirituality' in Late Modernity." *American Journal of Cultural Sociology* 10, no. 1 (2022): 1–33.
———. *The Spiritual Turn: The Religion of the Heart and the Making of Romantic Liberal Modernity*. Oxford: Oxford University Press, 2022.
Watts, Galen, and Dick Houtman. "Purification or Pollution? The Debate Over 'Workplace Spirituality.'" *Cultural Sociology* 17, no. 4 (2023): 439–56.
———. "The Spiritual Turn and the Disenchantment of the World: Max Weber, Peter Berger and the Religion-Science Conflict." *Sociological Review* 71, no. 1 (2023): 261–79.
Weber, Max. *The Protestant Ethic and the Spirit of Capitalism*. 1904–5. London: Routledge, 2005.
———. *The Religion of India*. New York: Free Press, 1958.
———. *The Sociology of Religion*. 1922. Boston: Beacon Press, 1963.
Wertheim, Margaret. "The Pope's Astrophysicist." *Wired*, December 1, 2002. https://www.wired.com/2002/12/pope-astro/.
Wheaton College. "Yoga at Wheaton?" January 2015. https://www.wheaton.edu/media/migrated-images-amp-files/media/files/athletics/Why-Yoga-at-Wheaton.pdf.
Whitehead, Andrew L., and Samuel L. Perry. *Taking America Back for God: Christian Nationalism in the United States*. Oxford: Oxford University Press, 2020.
Whorton, James C. *Nature Cures: The History of Alternative Medicine in America*. New York: Oxford University Press, 2002.
Wiese, Glenda. "Chiropractic History and Trivia." In *Chiropractic Secrets*, ed. Seth Gardner and John S. Mosby, 231–46. Philadelphia: Hanley and Belfus, 2000.
Wilkins-Laflamme, Sarah. "A Tale of Decline or Change? Working Toward a Complementary Understanding of Secular Transition and Individual Spiritualization Theories." *Journal for the Scientific Study of Religion* 60, no. 3 (2021): 516–39.
Williams, Leonard. "Ideological Parallels Between the New Left and the New Right." *Social Science Journal* 24, no. 3 (1987): 317–27.

Williams, Ruth. "Eat, Pray, Love: Producing the Female Neoliberal Spiritual Subject." *Journal of Popular Culture* 47, no. 3 (2014): 613–33.
Wilson, Bryan. *Contemporary Transformations of Religion*. Oxford: Oxford University Press, 1976.
———. *Religion in Sociological Perspective*. Oxford: Oxford University Press, 1982.
Wilson, Sarah. "The Wellness Realm Has Fallen Into Conspiritualism—I Have a Sense Why." *The Guardian*, September 14, 2020.
Wiseman, Richard. *UK Superstition Survey*. 2003. http://www.richardwiseman.com/resources/superstition_report.pdf.
Wolf, Ava, and Janet Wing. "How We Got Reiki Into the Hospital." Center for Reiki Research Including Reiki in Hospitals, April 13, 2010–November 7, 2016. https://web.archive.org/web/20100401000000*/https://www.centerforreikiresearch.org/Articles_HowWeGot.aspx.
Wolf, Gary. "Getting Things Done Guru David Allen and His Cult of Hyperefficiency." *Wired*, September 25, 2007. https://www.wired.com/2007/09/ff-allen/.
Wolfe, Tom. *The Electric Kool-Aid Acid Test*. 1968. New York: Picador, 2008.
Wolman, David. "Cairo Activists Use Facebook to Rattle Regime." *Wired*, October 20, 2008. https://www.wired.com/2008/10/ff-facebookegypt/.
Wood, Matthew. *Possession, Power and the New Age: Ambiguities of Authority in Neoliberal Societies*. Burlington, VT: Ashgate, 2007.
Wood, Richard L. *Faith in Action: Religion, Race, and Democratic Organizing in America*. Chicago: University of Chicago Press, 2002.
Wood, Richard L., and Mark R. Warren. "A Different Face of Faith-Based Politics: Social Capital and Community Organizing in the Public Arena." *International Journal of Sociology and Social Policy* 22, no. 9–10, (2002): 6–54.
Woodhead, Linda. "Afterword: To the Vagina Triangle and Beyond!" In *Secular Societies, Spiritual Selves? The Gendered Triangle of Religion, Secularity and Spirituality*, ed. Anna Fedele and Kim Knibbe, 233–38. New York: Routledge, 2020.
———. " 'Because I'm Worth It': Religion and Women's Changing Lives in the West." In *Women and Religion in the West: Challenging Secularization*, ed. Kristin Aune, Sonya Sharma, and Giselle Vincett, 147–63. Aldershot: Ashgate, 2008.
———. "The Gods of Modern Spirituality." In *Situating Spirituality: Context, Practice, and Power*, ed. Brian Steensland, Jaime Kucinskas, and Anna Sun, 49–71. Oxford: Oxford University Press, 2021.
———. "New Forms of Public Religion: Spirituality in Global Civil Society." In *Religion Beyond Its Private Role in Modern Society*, ed. Wim Hofstee and Arie van der Kooij, 29–54. Danvers: Brill, 2013.

———. "The New Spirituality and the World's Parliament of Religions." In *Reinventing Christianity: Nineteenth Century Contexts*, ed. Linda Woodhead, 81–96. Aldershot: Ashgate, 2001.

———. "Real Religion and Fuzzy Spirituality? Taking Sides in the Sociology of Religion." In Aupers and Houtman, *Religions of Modernity*, 31–48.

———. "The Rise of 'No Religion': Towards an Explanation." *Sociology of Religion: A Quarterly Review* 78, no. 3 (2016): 247–62.

———. "Tactical and Strategic Religion." In *Everyday Lived Islam in Europe*, ed. Nathal M. Dessing, Nadia Jeldtoft, Jørgen S. Nielsen, and Linda Woodhead, 9–22. Farnham, UK: Ashgate, 2014.

Woodhead, Linda, Hiroko Kawanami, and Christopher Partridge, ed. *Religions in the Modern World*. 2nd ed. London: Routledge, 2009.

Wuthnow, Robert. *After Heaven: Spirituality in America Since the 1950s*. Berkeley: University of California Press, 1998.

———. *After the Baby Boomers: How Twenty- and Thirty-Somethings Are Shaping the Future of American Religion*. Princeton, NJ: Princeton University Press, 2007.

———. *The Restructuring of American Religion*. Princeton, NJ: Princeton University Press, 1988.

———. *Sharing the Journey: Support Groups and America's New Quest for Community*. London: Free Press, 1996.

Wuthnow, Robert, and John H. Evans. *The Quiet Hand of God: Faith-Based Activism and the Public Role of Mainline Protestantism*. Berkeley: University of California Press, 2002.

Wyman, Scott. "Christian Minister Uses Reiki." May 23, 2006–December 24, 2016. https://web.archive.org/web/20161224112729/www.christianreiki.org/info/NunsPriestsMinisters/ChrisitanMinister.htm.

———. "Working with Wisdom & Compassion." 2013. www.scottwyman.com/Scott_Wyman/Integrating.html.

Yglesias, Matthew. "The Great Awokening." *Vox*. April 1, 2019. https://www.vox.com/2019/3/22/18259865/great-awokening-white-liberals-race-polling-trump-2020.

Yoga Alliance. "Brief of Amicus Curiae Yoga Alliance in Support of Respondents and Affirmance." October 16, 2014. In *Sedlock v. Baird*, Superior Court of San Diego County, No. 37-2013-00035910-CU-MC-CTL. (2013), 235 Cal. App. 4th 874 (2015).

———. "Spirit of the Standards—RYS 200." July 2016. https://www.yogaalliance.org/credentialing/standards/200-hourstandards.

Yoga Ed. "For Schools." https://yogaed.com/yoga-for-schools/#mindful-movement-program.

Yoga Journal and Yoga Alliance, with Ipsos Public Affairs. *The 2016 Yoga in America Study*. Boulder, CO: Yoga Journal, 2016.

York, Michael. "New Age Commodification and Appropriation of Spirituality." *Journal of Contemporary Religion* 16, no. 3 (2001): 361–72.

Young, Gale. "Becoming a White Foot-Soldier—Evolving Into Humanity: The Dangerous Intersections of the Personal, Professional, Political and Spiritual." *Initiative for Contemplation Equity & Action* 1, no. 1 (2017): 27–48.

Zaidman, Nurit, Ofra Goldstein-Gidoni, and Iris Nehemya. "From Temples to Organizations: The Introduction and Packaging of Spirituality." *Organization* 16, no. 4 (2009): 597–621.

Zandbergen, Dorien. "Silicon Valley New Age: The Co-constitution of the Digital and the Sacred." In Aupers and Houtman, *Religions of Modernity*, 161–85.

Zelevansky, Nora. "The Big Business of Unconscious Bias." *New York Times*, November 20, 2019.

Zijderveld, Anton C. *The Abstract Society: A Cultural Analysis of Our Time.* New York: Doubleday, 1970.

Žižek, Slavoj. "From Western Marxism to Western Buddhism." *Cabinet Magazine*, no. 2 (2001), https://www.cabinetmagazine.org/issues/2/zizek.php.

CONTRIBUTORS

Stef Aupers is a professor of media culture at the Institute for Media Studies, KU Leuven, Belgium. He has published widely in international peer-reviewed journals on religion and its mediatization, spirituality, conspiracy culture, and different forms of reenchantment.

Candy Gunther Brown is a professor of religious studies at Indiana University. She is author of *The Word in the World: Evangelical Writing, Publishing, and Reading in America, 1789–1880* (2004); *Testing Prayer: Science and Healing* (2012); *The Healing Gods: Complementary and Alternative Medicine in Christian America* (2013); and *Debating Yoga and Mindfulness in Public Schools: Reforming Secular Education or Reestablishing Religion?* (2019). She is editor of *Global Pentecostal and Charismatic Healing* (2011).

Colin Campbell is an emeritus professor of sociology at the University of York. He is the author of a dozen books and more than one hundred articles dealing with issues in the sociology of religion, consumerism, cultural change, and sociological theory. He is probably best known as the author of *The Romantic Ethic and the Spirit of Modern Consumerism* (1987; rpt. 2018). His other major publications include *Toward a Sociology of Irreligion* (1971; rpt. 2013), *The Myth of Social Action* (1996), and *Consumption and Consumer Society: The Craft Consumer and Other Essays* (2021).

Tim Dacey is an assistant professor of sociology at SUNY Oswego. His research examines how exposure to environmental risks associated with climate change has shaped political and cultural attitudes in the United States.

Jaron Harambam is an assistant professor of media, truth politics, and digitalization in the Department of Sociology of the University of Amsterdam. His research deals with conspiracy theories, news and platform politics, and AI (content moderation, search/recommender systems). Central to his research is the participation of multiple stakeholders to design our (future) digital worlds along democratic and public values. His *Contemporary Conspiracy Culture: Truth and Knowledge in an Era of Epistemic Instability* (2020) was awarded best dissertation 2017–19 by the Dutch Sociology Association (NSV).

Dick Houtman is a professor of sociology of culture and religion at KU Leuven, Belgium. His principal research interest is how the counterculture of the 1960s has sparked a romantic turn in the West that has transformed social realms ranging from politics and religion to work and consumption, and indeed sociology itself. He has published some two hundred articles and book chapters and twenty books, including *Science Under Siege: Contesting the Secular Religion of Scientism* (2021), *Religions of Modernity: Relocating the Sacred to the Self and the Digital* (2010), and *Class and Politics in Contemporary Social Science: 'Marxism Lite' and Its Blind Spot for Culture* (2003).

Jaime Kucinskas is an associate professor and chair of the Department of Sociology at Hamilton College. Her research examines the contexts in which people experience spiritual states and meaningfulness, as well as the conditions under which people engage in moral-sensemaking. She is the author of *The Mindful Elite* (2018) and coeditor of *Situating Spirituality: Context, Practice and Power* (2021).

Paul K. McClure is an associate professor and chair of the Department of Sociology and Human Services at the University of Lynchburg. His research interests include technology, religion, spirituality, and culture. His work has been published in *Poetics*, *Social Science Computer Review*, and *Journal for the Scientific Study of Religion*.

Michal Pagis is an associate professor of sociology at Bar Ilan University, Israel. She studies the transformations in self and identity in contemporary postindustrial culture with an emphasis on social spheres where religion, spirituality, and popular psychology meet. She is the author of *Inward: Vipassana Meditation and the Embodiment of the Self* (2019).

Christopher M. Pieper is a senior lecturer and director of the undergraduate program in sociology at Baylor University. His research interests include political sociology, social theory, religion, and technology/media. He is also the author of *Sociology as a Spiritual Practice* (2015) and *The Sociological Vision* (2019).

Evan Stewart is an assistant professor of sociology at University of Massachusetts Boston. His research examines the social forces that bring diverse groups of people together and break them apart, including work on religion, secularism, spirituality, and pluralism in public life. His work has been published in *American Sociological Review*, *Social Forces*, *Social Problems*, and *Sociological Theory*.

Orly Tal is a PhD candidate at the Department of Sociology and Anthropology, Bar-Ilan University, Israel. She studies the relations between modern psychology, religion, and spirituality, with a focus on the integration of Jewish and Buddhist ideas and practices in the clinical work of Israeli psychotherapists.

Galen Watts is an assistant professor in the Department of Sociology and Legal Studies at the University of Waterloo. His research focuses on cultural and institutional change in liberal democracies since the 1960s, with a focus on the spheres of religion, morality, work, and politics. His book *The Spiritual Turn: The Religion of the Heart and the Making of Romantic Liberal Modernity* (2022) won the Society for the Scientific Study of Religion's Distinguished Book Award in 2023.

Linda Woodhead is F. D. Maurice Chair in Moral and Social Theology and head of the Department of Theology and Religious Studies at King's College London. Her research focuses on religion, spirituality, and values in post-Christian societies. Her most recent books are *That Was the Church That Was: How the Church of England Lost the English People* (with Andrew Brown, 2016), *Gen Z, Explained: The Art of Living in a Digital Age* (with Robert Katz, Sarah Ogilvie, and Jane Shaw, 2021), and *Unknowing God: Toward a Post-Abusive Theology* (with Nicholas Peter Harvey, 2022).

INDEX

Abercrombie, Nicholas, 34, 262
Academic Consortium for Integrative Medicine & Health, 89, 114
accommodationism, 212, 219
Acevedo, David, 240
Achterberg, Peter, 31, 262, 263
Actually Free, 120
acupuncture, 87, 89, 90, 92, 96, 100, 273
Addley, Esther, 86
Adler, Margot, 56
Adorno, Theodor W., 242, 260
Aetherius Society, 74
Age of Aquarius, 3, 166
Albanese, Catherine L., 33, 113, 116, 119
Alexander, Brian, 163, 165, 175
Alexander, Jeffrey C., 26, 37, 207, 208
algorithms, 274, 277, 279
alienation, 18, 21, 154, 170, 217, 218, 245, 251, 252, 274
aliens, 73, 74
Allen, David, 167, 168
Alliance for Audited Media (AAM), 157, 174
Altglas, Véronique, 23, 35, 37, 235

American Association of Retired Persons (AARP), 114
American Hospital Association, 89, 114, 121
American Medical Association (AMA), 89, 233
American Psychological Association, 233
Ammerman, Nancy T., 2, 29, 35, 121, 148, 206
Anglican Church, 43, 44, 45, 67, 69, 76
Animal Liberation Front, 65
Ansolabehere, Stephen, 207
antibiotics, 253
anti-institutionalism, 18, 21, 22, 232, 243, 244, 245, 246, 247, 249, 251, 270, 273, 274, 287, 291
antivaccination protest, 27, 51, 241, 242, 243, 252, 255, 258, 259, 268, 271, 288
Apple, 154, 155
Arab Spring, 161
Arat, Alp, 58
Argentino, Marc-André, 295, 297
aromatherapy, 90, 100
AI (artificial intelligence), 165
Arya Samaj, 41

ascetic religion, 9
Asprem, Egil, 262, 274, 293, 294, 297
Association of Accredited Naturopathic Medical Colleges, 118
Association of American Medical Colleges, 233
Association of Religion Data Archives, 208
astrology, 63, 64, 73
Aupers, Stef, 23, 27, 30, 32, 35, 154, 158, 169, 173, 174, 176, 236, 237, 241, 260, 262, 264, 265, 270, 294, 295, 296, 297
authentic self, 136, 186, 210, 217, 219, 220, 221, 222, 223, 228, 229, 231, 235
authoritarianism, 248
awakening, 209, 270, 274, 275, 276, 280, 282, 285, 287, 291

Babbitt, Irving, 217, 237
Baggetta, Matthew, 207
Baker, Stephanie A., 279, 294, 295, 297
Bakker, Cok, 2, 30, 237
Barkun, Michael, 270, 293, 295, 296
Barrows, Henry, 55
Bartlett, Katharine T., 238
Bauder, Don, 120
Bauer, Brent A., 117
Bauman, Zygmunt, 260
Beal, Susan, 117
Bearman, Joshuah, 175
Beckford, James A., 32, 147
Bedesin, Elena, 113
Bell, Daniel, 80, 86
Bell, Emma, 36
Bellah, Robert N., 56, 148, 205, 207, 235
Bello-Gomez, Ricardo, 207

Bender, Courtney, 31, 33, 118, 125, 147, 205
Beres, Derek, 58, 293
Berger, Helen A., 52, 57, 58
Berger, Peter L., 31, 33, 151, 173
Berghuijs, Joantine, 2, 30, 237
Berman, Marshall, 209, 237, 238
Berman, Morris, 58
Berners-Lee, Tim, 151
Besant, Annie, 42, 43
Beyerlein, Kraig, 206
Bhagavad Gita, 109
Bible, 50, 93, 103, 104, 247
Bible Belt (The Netherlands), 258
Bill Gates, 269
Bin Khalifa Al-Thani, Hamad, 162
Binkley, Sam, 36, 153, 169, 173, 176
biofeedback, 90, 94
biomedicine, 24, 88, 90, 253, 254, 256, 270
BioNTech, 257
Birch, Stephanie, 278
black feminism, 225, 226, 227
black liberation, 226
Black Lives Matter movement, 248
Black Panthers, 65
Black, Lindsey I., 114
blackness, 229
Blake, William, 46
Blau, Max, 114, 117, 120
Blavatsky, Helena, 13, 44
Bloom, Mia, 295
Bloor, David, 32, 265
bodhisattva, 143
Bødker, Henrik, 174
bohemianism, 152, 153, 283
Boltanski, Luc, 36, 237, 262
Boon, Brooke, 109, 117, 121
Bowler, Kate, 35, 120
Brahmo Samaj, 41, 42
Branch Davidians, 65
Brand, Russell, 3, 58

Brand, Stewart, 151, 152, 153, 156, 168, 170, 172, 173, 174
Braunstein, Ruth, 206
Brenner, Philip S., 207
bricolage, 14, 20, 21, 22
British Empire, 40
Bromley, Patricia, 205
Brooks, David, 30
Brown, Callum G., 31
Brown, Candy Gunther, 24, 30, 35, 87, 113, 115, 117, 119, 120, 121, 123, 264
Brox, Trine, 121
Bruce, Steve, 4, 30, 31, 235
Bruley, Sue, 238
Bryner, Peter, 116
Buddhism, 3, 9, 12, 16, 39, 41, 42, 64, 74, 94, 99, 101, 102, 106, 108, 110, 126, 127, 128, 129, 130, 131, 132, 134, 135, 136, 138, 139, 140, 143, 144, 145, 155, 159, 180, 182, 247
Buddhist psychology, 129, 131, 144
Bullivant, Stephen, 58
Bultmann, Rudolph, 55
bureaucratization, 153, 248, 251
Burton, Tara Isabella, 173
business spirituality. *See* workplace spirituality
Butt, Riazat, 84
Butter, Michael, 295
Butzer, Bethany, 115
Byron Bay (Australia), 258

Cabanas, Edgar, 148
Cadge, Wendy, 148
Café Weltschmerz, 290
Callahan, David, 120
Calvinism, 16
camel racing, 162
Campbell, Colin, 12, 13, 19, 32, 33, 34, 35, 59, 83, 84, 85, 86, 237, 238, 261, 262, 263, 264, 265, 269, 272, 293, 294, 296

Campbell, David E., 206
cancel culture, 234
Canovan, Margaret, 251, 264
capitalism, 25, 26, 50, 107, 127, 145, 153, 181, 214, 217, 219
Capitol Hill insurrection, 270
Caplan, Eric, 147
Carley, Michael, 240
Carnes, Tony, 173
Carrette, Jeremy, 33, 36, 37, 120, 148, 212, 236
Casanova, José, 30, 113, 148, 212, 214, 215, 236, 237
Catholicism, 11, 16, 43, 44, 46, 48, 50, 51, 100, 103, 108, 159, 160, 165, 180, 198, 214, 246
Celtic Christianity, 46
Center for Mindfulness (UMass), 91, 106
Chait, Jonathan, 239
chakras, 49, 95, 97, 108, 109
Chandler, Siobhan, 237
channeling, 102, 128
charismatic Christianity, 1, 16, 18, 19, 20, 47, 48, 49, 56, 57, 66, 104
Charmaz, Kathy, 148
Chaves, Mark, 31, 32, 207
Chávez, Hugo, 250
cheiromancy, 95
Chen, Carolyn, 30, 169, 170, 173, 176, 182, 188, 206, 207
Chesterton, G. K., 43, 55, 180
Chia, Aleena, 296
Chiapello, Eve, 237, 262
Chiapello, Eve, 36
chiropractic healing, 87, 89, 90, 95, 96, 104
Chopra, Deepak, 219
Christian religion, 1, 7, 8, 9, 10, 11, 13, 15, 16, 20, 39, 40, 42, 43, 44, 45, 46, 47, 48, 49, 50, 51, 52, 53, 54, 88, 103, 104, 105, 159, 160, 165, 180, 245, 258, 275

Christocentrism, 6, 7, 8, 9, 10, 11, 13, 20, 26, 186
church attendance, 7, 186
Church of Satan, 65, 72, 74
church religion. *See* Troeltsch, Ernst
church sociology (Thomas Luckmann), 10, 11
civic behavior, 178, 179, 184, 186, 188, 189, 191, 192, 193, 194, 195, 196, 197, 198, 199, 200, 201, 202, 203, 204
civic decline, 178, 183, 203
civic engagement, 27, 177, 178, 179, 180, 181, 182, 183, 184, 186, 187, 188, 192, 195, 199, 201, 202, 203, 204, 211
civic identity, 179, 181, 184, 185, 186, 188, 189, 191, 192, 193, 194, 195, 196, 197, 198, 199, 200, 201, 202
civil rights movement, 225, 248
Clarke, Tainya C., 114
class struggle, 248
climate skepticism, 242
Clot-Garrell, Anna, 236
Coaston, Jane, 180
Cobbs, Price M., 225, 239
Cohen, Michael H., 123
Coleman, Simon, 35
Colker, Ruth, 222, 223, 224, 225, 227, 228, 229, 238
Collins, Francis, 163
Collins, Randall, 32
colonialism, 40, 43
Comaroff, Jean, 36
communism, 248
Complementary and Alternative Medicine (CAM), 3, 23, 64, 89
Complementary and Integrative Health. *See* Complementary and Alternative Medicine (CAM)

computational metaphor (Kevin Kelly), 166, 167, 170
computer technology. *See* digital technology
Condé Nast Publishing, 157
conformity, 15, 21, 246, 247, 273
Confucianism, 9
consciousness-raising, 223, 228
conspiracy culture, 28, 269, 270, 271, 272, 274, 276; positivism in, 289, 290, 291
conspiracy theories, 28, 51, 69, 79, 86, 242, 246, 268, 269, 270, 271, 272, 273, 274, 275, 276, 277, 278, 280, 281, 282, 284, 285, 286, 287, 288, 289, 290, 291, 292
conspirituality, 28, 51, 54, 270, 271, 272, 274, 275, 276, 277, 278, 279, 280, 286, 288, 289, 291, 292
content analysis, 151, 158, 169
contraction (Kabbalah), 140
Corcoran, Katie E., 205
Corn, Seane, 288
Corré, Anne, 292, 296
Cortois, Liza, 30
Coser, Lewis A., 206
counterculture, 48, 49, 53, 63, 79, 82, 152, 153, 155, 217, 218, 241, 242, 243, 244, 245, 247, 248, 249, 251, 263
COVID-19, 27, 51, 242, 243, 251, 252, 256, 257, 258, 267, 268, 271, 286, 287, 291
Cox, Harvey, 35
Coyne, George, 164
Cragun, Ryan T., 31
Creswell, J. David, 115
Crockett, Alasdair, 4, 30, 31, 235
Crouch, Andy, 174
Crowley, Aleister, 45, 46
cult, 12, 59, 71, 72, 80, 246, 270
cult of the individual (Emile Durkheim), 146

cultic milieu, 12, 13, 59, 60, 61, 62, 63, 64, 65, 66, 67, 68, 69, 70, 71, 72, 73, 74, 75, 77, 78, 79, 80, 81, 82, 246, 269, 272, 274
cultural boundaries, 292
cultural inclusion, 252
cultural liberation, 248
cultural mainstream, 13, 39, 51, 60, 63, 64, 68, 69, 70, 71, 72, 74, 75, 78, 79, 81, 270, 272
cultural orthodoxy, 69, 70, 71, 74, 75, 81
cultural otherness, 252
cultural pluralization, 11
cultural sociology, 5, 23, 210, 243, 272
cyberculture, 168

Dacey, Tim, 27
Dalai Lama Center for Peace-Education, 119
Daniel, Lillian, 237
Darwin, Charles, 166
David Lynch Foundation for Consciousness-Based Education and World Peace, 93, 111, 115, 116, 122
Davies, Owen, 56
Davies, Stephen, 61, 71, 78, 82, 83, 84, 86
Day, Abby, 57
De Blécourt, Willem, 56
De Certeau, Michel, 113, 118
De Keere, Kobe, 36, 262
De Koster, Willem, 265
De Waal, Martijn, 295
decline of religion, 8, 11
decolonization, 227
deep breathing, 90
dehumanization, 153, 244
DeLamater, John, 207
Delaney, Brigid, 293, 295, 297
Demerath III, N. J., 32

Denton, Melinda Lundquist, 205
Department of Veterans Affairs, 91
Derks, Anton, 262, 263
Descartes, René, 253
Desikachar, Sri T. K. V., 118
Desmond, Matthew, 204
Dessing, Nathal M., 113
Detweiler, Craig, 173
dharma, 102, 109, 111
Dharmapala, 42
DiAngelo, Robin J., 228, 229, 232, 239
dietary supplements, 90
digital technology, 152, 153, 154, 168
discourse analysis, 27, 151, 158, 159, 169, 211
disenchantment, 125, 151, 153, 170
diversity, 232, 234, 240
divine spark, 95, 134, 135, 137, 140
DNA, 282
Dorsey, Jack, 171
Douglas, Jack D., 257, 265
Douglas, Karen M., 294
Drescher, Elizabeth, 29
Drughi, Octavia, 118
drugs, 48, 100, 154, 253
druidry, 74
Dubé, Eva, 264
Duffy, Barbara J., 184, 204, 206, 208
Dupreem, Glen, 117
Durkheim, Emile, 10, 32, 146, 257, 259, 260, 265
Dyrendal, Asbjørn, 262, 274, 293, 294, 297

E&T Editorial Staff, 85
Earth First!, 65
East and West, 13, 41, 42, 55, 96, 247
Easterbrook, Gregg, 163, 164, 175
Eastern Orthodox religion, 44
Eccles, Janet, 57

echo chambers, 79
eclecticism, 152, 282
Edgell, Penny, 207
Edwards, Charlotte, 85, 86
Eisenberg, David M., 114
elective affinity, 26, 292
Eliasoph, Nina, 177, 188, 204, 207, 208
Ellul, Jacques, 176
Ellwood, Robert S., 261
empathy, 138, 140, 146, 149, 230
empowerment, 107, 143
energy. *See* sacred, in spirituality
enlightenment, 17, 64, 125, 242
environmentalism, 19, 48, 52, 63, 65, 252
episcopi vagantes. See wandering bishops
epistemological individualism. *See* romantic expressivism
Epperson, Hunter R., 172
Equal Employment Opportunity Commission (EEOC), 93, 94, 116
Erjavec, Karmen, 36
esotericism, 16, 44, 45, 48, 56, 246, 253
Estés, Clarissa Pinkola, 57
eugenics, 78
European Social Survey, 7
European Values Study, 7
evangelical Christianity, 56, 162
evangelical Protestantism, 104
Evans, John H., 206
Evans, Jules, 264, 265
evolution theory, 161, 162, 164
experience. *See* religious epistemology, in spirituality
experiential epistemology. *See* religious epistemology, in spirituality
experts, 68, 106, 244, 259

expressive individualism. *See* romantic expressivism
expressive revolution (1960s), 24, 216, 217, 227

Facebook, 160, 161, 172, 289
Faith Survey (UK Religion Survey 2017), 84
faith-healing, 47
fantasy, 244
far right, 52, 54, 86, 242, 269, 271, 283, 286, 287
Fedele, Anna, 121, 213, 236, 237, 238
femininity, 213
feminism, 48, 215, 221, 222, 223, 224, 225, 226, 227, 228, 229, 230, 248
Ferguson, Marilyn, 285
Fetto, John, 118
Fetzer Institute, 120, 122, 208
Fields, Karen E., 32
Findhorn (Scotland), 258
Fink, Matt, 107
First National Women's Liberation Conference, 223
Fischer, Claude S., 204
Fitzpatrick, Ruth, 262, 265
Five Star Movement (Italy), 250
Flat Earth Society, 77, 289
Flemish Interest (Belgium), 249
Folk, Holly, 117
Folk, Kenneth, 119
Forum for Democracy (The Netherlands), 249
Foucault, Michel, 25, 149, 232
Fox, John, 208
Francis of Assisi, 16
Frank, Thomas, 262, 263
Frankl, Victor, 131
Freemasonry, 44
Freud, Sigmund, 19, 134, 166, 219
Friedan, Betty, 238
Friedman, Gillian, 240
Froese, Paul, 176

INDEX ❧ 347

Frontline, 121
Fuchs, Christian, 295
Fuist, Todd N., 206
Fukuyama, Francis, 237
Fuller, Robert C., 33, 113, 116
Fulton, Brad R., 205

Gaddini, Katie, 57
Gaia (media platform), 279, 280
Gardner, Gerald, 45, 46
Gardner, Seth, 117
Gardner-Chloros, Penelope, 118
Garrett, William R., 32
Garwood, Kenneth, 85
Gauchat, Gordon, 261
Gauthier, François, 120, 148
Gavison, Ruth, 236
Gecewicz, Claire, 29
Gellner, Ernest, 264
gender, 49, 192, 213, 222, 234, 247
genetic engineering, 163
Gerstein, Julie, 293
Gerteis, Joseph, 207
Gevitz, Norman, 113
Gieryn, Thomas F., 292, 297
Gilhus, Ingvild Saelid, 32
Gilmore, James H., 262
Gilmore, Lee, 174
Glastonbury (United Kingdom), 258
Gleick, James, 176
Glendinning, Tony, 31
Glenny, Misha, 174
gnosis, 17
God particle. *See* Higgs boson particle
God within, 17, 48
Godrej, Farah, 37
Goffman, Erving, 118, 185, 206, 207
Gog, Sorin, 36
Golden Dawn (Greece), 249
Goldstein-Gidoni, Ofra, 118
Goleman, Daniel, 119

Goodman, Trudy, 119
Goodrick-Clarke, Nicholas, 270, 293
Google, 172
goth subculture, 65, 74
Goyal, Madhav, 115
Grateful Dead, 154
Great Reset, 268
greedy institutions, 187, 188
Greeson, Jeffrey M., 113, 122
Grier, William H., 225, 239
Griera, Mar, 236, 258, 261, 265, 271, 293, 294
Griffith, R. Marie, 113
Grindstaff, Laura, 37
Grogan, Jessica, 34
Guber, Tara, 102, 119
Guerin, Cécile, 278, 288, 293, 295, 296, 297
guided imagery, 90

Habito, Ruben, 99
Hadaway, C. Kirk, 29, 207
Hahnemann, Samuel, 117
Halafoff, Anna, 58, 262, 264, 265, 278, 279, 288, 294, 295, 296
half-belief, 73, 85
Hall, John R., 37
Hanegraaff, Wouter J., 34, 55, 56, 62, 63, 64, 65, 78, 82, 83, 238, 246, 263, 264, 296
Hanisch, Carol, 221, 238
happiness, 126, 127, 130, 131, 212. *See also* well-being
Harambam, Jaron, 28, 52, 86, 265, 267, 292, 293, 294, 295, 296, 297
Harris, Ruth, 55
Hartmann, Douglas, 207
Hatsune, Miku, 166
Hattaway Communications, 208
Hawn, Goldie, 111, 119, 122
healthcare, 3, 23, 24, 49, 90, 99, 102, 106, 107, 108, 112, 233, 254

Heath, Joseph, 262
heathenism, 52
Heelas, Paul, 12, 17, 31, 33, 34, 56, 57, 63, 82, 83, 147, 236, 238, 262
Heinze, Andrew R., 147
herbs, 89, 254
Hermetic Order of the Golden Dawn, 44, 45
Hersh, Eitan, 207
Hervieu-Léger, Danièle, 33
Hess, Frederick M., 120
heterosexism, 227, 231, 234
Higgs boson particle, 163
Hildegard of Bingen, 16
Hill Collins, Patricia, 204
Hinckle, Warren, 244, 261
Hinduism, 3, 9, 12, 16, 39, 41, 42, 64, 96, 102, 109, 155, 159, 164, 182
Hipp, John R., 206
hippies, 155, 256, 268
Hofstee, Wim, 235, 237
holism, 12, 15, 21, 24, 49, 50, 52, 54, 87, 88, 89, 90, 92, 93, 94, 95, 96, 97, 98, 100, 101, 103, 104, 105, 107, 108, 109, 110, 111, 112, 113, 253, 254, 259, 269, 274, 286, 288, 289, 291
holistic health, 24, 49, 87, 88, 89, 90, 92, 93, 94, 95, 97, 98, 99, 100, 101, 103, 104, 105, 107, 108, 109, 110, 111, 112, 113, 125, 253, 254, 255, 256, 270, 277, 279; mainstreaming, 3, 23, 87, 88, 89, 90, 91, 92, 94, 95, 101, 103, 108, 112, 113; tactical marketing through commodification, 105, 106, 107; tactical marketing through linguistics, 101, 102, 103, 104, 105
holistic milieu, 12, 21, 269, 286, 288, 289, 291
Höllinger, Franz, 35, 260, 261, 264
Holocaust, 78
Holy Spirit, 98, 103, 104

homeopathy, 90, 96, 100
homophobia, 209, 220
hooks, bell, 226, 227, 228, 229, 239
Horkheimer, Max, 242, 260
Horn, Emily, 119
Horn, Vincent, 119
Houston, Jaclyn D., 205
Hout, Michael, 204
Houtman, Dick, 1, 23, 27, 30, 31, 32, 33, 34, 35, 37, 58, 154, 173, 176, 186, 213, 236, 237, 241, 260, 261, 262, 263, 264, 265, 270, 273
Human Potential movement, 18, 19, 20, 21, 48
humanistic psychology, 19, 127, 130, 131, 133, 218
Humanists U.K., 84
Huss, Boaz, 2, 29
Husting, Gina, 294
Hutton, Ronald, 56
hypnotherapy, 90

Icke, David, 275, 280, 281, 282, 283, 284, 285, 295
identity politics, 49, 248, 249
idolatry, 40, 41, 159, 162
Ignazi, Piero, 263
Illouz, Eva, 145, 147, 148, 149
Illuminati, 281
imagination, 27, 66, 155, 186, 188, 211, 214, 216, 227, 231, 232, 233, 244, 251
immortality, 170
in vitro fertilization, 165
inclusion, 234, 240, 248
infectious disease, 258
Inge, Dean, 43
Inglehart, Ronald, 248, 262, 263
inner work, 221, 223, 224, 225, 227, 228, 229, 230, 231, 234, 235
inner-worldly religion, 9
institutional differentiation, 6, 8, 11
Intelligent Design, 161

internalized dominance, 228, 229, 231
International Association of Reiki Professionals, 97, 117
internet, 53, 54, 79, 100, 106, 154, 171, 191, 276
intuition. *See* religious epistemology, in spirituality
inwardness, 247
Isaacson, Walter, 155, 173
Islam, 41, 74, 159, 161, 162
Iyengar, Sri B. K. S., 118

Jackson, Paul, 83, 84
Jackson, Stanley W., 146
Jagat, Guru, 278
Jain, Andrea R., 30, 37, 120, 148
Jensen, Stine, 289, 296
Jentoft, Peggy, 117
Jephcott, Edmund, 260
Jeremiah, 160
Jeter, Pamela E., 115
Jewish psychology, 129, 131, 132
Jobs, Steve, 155, 173, 174
Johnson, Bryan, 165
Johnson, Hannah, 123
Johnson, Steven, 176
Jois, Pattabhi, 98, 99, 118
Jones, Paul Tudor, 106
Jones, Sonia, 120
Jordan, William, 84
Judaism, 127, 129, 130, 131, 132, 134, 135, 136, 140, 141, 142, 145, 159

K. P. Jois Foundation, 91, 106, 111, 122
ka. See sacred, in spirituality
Kabat-Zinn, Jon, 97, 102, 110, 117, 118, 119, 120, 122
Kabbalah, 44, 129, 132, 135, 140
Kahn, Richard, 281, 283, 295, 296
Kantor, Debra, 118
Kaplan, Dana, 148
Kaplan, Jeffrey, 62, 65, 66, 74, 83, 84, 86
Kaptchuk, Ted J., 116
Karan, Donna, 106
karma, 49, 109
Karpel, Richard, 119
Kasselstrand, Isabella, 31
Katz, Roberta, 58
Keeley, Allison, 175
Keil, David, 115, 121
Kelly, Kevin, 156, 166, 167, 168, 170, 174, 175, 176
Kendal (United Kingdom), 49
Kennedy, Jonathan, 261, 264
Khalsa, Sat Bir S., 115
ki. See sacred, in spirituality
King, David P., 184, 204, 206, 208
King, Richard, 33, 36, 37, 120, 148, 212, 236
Kingsford, Anna, 44
Klein, Ezra, 205
Klein, Naomi, 293
Klinenberg, Eric, 204
Knibbe, Kim, 121, 213, 236, 237, 238
Knight, Peter, 295
Kogan, Claudia, 149
Kohut, Heinz, 127, 135
Kong, Jian, 96, 117
Kopf, David, 55
Kral, Tammi R. A., 115
Krieger, Dolores, 96, 117
Kriesi, Hanspeter, 263
Kroes, Doutzen, 278
Kroes, Rens, 278
Kucinskas, Jaime, 27, 34, 36, 118, 125, 147, 148, 177, 183, 190, 192, 194, 204, 206, 207, 208, 236, 237
Kürti, László, 79, 86
Kurzweil, Ray, 165, 170, 175, 176

Laermans, Rudi, 32, 260, 264, 265
lagged cultural identities, 177, 185, 193, 195, 199, 203

Lago, Mary, 55
Lamont, Michèle, 207, 292, 297
LaMore Jr., George E., 120
Lanier, Jaron, 154, 173
Lasch, Christopher, 147, 237
Lau, Kimberley J., 36
Leach, Evan A., 58
Ledermann, Erich Kurt, 113
Lee, Lois, 29
Left Party (Germany), 250
Lega Nord (Italy), 249
Levinas, Emmanuel, 140
Levy, Steven, 175
Lewis, James R., 63, 64, 83
Lewis, Jim, 162, 175
Lewis, Rebecca, 294, 295
Lewis, Tyson, 281, 283, 295, 296
LGBTQ+, 184, 198, 248, 252
liberal Christianity, 40
Lichterman, Paul, 177, 188, 204, 205, 206, 207, 208, 237
life force. *See* sacred, in spirituality
life-hacking, 167
Lindahl, Jared R., 116
Lipinski, Kathie, 117
Lipka, Michael, 29
Llansó, Emma, 294
Lo, Ming-Cheng, 37
Lofton, Kathryn, 206
Lomas, Tim, 122
Lööw, Heléne, 62, 65, 66, 74, 83, 84, 86
Loria, Kevin, 115
LoRusso, James Dennis, 30, 36, 236
LSD, 154
Lucas, George, 94
Luckmann, Thomas, 10, 11, 13, 14, 28, 32, 261
Luhrmann, Tanya M., 147
Lyles, Margaret Lee, 100, 118

Lynch, Gordon, 35, 236, 238, 256, 261, 262, 264, 265
Lyon, David, 34

Macedo, Stephen, 239
Machold, Rhys, 294
MacKinnon, Catherine, 222
Madsen, Ole Jacob, 147
Madsen, Richard, 205
Magee, Ronda V., 230
magic, 16, 44, 45, 46, 47, 52, 64, 72, 73
Maharishi International University, 91, 115
Maharishi Mahesh Yogi, 118
mainstream media, 79, 273, 279
Mann, Charles C., 175
Mannheim, Karl, 251, 264
mantra, 91
market of ultimate significance (Thomas Luckmann), 11
Markovitz, Gayle, 240
Marler, Penny Long, 29, 207
marriage, 241, 243, 247
Martens, Jason P., 265
Martikainen, Tuomas, 148
Martin, Bernice, 36, 244, 261, 262
Martin, Craig, 36, 236
Martin, David, 35
Marwick, Arthur, 245, 262
Marx, Karl, 166
Marxism, 221
Mascini, Peter, 32, 37, 264
masculinity, 213, 233
Maslow, Abraham, 19
mass media, 47, 53
massage, 100
materialism, 163
mathematics, 166
Maxwell, Joel, 119
McClure, Paul K., 26, 151, 172, 183, 206, 207
McDonald, William P., 117

McDowell, John C., 116
McGee, Micki, 148
McGuire, Meredith B., 118, 121
McKellar, Peter, 85
McLuhan, Marshall, 156
McRoberts, Omar, 205
McWhorter, John, 239
Mead, George H., 206
Medin, R. Alexander, 118
meditation, 49, 50, 64, 87, 90, 91, 92, 93, 94, 99, 100, 102, 104, 106, 110, 111, 112, 126, 128, 132, 138, 139, 183, 190, 209, 230, 231, 247, 270, 273, 279
Mellor, Philip A., 247, 263
Melton, J. Gordon, 83
Mendelson, Tamar, 122
mental health, 145, 226
Meridians, 95, 109
Merry Pranksters, 153
mesmerism, 13, 47, 95
Metcalfe, Jane, 156
Methodism, 13
Meyers, Gert, 265
microaggression, 232
Miles, Pamela, 98, 117
Miller, Arlene, 107, 121
mind-body dualism, 24, 253
mind-body-spirit, 49, 87, 88, 100, 102
mindfulness, 3, 50, 51, 54, 87, 91, 92, 97, 102, 106, 109, 110, 111, 126, 209, 230, 239, 277, 289, 291
Mindfulness-Based Stress Reduction (MBSR), 91, 97, 102, 105, 106, 110
MindUP, 92, 111
modern science, 152, 241, 253, 260
Moderna, 257
modernization, 246
Mohler, R. Albert, 119
Molnár, Virág, 207, 292, 297
monism. *See* holism

Moore, Russell, 180, 205
moral individualism, 252
Morris, Aldon D., 205
Mosby, John S., 117
Moses, 167
Moskalenko, Sophia, 295
Moskowitz, Eva S., 147
Moss, Gabriel, 116
Mosurinjohn, Sharday, 30, 237
motives, 243, 257, 259
Mudde, Cas, 263, 264
multicultural societies, 76, 85
Murray, Margaret, 45
Musk, Elon, 170, 171
mystical religion, 9, 11, 12, 13, 16, 43, 44, 45, 48, 50, 56, 65, 80, 129, 155, 167, 273. *See also* Troeltsch, Ernst
myth, 11, 17, 27, 46, 244

Nadesan, Majia, 36
Nadis, 95
narcissism, 131, 134, 214
National Center for Complementary and Alternative Medicine, 89
National Center for Complementary and Integrative Health, 89, 114, 121
National Front (France), 249
National Health Interview Survey, 90
National Health Service, 50
National Institutes of Health, 89, 91
National Religion and Spirituality Survey (NRSS), 179, 184, 190, 191, 208
nationalism, 249, 267
natural food. *See* organic food
naturopathy, 90, 100
Nazism, 65, 78
Negroponte, Nicholas, 156, 174

Nehemya, Iris, 118
Nehring, Daniel, 147
neognosticism, 170
neoplatonism, 47, 53
Netflix, 279
neurology, 167
neuroscience, 98
New Age movement, 3, 18, 19, 20, 21, 34, 48, 49, 50, 54, 56, 62, 63, 64, 78, 79, 94, 126, 145, 153, 159, 168, 210, 218, 219, 220, 246, 282, 283, 285
New Earth Project (NEP), 278
new left, 210, 243, 247, 248, 249, 250, 251, 252, 263
new right, 248, 263
new social movements, 210, 217, 220, 232, 248, 249, 251
New Thought, 13
New World Order, 270, 274, 282
New Zealand First, 249
Nexus Magazine, 275
Nisbett, Richard E., 118
nonreligion, 1, 8
normalization of Christian religion. *See* Christocentrism
Norris, Pippa, 248, 263
Novella, Steven, 90
Numbers, Ronald L., 113, 114

O'Brien, John, 205
O'Reilly, Tim, 160
occultism, 16, 44, 45, 63, 73, 270
occulture, 60, 270
Offe, Claus, 263
Office of Alternative Medicine, 89
old left, 248
Old Testament, 159, 167
One Nation Party (Australia), 249
Ong, Jonathan Corpus, 287
oppositional subcultures (Jeffrey Kaplan and Heléne Lööw), 62, 65, 66, 74, 83

oppressive beliefs, 220, 228, 231, 233, 234
organic food, 270, 273
Orr, Deborah, 230, 239
Orr, Martin, 294
Orwell, George, 273
other-worldly religion, 9
Owen, Alex, 56

paganism, 46, 52, 54
Pagis, Michal, 24, 30, 118, 125, 126, 147, 148
Paglia, Camille, 156
palm reading, 95
Palmer, Daniel David, 95, 96, 116
Paltrow, Gwyneth, 3
Panayides, Fanos, 278
paranormal, 47
Park, Crystal L., 113, 122
Parsons, Talcott, 36, 217, 237
Parsons, William B., 33
Partridge, Christopher, 58, 60, 61, 82, 270, 293, 296
Party for Freedom (PVV, The Netherlands), 249
patriarchy, 221, 222, 223, 224, 228
Pattillo-McCoy, Mary, 205
Payne, Richard K., 121, 122
Pearson, Joanne, 46, 56
Pelkmans, Mathijs, 294
Penman, Stephen, 122
Pentecostalism, 16
People's Party (Switzerland), 249
People's Party (United States), 250
People's Party of Canada, 249
People's Party (Denmark), 249
perennialism, 21, 22, 41, 246
Perón, Juan, 250
Perreira, Todd LeRoy, 173
Perry, Samuel L., 30, 206
personal authenticity, 24, 141, 209, 220, 221, 222, 223, 224, 228, 244, 246, 248, 273

personal transformation. *See* self-realization
Peters, Ted, 163
Petersen, Jesper Aagaard, 60, 67, 82
Petty, Sheryl, 230, 239
Pew Research Center, 2, 29
Pfizer, 257
philanthropy, 106
Pickel, Gert, 31
Pieper, Christopher, 26
Pieper, Jos, 2, 30, 237
Pine, B. Joseph, 262
Platt, Gerald M., 36
Pless, Anna, 34, 58
Podemos (Spain), 250
Poell, Thomas, 295
political activism, 220, 224, 247, 283, 284, 285, 286, 292
political engagement. *See* civic engagement
politicization of the personal, 215, 221
politics of authenticity, 221, 222, 227, 233, 234
Pollack, Detlef, 31
polymorphous truth, 79
Pons, Anneke, 265
popular culture, 53, 73, 163, 219
populism, 12, 242, 248, 250, 251; leftist, 250;rightist, 27, 28, 242, 243, 248, 249, 250, 251, 252, 256, 258, 263
Porterfield, Amanda, 33
positive psychology, 127, 130, 131, 133
Possamai, Adam, 29, 34
posthumanism, 165, 166
postindustrial society, 171
postmaterialism, 19, 252
post-truth, 272
Potter, Andrew, 262
Powell, Walter W., 205
prana, 96. *See also* sacred, in spirituality

prayer, 93, 104, 108, 126, 137, 159, 190, 191
predestination, 16
prejudice, 220, 229, 231, 232
Price, H. H., 85
private versus public, 213, 214, 215
privatism, 243, 247
privatization of religion, 5, 6, 7, 11, 28, 88, 127, 128, 142, 145, 214
Prochaska, Frank, 57
Progress Party (Norway), 249
progressive politics, 19, 27, 184, 209, 210, 211, 217, 226, 232, 233, 234, 235, 241, 242, 243, 252, 256, 269
prosocial practices, 27, 179, 181
Protestantism, 9, 11, 13, 15, 16, 26, 43, 46, 47, 103, 159, 198, 214, 246, 258, 259
psychology, 125, 126, 127, 128, 129, 130, 131, 132, 133, 134, 135, 136, 137, 141, 142, 143, 144, 145, 146
psychotherapy, 24, 48, 125, 128, 129, 132, 138, 144; critiqued as hyperindividualistic, 128, 130, 133, 134, 135, 136, 137, 138, 140, 141, 146; spiritualization, 125, 127, 128
Pulignano, Valeria, 265
Pursuer, Ronald E., 37, 239
Putnam, Robert D., 178, 206

QAnon, 86, 270, 273, 278, 287, 290
qi. *See* sacred, in spirituality
quackery, 89, 90
Quakerism, 13
quantum physics, 98, 163
Quiet Time, 93, 112
quietism, 28, 43, 180, 212, 220, 232, 242, 243, 247

Raaphorst, Nadine, 35, 264
racism, 27, 52, 144, 160, 209, 220, 227, 228, 229, 230, 231, 234, 240

rainbow gatherings, 128
Rand, William L., 120
randomized controlled trial, 92
Raso, Jack, 117
rationalization, 9, 24, 153, 154, 241, 244, 246
Ratliff, Evan, 161, 175
Read, Bridget, 240
Redden, Guy, 36, 238
redemptive versus pragmatic politics (Margaret Canovan), 251
reenchantment, 54, 151, 153, 154, 167, 170
reiki, 3, 49, 87, 90, 92, 97, 98, 102, 103, 105, 106, 107, 108, 109, 273, 288, 291
reincarnation, 64, 69, 276
religion: conceptualization by Emile Durkheim, 10; conceptualization by Max Weber, 9
religion of the heart (Galen Watts), 34, 145, 187
religion-technology relationship: compatibility motif, 158, 163, 165, 169; conflict motif, 157, 161, 162, 165, 169; fulfillment motif, 152, 158, 164, 165, 166, 167, 168, 169, 170, 171
religious belief, 260
religious change, 14, 87
religious congregations, 181, 182, 187
religious diversity. *See* religious pluralism
religious dogmatism, 12, 21, 22, 42, 166, 255
religious dualism, 15, 16, 259
religious epistemology: in Christian religion, 16; in spirituality, 15, 17, 22, 88, 94, 97, 98, 99, 112, 256, 280, 289, 291
religious freedom, 76, 93

religious nationalism, 160
religious ontology. *See* sacred
religious orthodoxy, 67, 73, 74
religious pluralism, 8, 21, 54, 154
religious privatization. *See* privatization of religion
religious ritual, 10
religious soteriology, in spirituality, 15, 18, 22
religious universalism, 20, 21
Remski, Matthew, 58, 288, 293
Renaissance, 44, 46, 64
Rennison, Susan Joy, 62, 83, 84, 86
reptilian thesis (David Icke), 281, 282
Republican Party, 249
resistance, 212, 230
Reveley, James, 36
Rheingold, Howard, 156, 174
Richardson, John H., 175
Ricketts, Rachel, 230
Rieff, Philip, 147
Riis, Ole, 57
Riley, Kristen E., 113
Rimke, Heidi Marie, 36
Robertson, David G., 58, 293, 297
Robin DiAngelo, 228
Robinson, Brett T., 173
Robinson, John, 55
robotics, 162
Rogers, Carl, 19
romantic expressivism, 210, 216, 217, 218, 220, 221, 222, 223, 224, 225, 226, 228, 229, 232, 233, 234, 244
romantic individualism. *See* romantic expressivism
romanticism, 13, 167, 186, 187, 203, 210, 216, 217, 245
Roof, Wade Clark, 14, 33, 34, 148, 173, 205
Rosa, Linda, 116
Rose, Nikolas S., 37, 146, 148
Ross, Casey, 114, 117, 120

Rossetto, Louis, 156
Roszak, Theodore, 173, 244, 261
Rothschild, 281
Rountree, Kathryn, 52, 58
Rousseau, Jean-Jacques, 216, 217, 218
Roy, Rammohun, 41
Ruijs, Wilhelmina L. M., 265
Rutjens, Bastiaan T., 261, 264, 265

Sacks, Oliver, 167
sacred, 10: immanence, 15, 16, 17, 27, 94, 255, 256, 257, 258, 259; in Christian religion, 15, 16, 259; in spirituality, 15, 16, 17, 27, 94, 96, 154, 245, 247, 255, 256, 257, 258, 259; transcendence, 15, 16, 259; versus profane (Emile Durkheim), 10, 257, 265
Salam, Maya, 240
Sanchez, Gaëtan, 117
Sarachild, Katie, 223, 238
Saraswati, Dayananda, 41
Satin, Mark, 238
Sault, Samantha, 240
Scherer, Jochen, 61, 82, 86
Schmid Noerr, Gunzelin, 260
Schmidt, Lauren Chism, 29
Schmidt, Leigh Eric, 33, 55
Schnall, Marianne, 122
Schonert-Reichl, Kimberly A., 116
Schwab, Klaus, 268
scientific materialism, 42, 45
scientific orthodoxy, 67, 69, 73, 74
scientific reason, 241, 255, 260
scientific worldview, 244
scientism, 243, 260
Seager, Richard Hughes, 55, 118
sect religion. *See* Troeltsch, Ernst
secularism, 1, 2, 145, 162, 166, 183
secularization, 4, 5, 6, 7, 8, 9, 10, 11, 13, 14, 27, 28, 87, 151, 163, 211

secularization theory, 4, 5, 6, 7, 9, 10, 13, 14, 28, 151, 163, 211
Seddon, Philip, 64, 83
Sedona (Arizona), 259
seekership, 14, 20, 21, 22, 27, 28, 127, 181, 186, 242, 246, 247, 252, 256, 258, 259, 268, 276, 279, 286, 287, 289, 291
Seidman, Steven, 260
self-actualization. *See* self-realization
self-attainment. *See* self-realization
self-development. *See* self-realization
self-expression. *See* self-realization
self-improvement. *See* self-realization
selfishness, 27, 127, 179, 180, 182, 185, 202, 214
self-realization, 17, 22, 24, 27, 141, 142, 153, 209, 210, 211, 212, 214, 215, 216, 218, 219, 220, 221, 222, 223, 224, 226, 228, 230, 231, 232, 233, 234, 235, 244, 246, 248, 252, 273
self-recovery, 227
self-transformation. *See* self-realization
self-work, 224, 228, 229, 233, 234, 235
Semmes, Clovis E., 225, 239
sexism, 27, 209, 220, 221, 223, 226, 227, 228, 231, 234
sexuality, 46, 192, 247
Shaffer, Leigh S., 58
Shapiro, Dean H., 122
Shaw, Jane, 55, 56
Sheldrake, Philip, 29
Sheridan, Kate, 114, 117, 120
Shils, Edward, 264
Shook, Andria, 123
Shropshire, Kitty, 84
Sibinga, Erica M. S., 122

Siegel, Aryeh, 115
Silberman, Steve, 175
silent revolution (Ronald Inglehart), 248
Silicon Valley, 27, 151, 152, 153, 154, 155, 156, 167, 168, 169, 170, 171, 172, 182
Simionca, Anca, 36
sin, 42
Singler, Beth, 293
Singleton, Andres, 262, 265
sixties, 1, 12, 18, 19, 23, 24, 27, 63, 96, 126, 153, 187, 210, 211, 216, 217, 223, 224, 227, 228, 232, 241, 242, 243, 245, 248, 249, 251
slavery, 225
Smith, Christian, 205, 206
Smith, Philip, 26, 37, 207, 208
Smithuijsen, Doortje, 293, 296
social change, 143, 146, 168, 218
social control of deviant beliefs, 72, 73, 75, 76, 77, 79
social desirability bias, 185, 186, 201, 202
social justice, 209, 211, 216, 220, 221, 228, 230, 231, 235
social media, 53, 77, 79, 154, 170, 273, 276, 277, 278, 279, 286
social roles, 185, 247, 275
socialism, 248
Socialist Party (The Netherlands), 250
socialization, 217, 223, 229, 231
sociology of religion, 4, 6, 10, 11, 22, 26, 30, 81, 186
Sointu, Eeva, 57
Somin, Ilya, 78, 84, 86
Sonima/Pure Edge. *See* K. P. Jois Foundation
Sood, Amit, 117
SpaceX, 170
spiritual awakening, 209, 270
spiritual but not religious (SBNR), 2, 6, 15, 19, 20, 53, 110, 126, 183, 185, 212, 242, 243, 252, 256, 258
spiritual experience, 12, 15, 16, 17, 22, 45, 48, 50, 98, 99, 104, 109, 112, 131, 134, 136, 138, 139, 140, 183, 202, 203, 223, 247, 251, 255, 273, 280, 282, 289. *See also* religious epistemology, in spirituality
spiritual supermarket. *See* spiritual marketplace
spiritual turn, 2, 3, 5, 6, 8, 14, 19, 20, 28, 60, 80, 125, 141, 186, 243, 245
spiritualism, 13, 47, 95
spirituality: as "unreal" religion, 4, 6, 14; as capitalist ideology, 26; as consumption, 11, 14, 22, 211; as cultural criticism, 18; as culturally coherent, 23, 88; as culturally incoherent, 4, 8, 13, 14, 22, 25, 35, 213, 237; as mainstream, 53, 54, 60, 63, 64; as neoliberal ideology, 25, 26, 127; as postmodern religion, 14, 22; as privatized religion, 4, 8, 181, 188, 201, 209, 210, 211, 212, 220, 237, 242; as publicly insignificant, 4, 5, 8, 25, 35, 210, 214, 215; as religious metanarrative, 22, 23; as selfish, 27, 179, 180, 182, 185, 202; female dominance, 49, 54, 57; social vision, 141, 145, 146; sociological significance, 28
Star Wars, 94
Starhawk, 57
Starlink, 171
Steensland, Brian, 29, 34, 148, 184, 192, 199, 201, 204, 206, 208
Stein, Diane, 120
Steinem, Gloria, 224, 225, 227, 228, 229, 238

stereotypes, 232
Stewart, Evan, 27, 148, 151, 153, 156, 168, 170, 177, 183, 190, 192, 194, 204, 206, 207, 208, 237
Stewart, V. Michelle, 113
Stolz, Jörg, 31
Stone, Sacha, 278
substance abuse recovery groups, 203
Suellentrop, Chris, 174
Sun, Anna, 34, 148
Sunstein, Cass, 239
supernatural beings, 16
superstition, 47, 69
Sutcliffe, Steven J., 32, 56
Swedenborgism, 13
Syman, Stefanie, 114, 116
syncretism, 14, 21, 22
Syriza (Greece), 250
System, The, 247, 249, 274
system-following versus system-challenging politics, 251

Taggart, Paul, 250, 263
Tagore, Dwarkanath, 41
Takata, Hawayo, 105
Tal, Orly, 24, 125, 148
Taoism, 12
Taylor, Charles, 1, 29, 126, 145, 146, 147, 149, 216, 237
Taylor, Scott, 36
technoanimism, 169
technocracy, 241, 244, 268
technology journalism, 152, 153
techno-utopianism, 170, 171
Ten Kate, Josje, 265
Tesla, 170
The Force (*Star Wars*), 94. *See also* sacred, in spirituality
theodicy, 9
Theosophy, 13, 42, 43, 44
Therapeutic Touch, 92, 96, 104, 107, 108

therapy, 54, 102, 105, 125, 126, 127, 128, 129, 130, 131, 133, 144, 145, 181, 209, 219, 221, 226, 276, 283
Thiessen, Joel, 29, 31
thumbtack, 120
Tibet, 43
Tiffany, Kaitlyn, 295, 297
Tikkun Olam (Judaism), 142
Tipton, Steven M., 56
TM.org, 112, 120, 123
Toastmasters, 203
Tobias, Andrada, 37
Tocqueville, Alexis de, 177, 202, 204
Todd, Nathan R., 205
Tolkien, J. R. R., 244
Tomasi, Marta, 261, 264
Torah, 140
Tosoni, Simone, 295
totalitarianism, 76
Toulmin, Stephen, 260
Tracy, Marc, 240
Transcendental Meditation (TM), 91, 93, 105, 111, 112
Transcendentalism (New England), 13
transhumanism, 165, 166, 170
trauma, 221
Travis, Adam, 204
Trinitarianism, 40
Troeltsch, Ernst, 11, 13, 17, 32, 33, 65, 81, 83
Tromp, Paul, 34, 58
True Finns, 249
Trump, Donald, 287
Truth Movement 9/11, 289
Tschannen, Oliver, 31
Tufekci, Zeynep, 294
Tumber, Catherine, 33
Turner, Bryan S., 4, 30, 148, 211, 235
Turner, Fred, 153, 155, 156, 157, 170, 173, 174, 175, 176
Tweed, Thomas A., 205

Twitter, 170, 171, 271
Tzimzum. See contraction

UFOs, 63, 74
UK Independence Party, 249
UMass Memorial Medical Center, 120
unconscious bias, 220, 231, 232
Underhill, Evelyn, 43, 45
Unitarianism, 13, 40, 41
United States Conference of Catholic Bishops, 108, 121
Universalism, 13
unlearning, 224, 227, 228, 229, 230, 233
Urban Zen Foundation, 106, 120
utopianism, 48, 170, 216, 219, 251, 288

vaccination, 100, 242, 243, 251, 252, 253, 255, 256, 257, 258, 259, 288
vaccine hesitancy, 27, 242, 258, 270
Valaskivi, Katja, 295
Van de Ven, Coen, 292, 295, 296
Van der Kooij, Arie, 235, 237
Van der Lee, Romy, 261, 264
Van der Veer, Peter, 33
Van der Waal, Jeroen, 265
Van Dijck, José, 295
Van Gool, Rosa, 292, 295, 296
Van Hoyweghen, Ine, 265
Vatican, 164
vegetarianism, 63
Verini, James, 166, 175
Versluis, Arthur, 33
Vincen-Brown, Frances, 117
virtual reality, 154
vitalism, 88, 94, 95, 96, 101, 112. *See also* sacred, in spirituality
Vivekananda, 42, 43, 55
Voas, David, 4, 30, 31, 37, 235, 270, 271, 274, 275, 276, 286, 287, 291, 293, 294, 296, 297

Vogelstein, Fred, 175
Volčič, Zala, 36
voluntary association, 93, 177, 180

Waksler, Frances C., 257, 265
Waldersee, Victoria, 84
Walker, Julian, 58, 293
Walzer Leavitt, Judith, 114
wandering bishops, 46
Wang, Xiaoyun, 29
Ward, Charlotte, 37, 270, 271, 274, 275, 276, 286, 287, 291, 293, 294, 296, 297
Ward, Robert, 160
Warde, Alan, 34, 262
Warren, Mark R., 206
Warren, Rick, 48, 56
Watts, Galen, 1, 27, 30, 33, 34, 35, 37, 57, 58, 82, 83, 147, 149, 186, 187, 203, 206, 207, 208, 209, 213, 236, 237, 238, 261, 262, 263, 273, 296
Wayne Dwyer, 219
Weber, Max, 9, 10, 11, 15, 32, 33, 34, 151, 167, 180, 205, 292
well-being, 49, 50, 126, 128, 133, 138, 141, 145, 226. *See also* happiness
Werczberger, Rachel, 148
Wertheim, Margaret, 164, 175
Whitehead, Andrew L., 206
whiteness, 229, 230
Whole Earth Catalog, 151, 152, 153, 168, 169
Whorton, James C., 114, 116
Wicca, 45, 46, 52, 74
Wiese, Glenda, 117
Wilkins-Laflamme, Sarah, 29, 37
Williams, Justin Michael, 230
Williams, Leonard, 263, 264
Williams, Rhys H., 206
Williams, Ruth, 37
Williams-Oerberg, Elizabeth, 121

Williamson, Marianne, 3, 236
Wilson, Bryan, 4, 30, 32
Wilson, Sarah, 58, 288
Wilson, Timothy DeCamp, 118
Wing, Janet, 102, 119
Winnicott, Donald, 127
Wired magazine, 27, 151, 152, 153, 154, 156, 157, 158, 159, 160, 161, 162, 163, 164, 165, 166, 167, 168, 169, 170, 269
Wirth, Louis, 264
Wiseman, Richard, 84
witchcraft, 45, 46, 52, 64
Wolf, Ava, 102, 119
Wolf, Gary, 167, 176
Wolfe, Tom, 153, 173
Wolman, David, 175
Wood, Matthew, 36, 37
Wood, Richard L., 206
Woodhead, Linda, 7, 8, 12, 13, 29, 32, 33, 39, 55, 57, 113, 118, 121, 147, 211, 235, 236, 237, 262, 263
workplace spirituality, 3, 24, 25
World Economic Forum (WEF), 268
World Values Survey, 7
World's Parliament of Religions, 40, 42, 43
world-affirming religion, 219

Wuthnow, Robert, 14, 34, 147, 205, 206
Wyman, Scott, 109, 121

xenophobia, 249

Yang, Fenggang, 173
yin and yang, 95
yoga, 3, 49, 50, 57, 87, 89, 90, 91, 92, 93, 94, 98, 99, 100, 102, 103, 104, 106, 109, 110, 111, 112, 183, 190, 209, 230, 268, 269, 270, 273, 277, 278, 279, 288, 289, 291
Yoga Alliance, 101, 109, 114, 118, 119, 121
Yoga Journal, 114, 118, 121
York, Michael, 36
Young, Gale, 230, 240
YouTube, 275, 277

Zaidman, Nurit, 118
Zandbergen, Dorien, 153, 173
Zarzeczna, Natalia, 261
Zeitgeist (documentary series), 275
Zelevansky, Nora, 240
Zijderveld, Anton C., 261, 263
Žižek, Slavoj, 236
Zuckerberg, Mark, 160
Zuckerman, Phil, 31

GPSR Authorized Representative: Easy Access System Europe, Mustamäe tee
50, 10621 Tallinn, Estonia, gpsr.requests@easproject.com

www.ingramcontent.com/pod-product-compliance
Lightning Source LLC
Chambersburg PA
CBHW022026290426
44109CB00014B/772